# The Economics of Voting

The economics of voting is about when, and subject to what qualifications, electoral markets are like ideal commercial markets where universally self-interested behaviour yields outcomes that are in some sense best for society as a whole. Self-interest can be relied upon in voting about the redistribution of income, narrowing the gap between rich and poor, without removing the gap completely, altering people's ordering on the scale of rich and poor or destroying incentives to work and save. Elsewhere, self-interested voting can lead to inconsistent collective behaviour, and must be supported by bargaining, duty and rights.

Bargaining is indispensable in the formation of platforms of political parties, passage of laws in the legislature and other situations where two or more magnitudes must be voted upon simultaneously. Bargaining is ubiquitous but mysterious, with no plausible equilibrium comparable to the equilibrium in competitive markets. A duty to vote arises because the chance of any person's vote influencing the outcome of an election is too small to justify the time and trouble of voting. Widespread abstention is corrosive, but the purely self-interested person abstains. A duty to vote need not require a person to vote for the party seen as best for society as a whole. It may be sufficient to vote for the party seen as best for oneself alone.

Rights are the citizen's defence against exploitation. Unconstrained, majority rule voting allows any majority of the electorate that can vote as a block – a majority identified by race, religion or social class – to expropriate the corresponding minority completely. No government in office, and its supporters, would risk losing office in an election if loss of office meant destitution at the hands of its successors. Constraints include property rights that may be modified by systematic redistribution but not discarded or altered indiscriminately if democratic government is to be preserved.

This book will be of interest to political scientists, economists and philosophers, and would serve as a text for senior undergraduate or graduate courses.

**Dan Usher** is Professor Emeritus at Queen's University, Kingston, Ontario, Canada.

# Routledge Frontiers of Political Economy

# The Economics of Voting

Studies of self-interest, bargaining,
duty and rights

**Dan Usher**

LONDON AND NEW YORK

First published 2016
by Routledge
2 Park Square, Milton Park, Abingdon, Oxon OX14 4RN

by Routledge
711 Third Avenue, New York, NY 10017

First issued in paperback 2017

*Routledge is an imprint of the Taylor & Francis Group, an informa business*

*British Library Cataloguing in Publication Data*
A catalogue record for this book is available from the British Library

*Library of Congress Cataloging in Publication Data*
Usher, Dan, 1934-
The economics of voting : studies of equilibrium, bargaining, duty and rights / Dan Usher.
   1. Voting–Economic aspects.  2. Voting research.
   3. Self-interest–Political aspects.  4. Political participation–Social aspects.
   5. Citizenship. I. Title.
   JF1001.U79 2015
   324.9–dc23                        2015023548

Even where gender-neutral formulations are not explicitly used in the text, all gender-
specific terms are to be considered to refer to both the feminine and the masculine form.

ISBN 13: 978-1-138-49543-2 (pbk)
ISBN 13: 978-1-138-93255-5 (hbk)

Typeset in Times New Roman
by Sunrise Setting Ltd, Paignton, UK

**Dedicated to**

Samphan

Ann and David

Luna, Sasha, Coco and Océane

# Contents

# Figures

# Tables

# Acknowledgements

Many thanks for help in preparing this book to Mark Babcock, Jill Hodgson, Elvira Posthumus and Changuk Sohn. I am grateful for comments and suggestions by my colleagues at the Queen's Economics Department, especially, John Hartwick, Steve Kaliski and Scott Gordon.

# 1 Introduction

A decentralized economy motivated by self-interest and guided by price signals would be compatible with a coherent disposition of economic resources ... It is important to understand how surprising this claim must be to anyone not exposed to this tradition. The immediate 'common sense' answer to the question 'What will an economy motivated by a very large number of different agents look like?' is probably: There will be chaos ... quite a different answer has long been claimed true and has indeed permeated the economic thinking of a large number of people who are in no way economists.

Arrow and Hahn (1971: vi–vii)

Why the *economics* of voting? The central proposition in economics is that the world's work gets done satisfactorily when each person does what is best for himself alone. The common sense view of the matter is that the outcome when each person does what is best for himself alone would be chaos. By contrast, the great lesson of economics is that, subject to strong qualifications which it is the business of economists to study, the outcome is order rather than chaos and that the resulting order is in some sense desirable. Self-interest generates a satisfactory outcome in markets for ordinary goods and services within an appropriate framework that only government can provide, including the protection of life and property, resolution of disputes, provision of roads, bridges and schools, dealings with other countries and the mitigation of inequality of income when deemed in the interest of the community as a whole. The economics of voting is the study of whether – subject to what qualifications and to what extent – an equally satisfactory outcome is attained in government, too, when laws and leaders are chosen by majority rule voting and when each person votes for whatever seems best for himself alone. The economics of voting is about when self-interest may be relied upon in voting as well as in markets, and, if not, what other considerations must be introduced.

The principal themes of this book are suggested by the terms in the subtitle. Under the heading of 'Self-interest' is an examination of voting about the redistribution of income: whether an equilibrium emerges when everybody votes selfishly, whether that equilibrium is desirable, whether there would be full or partial redistribution, how outcomes might be affected by campaign advertising and whether redistribution is seriously constrained by inefficiencies in taxation. Under the heading of 'Bargaining' is an analysis of how voting and bargaining are inextricably intertwined, where bargaining is seen as fundamentally different from ordinary self-interested behaviour, so that the one cannot be subsumed in the other. Under the heading of 'Duty' is the argument that citizens must recognize a duty to vote because the expected gain to the voter is never sufficient to cover the full cost of voting. There is some discussion of the chance of one's vote being influential and of what exactly the duty to vote requires. Under the heading of 'Rights' is an exposition of the different roles of property rights in politics and in markets. The virtues of the competitive economy are only realized when there is a prior allocation among citizens of property rights with a sufficiently well-specified rule of law that people know exactly what their property entitles them to do. Property rights include ownership of money, land, capital goods, patents and shares of corporations. Ownership in this idealized description of the competitive economy is given, as it were, by the hand of God with no explanation of why different people's allocations are what they turn out to be. Political markets are different. Majority rule voting would be a sham if people were somehow stopped from voting about the content and allocation of property rights; the defence of property rights under majority rule voting must rest upon voters' unwillingness to vote away property rights for fear of what might happen not just to the economy, but to the institution of majority rule voting itself. Formal constitutional constraints surely help, but would be a poor defence of property rights if not bolstered by the long-term interest of the great majority of voters.

This book is a cross between a collection of essays and a systematic treatise. It is a collection of essays in that half of the chapters have appeared as academic articles. It is a systematic treatise in that a good deal of material has been added and the chapters are ordered to tell a coherent story about behavioural and institutional requirements for government by majority rule voting. Following this introduction and a chapter on voting patterns, the book consists of five pairs of chapters, a pair on each of the four themes and a final pair on attempts in the literature to explain politics on the strength of self-interest alone. Chapter by chapter, the content of the book is as follows.

Chapter 2, called 'Voting patterns', is a collection of well-known paradigms, beginning with circumstances where voting works well, and proceeding to other circumstances where voting is inefficient and intransitive. There is a unique electoral equilibrium, comparable to the equilibrium in a competitive market, in the world of the *median voter theorem* where all options can be represented as points on a line, each voter has a preferred option and, between any two options both to the right or both to the left of one's preferred option, one always votes for the option closest to one's first best. The theorem itself is that the preference of the median voter, the person in the middle of the line, beats any other option in a pair-wise vote and can be expected to emerge as the winner in the election. Subject to several qualifications, the median voter theorem holds for the acquisition of public goods and for the redistribution when voted upon separately, but not for both together. A second favourable circumstance is the world of the *Condorcet jury theorem* where one among many available options is best for everybody but voters may be mistaken about which option that is. The theorem is that the best option is likely to be selected when each voter's probability of choosing the better of two options is over fifty percent.

Otherwise majority rule voting is less satisfactory. Outcomes may be inefficient because no account is taken of voters' *intensity of preference*. Voting takes account of how many people favour each option in an election, but not by how much. It may be that everybody – supporters of the winning option and supporters of the losing option – could be made better off by a reversal of the outcome of an election together with an appropriate compensation from all supporters of the losing option to all supporters of the winning option. This peculiar feature of majority rule voting is part of the rationale for vote trading and cost–benefit analysis.

Majority rule voting may be intransitive, giving rise to a *paradox of voting* where no option in an election can beat every other option in a pair-wise vote. Option A beats option B, option B beats option C, but option C beats option A. Majority rule voting may well be intransitive even if each voter's preferences are transitive. Transitivity being an essential ingredient of what we see as rationality, public decision-making by majority rule voting displays characteristics which if observed in a person's decision-making would lead one to suppose that the person is insane. Voting about platforms of issues is especially likely to be intransitive, giving rise to strategic voting, to bargains among voters and to the empowerment of the agenda setter to lead the legislature by the nose to whatever outcome the agenda setter prefers.

Another disturbing feature of majority rule voting is the *exploitation problem*. Voting about the allocation of the entire national income creates an almost irresistible temptation for a majority of voters to grab the entire national income for itself, with nothing left for the excluded minority. Such a majority would normally conform to pre-existing cleavages among citizens on religious, ethnic, social, economic or geographical lines, but may be composed of any group that can coordinate its votes. Recognition of the exploitation problem is the core of a political argument for strong property rights that can be moderated by systematic redistribution but cannot be voted away altogether if government by majority rule voting is to be preserved. Recognition of the exploitation problem is part of the case for the bicameral legislature and for the division of power among legislature, executive and judiciary.

Voting is by citizens for legislators and executives, and by legislators for laws. Three troubling aspects of voting by citizens are the *paradox of not voting*, *voting externalities* and the *spoiler problem*. The paradox of not voting is that a rational, self-interested person would never bother to vote because one's expected benefit from voting – the dollar value of a win by the party one prefers weighted by the minute probability of one's vote determining the outcome of the election – falls well short of any reasonable estimate of the cost of the time required in going to the polling station and casting one's vote. A rational self-interested person would prefer to abstain. A person's vote can have no effect on the welfare of that person or anybody else unless it is pivotal, swinging the outcome of the election from the party or candidate one votes against to the party or candidate one votes for. The chance of one's vote being pivotal is too small to justify voting from self-interest alone. On the other hand, a vote that is pivotal creates two massive externalities: a positive externality of benefits to thousands and thousands of other supporters of the party one votes for and a negative externality of costs to thousands and thousands of supporters of the party one votes against. The spoiler problem is that, though candidate A beats candidate B when these are the only candidates running, the addition of candidate C causes candidate B to win instead. There are very brief discussions of alternative voting schemes, plurality voting as in the United Kingdom, the United States and Canada and proportional representation as in France and Israel. Voting by legislators for laws requires an ordering of votes for amendments and amendments to amendments on any given bill, and processes, since time is limited, for choosing which bills to bring to a vote and for examining bills in detail. These voting patterns are discussed briefly as preface to the more limited and focussed discussions to follow.

Chapter 3, entitled 'Voting about the redistribution of income', is a theme and variations. A core model portrays redistribution as undertaken by a negative income tax, where tax evasion makes redistribution costly so that each voter, depending on his initial income, has a preferred tax rate and the preference of the median voter prevails. There is an unambiguous political equilibrium where income disparities are reduced without equalizing incomes altogether and without altering people's places on the scale of rich and poor. It is then shown how the implications of the model are modified or reversed altogether by changes in the assumptions: recognition of political parties, progressive taxation, abstention, campaign advertising and additional impediments to taxation including the switch from paid labour to leisure or do-it-yourself activities.

It is shown how campaign advertising can reverse the correlation between the initial inequality of income distribution and the amount of redistribution that majority rule voting prescribes. In the core model without campaign advertising, a widening of the distribution of income, increasing the gap between rich and poor, automatically increases the spread between average and median incomes, making redistribution more advantageous to the median voter. With campaign advertising, a greater disparity between the incomes of rich and poor is likely to be reflected in a greater disparity between campaign contributions to the party of the rich and the party of the poor, together with a greater disparity in the parties' campaign advertising, influencing perceptions of the efficiency of tax collection and persuading the median voter to favour less rather than more redistribution. It is shown how more inequality *may* lead to less, rather than, more redistribution. Whether this actually happens depends upon the magnitudes of the different effects, but the simple connection between distribution and redistribution is destroyed.

Chapter 4, called 'How high might the revenue-maximizing tax rate be?', examines the proposition that extensive redistribution is impossible because there is an upper limit to taxation beyond which a tax increase yields less rather than more tax revenue. There is a political edge to this proposition, conservatives tending to argue that the revenue-maximizing tax rate is low and liberals tending to argue that the revenue-maximizing tax rate is high. The chapter contains a critical discussion of the 'new tax responsive literature' about how to measure the revenue-maximizing tax rate. The Laffer curve, showing how tax revenue varies with tax rate, is derived first from the assumption that a tax increase provokes increased tax evasion and then from the assumption that a tax increase provokes a switch in the usage of time from labour to leisure. It is commonly supposed that the Laffer curve is humped with a peak revenue at a tax rate well short of 100 per cent. That is not always so. It is shown that the peak of the Laffer curve may be close or even equal to 100 per cent. The crux of the argument in this chapter is that though redistribution may be expensive in the sense that there is a high marginal cost of public funds, it is rarely if ever impossible at rates the median voter would like to impose.

Chapter 5, entitled 'Bargaining and voting', shows how the two activities are intertwined. The chapter is essentially a list of circumstances where public decision-making requires that bargains be struck because there is no determinate equilibrium in purely self-interested voting by all parties concerned. Bargaining becomes indispensable for the formation of party platforms when stances on two or more issues must be combined and no platform beats every other platform in a pairwise vote. Members of every political party must bargain about what its platform should be. With proportional representation, parties in a majority coalition of the legislature must bargain about the allocation of places in the cabinet and about a common set of policies to follow. Only by bargaining among interested parties can a complete tax schedule be chosen. Bargaining is a major concern in the design of governments. A tyranny of the majority might be averted through a bicameral legislature with excesses of a majority in each house checked by a different majority in the other house where members are elected on somewhat different principles, but only at the cost of some risk of gridlock if majorities in the two houses cannot strike a deal. Democracy is a trade-off between efficiency in the design and execution of public policy and the risk of exploitation of minorities by majorities, with bargaining as an impediment to the one and a defence of the other. A willingness to compromise is required if democracy is to work at all. Two paradigms are somehow intertwined: the collective choice of a point on a line, and the division of a pie by unanimous consent of two or more parties. There is normally an equilibrium in majority rule voting for the one but not the other.

Chapter 6, called 'Bargaining unexplained', is a defence of the odd proposition that bargaining works in practice but not in theory. There is no denying that people bargain successfully – not always, for wars do begin from time to time – but over and over again in the ordinary business of life. This chapter is an examination of the principal bargaining models – based upon a sense of fairness, a hypothetical sequence of concessions or time-preference where each party accepts a deal today rather than waiting for a better deal tomorrow – arguing that, in each case, the assumptions of the model are too far from the circumstances of actual bargaining to warrant confidence that bargains will actually be struck. Models based upon a sense of fairness start with the premise that, wherever possible, bargainers agree upon a fifty-fifty split, generalizing to a Nash bargaining solution in more complex situations. Models based upon a postulated sequence of concessions are open to the objection that nothing forces bargainers to concede as the models presume them to do. Models connecting bargains to time preference postulate a pre-assigned timed sequence of offers and counter offers going on for ever and ever unless a bargain is struck. Understanding the process, bargainers strike a deal, called the Staahl–Rubinstein bargaining solution, in the first moment of bargaining, a deal preferable for both parties to what they might have had by waiting. As shown in an appendix, the deal is conditional on both parties believing that, but for the deal, the sequence of offers and counter-offers would never end. All three models require that nobody is just plain stubborn. Nobody is able to promise that, unless he gets such-and-such which may exceed what any of the models would assign, no bargain will ever be struck even if the pie is wasted altogether. Of course, to deny that bargains can be accounted for by pure self-interest – each party to the bargain maximizing some measure of his own welfare subject to constraints – is not to deny that bargains do get struck.

Chapter 7, called 'What exactly is a duty to vote?', investigates whether there really is any such duty and compares several interpretations of what that duty might be. Since voting is costly, widespread abstention would be socially desirable as long as the outcome of the election is unaffected, as would be the case if votes for all competing parties were reduced proportionally. If abstention were independent of party preference, there would be no duty to vote. Duty arises when abstention is likely to be biased. There are several reasons why that may be so. Supporters of one party may have a lower cost of voting or more to gain from a win by the party they prefer. Once large numbers of voters abstain it becomes that much easier for pacts among like-minded voters to swing the outcome of the election by acting collectively. Among like-minded voters, the probability of influencing the election is a public good; if one voter's chance of changing the outcome of the election is 1/1,000, then 10 like-minded voters' chance, when they all agree to vote rather than abstain, rises ten-fold to 1/100 which may be sufficient to make voting advantageous for each member of the pact despite the fact that voting is disadvantageous in the absence of any such pact. If everybody votes, there can be no such pacts. The more people vote, the less influential any such pact will be. Similarly, the more people abstain, the greater is the opportunity for representatives of one party to bribe supporters of the other party to change their votes. Just as a person's vote supplies a public good to all like-minded voters, so too does it supply a public bad to all supporters of the opposing party, which is why vote buying is everywhere illegal.

In view of these harms from widespread abstention, a distinction can be drawn among several possible variants of a duty to vote. One may feel obliged to vote for the party expected to maximize total output, or perhaps total utility, in the nation as a whole. One may feel obliged to vote in the interest of the poor or of the social class to which one belongs. One may feel obliged to vote but with no corresponding obligation about which party to vote for, provided only that the party is not vicious of cruel. One may look upon the duty to vote as nothing more than an obligation to do one's part to ensure that the will of the majority of the electorate prevails. Pros and cons of each variant are discussed. A case is made for the more limited interpretation of duty on several grounds: that whether one votes is observable, but how one votes is not, that outcomes where some people vote altruistically and others vote selfishly may be worse than outcomes where everybody votes selfishly, that a mere willingness to vote dispenses with problems of voting pacts, and that, even if everybody votes selfishly, the outcome when everybody votes is like a census of opinion which may be satisfactory as a foundation for democratic government.

Chapter 8, called 'An alternative explanation of the chance of casting a pivotal vote', is about a technical problem. Voting can never be advantageous to the voter unless there is some chance that one's vote makes a difference to the outcome of the election. The only way for that to happen is if one's vote is pivotal, swinging the outcome of the election from the party one opposes to the party one favours. And the only way for one's vote to be pivotal is for there to be a tie among all other voters because otherwise the outcome of the election is the same regardless of whether or not one votes. The problem is that two ways of inferring one's chance of casting a pivotal vote, called historical and theoretical methods, yield vastly different estimates. Consider an election between left and right parties in a constituency with 100,000 voters and where in past elections between 47,000 and 51,000 have voted for the left party. The theoretical method is to reason that, since 49 per cent of all voters have favoured the left party, the chance of a tied election is the chance of picking exactly 50,000 red balls in 100,000 draws from an urn containing 49 red balls (reflecting the percentage of votes for the left party) and 51 blue balls. This chance is very, very small. Specifically, it is about *one in fifty billion*. The theoretical method creates the impression that the chance of casting a pivotal vote is always small enough to be ignored in practice.

By contrast, one might reason historically that if outcomes of past elections have been within a range of 4,000 votes and on the assumption that all outcomes between the historically observed extremes are equally likely, then one's chance of casting a pivotal vote becomes *one in four thousand*, still small but large enough to be relevant in some circumstances. Uncertainty in the outcome of elections might be modelled not by *person-by-person* randomization as in the theoretical model, but by *nationwide* randomization. Think of all voters placed on a scale according to their valuations of a win for the left party, where valuations are negative when the right party is preferred. Randomness in voting is seen as shifts of the entire schedule in response to unanticipated events. A model of nationwide randomization yields estimates of the chance of casting a pivotal vote that are broadly consistent with the historical estimates, and is easily modified to account for people's decisions whether to vote or abstain. Such a model is used in the discussion of the duty to vote in Chapter 7. Depending on the shape of the voters' valuations schedule, a majority of the people who vote might favour one party even though a majority of eligible voters favours the other.

Chapter 9, called 'The problem of equity', is about the defence of voting against the exploitation problem that citizens will not trust themselves to government by majority rule voting where any majority of the electorate is automatically empowered to dispossess the corresponding minority completely, in the extreme taking every penny they have. Government by majority rule voting does not work if there is too much at stake in elections. No government in office will willingly hold elections if loss in an election means descent for the office-holders and their supporters in the population at large from the top to the bottom of society, from prosperity to destitution. It is argued that a democratic society requires a system of *equity* as a constraint upon voting and as a way of dealing with matters that must not be voted about. The word 'equity' is used in this context because of its association with possessions and entitlements. The chapter contains a description of the exploitation problem, a discussion of property rights as a system of equity and an explanation of how public policy may exacerbate or diminish the exploitation problem.

The story continues in Chapter 10, called 'Voting rights, property rights and civil rights', with a review of attempts to justify property rights despite their inevitable inequality and despite their origin in ancient theft, a description of the porous boundary between the domain of civil rights and voting rights where all people are equal and the domain of property rights where all dollars are equal, and discussions of the origin of rights and the path to universal suffrage, raising the odd possibility that some of the requirements for democracy can only be supplied by preceding autocratic regimes.

The book concludes with a defence of its central theme – that bargaining, duty and rights are indispensable requirements the maintenance of government by majority rule voting – against the implicit assumption in certain models of voting that an equilibrium is attainable without these requirements. Chapters 11 and 12, called 'Assessing the citizen-candidate model' and 'The significance of the probabilistic voting theorem', are critical examinations of models of political equilibrium where, on certain strong assumptions, outcomes in democratic politics are as determinate as outcomes in the competitive economy. In the *citizen-candidate* model, anybody can stand as a candidate, each candidate promises to enact one of a given set of options, the promised option is always that which is best for the candidate, and each person votes for the candidate whose chosen option is best for that person. All candidates are utterly selfish but completely truthful, at least in the sense that a candidate promising something other than what is best for him- or herself would never be believed. When politics is about the choice of a single number – such as the rate of the negative income tax – the citizen-candidate model becomes an extension of the median voter theorem because no candidate can win the election if his promised number is too far away from the first preference of the median voter. When politics is about the allocation among voters of a sum of money, everybody runs for office, the winner of the election grabs the entire sum for himself, all candidates are tied and the outcome of the election is determined by the flip of a many-sided coin. In the *probabilistic voting* model, political parties seek nothing other than to be elected, and voters have enough attachment to political parties that groups with otherwise identical preferences share votes between parties rather than all voting for one party even if the parties' offers to any given group are not identical. Platforms of political parties allocate income among groups to equalize votes per dollar of income supplied.

The models are criticized on the technical grounds that they supply very odd results in some circumstances and that all bargaining is assumed away. It is shown by example that the probabilistic voting model is not immune to the exploitation problem. There may be an equilibrium where every group gets a part of the pie, but that is not always so. In both models, a prohibition on bargains and commitments is essential. The critical assumption in the citizen-candidate model is that no candidate can commit today to an action that may not be in his interest tomorrow, for a candidate who can make such commitments can win an election with the support of some predatory majority. The critical assumption in the probabilistic voting model is that groups constituting a majority of the electorate cannot agree on some allocation of income among themselves and promise one another to vote for a party which incorporates that allocation as its platform, no matter what the alternative. Both models fall apart and the full force of the exploitation problem is restored when promises cannot be believed and when predatory bargains are not assumed away.

My interest in the economics of voting began in the early 1970s with the realization – by no means original, but new to me – that the attempt to allocate income by voting would destroy democratic government and that 'a system of equity' (an allocation of income prior to and independent of voting) is required if majority rule voting is to be maintained. 'The problem of equity' first appeared in 1975, was reprinted in *The Collected Papers of Dan Usher*, (Usher, 1994a) and was the basis of *The Economic Prerequisite to Democracy* (Usher, 1981). That same insight was the basis of 'The significance of the probabilistic voting theorem' (Usher, 1994b) and 'Assessing the citizen-candidate model' (Usher, 2005). Recent essays have been about the behavioural requirements of majority rule voting: 'Bargaining and voting' (Usher, 2012a), 'Bargaining unexplained' (Usher, 2012b) and 'An alternative explanation of the chance of casting a pivotal vote' (Usher, 2014).

## References

Arrow, K. J. and Hahn, F. H. (1971) *General Competitive Analysis*, San Francisco: Holden-Day, pp. vi–vii.

Usher, D. (1975) The problem of equity, Discussion Paper 181, Economics Department, Queen's University.

Usher D. (1981) *The Economic Prerequisite to Democracy*, Oxford: Blackwell.

Usher, D. (1994a) *National Accounting and Economic Theory: The Collected Papers of Dan Usher*, Vol. 1, Cheltenham: Edward Elgar.

Usher, D. (1994b) The significance of the probabilistic voting theorem, *Canadian Journal of Economics*, 27(2), 433–45.

Usher, D. (2005) Assessing the citizen-candidate model, *Public Choice*, 125(1–2), 43–65.

Usher, D. (2012a) Bargaining and voting, *Public Choice*, 151(3–4), 739–55.

Usher, D. (2012b) Bargaining unexplained, *Public Choice*, 151(1–2), 23–41.

Usher, D. (2014) An alternative explanation of the chance of casting a pivotal vote, *Rationality and Society*, 26(1), 105–38.

# 2 Voting patterns[1]

One would like to think of majority rule voting as reflecting the will of the people, and it does so, imperfectly. It is indispensable in bringing forth leaders and law-makers who can be expected to serve some notion of the common good, in enabling citizens to choose among candidates, and in keeping the dictator at bay. But majority rule voting is less than fully efficient, and is at times irrational. The well-known stories – or voting paradigms – to be retold in this chapter illustrate the irrationality as well as the virtues of majority rule voting and help to explain the rules and customs within which voting takes place.

Voting may be by people for options, by citizens for candidates or by legislators for laws. These contexts are not entirely distinct because voting for candidates is at least in part for the laws and policies candidates would adopt as legislators or executives. The emphasis here is on people voting for options, discussed in the first two-thirds of this chapter. Voting for candidates and laws inherit some of the character of voting for options, but have distinct features of their own. Options are looked upon as given exogenously. Candidates choose themselves. Legislators craft laws in addition to choosing among them.

The chapter begins with the *median voter theorem* and the *Condorcet jury theorem* where voting works very well. The median voter theorem establishes that there is a unique voting equilibrium, one option that beats every other in a pairwise vote as long as all options in an election can be lined up so that every voter has a best place on the line and, as between any two options both to the right or both to the left of the best place, prefers the option closest to the best place. The Condorcet jury theorem pertains to situations where people differ in opinions rather than interests. One among a set of options is best for everybody but people disagree about which option that is. The theorem establishes that voting is likely to find the best option when each person has a better than even chance of being right. Depiction of contemporary politics as a contest between left and right can be seen as an attempt to confine platforms of political parties within the boundaries of these theorems. Otherwise, majority rule voting may be intransitive and inefficient: intransitive in succumbing to a *paradox of voting* where none of the options in an election defeats all other options in a pairwise vote, and inefficient in that the loser in an election may, in a sense to be described, be preferable to the winner.

The potential inefficiency and intransitivity of majority rule voting may be mitigated by vote trading which is at once the rationale for cost–benefit analysis and a way for minorities of voters who care passionately about one issue above all others to thrust their cherished policies onto the platforms of competing parties, even when those policies are opposed by the great majority of voters.

Much depends on what people vote about. An *exploitation problem* has for centuries stood as the principal objection to majority rule voting. A majority of voters – any majority whatsoever – can employ the power of the vote to dispossess the corresponding minority completely. A majority of the poor can totally dispossess the rich. A majority of one religion can totally dispossess the minority of other religions. Fear of exploitation is the rationale for divided government and for the constitutional protection of civil and property rights. The exploitation problem is compounded by the danger of the emergence of an *elected dictator* who will employ the powers of government to preserve his tenure in office indefinitely.

Much also depends on who votes and who abstains. A person's vote can have no impact on anybody unless that vote is *pivotal*, swinging the outcome of the election from one party to another, but, if one's vote is pivotal, the *voting externalities* – positive to like-minded voters and negative to others – can be enormous. That the chance of a person's vote being pivotal is almost never large enough to justify voting on purely selfish grounds is called the *paradox of not voting*. Government by majority rule voting does not work if too large a proportion of the eligible voters abstains.

Democratic politics is more than the choice by voting among a given set of options. It is also a set of rules about how people vote. The outcome of majority rule voting depends on what people vote about and how votes are counted. Voting may be about the choice of one option (the president) from a set of options, the choice of several options (legislators) at once from a larger set, or the formation of laws within the legislature. Voting for candidates is conducted within established rules – among them *plurality voting*, *proportional representation*, the *single transferable vote* and the *Borda count* – where the pros and cons of the different voting rules depend on the context in which they are applied. Among the concerns in the choice of voting rules is the possibility of a *spoiler*, a candidate who has no chance of winning the election but whose presence switches the outcome among other candidates, often causing the most popular candidate to lose the election.

## The median voter theorem

The median voter theorem[2] is best introduced by an example. A small tribe protects itself with guns from predation by neighbouring tribes. Its one and only political decision is how many guns to acquire. The decision is made by majority rule voting. The tribe consists of five people – $A$, $B$, $C$, $D$ and $E$ – with different preferences about the number of guns for the tribe to acquire. Person $A$ wants the tribe to acquire to acquire 10 guns, person B wants 5 guns, and so on, as shown in Table 2.1.

A key assumption here is that people's preferences for guns are 'single peaked', meaning that having to choose between two numbers of guns, both above or both

*Table 2.1* Each person's preferred number of guns

| People | A | B | C | D | E |
|---|---|---|---|---|---|
| Preferred number of guns | 10 | 5 | 7 | 12 | 2 |

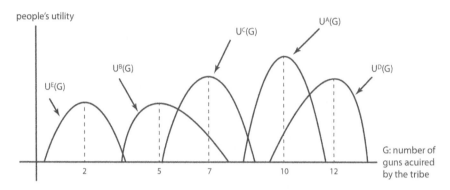

*Figure 2.1* Preferences of the five members of the tribe.

below one's preferred number, a person always chooses the number closest to his preferred number. The assumption says nothing about a person's choice between options on either side of his first preference, but, among options on the same side, all the left or all to the right, a person becomes less and less well-off the farther away from his first preference the tribe's choice turns out to be. For example, person *A*, who would like the tribe to acquire 10 guns, would prefer 8 guns to 6 guns, and would prefer 12 guns to 15 guns.

Single-peaked preferences can be represented by humped utility functions as illustrated in Figure 2.1, where, since utility is intrinsically ordinal rather than cardinal, it is the location of the peak that matters rather than its height. On the understanding that all public expenditure is borne equally among all five people, the utility functions of persons *A*, *B*, *C*, *D* and *E* are $U^A(G)$, $U^B(G)$, $U^C(G)$, $U^D(G)$ and $U^E(G)$ where *G* is the number of guns that the tribe acquires. The ordering of the five people in accordance with the number of guns they prefer the tribe to acquire is *E*, *B*, *C*, *A* and *D*.

The 'median voter theorem' specifies conditions where the first preference of the median voter wins in a pairwise vote with any other option, the median voter being the person in the middle with equal numbers of voters to the left and to the right when all voters are lined up accordance with their preferences as in Figure 2.1. The median voter wins because the median voter and the two voters who want *more* guns vote for the median voter's preferred number in a contest with any *smaller* number, and because the median voter and the two voters who want *fewer* guns vote for the median voter's preferred number in a contest with any *larger* number. In this example, the median voter is person *C* whose first preference, 7 guns, prevails in a pairwise vote with any other number. Persons $E$ and $B$ join person $C$ in voting for 7 guns when the alternative is 8, and persons $A$ and $D$ join person $C$ in voting for 7 guns when the alternative is 6.

The theorem holds true for a population of any number of voters as long as there is some ordering of society's options over which every voter's utility function is humped as shown in the figure. As will be discussed later, actual voting may, but does not always, conform to the requirements of the median voter theorem. When it does, one would expect the first preference of the median voter to emerge as the outcome of two-party elections.

The simple example shown in Table 2.1 and Figure 2.1 can be generalized by expanding the tribe from 5 to $N$ people whose welfare depends upon their own consumption of private goods (butter) and the tribe's acquisition of public goods (guns). Suppose

- Prior to the acquisition of guns, every person has an income of $y$ pounds of butter.
- The price of guns to the tribe is $P$ pounds of butter.
- The tribe's expenditure on guns is financed by a head tax, so that the price of guns per person is $P/N$.
- Every person's budget constraint is

$$y = b + PG/N \tag{2.1}$$

where $b$ is each person's consumption of butter and $G$ is the tribe's acquisition of guns.
- Differences in people's preferences for guns and butter are represented by the parameter $\alpha_i$ in their utility functions

$$U_i = \log b + \alpha_i \log G \tag{2.2}$$

where, the larger $\alpha_i$, the more guns person $i$ wants the tribe to acquire. This utility function gives rise to the usual concave indifference curves in $b$ and $G$.

A person's demand price for guns (the amount of butter he is prepared to sacrifice for the tribe to acquire an extra gun) when the tribe has acquired $G$ guns and the person consumes $b$ pounds of butter is the slope of the indifference curve at the point $(b, G)$. It follows at once from Equation (2.2) that person $i$'s demand price for guns at $(b, G)$ becomes

$$(\delta U_i/\delta G)/(\delta U_i/\delta b) = (\alpha_i/G)/(1/b) = \alpha_i b/G \tag{2.3}$$

so that, the larger $\alpha_i$, the higher person $i$'s demand price for guns must be.

The humped utility functions in Figure 2.1 show utility as a function of $G$ alone rather than as a function of $G$ and $b$ as in Equation (2.2) above. The functions are derived by plugging the budget constraint into the utility function,

$$U_i = \log(y - PG/N) + \alpha_i \log G \tag{2.4}$$

so that a person's marginal utility of guns, allowing for the loss of bread to procure them, becomes

$$dU_i/dG = -(P/N)/(y - PG/N) + \alpha_i/G = (1/b)[\alpha_i b/G - P/N]$$

or, equivalently,

$$(dU_i/dG)(\delta U_i/\delta b) = [\alpha_i b/G - P/N] \tag{2.5}$$

Equation (2.5) means that, when expressed in pounds rather than in utils, a person's gain or loss from an extra gun is the difference between that person's demand price for guns, $\alpha_i b/G$, and the supply price per person, $P/N$.[3] Person $i$'s utility is maximized when $(dU_i/dG) = 0$ at which

$$G_i = \alpha_i bN/P \tag{2.6}$$

where $G_i$ is the number of guns that person $i$ would prefer the tribe to acquire. With $G$ less than $G_i$, the utility of person $i$ is an increasing function of $G$ because the demand price exceeds the supply price. With $G$ greater than $G_i$, the utility of person $i$ is a decreasing function of $G$ because the supply price exceeds the demand price.

Returning to the original five person example, the ordering of the humped shaped curves in Figure 2.1 is derived from the assumption that $\alpha_E < \alpha_B < \alpha_C < \alpha_A < \alpha_D$ as long as everybody's income is the same. The median voter is $C$. The tribe's demand for guns, $G$, is

$$G = (\text{median } \alpha)bN/P \tag{2.7}$$

Voters' preferences are illustrated on the demand and supply diagram in Figure 2.2 with the price of guns on the vertical axis and the number of guns acquired on the horizontal axis. The flat line a distance $P/N$ above the horizontal axis is the supply curve of guns to voters who must all pay the same share of the total cost of all guns acquired. The five downward sloping lines are the demand curves of the five members of the tribe showing the each person $i$'s demand price, $\alpha_i b/G$, for each value of $G$. Each person's preferred quantity of guns is indicated by the crossing of that person's demand curve with the supply curve for the tribe as a whole.

When the tribe acquires the median voter's preferred number of guns, every person but the median voter is somewhat worse off than if that person's own first preference were chosen instead. Person $A$'s loss from the having the median voter's first preference rather than his/her own is represented by the area of the

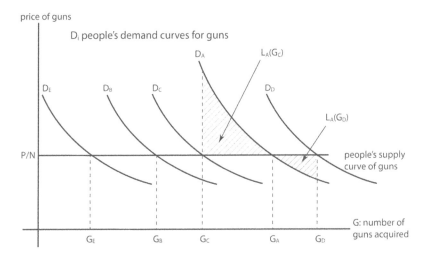

*Figure 2.2* People's preferences represented by the crossing of demand and supply curves.

shaded triangle $L_A(G_C)$. Person $A$'s loss would be the area of the shaded triangle $L_A(G_D)$ if person $D$'s first preference had been chosen instead.

The first preference of the median voter becomes the equilibrium number of guns in a two-party election where nothing but the number of guns is at stake. The party choosing that number of guns as its platform automatically wins the election against an opposing party that chooses a different number. Both parties are driven to choose that number of guns in their platforms, leaving voters indifferent between them.

The resulting equilibrium is probably close to the efficient outcome, but not exactly the same. The efficient number of guns – efficient in the sense that no change in the number of guns with compensation from gainers to losers can make everybody better off – is identified by the Samuelson rule that the sum of the marginal utilities of a public good is just equal to the marginal cost, specifically that

$$\sum_{i=1}^{N} \alpha_i b / G = P$$

or, equivalently,

$$G = (\text{average } \alpha) bN / P \tag{2.8}$$

in which the median value of $\alpha$ in Equation (2.7) has been replaced by the average. The equilibrium $G$ could differ substantially from the efficient $G$ if more than half of voters' values of $\alpha$ were concentrated tightly at one end of the scale.

Nothing in the median voter theorem speaks of why voters' preferences are what they are postulated to be. People who vote for a large number of guns may do so self-interestedly because they live in a part of the country that is especially susceptible to attack from neighbouring tribes, or, though neither more nor less in danger than anybody else, because they place a high value on safety by comparison with ordinary goods, or, altruistically, because they are concerned about the safety of fellow citizens in dangerous circumstances, or from a sense of fear that fellow tribesmen will prove unpatriotic if not well protected. Similarly, in voting about redistribution to be discussed in the next chapter, the median voter theorem remains valid regardless of whether voters' preferences for redistribution differ because of differences in what they stand to gain or lose from redistribution, in their concern for other people, or in fear of rebellion if the gap between rich and poor becomes too wide.

Nor is it a requirement of the median voter theorem that voters be correct in their judgments about what is best for themselves or for their fellow citizens. People may favour a large armory to protect themselves from imaginary dangers, or they may favour a small armory because of a false sense of security. There is, however, an interesting case where voting resolves differences of opinion to produce the outcome that is best for everyone.

## The Condorcet jury theorem

Voting in the context of this theorem is not to reconcile conflicting interests, but to discover a common interest presumed to exist. Imagine an election with two candidates where it is in every voter's interest to elect the better candidate, where voters differ in their opinions about which candidate is best, but where every voter has a better than fifty-fifty chance of recognizing the better candidate. The theorem is that when all voters are equally likely to identify the better candidate, when there is no correlation among voters' judgments and when the electorate is large enough, the better candidate is almost certain to win the election.[4]

Suppose the election is between Abe and Beth where Abe is in fact the better candidate and where each voter has a 60 per cent chance of recognizing Abe as such. Voting in this context is like choosing a ball at random from an urn containing six balls marked Abe and four balls marked Beth. An electorate with only one voter would have a 60 per cent chance of electing Abe, an electorate with three voters would raise the probability to 64.8 per cent, an electorate with five voters would raise the probability to 68.3 per cent and a very large electorate would give Abe a sure majority of the votes. It is essential for this example that voters' judgments be uncorrelated. At the opposite extreme where voters' judgments are perfectly correlated, Abe's chance of winning the election remains at 60 per cent regardless of the size of the electorate. Also, in sharp contrast to other circumstances to be discussed later on in this chapter, it might be beneficial to everybody for people to abstain when they are unsure about which candidate is best and when they believe that other voters are better informed.

The line between the median voter theorem and the Condorcet jury theorem is not as clear-cut as one might at first suppose. The guardian of the ballot box sees how many people voted for each candidate, but does not see why people voted as they did. Voting is partly a game played among voters with different objectives, partly a struggle to identify policies that are best for everybody, partly a conflict among politicians seeking office for its own sake and partly an attempt to elect the most competent[5] and honest leaders. The most that can be expected of the theorems is that each, in its own way, sheds some light on the process. Other voting patterns identify other difficulties that must in practice be tolerated or overcome.

## Intensity of preference

The central proposition in economics is that, depending on initial conditions and subject to well-known qualifications, a competitive economy yields an efficient output of goods and assignment of goods to people, so that no planner, however wise, powerful or benevolent, could rearrange the economy to make everybody better off. A planner may favour some people at the expense of others, but cannot make everybody better off at once. By contrast, majority rule voting may be inefficient, recognizing only the numbers of people favouring each option in an election, but placing no weight on how deeply voters are concerned about the options they support. Sometimes this inefficiency is borne as a regrettable but necessary cost of democracy. Sometimes it is modified by the rules within which majority rule voting takes place. Sometimes it is avoided altogether by removing certain matters from the political arena. Several simple examples show what might be at stake.

Consider once again the election with two candidates, Abe and Beth, who differ not in innate ability, but in the groups of people who can expect to benefit from the policies they will adopt if elected. There is no longer any uncertainty about the meaning of the election. Perhaps Abe, whose supporters are relatively rich, promises less progressivity of taxation, or perhaps Abe is expected to adopt policies that are advantageous to people in the west, while Beth is expected to adopt policies that are advantageous to people in the east. Suppose there are $n$ voters among whom $n_A$ voters would become better off if Abe wins the election, $n_B$ voters would become better off if Beth wins the election. Everybody votes self-interestedly and the winner is whoever gets the most votes. Abe is elected if $n_A > n_B$, Beth is elected if $n_B > n_A$, and the election is decides by the flip of a coin if $n_A = n_B$.

Suppose $n_A > n_B$ so that Abe wins the election. To see why the outcome of the election need not be efficient, suppose that supporters of the two candidates differ in their valuations of the outcome of the election. Suppose everybody who votes for Abe places a value of $\$A$ on Abe winning the election, while everybody who votes for Beth places a value of $\$B$ on Beth winning the election. Each supporter of Beth would be prepared to pay a maximum of $\$B$ and each supporter of Abe would be prepared to accept a minimum of $\$A$ to have Beth in office instead of Abe. Whether or not the outcome of the election is efficient depends on the magnitudes of $A$ and $B$.

Imagine a benevolent planner who cannot alter the national income but can transfer income from Beth's supporters to Abe's supporters in return for the substitution of Beth for Abe as the winner of the election. The planner could transfer $T_B$ *from* each supporter of Beth yielding a transfer of $T_A$ *to* each supporter of Abe, where $T_A$ and $T_B$ are subject to the constraint that[6]

$$n_A T_A = n_B T_B \tag{2.9}$$

The transfer is advantageous to both groups if and only if

$$T_A > A \quad \text{and} \quad T_B < B \tag{2.10}$$

that is, as long as

$$A < T_A < [n_B/n_A]B \tag{2.11}$$

supplying upper and lower limits to what each of Abe's supporters must be paid to keep people in both groups better off than they would be if the outcome of the election were allowed to stand. The payments must be at least $A$ and not more than $[n_B/n_A]B$ which is somewhat less than $B$ because Abe won the election. For example, if twice as many people vote for Abe as for Beth, if the least that each of Abe's would be willing to accept in return for having Beth in office rather than Abe is $100, and if each of Beth's supporters would pay up to $300 to place Beth in office, then a planner can make everybody in both groups better off by a transfer to each of Abe's supporters of not less than $100 and not more than $150.

Whether such a transfer is feasible depends on valuations of voters' preferences and the size of the majority. The closer the vote, the more likely it becomes that the outcome of the election is inefficient, rising to a fifty-fifty chance as the share of votes for the losing candidate approaches 50 per cent. The office about which people vote must be filled, and the risk of inefficiency is an unavoidable consequence of the process by which a candidate is selected.

Differences in people's intensities of preference is the rationale for vote trading or, as it is sometimes called, logrolling. If a group cares a great deal about one thing and another group cares a great deal about another, they may trade votes, each getting its way in the matter it cares most about. Sometimes, vote trading is at the expense of voters who are not part of the trade, but, like the planner's imaginary transfer of income as described above, vote trading may be beneficial for everybody at once.

Three friends, Allan, Bill and Carol, are ordering lunch consisting of soup, sandwiches and pie, where, never mind why, they must all have the same lunch and where, being democratically minded, they select their lunch by majority rule voting. Collectively, they must choose between tomato soup and chicken soup, between ham sandwiches and cheese sandwiches and between apple pie and cherry pie. Suppose Allan prefers tomato soup, ham sandwiches and apple pie, Bill prefers chicken soup, ham sandwiches and cherry pie, and Carol prefers

*Table 2.2* Voters' preferences for soup, sandwiches and pie

|  | *Soup* | *Sandwich* | *Pie* |
| --- | --- | --- | --- |
| Allan | tomato | ham | apple |
| Bill | chicken | ham | cherry |
| Carol | chicken | cheese | apple |
| Winner | chicken | ham | apple |
| Best choice | tomato | cheese | cherry |

chicken soup, cheese sandwiches and apple pie, as shown in the first three rows of Table 2.2. In three item-by-item votes, one for soup, one for sandwiches and one for pie the winners, two-to-one, are chicken soup, ham sandwiches and apple pie, as shown in the fourth row of the table.

This outcome may, in fact, be very unsatisfactory for everybody because, as is always the case in voting, people's intensities of preference are not taken into account. Suppose it just so happens that Allen detests chicken soup but, although he has a slight preference for ham sandwiches over cheese sandwiches, would be quite content with either, and that he would also be content with either apple pie or cherry pie. Suppose also that Bill detests apple pie but would be quite content with either soup and either sandwich, and that Carol detests ham sandwiches but would be quite content with either soup and either pie. Were that so, all three voters would be better off with the combination of tomato soup, cheese sandwiches and cherry pie than they would be with the winning combination of chicken soup, ham sandwiches and apple pie that would win in the three separate votes. The best outcome may be attained by a vote trade in which each person votes for his second choice in two elections in return for the other people's votes for his first choice in the election that matters. Alternatively, there may be one comprehensive vote for all three items together in which (tomato, cheese, cherry) beats (chicken, ham, apple).

A related example has implications for cost–benefit analysis. A community of five people – Allan, Bill, Carol, Donald and Elizabeth – is considering whether to build any or all of five roads. Each road is near one of the five people's houses, but all roads are somewhat beneficial to all five people. Suppose each road costs $10 to build, yields benefits of $8 to one of the five people (a different person for each road) and of $1 to each of the other four people, so that the sum of the benefits from each road is $12, as shown in Table 2.3. The principal feature of this example is that it is in no person's interest to build the road near his house all by himself, but it is in the interest of all five people that all five roads be built.

Decisions about road building could be left entirely to the private sector (each person choosing whether or not to build the road near his own house), the community might vote on each of the five roads, one by one, or the community might decide whether to build all roads or none in a single comprehensive vote. No roads would be built if road building were left to the private sector. If Allan alone had to decide whether or not to build (and pay for) the road near his house, he would

*Table 2.3* Benefits of each road to each person

|  | Alan | Bill | Carol | Donald | Elizabeth |
|---|---|---|---|---|---|
| Road near Allan's house | $8 | $1 | $1 | $1 | $1 |
| Road near Bill's house | $1 | $8 | $1 | $1 | $1 |
| Road near Carol's house | $1 | $1 | $8 | $1 | $1 |
| Road near Donald's house | $1 | $1 | $1 | $8 | $1 |
| Road near Elizabeth's house | $1 | $1 | $8 | $1 | $8 |

Note: Each road costs $10 to build.

choose not to do so because his gain, $8, from the road is less than the cost, $10, of building it. All other roads would remain unbuilt for the same reason. Nor would any of the five roads be built if decisions about road building were made by majority rule voting, one road at a time. Every road would be voted down four-to-one because four out of the five people would be better off without it. Everybody but Allan is made worse off when the road near Allan's house is built. If all five people voted whether or not to build the road near Allan's house on the understanding that the cost of the road would be shared equally among them, the building of the road would be rejected four-to-one because everybody but Allan would bear $2 of cost for only $1 of gain.

There is a different outcome in voting about all five roads together, or when a deal is struck among the five people, each to vote for the others' roads in return for their voting for his. All five people gain from such a deal, for each person's gain, $12, from having all five roads is greater than each person's share, $10, of the cost of building them, though any three people could do even better by a predatory vote trade to build their roads alone.[7]

A comprehensive trade is implicit when authority to build roads is assigned to the Ministry of Transport in accordance with the principles of cost–benefit analysis. Actual cost–benefit analysis differs from this example in several ways. Not all projects are equally expensive, and not all projects pass the standard test that cost must be exceeded by benefits 'to whomsoever they may accrue'. The test serves to maximize total net benefits, but it may allocate benefits unequally. People everywhere may nonetheless tolerate such inequality of outcomes because it is not known when the rule is adopted who the net beneficiaries will be. Cost–benefit is a comprehensive once-and-for-all vote trade, avoiding predatory vote trading and supplanting the many possible electoral deals that might otherwise be required.

The lunch story in Table 2.2 and the roads story in Table 2.3 are alike in that voting on distinct items can be bundled to yield an outcome that is better for everybody than the outcome of voting for one item at a time. The lunch story is about vote trading in parliament and might also be applicable to the formation of platforms of political parties. The roads story is about cost–benefit analysis. Both are analytically the same. The stories are alike in another much less satisfactory way. Even when small issues can be combined into one large issue, the efficient outcome may be unstable in that it cannot beat all other outcomes in a pairwise vote. This will be explained later once certain other matters have been discussed.

## The paradox of voting[8]

For some constellations of individual preferences, a community's preferences as expressed by majority rule voting may be intransitive, despite the fact that each and every voter's preferences are transitive. To say that a person's preferences are transitive is to say that, if $x$ is preferred to $y$ and $y$ is preferred to $z$, then $x$ must be preferred to $z$. A person whose preferences are intransitive would be considered irrational or insane. The paradox of voting is that electoral preferences may be intransitive, even though voters's preferences are not.

Once again, three friends, Allan, Bill and Carol, are ordering lunch but now lunch consists only of sandwiches, with no soup or pie, and there are three, rather than just two, choices: ham, cheese and tuna. Again, the same type of sandwich must be chosen for everybody, and the three friends must agree among themselves which type to order. It is, of course, entirely possible that all preferences are the same, in which case the common first preference would win in a pairwise vote with either of the other two options. It is also possible for preferences to be as shown in Table 2.4 where each person's preferences are transitive but the group's preferences as expressed by majority rule voting are not.

Since Allan prefers ham to cheese and cheese to tuna, he must prefer ham to tuna. Bill's and Carol's preferences are consistent as well. Voting is different. In a vote between ham and cheese, ham wins two-to-one because Allan and Carol both prefer ham to cheese. In a vote between cheese and tuna, cheese wins two-to-one because Allan and Bill both prefer cheese to tuna. But in a vote between tuna and ham, tuna wins two-to-one because both Bill and Carol prefer tuna to ham. Individual rationality gives rise to collective irrationality because different pairs of people are on the winning side in each of the three votes.

With individual preferences as shown in Table 2.4, the community's preferences expressed by majority rule voting are summarized in the directed graph in Figure 2.3, where an arrow from one option to another signifies that the former beats the latter in a pairwise vote.

The paradox of voting means that there is no *Condorcet winner*, no option that defeats any other option in a pairwise vote. Absence of a Condorcet winner has two very important consequences: the empowerment of the *agenda setter* and the incentive for *strategic* rather than *sincere* voting.

*Table 2.4* None of the three options beats both of the others in a pairwise vote

| Person | First preference | Second preference | Third preference |
|--------|------------------|-------------------|------------------|
| Allan | ham | cheese | tuna |
| Bill | cheese | tuna | ham |
| Carol | tuna | ham | cheese |

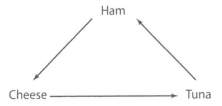

*Figure 2.3* A directed graph for voting among three options.

To illustrate the power of the agenda setter, suppose voting for sandwiches is conducted in two stages. A first vote is between two arbitrarily chosen sandwiches. A second vote is between the winner of the first vote and the one remaining sandwich. It turns out that, regardless of which two sandwiches are included in the first round, the winner in the first round is always the loser in the second. The sandwich introduced in the second round must always win. If the first round is between ham and cheese, the ultimate winner is tuna. If the first round is between ham and tuna, the ultimate winner is cheese. If the first round is between tuna and cheese, the ultimate winner is ham. Whoever is entitled to set the ordering of the votes is, in effect, entitled to determine which sandwich is ultimately chosen by the group.

The influence of the agenda setter is eliminated when there is a Condorcet winner and is weakened when voters defend themselves against the agenda setter by voting strategically. The agenda setter is powerless when there is a Condorcet winner because a Condorcet winner must sooner or later be introduced into the sequence and, once introduced, wins every subsequent vote. If, for example, Allan's preferences were for ham, tuna and cheese in that order (rather than for ham, cheese and tuna as shown in Table 2.4), then, without changing anybody's first preferences, the direction of the bottom arrow in Figure 2.3 is reversed and tuna becomes the unique Condorcet winner.

A person's vote is *strategic* rather than *sincere* when that person votes for an option other than his first preference in order to obtain a better outcome in the entire sequence of votes.[9] Suppose that Carol is the agenda setter and that, to engineer a win for her first preference, she chooses a sequence with a first-round vote between ham and cheese and followed a second between the winner in the first round against tuna. If everybody votes sincerely, the community's choice is tuna, as Carol prefers. But what is best for Carol is worst for Allan whose first preference, ham, emerges victorious in the first round, only to lose out in the second to his least preferred sandwich which is tuna. As long as Allan votes sincerely in the first round, this outcome is inevitable.

Allan's defence against the agenda setter is to vote strategically. Instead of voting for his preferred sandwich in the first round, he might cast his vote to get the best attainable outcome in the second. As between ham and cheese, Allan prefers ham, but, by voting for ham, he obtains not ham, but tuna. A better strategy for Albert is to vote for cheese. Then, cheese beats ham in the first round because

Allan and Bill both vote for cheese, and cheese beats tuna in the second round because, once again, Allan and Bill vote for cheese. By voting strategically, Allan cannot get his first preference, ham, but he derails his last preference, tuna. Carol, on the other hand, is foiled completely. Manoeuvring to procure a vote for her first preference, tuna, she procured a vote for her least preferred sandwich, cheese, instead. In more realistic voting situations, the relation between the power of the agenda setter and strategic voting can be quite complex. Though it is in every-body's interest to vote sincerely in the last round, there may be an incentive to vote strategically in preceding rounds.

Sequential voting can be seen as a stripped-down version of parliamentary procedure where a choice has to be made among an original bill, the bill as amended, alternative amendments and the status quo with no bill at all. Parlia-mentary procedure is a sequence of pairwise votes with elaborate supplementary rules determining which pairs of options belong at each round of voting.

Sequential voting may be contrasted with *plurality voting* where all options are on the table at once, each person votes for one and only one option and the option with the most votes wins. Under plurality voting, Allan would cast his ballot for ham, Bill for cheese and Carol for tuna, so the outcome would be a three-way tie. Alternatively, with three Allans, two Bills and two Carols, whose preferences are as shown in Table 2.4, the winner under plurality voting would be ham, with three votes as against two for each of cheese and tuna, but the winner under sequential voting would still be whichever option is introduced in the second round.

## Vote trading among the extremists

Similar difficulties arise in the formaion of multidimensional public policy. Imag-ine a society in which two reforms are being considered, the abolition of the death penalty and the establishment of free trade, neither of which is favoured by a majority of the population. Suppose, 70 per cent of the population would vote 'no' in a referendum on the question 'Should we abolish the death penalty?' and 70 per cent of the population would also vote 'no' in a referendum on the question 'Should we establish free trade?' There are, nevertheless, circumstances where a majority in this society might vote 'yes' in a referendum on the question 'Should we abolish the death penalty *and* establish free trade?' Equivalently, there are cir-cumstances where the inclusion of both the abolition of the death penalty and the establishment of free trade in the platform of a political party might enable that party to win the election.

Two extreme cases can be disposed of easily. If the very same group of people are the advocates of both reforms, a referendum to adopt both reforms together would automatically be rejected by the very same 70 per cent of the population that rejects each reform separately. Alternatively, if advocates of the two reforms are different groups of people but advocates of each reform are in favour of, though perhaps less enthusiastic about, the other, then a referendum to adopt both reforms together would be automatically be passed by a majority of 60 per cent, the two groups' combined share of the electorate. The interesting case is where the reformers are two distinct groups of people, each of which would prefer the other's reform to be rejected, people favouring the abolition of the death penalty preferring not to have free trade, and free traders preferring not to abolish the death penalty. The problem is to specify the conditions in which these groups come together to vote as a block.

Designate abolition of the death penalty as $D$, preservation of the death penalty as $D^*$, establishment of free trade as $F$, and rejection of free trade as $F^*$. There then four possible options for the two policies together: $(D, F)$, $(D, F^*)$, $(D^*, F)$ and $(D^*, F^*)$.

Suppose the electorate is composed of three distinct groups:

- traditional people whose first preference is $(D^*, F^*)$ and who constitute 40 per cent of the population;
- opponents of the death penalty whose first preference is $(D, F^*)$ and who constitute 30 per cent of the population; and
- free traders whose first preference is $(D^*, F)$ and who also constitute 30 per cent of the population.

By definition, the three groups' least preferred options must be $(D, F)$, $(D^*, F)$ and $(D, F^*)$, the opposites of their most preferred options.

The problem at hand is to discover what, if any, are the circumstances in which $(D, F)$ defeats $(D^*, F^*)$ in a head-to-head vote or vicariously as platforms of political parties. It turns out that $(D, F)$ can defeat $(D^*, F^*)$ when the abolitionists and the free traders are extremists rather than moderates in a sense to be defined.

For the purposes of this example, a person who favours both of two policies is a moderate if he is as content with one policy as with the other, and is an extremist if one of the two policies is very much preferred. In this example, the two policies favoured by the group opposing the death penalty are the abolition of the death penalty and the rejection of free trade, and the two policies favoured by the group advocating the establishment of free trade are the establishment of free trade and the maintenance of the death penalty. Thus, an opponent of the death penalty is an extremist if he continues to support the abolition of the death penalty even at the expense of establishing free trade too, and a free trader is an extremist if he continues to support the establishment of free trade even at the cost of abolishing the death penalty too. A moderate opponent of the death penalty would just as soon not have the death penalty abolished if that could only be procured together with the establishment of free trade. A moderate advocate of free trade would just as soon not have free trade if that could only be procured together with the abolition of the death penalty. The distinction between moderation and extremism has no relevance to a person (there are assumed to be no such people in this extreme example) who favours both reforms. The distinction between extremism and moderation is reflected in voters' second and third preferences among the four options, as shown in the comparison of Tables 2.5 and 2.6.

*Table 2.5* Orders of preference when reformers are moderates

| Groups of identical people population | Per cent of population | Orders of preference |
|---|---|---|
| Opponents of the death penalty | 30 | $(D, F^*), (D, F) = (D^*, F^*), (D^*, F)$ |
| Free traders | 30 | $(D^*, F), (D, F) = (D^*, F^*), (D, F^*)$ |
| Traditional people | 40 | $(D^*, F^*), (D^*, F) = (D, F^*), (D, F)$ |

*Table 2.6* Orders of preference when reformers are extremists

| Groups of identical people population | Per cent of population | Orders of preference |
|---|---|---|
| Opponents of the death penalty | 30 | $(D, F^*), (D, F), (D^*, F^*), (D^*, F)$ |
| Free traders | 30 | $(D^*, F), (D, F), (D^*, F^*), (D, F^*)$ |
| Traditional people | 40 | $(D^*, F^*), (D^*, F) = (D, F^*), (D, F)$ |

The tables are almost the same. In each row, a group's preferences among the two-dimensional options are listed in order from best to worst, except that '=' signifies indifference between the two adjacent pairs of options, indicating moderation. In both tables, traditional people who prefer neither the abolition of the death penalty nor the establishment of free trade are assumed for convenience to be moderate in their preferences. The only difference between the tables is that, in Table 2.5, the reformers are assumed to be moderate too, while, in Table 2.6, they are assumed to be extremists, both abolitionists and free traders preferring $(D, F)$ to $(D^*, F^*)$.

With one additional assumption, it is possible to go from the tables of preference to directed graphs, comparable to that in Figure 2.3, showing how each of the four options, $(D, F)$, $(D^*, F^*)$, $(D, F^*)$ and $(D^*, F)$, holds up against each of the others in a head-to-head vote. The additional assumption is that when a group is indifferent between two options it supplies half of its votes to one and half to the other. For example, in a vote between $(D, F)$ and $(D^*, F^*)$, moderate abolitionists cast half their votes for $(D, F)$ and the other half for $(D^*, F^*)$, supplying each option with 15 per cent of the total national vote. Figure 2.4 is the directed graphs for a society where both groups of reformers are moderates, and Figure 2.5 is the directed graph for a society where reformers are extremists. In both graphs, a pointed arrow from one option to another indicates that the first beats the second in a pairwise vote, and the line without an arrowhead signifies a tie.

Figure 2.4 shows preferences in a society of moderates. Reflecting the votes in referendums on one issue at a time, $(D^*, F)$ gets 70 per cent of the votes in a contest with $(D, F)$, and $(D^*, F^*)$ gets 70 per cent of the votes in a contest between $(D, F^*)$ and $(D^*, F^*)$. As one might expect, $(D^*, F^*)$ also gets 70 per cent of the votes in a contest with $(D, F)$, capturing all of the votes (40 per cent of the total) of opponents of both reforms, as well as half the votes (15 per cent attributable

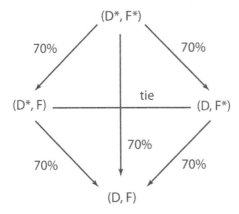

*Figure 2.4* Outcomes of all votes between combinations of options when reformers are moderates.

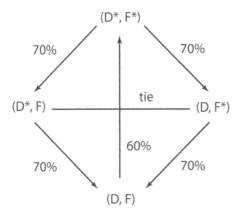

*Figure 2.5* Outcomes of all votes between combinations of options when reformers are extremists.

to each group) of both groups of reformers who, by assumption, are indifferent between $(D^*, F^*)$ and $(D, F)$.

The only change in passing from a society where reformers are moderate to a society where reformers are extremist is that $(D, F)$ is now the winner in a contest with $(D^*, F^*)$, capturing all, rather than just half of the votes of the both groups of reformers. The two issues can be bundled into one platform which beats the status quo in a pairwise vote.

Imbedded within the directed graph in Figure 2.5 are several paradoxes of voting, so that one cannot say a priori what deal will be struck. Typically, though not invariably, the prospect of vote trading introduces an indeterminacy into majority rule voting, with no unique electoral equilibrium because the outcome depends on who cooperates with whom. Organization as well as pure voter preference influences the outcome of the vote. Context is important. It has so far been implicitly assumed that all members of any group can vote together as a block and can agree among themselves where to sacrifice a first preference on one issue in return for similar behaviour on the part of all members of some other group. That may be difficult when there are tens, even hundreds, or thousands of voters. There are two ways around this difficulty.

Deals may be struck not among voters directly, but among legislators representing groups of voters with similar preferences. If members of each group are concentrated in a distinct constituency, deals among legislators can replicate the deals among voters as described above. This is not always possible, for members of all three groups may be spread over all constituencies in the proportions shown in Tables 2.4 and 2.5.

Deals may be struck within political parties. A reform party may incorporate both the abolition of the death penalty and free trade as planks in its platform. By identifying themselves with the reform party, candidates throughout the country would signal to voters what policies they would support if elected, allowing nationwide voting to determine national policy without recourse to (or with less need than otherwise) deals among elected legislators. It may be easier to strike deals in the formation of party platforms than in other contexts. Sometimes there is a natural affinity among policies making it relatively simple to bundle them together. It is convenient for candidates to speak as though this were so.

In the example, the reform party wins with 60 per cent of the vote, but that is a consequence of some very strong assumptions. No account was taken of the competence of politicians, of random events altering voters' opinions, or of modifications in each party's platform to gain an advantage over its rivals. The anti-reform party may well incorporate extra planks in its platform in the hope of beating the reform party in a pairwise vote.

The principle in this example extends to many other cases. Consider for example a society where the issues at stake are economic and religious, with two alternative policies in each dimension. Economic policy is either socialist or libertarian. Religious policy is either to preserve or not to preserve the establishment of the one true religion. Suppose socialism and preservation of the establishment of the one true religion are both opposed by a minority of the population, so that neither would be supported in a referendum on that issue alone. Whether or not they might both be supported in a joint referendum or might be combined in the platform of a successful political party depends on whether their adherents are moderates or extremists.

Political parties can be seen at once as a vehicle for implicit vote trading and as a substitute for vote trading within the legislature. Three considerations come together in the establishment of political parties and in the choice of party platforms. The first is to formulate a grand bargain among like-minded candidates for office about which policies to adopt and which to reject. As in the death penalty–free trade example, legislators are likely to get more of their preferred policies adopted when they vote as a block than when they vote independently for the policies they most prefer. The second is to let people know when they vote what they are really voting about. There is a far more direct connection between votes and policies when the candidate's policies are the policies of a political party with some chance of being elected, in the current election or in elections to come, than when each legislator acts entirely on his own. The third consideration is the connection between the legislature and the executive. One way or another, a head of state must be chosen with authority over the army, the police and the civil service. In parliamentary government, as in the UK and Canada, the head of state is the leader of the majority party, occupying that position for only as long as he has the support of a majority in the legislature and bound, at least to some extent, by the platform of the party he leads, so that, in voting for candidates, people are also voting for the policies that the head of state is pledged to adopt. The connection is less strong in congressional government where the president is directly elected, but, there too, candidates for executive positions are identified with one party or another.[10]

How important is all this for actual competition between political parties seeking office and in the evaluation of outcomes in the political arena? Much may depend on what extremists are extreme about. Extremism may reflect intensity of preference, and the triumph of extremism may be seen as a correction for the failure of ordinary voting to take intensity of preference into account. Perhaps the opponents of the death penalty are deeply passionate about this issue, while traditional folk do not care much either way. The triumph of the extremists may in that case contribute to the welfare of society as a whole. Other instances of the triumph of the extremists may be less innocuous. The phenomenon may shift the burden of public policy about broad issues of war, peace and poverty away from relatively selfish people and onto the shoulders of other people who are more altruistically inclined. In a society more or less evenly split into two camps, extremists – not members of either camp but who are exclusively concerned, for example, about tariffs on foreign goods competing with the goods they produce – may offer their support to whichever camp is prepared to back their claims. Questions of war and peace may be resolved in accordance with the views of whatever group is prepared to supply the largest advantages to narrowly focused factions of voters or to industry in certain regions of the country. Formation of platforms of political parties is the pulling together of groups whose extremist interests are not too costly to one another.

In short, extremism can have three large effects upon the outcome of majority rule voting. It can facilitate the formation of coalitions among interest groups on different issues to procure objectives that could never be attained through voting on one issue at a time. It may distort outcomes on other matters by dislodging what would otherwise be the Condorcet winner. By dislodging the Condorcet winner, it may cause outcomes in majority rule voting to be far more dependent upon strategy and bargaining than would otherwise be the case. Note the strong resemblance between the vote trading story in this section and the five roads example in the preceding section. In both, and in the exploitation problem to be discussed below, policies that would all be rejected if voted on one at a time may be accepted in one large vote on several policies at once.

# Left, right and the need for compromise

One might suppose that the combination of two single-peaked issues – as in the platform of a political party – would itself be single peaked, but that turns out not to be so. To see why, imagine a society where public choice is restricted to two items, expenditure on defence and expenditure on redistribution, and where, to keep matters simple, there is assumed to be no dispute among voters about the composition of expenditure within each category or about the tax system to finance total public expenditure. Knowing the effect of total public expenditure on their post-tax income, every person has a preferred combination of expenditures on defence and redistribution.

A person's preferences for defence and redistribution together are illustrated as a set of indifference curves in Figure 2.6 with defence expenditure on the horizontal axis and redistributive expenditure on the vertical axis. The most preferred pair of expenditures is represented by the point $\delta$, and the person becomes progressively worse off the farther away in any given direction the actual combination of expenditures turns out to be. The person's indifference curves must therefore be loops around the point $\delta$, such that, the larger the loop, the worse off this person must be. If everybody's preferences were the same, they would unanimously choose the combination of defence and redistribution represented by the point $\delta$.

But it is most unlikely that everybody's preferences are the same. Far more likely is that each voter has his own unique value of $\delta$ and of the surrounding indifference curves.[11] Consider once again the community consisting of Allan, Bill and Carol who may be thought of equally well as three particular people or as representatives of groups of people with identical preferences. In Figure 2.7, their

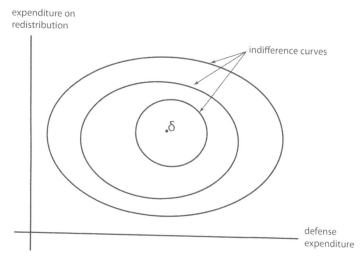

*Figure 2.6* A person's indifference curves for expenditures on defence and redistribution.

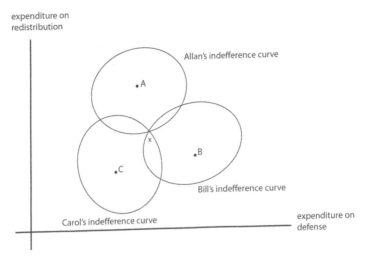

*Figure 2.7* Three persons' indifference curves for public expenditures on defence and redistribution.

preferred combinations of expenditures on defence and redistribution are indicated as *A*, *B* and *C*. Three indifference curves, one for Allan, one for Bill and one for Carol, are also shown.

That there may be no equilibrium platform or menu of defence expenditure and redistributive expenditure together can be shown by contradiction. Suppose there were such an equilibrium, a point *x* representing a combination of defence and redistribution beating any other combination in a pairwise vote. Through any such point there must be three indifference curves, one for each of the three people. Normally, the three indifference curves cross, creating three leaf-shaped areas emanating from the point *x*. Necessarily, all points within each of the three leaves represent combinations of defence and redistribution preferred to the point *x* by a some pair of voters, Allan and Bill for one leaf, Bill and Carol for another and Carol and Bill for the third. Hence the combination of defence and redistribution represented by the point *x* cannot be a Condorcet winner. As *x* is any arbitrarily chosen point, there can be no Condorcet winner at all. From this it follows that, in an election between two parties where voters care about party platforms and nothing else and where one of the parties must set its platform first, the other party can always choose some different platform that will enable it to win the election. Voting equilibria for each of two issues separately does not guarantee an equilibrium when the issues are combined.

There is such an equilibrium for three special cases illustrated in Figures 2.8, 2.9 and 2.10. In the first case as shown in Figure 2.8, a fixed resolution of one issue leads to a voting equilibrium in the other. The figure shows each person's preferred expenditure on defence for some arbitrarily given expenditure on redistribution.

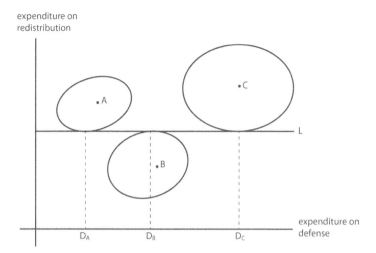

*Figure 2.8* Demonstration that defence expenditure is a single-peaked issue.

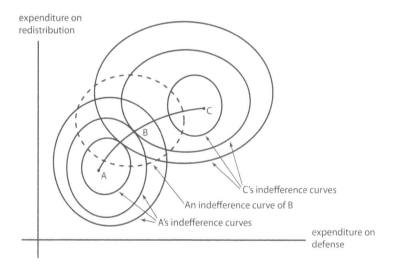

*Figure 2.9* A left–right continuum.

Suppose the community's expenditure on redistribution is set at $L$, represented by the height of the flat line above the horizontal axis. Unconstrained, three persons' preferred combination of expenditures would be as indicated by the points $A$, $B$ and $C$. Subject to this constraint, each person's preferred defence expenditure is at the tangency of an indifference curve to the flat line. Their preferred defence expenditures are shown on the horizontal axis as $D_A$, $D_B$ and $D_C$. That defence is a single-peaked issue is evident from the figure because every person becomes progressively worse off the farther in either direction is the actual defence expenditure from their first preference. As Figure 2.8 is drawn, the median voter is Bill whose preferred defence expenditure, $D_B$, becomes the unique equilibrium defence expenditure in majority rule voting. A parallel demonstration reveals that there is a unique equilibrium redistributive expenditure corresponding to any arbitrarily chosen defence expenditure.

The second, more interesting exception arises from a special configuration of preferences illustrated in Figure 2.9. For any two people – say Allan and Carol – there must be a *contract curve*, defined as the locus of all tangencies between their indifference curves. As is evident from the figure, the contract curve identifies combinations of defence and redistributive expenditures that are efficient for Allan and Carol (thought not necessarily for Bill) in that any combination of expenditures corresponding to a point off the contract curve is worse for both parties than some combination represented by a point on the contract curve.

Intransitivity vanishes when Bill's first preference lies somewhere on the contract curve connecting preferences of Allan and Carol, or, more generally, when one person's first preference lies on the contract curve of the other two. The first preference of the person in the middle must be a Condorcet winner because a movement to any other point is disadvantageous for that person and for at least one (and possibly both) of the other two people. As long as people's preferences yield a left–right continuum as illustrated in Figure 2.10, a median voter can be identified and platforms of competing political parties can be expected to hover about the first preference of the median voter. But if there is no such continuum and if people's preferences over two or more single-peaked issues are as described in Figure 2.8, there emerges a paradox of voting that must somehow be resolved politically. Absence of political equilibrium – of a Condorcet winner among possible platforms of political parties – creates an inescapable need for bargaining among politicians in each political party to determine what the party's platform is to be. Bargaining is also required in coalition government to determine which bits of the platforms of each party in the coalition are to emerge in the policy of the coalition as a whole. Majority rule voting is no longer self-sufficient. A mixture of voting and bargaining is required.

Strictly speaking, there need be no left–right continuum, but the language of the left–right continuum tends to be preserved as a way of distinguishing one's preferred party from the opposition. Designation of public decisions as left or right may have more to do with the requirements of politics than with people's preferences. When parties choose platforms of policies, it becomes tempting to imagine that the components of a party's platform have a closer affinity than is really the case. It may be easier to castigate one's political opponents as weak-minded lefties or as nasty right-wingers than to criticize elements of platforms one at a time.

A third equilibrium arises when all voters' preferences are appropriately bunched together.[12] Suppose: i) voting is to choose a combination of expenditures on redistribution and defence from among the set of all possible combinations; ii) each voter has a first preference among all combinations, and indifference curves are circles (rather than just loops) around the voter's first preference; and

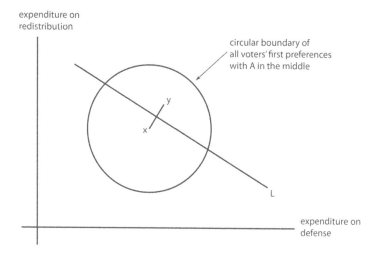

*Figure 2.10* Another equilibrium among two-dimensional platforms.

iii) All voters' first preferences are evenly spread out on a circular disc. (It is convenient to suppose there to be an infinity of voters so that the density of voters' first preferences is the same throughout the disc.) On these assumptions, there is an electoral equilibrium at the center of the disc; the combination at the centre of the disc beats any other combination in a pairwise vote.

The electoral equilibrium is illustrated in Figure 2.10. All voters' first preferences are evenly spread out within the disc and the combination represented by the point *x* at the centre of the disc beats any other combination, such as the combination represented by the point *y*, in a pairwise vote. To see why, draw a line from *x* to *y*, and then draw a second line, shown as *L*, perpendicular to and passing through the middle of the first line. It follows from the simple geometry of the figure that all points in the disc on the same side of the line *L* as the point *x* are closer to the point *x* than to the point *y*, while all points on the other side of the line *L* are closer to the point *y* than to the point *x*. Since first preferences of voters are distributed evenly throughout the disc and since the portion of the disc on *x*'s side of the line *L* is larger than the portion of the disk on *y*'s side of the line *L*, it must be the case that combination *x* beats combination *y* in a straight up-or-down vote. Since *y* might be any point within the disc, the combination represented by the point *x* beats any other combination. The combination in the middle of the disk is the unique electoral equilibrium.

It is difficult to say how far these examples can be generalized. At one extreme, there is a voting equilibrium when everybody's preferences are single peaked or when all first preferences are appropriately bunched together. At the other extreme, there need be no equilibrium, as illustrated in Figure 2.8, when the numbers of voters and options are the same or, as will be shown later, in voting about the allocation of the entire national income. A voting equilibrium is a substitute for compromise. When there is no such equilibrium, compromise becomes essential.

## The exploitation problem

Tables 2.2 and 2.3 portrayed situations where voting on issues one at a time was inefficient and where a universally preferred outcome could be obtained by mutual concessions in the lunch story or by cost–benefit analysis in the roads story. But those efficient outcomes are unstable because members of any majority coalition can make themselves better off at the expense of the excluded minority by coordinated voting for a different outcome instead. In the lunch story in Table 2.2, Allan and Bill can form a predatory coalition at the expense of Carol by agreeing to vote for ham sandwiches rather than cheese sandwiches as would be warranted by the 'best choice' as indicated in the last row of the table. The resulting outcome – tomato soup, ham sandwiches and cherry pie – is the worst possible combination for Carol, but Allan and Bill may not care. Majority rule voting allows them to act as they do. Similarly, Allan and Carol could form a coalition at the expense of Bill, or Bill and Carol could form a coalition at the expense of Allan. There is no telling a priori who the members of the majority coalition will be. Any of the three possible bargains might be struck.

In the roads story in Table 2.3 where each of five people was the principal beneficiary of one of five roads, it was never advantageous for any person to finance and build a road alone, but externalities made it advantageous for the five people to build all five roads together. Each road cost $10, yielded a benefit of $8 to one of the five people together with benefits of $1 to each of the other four, so that everybody gains $2 when all five roads are built. But any three people could do better still at the expense of the other two. As long as all roads are financed collectively, it becomes advantageous for any three of the five people to vote for their roads and against the other two. By voting for their roads alone, Allan, Bill and Carol increase their total benefits from road building from $2 to $4, saving $4 by not having to pay a share for Donald and Elizabeth's roads and losing only $2 from not having those roads available. As the exploited minority, Donald and Elizabeth each lose $3, having to pay $6 as their shares of the total cost of road building and gaining only $3 from their usage of the three roads actually built. Once again, there is no telling who the participants of the predatory coalition will be. Any three of the five people will do.

A third story is more disturbing. Majority rule voting is unsuitable for allocating a sum of money among a group of people or for allocating the national income among the entire population, for no allocation beats every other allocation in a pairwise vote. When voters are short-sighted, whoever sets the voting agenda is, in effect, empowered to select the allocation of income. When voters are not short-sighted, any majority of voters acting in concert can grab the entire national income for itself. The problem will be examined in two stages, first for a community with five people and then for a large electorate.

*Table 2.7* A sequence of allocations, each defeating the preceding allocation in a pairwise vote

|  | Allan | Bill | Carol | Donald | Elizabeth |
|---|---|---|---|---|---|
| Original fair allocation | 150 | 150 | 150 | 150 | 150 |
| Allan, Bill and Donald's coalition | 250 | 250 | 0 | 250 | 0 |
| Allan, Bill and Carol's alternative | 350 | 350 | 50 | 0 | 0 |
| Donald and Elizabeth's alternative | 150 | 150 | 150 | 150 | 150 |

Note: Numbers in $000s.

An income of $750,000 is to be allocated by majority rule voting among Allan, Bill, Carol, Donald and Elizabeth. The income is owned collectively, but none of it can be appropriated by anybody until the community determines each person's share. Five decent and fair-minded people might choose to allocate the combined income equally, supplying each person with an income of $150,000 as shown in the first row of Table 2.7. If at least three of the five people believe that allocation to be just and right, and, if they are prepared to vote in accordance with their beliefs, then an allocation of $150,000 to each person wins over any other allocation.

Majority rule voting allows for a very different possibility. Since three people constitute a majority, any three voters can employ the power of the vote to increase their incomes at the expense of the other two. If they are greedy, as economists postulate everyone to be, Alan, Bill and Donald might conspire to vote for an allocation raising each of their incomes to $250,000 with no income left over for Carol or Elizabeth, as shown in the second row of Table 2.7. Nothing in the rules of majority rule voting blocks exploitation of this kind. Allan, Bill and Donald might try to justify their manoeuvre to themselves on the grounds that men are worthy but women are not.

But that is not the end of the story. Carol, who would have no income at all when there is a predatory coalition of Allan, Bill and Donald, might try to break the coalition by offering $350,000 to each of Allan and Bill, accepting $50,000 for herself, and cutting out Donald and Elizabeth altogether. Being greedy, Allan and Bill would accept Carol's proposal if they could be assured that the new alliance would hold, but they have reason to fear that it may not. Carol may betray them just as they betrayed Donald, by striking a deal with Donald and Elizabeth in which they each get $100,000 and she gets the remaining $550,000. Or Donald and Elizabeth who have been dispossessed altogether under Carol's proposed allocation may reintroduce the original fair allocation which beats Carol's allocation three votes to two. This sequence of votes, as set out in Table 2.7, gives rise to a paradox of voting, for the allocation in each row of the table defeats the allocation in the preceding row even though the first and last rows are the same. The sequence of alliances is potentially interminable. Every allocation of income is beaten by some other allocation in a pairwise vote. Majority rule voting may well give rise to a 'tyranny of the majority', but there is no telling which majority prevails; it is whatever majority can hold together and vote as a block.

*Table 2.8* How the agenda setters grab most of the pie for themselves

|  | Allan | Bill | Carol | Donald | Elizabeth |
|---|---|---|---|---|---|
| Original fair allocation | 150 | 150 | 150 | 150 | 150 |
| Allan's first alternative | 250 | 250 | 250 | 0 | 0 |
| Allan's second alternative | 40 | 40 | 590 | 40 | 40 |
| Allan's third alternative | 550 | 50 | 50 | 50 | 50 |

Note: Numbers in $000s.

Another aspect of the exploitation problem is illustrated in the sequence of allocations in Table 2.8. Choosing among a set of possible allocations would typically require a sequence of votes, and an *agenda setter* may be delegated to choose the sequence as long as majority rule prevails at each step. When voters are myopic, opting for their preferred outcome at each step, this authority entitles the agenda setter to engineer any outcome whatsoever in the final vote. Suppose Allan is the agenda setter and suppose, starting from a status quo of {150, 150, 150, 150, 150}, Allan wishes to drive the allocation to {550, 50, 50, 50, 50} where he keeps most of the pie for himself. As long as voters are short-sighted, Allan can do so by an appropriate sequence of votes. However, for the agenda setter to obtain this outcome, the population of voters must be radically myopic, each voter failing to realize that what would serve his interest if the current vote were final need not do so when the current vote is just one component in a sequence. Thwarting the agenda setter is an important concern in the design of the rules of parliamentary procedure.

An extension of these examples shows more clearly why majority rule voting cannot be entrusted with the allocation of the national income. Imagine a country with a million people and a national income that is somehow fixed at $50 billion. If everybody was decent and fairminded, they might all agree to apportion the national income equally, each person receiving an income of $50,000. If not, and if every person voted self-interestedly, any majority of over half a million people might form a coalition using the power of the vote to grab the entire national income for its members, raising average incomes of the members of the coalition – for they need not agree to divide the spoils equally – from $50,000 to just under $100,000 with nothing left over for the excluded minority.[13] Why not? There is no reason to suppose that voters are saints, and if I am unwilling to join a predatory majority coalition, what assurance have I that others will not form a coalition from which I am excluded? If that is what is to be expected from majority rule voting, why should people tolerate such a system of government? Is it not better to trust one's fortune to the dictates of a king in whose interest it may be to keep the nation prosperous and who has no special connection with any sub-group of the population?

The principal answer to this question is that the exploitation problem is circumvented by a general agreement to remove the allocation of the national income from the political sphere. Subject to qualifications discussed later on in this book, the national income is allocated before voting takes place. Maintenance of the system of majority rule voting requires there to be some non-political method of allocation – some *system of equity* – which voters respect because they know that a failure to respect the system of equity spells the end of democratic government.

What might the system of equity be? In the sandwich example in Table 2.2, it is an understanding that intensities of preference are to be respected; otherwise the three friends will not remain friends for long. In the five roads example in Table 2.3, it is the principle of cost–benefit analysis which is efficient in the long run and averts massive conflict over the choice of public projects. In the allocation of the national income, it might conceivably be a regime of equality, a sort of ideal communism 'from each according to his ability, to each according to his needs'. This candidate for a system of equity has been rejected, even in countries that call themselves communist: Supplying no automatic incentive to work and save, it requires an extensive control of the worker by the administration. By definition, positions of authority cannot be allocated equally, and, in any case, people in authority would take the lion's share for themselves.

The system of equity in every country where majority rule voting is maintained is the allocation of the national income in markets with historically given property rights, including the right to the produce of one's labour. Property rights may well have originated in ancient theft, but, once established, are maintained because we need them, because an economy based upon private property yields a higher national income than any conceivable alternative and because they are a necessary condition for the maintenance of government by majority rule voting. Property rights are a requirement not just for prosperity, but for democracy as well.

There are several qualifications and exceptions. First, the barrier between voting and the distribution of income is at best imperfect. Provision of the army, the police, schools and roads, together with the taxation to pay for them, cannot be altogether distributionally neutral, though the ideal is to preserve people's ordering on the scale of rich and poor. Government by majority rule voting can withstand a good deal of systematic redistribution of income, narrowing the disparity between the incomes of rich and poor without at the same time altering people's positions on the scale, for, as will be discussed in the next chapter, there is a natural stopping pace for redistribution well short of full equality of income, beyond which the median voter does not wish to go. In practice, government can take small steps increasing one person's income at the expense of the rest of the nation, though large steps in this direction might prove dangerous.

Second, the system of equity contains more than just property rights. There must also be a rule of law specifying everybody's rights and obligations, and placing limits on the ability of people in office to penalize their prospective opponents in the next election. No government in office can be expected to risk loss of office in an election if the loss of office is a descent from the top to the bottom of the income scale, leaving one completely at the mercy of one's successors who can punish and impoverish at will. By restricting punishment to people breaking well-specified laws, the rule of law is beneficial to everybody, but it plays a special role in the preservation of democratic government.

Third, there is a natural defence against the exploitation problem in the difficulty of would-be exploiters to recognize one another and to vote in unison as exploitation requires. Members in the majority coalition must agree on the allocation of the spoils among themselves where, presumably, the leaders of the coalition will be entitled to more than a per capita share of the loot. Identifying and coordinating a coalition may be very difficult in a society where everybody is much alike, but less so in a society already sharply divided by race, religion, ethnicity, wealth or even geography if there is little mobility from place to place. Antagonism among people of different religions may be due more to the role of religion as a badge of membership in a predatory coalition of voters than to any natural animosity among people of different faiths. The more sharply people are divided socially, the easier it becomes to maintain the discipline that the exploitation of minorities by majority requires.[14]

Fourth, government may be designed to constrain predatory voting by making it more difficult for coalitions to form and, once formed, to influence public policy. Legislation is usually entrusted to two houses: the Senate and the House of Representatives in the United States, the House of Commons and the House of Lords in Great Britain, and the House of Commons and Senate in Canada. The rationale for this practice is that two heads are better than one, as when the Canadian Senate and the British House of Lords are seen as contributing 'sober second thoughts', but it is also, at least in part, to balance predatory interests in one house with different predatory interests in the other. The establishment of countervailing power is also a part of the rationale for the division of authority among legislature, executive and judiciary.[15]

Note finally, that bargaining in democracy is a two-edged sword, at once indispensable when diverse views must be reconciled in platforms of political parties or in crafting law and policy, but potentially destructive as a vehicle for exploitation of minorities by majorities. Legislators must be able to strike deals but not too easily.

## Delegation

In ancient Athens, citizens voted for laws and policies directly. Populations of modern democracies are too large and current policy is too complex for direct democracy. Citizens must vote for delegates to formulate legislation, choose laws and conduct the nation's business on the citizens' behalf. Politicians identify themselves with political parties if only to tell citizens what they can reasonably expect if a candidate is elected. Parties have several roles to play.

Parties may be groups of would-be leaders who will be confronted with unforseen events requiring decisions such as whether to go to war or how to take the country out of depression, where nobody can be absolutely sure which group of leaders is best and every party seeks to persuade voters that its leaders are the most honest and most competent of all.

Parties may be thought of as occupying a place on a left–right scale where, as discussed earlier, all points of contention can be fitted onto that scale so that every plank in a party's platform – its stance on the old age pension, its aggressiveness to its neighbours, and so on – can be inferred from its place between extreme left and extreme right. People commonly talk as though politics conformed to this pattern, though nobody believes that to be the whole truth.

Parties may be vehicles for exploitation, supplying goodies to a majority of voters at the expense of the corresponding minority. As discussed earlier in connection with the exploitation problem, there are two impediments, one administrative and the other constitutional. The administrative impediment is the difficulty in deciding and publicizing who is to be included among the privileged majority and who is to be left out. Sometimes this is easily resolved, as when the population is sharply divided into two hostile religious groups. Exploitation is increasingly difficult the more homogeneous society becomes. The constitutional impediment lies in the protection of civil and property rights. Recognizing that unchecked exploitation is a recipe for civil war, successful democratic societies adopt constitutional prohibitions that are respected because the anticipated harm from civil war outweighs the expected benefit from exploitation. The ceremony of the law conveys confidence that the rules will be respected.

Parties may reflect social preference as, for example, where one party favours for the legalization of abortion and the other does not. Candidates for president or for the legislature would be selected accordingly. Parties may engineer vote trades or compromise to reflect voters' intensities of preference as discussed in the death penalty–free trade example where neither policy is preferred by a majority of voters but a party with both policies in its platform can expect to win the election.

One way or another, politicians seeking office, for its own sake or to advance some cause, come together to forge a written or unwritten platform of policies. The process cannot be explained mechanically as outputs of goods and services are determined from the prior distribution of property rights in general equilibrium. Parties' choices of candidates and platforms require compromise among reasonably like-minded participants.

## Voting externalities

An analogy is sometimes drawn between politics and markets, but there is one enormous difference. When someone buys an orange, the only people significantly affected are the buyer and the seller, both of whom must benefit because the transaction is voluntary. Everybody else is unaffected, except minutely through the impact of the transaction on the price of oranges worldwide. When one votes, there is a near certainty that one's vote has no impact on oneself or anybody else, coupled with a tiny chance of an enormous impact on the entire population. There is a near certainty of one's vote having no impact because the only possible impact is to change the outcome of the election from a win by the party one votes against into a win by the party one votes for, and the probability of that happening is minute. The tiny chance of an enormous impact on the entire population arises because the benefit to oneself if one's preferred party wins the election is matched by more or less the same benefits to thousands and thousands of like-minded citizens and by costs to thousands and thousands of other citizens who prefer the opposing party. There is, in other words, a minute chance of one's vote being pivotal. Unless one's vote is pivotal, it can have no impact at all. If one's vote is pivotal, it creates two massive externalities, a positive externality to all like-minded citizens, and negative externality to all citizens who would be made better off by a win for the opposing party. A voter's gain if his vote is pivotal is his valuation of a win for his preferred party. The massive positive externality is the sum of the gains to all like-minded voters. The massive negative externality is the sum of the harms to everybody who prefers a win by the other party.

Imagine an election with just two political parties, Liberal and Conservative, in a country with a million eligible voters, approximately equally divided between pro-Liberals and pro-Conservatives, where a win for the Liberal party is worth $4,000 to each pro-Liberal person and a win for the Conservative party is worth $6,000 to each pro-Conservative person. To keep the story simple, suppose the outcome of the election is universally expected to be somewhere between a win by 10,000 votes for the Liberal party and a win by 10,000 votes for the Conservative party, with equal chances of each and every outcome in between, so that the chance of any particular outcome – such as a Liberal win by 625 votes, a Conservative win by 4,789 votes, or a tie – is 1/20,000. A tie is broken by the flip of a coin. The cost of voting, of going to the ballot box and casting one's vote, is assumed to be $20.

Introduce one extra person who is strictly self-interested, who, let it be supposed, is pro-Liberal and who must decide whether to vote or abstain. This person votes if and only if his expected benefit from voting exceeds the cost. The expected benefit from voting is the valuation of a win by the Liberal party ($4,000), weighted by the probability of the person's vote being 'pivotal', meaning that it swings the outcome of the election from Conservative to Liberal, for only if one's vote is pivotal can voting be beneficial to oneself or anybody else. With equal likelihoods of electoral outcomes anywhere between a Liberal win by 10,000 votes and a Conservative win by 10,000 votes, the probability of this person's vote being pivotal is 1 in 20,000.[16] This pro-Liberal person's expected benefit from voting is only 20¢ (equal to $4,000 × 1/20,000) which is a mere one hundredth of the cost ($20). As each pro-Conservative's value of a win for the Conservative party is $6,000, a Conservative voter's expected benefit from voting would be 30¢.

Several implications of this example carry well beyond the example itself.

- To the self-interested person, voting does not pay. Better to abstain, for the expected benefit of voting falls well short of the cost. The probability of one's vote being pivotal is just too small. This is shown here with arbitrarily chosen numbers, but it seems unlikely that any plausible numbers would reverse the result. In what is known as 'paradox of not voting', a rational person abstains, though, if everybody abstains, voting becomes advantageous once again.[17]
- A duty to vote is indispensable. Self-interest alone will not suffice in voting as it does in markets. Some authors have given up on self-interest altogether as an

explanation of why people vote, in part because the chance of casting a pivotal vote is deemed very much smaller than is assumed here. The decision to vote rather than to abstain is then seen as an act of self-expression, analogous to participation in sports or voting for the American Idol. A duty to vote may be narrowly or broadly conceived. Narrowly conceived, it is nothing more than an obligation to vote cast one's ballot with no additional obligation about whom to vote for. Broadly conceived, it includes a requirement to vote in the interest of one's social class or the nation as a whole.

- Benefits arising from a person's decision to vote rather than abstain extend automatically to all like-minded people regardless of whether or not they vote. An increase in the Liberal party's chance of winning the election is equally advantageous to all pro-Liberals, and equally disadvantageous to all pro-Conservatives. The decision by one pro-Liberal to vote rather than abstain provides a positive externality of 20¢ to each and every pro-Liberal person together with a negative externality of 30¢ to each and every pro-Conservative person.
- The combined benefits of one person's vote to all like-minded people is likely to be very much larger than this person's cost of voting. The combined benefit to the approximately half a million pro-Liberals arising from the decision of one pro-Liberal person to vote rather than abstain is $10,000 (equal to 20¢ × 500,000), which is 500 times the cost to this one pro-Liberal person of casting their vote. One pro-Liberal person's decision to vote rather thaan abstain creates a positive externality of $10,000 to all pro-Liberals, together with a negative externality of $15,000 to all pro-Conservatives. Voting generates a modest benefit not just to voters themselves but to all like-minded voters, an externality outweighing the gain to the voter by a factor equal to the number of like-minded voters.
- Though voting does not pay to the individual voter acting alone, it may nevertheless be advantageous to a group of like-minded voters, each of whom agrees to vote on condition all the others do so too, a voting pact where each member of the group conveys an externality on all of the rest. Imagine a voting pact among 2,000 pro-Liberal people. Each person's vote increases the probability of a win for the Liberal by 1/20,000; together, they increase the probability of a win for the Liberal party by 1/10 (equal to 2,000 × 1/20,000), worth $400 (equal to $4,000 × 1/10) to each member of the pact, or 20 times the cost of casting one's vote. A voting pact of as few as 100 members would be sufficient for each person's expected benefit from the pact to exceed the cost of voting.

The numbers in this example are chosen to tell a simple story about voting externalities, but the contrast between private and social benefits of voting is almost certainly large enough to withstand plausible changes in the numbers. The assumptions are unrealistic in several important respects. It is unrealistic to suppose that everybody places the same value on a win for their chosen party; one would normally expect undecided voters to place lower values on a win by the party they ultimately vote for than are placed by people with no reservations about which party they prefer. Since everybody's chance of casting a pivotal vote is the same, one might expect a correlation between people's valuation of a win by their preferred party and their willingness to vote rather than abstain. These matters are discussed in Chapter 7 where a schedule of voters' preferences is postulated and uncertainty is generated by random shifts in the schedule as a whole.

The example illustrates the rationale for the prohibition of the buying and selling of votes. Consider once again a pro-Liberal person who would ordinarily abstain because his expected benefit from voting is less than the cost. This person could profitably be bribed to vote Conservative by a committee of – say – 1,000 Conservative supporters, each of whom would acquire an expected gain of 30¢ from this person's vote. They could profitably offer up to $300, and, unless the intended recipient was deterred by ethical considerations, the bribe would be accepted because the recipient's cost of voting Conservative is only $20.20, the sum of the cost of voting and the valuation of the slight reduction of the chance of a win by the Liberal party. Temptations to offer and accept bribes would seem irresistible. Bribes might be paid out of campaign funds acquired from willing partisans or from interest groups expecting favourable laws in the event that the recipient party wins the election. If both political parties can play this game, then the outcome of the election comes to depend on which party is best organized rather than which is seen as best for the electorate as a whole. It is to avoid such outcomes that electoral bribery, the buying and selling of votes, is illegal.

Reasons for the prohibition of the buying and selling of votes carry over to campaign financing and advertising. Outright purchase of votes must be illegal if democracy is to be preserved. It is an open question how far the prohibition of vote buying extends to the acquisition of party funds from campaign contributions, especially as large contributors can expect to be rewarded one way or another if the recipient party wins the election. Expenditure by political parties on campaign advertising and on organizing voters has something in common with vote buying, but its role in supplying genuine information can outweigh this consideration as long as the parties' expenditures are not too disproportionate. Like all advertising, campaign advertising is at once informative and persuasive. Informative advertising is generally deemed socially advantageous, especially if information is equally supplied on both sides of the case. Persuasive advertising is something like bribery, spending money to acquire votes. That is far from the whole story, but it is at the core of proposals to equalize advertising expenditures by competing candidates or parties, and to supply public funds to candidates who agree not to accept private funds at all.

Vote buying and the exploitation problem are two sides of the same coin. Both recruit majority rule voting for the victimization of one part of the population by another, both involve a more comprehensive organization of voters than is otherwise necessary and both are, in different ways, deterred by the surrounding rules. Vote buying is illegal. Exploitation of minorities by majorities is constrained by an implicit or explicit constitutional protection of property rights. There is what might be called a paradox of organization in voting. Political parties are necessary if only to tell voters what they are really voting about, for a candidate's promise to support such-and-such a programme is almost meaningless unless that candidate is speaking for a party with the authority to enact the programme if elected. Unchecked, that organization may be predatory, for laws and customs can be changed by a determined and disciplined majority. Organization of political parties must be strong enough to enact legislation, but legislators must be prepared to break ranks with their parties in defence of rules required for the maintenance of democratic government.

## The spoiler

> Customer: What sandwiches do you serve?
> Waiter: Ham or cheese.
> Customer: I'll take ham.
> Waiter: Sorry, I forgot, we serve tuna sandwiches too.
> Customer: In that case, let me have cheese.

The customer is crazy. If rationality means anything at all, it requires a consistency of preference. A rational person who chooses ham when only ham and cheese are available would never choose cheese when all three sandwiches are available. The spoiler problem is that majority rule voting may lead a community to do so. Voting may be irrational even though voters are not. A variant of preceding examples shows what is at stake.

A community of 100 people are having lunch together. Lunch consists of sandwiches without soup or dessert, and, never mind why, the community must choose one and the same type of sandwiches for everybody. The choice is by majority rule voting. The community consists of three groups with numbers of people and orders of preference among three types of sandwiches, ham, cheese and tuna, as shown in Table 2.9. People in the different groups have different orders of preference, but everybody's preferences are consistent. The choice of sandwiches is to be made by plurality voting first-past-the-post, where each person votes for one, and only one of the available options, and the option with the most votes is chosen.

Suppose that, initially, only two rather than three types of sandwiches are available, ham and cheese but not tuna. If so, there is straight vote between ham and cheese in which ham defeats cheese by 55 to 45 votes because groups 1 and 3 both vote for ham. But if tuna becomes available, and as long as everybody votes sincerely, tuna does not win but it spoils ham's win by diverting the 20 voters in group 3 from ham to tuna, allowing cheese to win with 45 votes, as against

*Table 2.9* The community's preferences for sandwiches

| Name of group | Number of voters | Most preferred | Second choice | Least preferred |
|---|---|---|---|---|
| 1 | 35 | ham | tuna | cheese |
| 2 | 45 | cheese | ham | tuna |
| 3 | 20 | tuna | ham | cheese |

35 votes for ham and 20 votes for tuna. Choices which for an individual would be completely irrational are made collectively through majority rule voting.

In most contexts, the availability of additional options is beneficial to everybody, but not so here. The availability of tuna sandwiches is harmful to people in groups 1 by switching the outcome of the election from their most preferred (ham) to their least preferred (cheese) option, and to people in group 3, switching the outcome of the election from their second choice (ham) to their least preferred option (cheese). People in group 2 benefit at the expense of people in the two other groups. People in group 3 would be better off if their first preference were off the ballot!

The spoiler problem is endemic in elections of candidates for office. Replacing ham, cheese and tuna with candidates Harry, Charles and Tom in a constituency with 100 voters, the story becomes about how the appearance of an additional candidate, Tom, in a contest that was originally between Harry and Charles switches the outcome from a win by Harry to a win by Charles. With only Harry and Charles in the race, Harry wins with a plurality of 55 per cent. With all three candidates in the race, Charles wins with a plurality of 45 per cent. The spoiler is a candidate with no chance of winning the election but who nevertheless alters the outcome of the election.

A classic example is the contest among Bush, Gore and Nader in the US presidential election of 2001. Voting for the US president is a variant of first-past-the-post. Each state is entitled to a certain number of delegates to the electoral college, the winner in a first-past-the-post election in each state gets all the delegates in that state, and the candidate with the most delegates nationwide becomes the president. The delegates were originally intended to be wise men who would vote for the president independently, but they are now expected to vote for the winners of the elections in their states. Bush won the presidency with 271 electoral votes, against 266 electoral votes for Gore and none for Nader. The critical state was Florida with 25 electoral votes, enough that Gore rather than Bush would have won the presidency if Gore rather than Bush had won a plurality of votes in that state. The vote in Florida was 2,912,790 for Bush, 2,912,253 for Gore and 97,488 for Nader. Bush won Florida by less than 600 votes. Had Nader withdrawn from the race and if, among people who would otherwise have voted for Nader, the vote for Gore would have exceeded the vote for Bush by 600 or more, Gore would have won the election and become the president instead of Bush.

One cannot be certain that Nader really was a spoiler because one cannot be certain how people who voted for Nader would have behaved had he not been in the race, but there is reason to suppose that Gore would have won. Think of politics on a left–right scale, with Bush to the right, Gore to the left of Bush and Nader to the left of Gore, so that people who voted for Nader did so because Gore was not left enough. If so, then most people who voted for Nader would prefer Gore to Bush, and would vote accordingly. There may be just enough truth in this story to have provided Gore with the extra 600 votes in Florida needed for Gore to win the presidential election.[18]

A distinction may be drawn between two variants of the spoiler problem. The classic spoiler problem is where the entrance of the spoiler alters the outcome of the election even though the spoiler himself has no chance of being elected. The other variant is where each of two candidates is the spoiler of the other, where each would win the election if the other withdrew from the race. This seems to have been the case in Canada some years ago when the conservative side of the political spectrum was occupied by two parties, the Progressive Conservative Party and the Reform Party. The ruling Liberal Party was able to obtain a plurality of votes in many constituencies where either conservative party might have won if the other had withdrawn from the race. That situation came to an end when the Progressive Conservative Party and the Reform Party were combined into a single Conservative Party which constitutes a majority in the Canadian Parliament today.

One would like to think that the spoiler problem could be dispensed with altogether by the replacement of plurality voting with some other method, but that turns out not to be so. It is an implication of Arrow's Impossibility Theorem that no method of voting avoids the spoiler problem altogether. The theorem establishes that no method of public choice is guaranteed never to violate any of several axioms for any and every constellation of voters' preferences. Among these axioms is the 'independence of irrelevant alternatives'. Arrow speaks of the axiom as follows:

> Suppose that an election is held with a certain number of candidates in the field, each individual filing his list of preferences, and then one of the candidates dies. Surely the social choice should be made by taking each of the individual's preferences lists, blotting out completely the dead candidate's name, and considering only the orderings of the remaining names in going through the procedure of determining the winner. That is, the choice to be made among the set S of surviving candidates should be independent of the preferences of individuals for candidates not in S.
>
> Arrow (1963: 26)

Otherwise the dead candidate would be a spoiler. Independence of irrelevant alternatives means that there can be no spoiler. The impossibility in Arrow's Impossibility Theorem is to design a voting system, or method of social choice other than dictatorship, where no spoiler can ever emerge.

A variant of Arrow's Impossibility Theorem (Theorem I, Arrow (1963: 63)) is that no social ordering of options can be derived from individual orderings in such a way that all of the following conditions are valid:[19]

a) all logically possible individual orderings are admissible;
b) independence of irrelevant alternatives;
c) unanimity of individual preference between any two options implies social preference as well; and
d) there is no dictator whose preferences automatically become the social ordering.

It is important to recognize what has and has not been proved. It has been proved that no system of voting avoids the spoiler problem altogether for any and every structure of individual preferences. It has not been proved that the problem is equally troublesome in all voting systems. Virtues and vices of several alternatives to plurality voting are discussed briefly in the next two sections.

## Voting for president

Voting may be used to select one person among a number of candidates for a single office, or to select a group of people from among a larger number of candidates. The former, exemplified by voting for president, is discussed here. The latter, exemplified by voting for legislators, is discussed in the next section. The ideal in the design of voting rules for selecting a president is to find the Condorcet winner, the candidate who can beat every other candidate in a pairwise, head-to-head vote. A candidate chosen over every other candidate can reasonably be said to be the community's choice. The ideal is sometimes but not always attainable.[20] The paradox of voting implies that there need not always be a Condorce winner, The ideal is to find the Condorcet winner if there is one.

The simplest and most common procedure is *plurality voting*. Voters are presented with a list of candidates, each voter indicates their first preference among the candidates on the list, and the candidate who is first past the post with the most votes is elected. A candidate with more than half the votes must be the Condorcet winner, but a candidate might win the election with less than half the votes in which case that candidate need not be the Condorcet winner as well. Except when one candidate wins over half the votes, plurality voting is susceptible to both versions of the spoiler problem; the entry of a candidate who has no chance of winning may nevertheless change the outcome of the election, and each of two candidates may be spoilers of the other.

When no candidate has a clear majority, victory for the Condorcet winner might be secured by the replacement of simple plurality voting with a *two-stage* election, with ordinary plurality voting at the first stage followed by a run-off election between the two top candidates. Had there been a two-stage election, Bush and Gore would have been advanced to the run-off, and, since both Bush and Gore could beat Nader easily, the Condorcet winner, who might well have been Gore, would have been elected. Similarly, with two relatively strong Conservative candidates and one even stronger Liberal candidate, the Liberal candidate would win under plurality voting but the stronger of the Conservative candidates might win in the second round of a two-stage election.

Outcomes in a two-stage election can be replicated without actually holding a second election through a procedure using information acquired by replacing the *single ballot* with a *ranked ballot*. With the single ballot, each person votes for only one candidate. With a ranked ballot, each person orders all candidates, or as many candidates as the person chooses to order, from most to least preferred. The president is then elected in two successive vote counts. In the first, the two candidates with the most first preferences are selected. Then, an imaginary election is conducted between these two candidates in which each voter is presumed to select the candidate who ranks higher on that person's ordering. The candidate with the most votes in this imaginary election becomes the president. This notional two-stage election differs from an actual two-stage election in that voters can no longer acquire new and vote-changing information between the first and second stages, but, as long as voters' preferences are unchanged, outcomes in notional elections and in actual elections would be the same.

Ranked ballots may be used in a slightly different way that is sometimes called the *alternative vote*. Instead of deleting all but the two leading candidates for an imaginary run-off election, candidates can be deleted one by one until there is only one candidate left, who is then declared to be the winner of the election. First, the candidate with the fewest first preferences is deleted, and all voters' orders of preferences for the remaining candidates are observed, so that no voter's ranking of the remaining candidates is changed. The process is repeated over and over again, as many times as is necessary to identify the winner of the election. The winner can always beat the runner-up in a pairwise election, and can usually, but not necessarily, beat every other candidate as well.

These alternatives to plurality voting – the run-off election, and the process by which candidates are rejected one by one – are kind to the spoiler and their supporters. When the presence of a spoiler alters the outcome of an election, it is usually by transferring votes from a candidate who is similar to the spoiler to a candidate who is different; more likely than not, people who vote for the spoiler prefer the candidate displaced to the candidate who is elected. The spoiler may run for election regardless, to proclaim a special point of view or to build up support for future elections. The alternatives to plurality voting allow the ideologue to run without actually influencing the outcome of the election and they relieve the ideologue's supporters of the unfortunate choice between suppressing their opinions and harming a candidate they favour.

These alternatives to plurality voting fail to procure the Condorcet winner when the candidate with the fewest first preferences is all other voter's second choice. Imagine an election with candidates Abe, Bill and Carol and with preferences of four groups of voters as illustrated in Table 2.10.

With these preferences, Carol is the Condorcet winner, with 55 per cent of the votes in a head-to-head contest with Abe and 65 per cent of the votes in a head-to-head contest with Bill. Yet Carol fails to win the election, not just in a system

*Table 2.10* How the Condorcet winner fails to be elected

| Groups of voters | Percentage of electorate | Most preferred | Second choice | Least preferred |
|---|---|---|---|---|
| 1 | 45 | Abe | Carol | Bill |
| 2 | 35 | Bill | Carol | Abe |
| 3 | 10 | Carol | Abe | Bill |
| 4 | 10 | Carol | Bill | Abe |

of plurality voting, but in any of the alternatives discussed here. Having the fewest number of first preferences, Carol is eliminated in the first round of counting, and the winner is one of the other two candidates. The alternative vote can be expected to procure the Condorcet winner when two or more candidates appeal to the same constituency of voters, as in the Bush, Gore and Nader example, but not necessarily where one candidate is everybody's second choice.

Prospects for a candidate who is everybody's second choice are brighter under a system of voting called the *Borda count*, where, for example, voters' first preferences are given a weight of 2, second preferences are given a weight of 1 and lower orders of preference are ignored. With this system in place and with voters' preferences as shown in Table 2.10, the count for Abe would be 100 {equal to $(45 \times 2) + (10 \times 1)$}, the count for Bill would be 80 {equal to $(35 \times 2) + (10 \times 1)$}, and the count for Carol would be 120 {equal to $(45 \times 1) + (35 \times 1) + (20 \times 2)$}, so that the winner of the election would be Carol who is the Condorcet winner in this example.

## Voting for legislators

In Britain, Canada and the United States, each member of the legislature – members of parliament, senators and congressmen – is elected in a separate constituency, more or less as the president is elected in plurality voting as described above. The ballot contains the names of all candidates, each voter opts for one of the candidates and the candidate with the most votes is elected.

A common objection to this method of voting for legislators is that it is unrepresentative of the diversity of opinion in each constituency and in the nation as a whole. To take an extreme example, imagine a legislature with 100 members, each elected from one of 100 constituencies. Suppose there are only two political parties, Liberal and Conservative, and that 51 per cent of the electorate votes Liberal in each and every constituency. Were that so, the Liberals would win every seat in the legislature despite the fact that almost half the nation is Conservative. More generally, plurality voting can be expected to under-represent small parties with some support everywhere but a plurality of votes in few, if any, constituencies.

The legislature might be made more representative by *proportional representation*. The division of the country into one-seat constituencies is replaced by a division into a smaller number of multi-seat constituencies or by just one constituency in the nation as a whole. With nationwide proportional representation, people everywhere would vote for parties rather than candidates, each party would present an ordered list of candidates, seats in the legislature would be allocated to parties in proportion to their shares of the total vote and each party would appoint legislators in accordance with their positions on the list. If the liberals won 60,000 out of total of 100,000 votes in the nation as a whole, and with 200 seats in the legislature, the Liberal party would be entitled to 120 seats. Alternatively, with 51 per cent of the vote, the Liberals would be entitled to 104 seats. An adjustment to the formula is required when proportions of votes and seats cannot be equated exactly.

Proportional representation is meaningless in a one-member constituency. Choice of the number of seats per constituency is a trade-off between representation and responsibility. The larger the constituencies, the closer the proportions of seats to votes are likely to be, but the weaker the ties between legislators and the people in the districts that elect them.

A common objection to proportional representation is that it enhances the power of political parties over legislators. When people vote for parties rather than candidates, a party can almost assure the election of any given candidate by placing that candidate high on the party list, and can punish a candidate accordingly. The leader of a party may be placed first on the list, ensuring their election as long as the party's vote is large enough to supply at least one seat in the legislature. Whoever is empowered to set the ordering of candidates on a party's list may, in fact, be entitled to decide what the party's policy will be.

An escape from this unfortunate feature of proportional representation – to preserve fair representation without the subservience of legislators to the party hierarchy – is the *single transferable vote*. As in proportional representation, the single transferrable vote may be conducted for the entire legislature at once or for groups of legislators in multi-seat constituencies. As in plurality voting, citizens vote for candidates rather than parties. The main concern in the design of this system of voting is to promote candidates of great ability,[21] or with nationwide support but less than a majority in any constituency, while at the same time avoiding the wastage of votes for especially popular candidates. To see what is at stake, imagine a single ballot election for five members of parliament in which each voter specifies a preference for one and only one candidate and seats in the legislature are awarded to candidates with the largest number of votes. Suppose ten candidates are competing for the five seats and that, among these ten candidates, Joe is the preferred candidate of 90 per cent of the electorate. If all of Joe's supporters voted for Joe, he would surely be included among the five winners in the election, but Joe's supporters would be grossly under-represented in the legislature because the other four legislators in this five-candidate constituency would be selected by no more than 10 per cent of the electorate; 10 per cent of the electorate would be choosing 80 per cent of the legislators. On the other hand, people who have already obtained their first preference, Joe, should be given less weight in the selection of the other four candidates than people who did not vote for Joe.

The single transferable vote is designed to avoid two opposite extremes: under-representation of supporters of the most popular candidate when the five candidates with the most first preferences are elected, and over-representation of supporters of the most popular candidate when they are given the same weight as other voters in the selection of the other legislators. The single transferrable vote gives supporters of very popular candidates some weight in the selection of the remaining legislators, but less than is given to other voters. The single transferable vote is based upon ranked ballots rather than single ballots. Instead of selecting just one candidate, voters order all candidates from most preferred to least preferred. A 'quota' of first preferences is established, as will be explained presently. The candidate with the largest number of first preferences is elected if and only if that number exceeds the quota. When that happens, the elected candidate is dropped from the list, all voters' rankings are adjusted accordingly and there is recount in which only the 'excess votes' of people who selected the successful candidate as their first choice – excess votes being the difference between the number of votes for that candidate and the quota – are recognized. Otherwise, if no candidate acquires enough first preferences to meet the quota, the candidate with the smallest number of first preferences is dropped from the list, votes among all other candidates are re-ranked as though the excluded candidate had not run at all, and the process is repeated as often as necessary until – as must happen eventually – the designated number of legislators is elected.

For this process to work, the quota must be set equal to

$$[(\text{number of votes})/(\text{number of seats to be filled} + 1)] + 1$$

The quota is set just high enough to ensure that the right number of candidates, no more, no less, is elected. With three million votes cast in an constituency where two legislators are to be selected, the quota is 1,000,001 votes [{3,000,000/(2 + 1)} + 1]. Each of two winning candidates can meet the quota with votes left over, but each of three candidates cannot. If 2,000,001 voters select Joe as their first preference, then Joe's 'excess votes' would be 1,000,000, and anybody who voted for Joe would henceforth be treated as approximately half a person (1,000,000/2,000,001, which is the ratio of excess first preference votes to total first preference votes among the supporters of Joe). In the next stage of the single transferable vote, one more legislator is selected in a recount with Joe off the list of candidates, with voters' orders of preference adjusted accordingly and with only 2,000,000 voters, the 1,000,000 voters who did not select Joe as their first preference together with the 1,000,000 excess votes – 2,000,000 people each given a weight of ½– of people who selected Joe in the preceding stage. If no candidate meets the quota at this stage, the candidate with the lowest number of first preferences is dropped from the list and the process is repeated, as many times as necessary, until a second legislator is selected.

Being kinder to small parties, proportional representation and the single transferrable vote are less likely to supply any party with a clear majority in parliament, so that a coalition among several parties would likely be required to form a government. The general principle here, known as Duverger's law,[22] is that plurality voting creates a strong incentive for the formation of a small number – ideally two – of large political parties with platforms appealing to a large proportion of the electorate and with a significant chance of winning a majority of the seats on the legislature, while proportional representation creates an incentive for the formation of a relatively large number of ideologically pure parties, each unlikely to win more than a small minority of the seats in the legislature, so that a majority government must be formed by a coalition of parties.

Plurality voting may be less unfair to people than to parties. People's preferences tend to be multi-dimensional and not always well-represented by the small ideological parties that proportional representation tends to encourage. With two large political parties, people know exactly what they are voting for, while, with many parties from which a majority coalition will be formed after the election, it becomes difficult to predict what the ultimate effect of one's vote will be.

Comparison of representation under the different voting systems is complicated by the fact that the mix of parties is unlikely to be the same. With plurality voting, there can be no doctors' party or teachers' party because such parties could never win a majority of votes in any constituency. With proportional representation or the single transferable vote in the nation as a whole, a doctors' party or a teachers' party might be formed if doctors or teachers cared enough about their special interests to organize a party and vote as a block. Every religion, every ethnic group and every social class might form what has been called a 'voluntary', as distinct from 'compulsory' constituency not just to influence members of parliament as they do today, but to elect members of parliament devoted to their special concerns. There may be a catholic party and a protestant party, each justifying its existence as a defence against the other. By contrast, the winner in a first-past-the-post election with one seat per constituency would be more likely to be a moderate appealing, or at least tolerable, to people of both religions. As it is difficult to say whether the electorate is better represented by a few large comprehensive parties or by many narrowly focused parties. Equality of political parties' ratios of seats to votes is a questionable virtue.

An immediate corollary of Duverger's law is that voting arrangements can have a profound effect upon the role of bargaining in the formation of laws and policies. Plurality voting promotes bargaining in the establishment of platforms of large political parties *before the election*, while proportional representation promotes bargaining among smaller relatively more homogeneous parties in the formation of government and the choice of policies *after the election*. The latter can be much more dangerous. Failure of a political party to bargain its way to a common platform may cost that party the election. Failure of a collection of small parties to bargain their way to a common set of policies may stop government altogether, blocking the passage of laws, the financing of the bureaucracy and the selection of the executive. Failure to compromise may be less of a threat under plurality voting than under proportional representation. Much depends on whether there is a broad consensus in society about what public policy ought to be, a consensus determining the platforms of large political parties or the policies agreed upon by coalitions of smaller parties that come together to form a majority government. With such a consensus, both plurality voting and proportional representation can be expected to work rather well. Otherwise, plurality voting may still yield a viable majority government, albeit a government that is very unpopular with a large minority of the population, but proportional representation can be a recipe for stalemate.

It is for this reason that proportional representation is believed by some authors to have facilitated the triumph of the Fascist party in Italy and the Nazi party in Germany.[23] Neither was the creation of proportional representation, but both may have been stopped had there been plurality voting instead. Both parties might have had substantially smaller representation in the national legislatures. Stalemate due to ideological differences among other parties is said to have crippled government to the point where, as Finer (quoted in Riker (1982: 757)) said 'people became so distracted by fumbling governments, that they will acquiesce in any sort of dictatorship'.

Much depends on how bargains in the legislature are struck. Diversity of opinions and interests may be seen as analogous to occupancy of positions on a left–right scale where the preference of the median voter can be expected to prevail, as facilitating tyranny of whatever majority can come together to vote as a block, or as giving rise to a nationwide compromise in which all voters' interests are somehow taken into account. Desirability of the different voting systems discussed here depends very much on how conflict of interest is, or is not, resolved and on what the legislature is expected to do.[24]

Long ago, in a classic description of British parliamentary government, Walter Bagehot (1966[1867]: 151–3) classified the functions of parliament as elective, expressive, teaching, informing and legislating, to which might be added the task of holding the executive's feet to the fire to keep it from perpetuating itself indefinitely. It may be that voting arrangements which are best for some functions of parliament are not best for all. The 'voluntary' constituencies in the single transferrable vote may be better for the expressive, teaching and informing functions of government than the geographically defined constituencies in plurality voting. Proportional representation and the single transferrable vote may supply parliament with the diversity of opinion and interests that these functions of government require. On the other hand, the elective function of choosing the prime minister who in turn chooses the cabinet to watch over the bureaucracy and to govern the country might be better served by plurality voting which is more likely to yield the majority required to get things done. Bagehot saw the elective function as the most important task of parliament. The case for first-past-the-post may be stronger in parliamentary government where the prime minister is chosen in parliament than in societies where the president is chosen in a separate election.[25]

## Legislators voting for laws

Citizens voting for candidates is never more than half the story because what citizens are really voting for is the legislation and the policy that the candidates, as legislators and executives, can be expected to adopt. Voting by legislators for laws differs from voting by citizens for legislators – for members of parliament in Canada and the United Kingdom, for president, senators and members of the US House of Representatives – in several essential respects.

Voting for laws is against the background of a status quo that persists if no new law is enacted. There is no analogue to the status quo in voting for candidates because one of the candidates must win, and nothing in the voting mechanism favours one candidate over another. Some candidate must be elected; no new law need be passed. Nor is there a clear set of options to vote about. Laws must be crafted by legislators and proposed amendments must be taken into account.

When amendments are proposed, there is a prescribed order of votes, on the principle of 'first in–last out'. Consider a bill with two amendments, amendment *x* that was proposed first and amendment *y* that was proposed afterwards. The prescribed sequence of votes is

i)    an up-or-down vote on amendment *y*;
ii)   an up-or-down vote on amendment *x*;
iii)  a vote between the bill as amended at stages (i) and (ii) and as originally proposed; and
iv)   a vote between the survivor at stage (iii) and the status quo (that is, a vote whether to accept or reject the bill as amended).

The logic of the sequence is that, should a paradox of voting occur among the versions of the bill, the advantage goes first to the status quo, then to the bill as first proposed, then to the fully amended bill and lastly to partly amended versions of the bill depending on the sequence of amendments. Parliamentary procedure can be looked upon as a defence against the agenda setter who, in the ham, cheese and tuna example, could bamboozle voters into choosing whichever sandwich the agenda setter wants through the appropriate ordering of votes. Actual parliamentary procedure is a complex generalization of the example in this paragraph.[26]

Bills in parliament are crafted and modified at the same time as they are being judged worthy or otherwise. Typically, when a proposed bill is taken seriously, it is assigned to a committee of the legislature to be examined in detail, modified as the committee sees fit and only then committed to the legislature to be amended, passed or rejected as the legislature sees fit. Bills are often long and detailed with add-ons favouring special interests that must be placated if the bill is to be passed at all.

Passage of bills is time-consuming and requires an elaborate network of rules specifying when a bill is to be considered at all, who may speak for and against a bill, how much time is to be allocated for each speech, and so on. The government of the day may exert more or less influence on these matters. In Canada, a distinction is drawn between government bills that are always discussed in parliament and private members' bills that are considered or not considered at random because there is no time to consider all of the bills that are proposed. Bills are given three readings. The first reading is to decide quickly whether the bill is to be considered at all. The pros and cons of the proposed bill are seriously and extensively discussed at the second reading after which the bill is sent to committee for detailed analysis. At the third reading, the bill is given a final up-or-down vote. Rules are arcane and complex, specifying the composition of committees, whether the committee chair is appointed by the prime minister or elected, whether, and for which bills, rejection of a government-sponsored bill requires the government to resign, whether debate can be terminated, whether parliament can be prorogued requiring bills in process be evaluated all over again when parliament resumes, the authority to appoint the speaker, the powers of the speaker, authority to appoint senators and judges, and so on. Rules are always fuzzy at the edges, and are gradually refined and changed.

## The elected dictator

Democracy is fragile. Especially when society is sharply polarized, elected governments may be terminated by the army and the bureaucracy, by organized groups of people who honestly believe they know what is best for society, or by voters so disenchanted with bickering and inactivity in the legislature that they are prepared to vote for a strong man to dispense with elections and get things done. Neither Hitler nor Mussolini disguised their anti-democratic sympathies, but both came to office legitimately in countries where voters knew, or thought they knew, what they were doing. Both were appointed – Hitler by President Hindenberg in 1932 and Mussolini by King Victor Emmanuel III in 1923 – to lead coalitions of political parties at a time of gridlock when no party held a clear majority of the seats in the legislature.

This brief review of voting patterns suggests how democracy may be defended. Part of that defence is behavioural. Citizens must recognize a duty to vote. Legislators must strike bargains in ways that cannot be explained by self-interest alone. Part of that defence is institutional. Democracy requires strong property rights, but with as much redistribution of income as in the interest of the median voter, for its own sake to alleviate poverty and reduce gross inequality, and so that a majority of the poor does not become disillusioned with the system as a whole.

## Notes

1 Throughout this chapter, the terms 'majority rule voting' and 'democracy' are used interchangeably. In general, the term democracy may refer to rule by the many as distinct from rule by the few, or it may refer to majority rule voting as a means of public decision-making. The terms part company when franchise is restricted to a portion of the population as will be discussed in later chapters. For the present, restricted franchise is ignored.

2 For the original statement of the theorem, see Black (1948).

3 The derivative $\delta U_i/\delta b$ is *partial*, the change in $U_i$ in response to a change in $b$ when $G$ is held constant, and it is necessarily positive. The derivative $dU_i/dG$ is *total*, the change in $U_i$ in response to a change in $G$ when $b$ changes in accordance with the budget constraint in Equation (2.1). It is positive when $G$ is low and negative when $G$ is high.

4 On the Condorcet jury theorem, see Austen-Smith and Banks (1996). The theorem is named after the mathematician and political scientist, Nicolas de Caritat, Marquis de Condorcet, 1743–1794, who is also credited with the notion of the Condorcet winner to be discussed later.

5 In 'Policy gambles' Sumon Majumdar and Sharon W. Mukand (2004) show how politicians' need to appear competent in the eyes of voters creates an incentive to stick with policies that have very little chance of success.

6 The formula as it stands makes no allowance for deadweight loss in taxation. Allowance for deadweight loss would alter the formula without changing the story in any essential way.

7 This example and its implications for public policy was introduced by Tullock (1959).

8 The paradox of voting has been recognized at least since the eighteenth century. On early references, see Black and Newing (1958).

9 On strategic voting, see Downs (1957).

10 That vote trading may be benign or predatory was recognized by Buchanan and Tullock (1962). They refer to what is here called vote trading as logrolling, but the analysis is essentially the same.

11 Indifference curves are drawn as loops, not circles. For any given distance from $\delta$, a person may be better off in some directions than in others.

12 See Tullock (1967). On voting equilibrium, see Plott (1967).

13 More realistically, people outside the majority coalition might be left with a bare subsistence income, just enough to keep them alive and working. They might be supplied with whatever income serves to maximize the income of the majority coalition. This changes the detail but not the essence of the example.

14 Aristotle recognized the danger: 'Heterogeneity of stocks may lead to sedition – at any rate until they have had time to assimilate. A state cannot be constituted from any chance body of persons, or in any chance period of time. Most of the states which have admitted persons of another stock, either at the time of their foundation or later, have been troubled by sedition' Baker (1958: 210).

15 In *The Federalist Papers* no. 51 (Hacker, 1964), James Madison argued that the proposed American constitution would 'divide and arrange the several offices in such a manner as that each may be a check on the other'.

16 A pro-Liberal's person's vote can be pivotal in either of two circumstances: i) but for this person's vote, the election would have been tied, and the winner of the election, as determined by the flip of a coin, would have been the Conservative party, and ii) but for this person's vote, the outcome of the election would have been a win by one vote for the Conservative party and the coin toss required in the event that this person votes is won by the Liberal party. The probability of each of these pairs of events is 1/40,000. The probability of either one or the other is 1/20,000. The example needs to be tweaked slightly to allow for the possibility of the Conservatives winning the election by exactly one vote.

17 The paradox of not voting was introduced in Riker and Ordeshook (1968).

18 *United States Presidential Election in Florida, 2000*, Wikipedia. It is at least arguable that, had Nader dropped out of the race, Gore would have won the presidency, and there would have been no Bush tax cuts, no invasion of Iraq and no crash of the economy in 2008, though who knows what might have happened instead?

19 These four conditions are enumerated in Arrow (1963) as 1', 3, P and 5.

20 For simple expositions of the different vote-counting arrangements, see Mackenzie (1958) and Rae (1967). For a thorough examination of ways of counting votes for candidates, see Tideman (2006). Tideman also discusses proposals for identifying voters' intensity of preferences and incorporating that information in rules for choosing among candidates. For a briefer treatment of voting methods in the context of a general study of politics, see Riker (1988). Riker's (1986) contains some very enlightening examples.

21 John Stuart Mill (1948[1861]), emphasized this consideration in his classical defence of what is now called the single transferrable vote.

22 For a history and exposition of Duverger's law, see Riker (1982). Riker distinguishes between Duverger's hypotheses that 'the simple majority ... favours a two-party system' and Duverger's law that 'proportional representation favours multi-partyism'.

23 See Hermens (1941). The book contains a detailed account of the development of proportion representation in Italy, Germany and several other countries, together with the argument that, but for proportional representation, the regimes of Mussolini and Hitler would not have emerged.

24 Robert Dahl (1956) speaks of 'polyarchy' where democracy is a resolution of the interests of diverse minority groups: 'Prior to politics, beneath it, enveloping it, restricting it, conditioning it, is the underlying consensus on policy that usually exists in the society among the predominant proportion of the politically active members. Without such a consensus, no democratic system would long survive ...'

25 Speaking of the Canadian House of Commons, C. E. S. Franks (1987) identified four functions: 'to make a government, that is, to establish a legitimate government through the electoral process, to make government work, that is, to give government the authority, funds, and other resources necessary for governing the country, to make a government behave, that is, to be watching over the government, and fourth, to make an alternative government, that is, to enable the opposition to present its case to the public and become a credible choice for replacing the party in power.'

26 The process is described in Riker (1988) section 4C.

# References

Arrow, Kenneth J. (1963) *Social Choice and Individual Values*, 2nd edn, New Haven: Yale University Press, p. 26.

Austen-Smith, D. and Banks, J. (1996) Information aggregation, rationality and the Condorcet jury theorem, *American Political Science Review*, 90, 34–45.

Bagehot, Walter (1966[1867]) *The English Constitution*, Ithaca, NY: Cornell Paperback, pp. 151–3.

Baker, Ernest, (ed. and trans.) (1958) *The Politics of Aristotle*, Oxford: Oxford University Press, p. 210.

Black, D. (1948) On the rationale of group decision-making, *Journal of Political Economy*, 56(1), 23–34.

Black, Duncan and Newing, R. A. (1958) *The Theory of Committees and Elections*, Cambridge: Cambridge University Press.

Buchanan, James and Tullock, Gordon (1962) *The Calculus of Consent: Logical Foundations of Constitutional Democracy*, Indianapolis, IN: Liberty Fund Inc.

Dahl, Robert A. (1956) *A Preface to Democratic Theory*, Chicago: University of Chicago Press, p. 122.

Downs, Anthony (1957) *An Economic Theory of Democracy*, New York: Harper and Row.

Franks, C. E. S. (1987) *The Parliament of Canada*, Toronto: University of Toronto Press, p. 5.

Hacker, A., (Ed.) (1964) *The Federalist Papers by Alexander Hamilton, John Jay and James Madison*. New York: Washington Square Press, no. 51.

Hermens, F. A. (1941) *Democracy or Anarchy: A Study of Proportional Representation*, Notre Dame, IN: University of Notre Dame.

Mackenzie, W. J. M. (1958) *Free Elections:An Elementary Textbook*, London: George Allen and Unwin Ltd.

Majumdar, Sumon and Mukand, Sharun W. (2004) Policy gambles, *American Economic Review*, 94(4), 1207–22.

Mill, John Stuart (1948[1861]) *Considerations on Representative Government*, Oxford: Basil Blackwell, chapters VII and X.

Plott, Charles R. (1967) A notion of equilibrium and its possibility under majority rule, *The American Economic Review*, 57(4), 787–806.

Rae, Douglas W. (1967) *The Political Consequences of Electoral Laws*, New Haven, CT: Yale University Press.

Riker, William H. (1982) The two party system and Duverger's law: an essay on the history of political science, *The American Political Science Review*, 76(4), 753–66.

Riker, William H. (1986) *The Art of Political Manipulation*, New Haven, CT: Yale University Press.

Riker, William H. (1988) *Liberalism Against Populism: The Confrontation Between the Theory of Democracy and the Theory of Social Choice*, Long Grove, IL: Waveland Press.

Riker, William H. and Ordeshook, Peter C. (1968) A theory of the calculus of voting, *American Political Science Review*, 62(1), 25–42.

Tideman, Nicolaus (2006) *Collective Decisions and Voting: The Potential for Public Choice*, Farnham, UK: Ashgate Publishing Company.

Tullock, Gordon (1959) Problems of majority voting, *Journal of Political Economy*, 67(6), 571–9.

Tullock, Gordon (1967) The general irrelevance of the general impossibility theorem, *Quarterly Journal of Economics*, 81(2), 256–70.

# 3   Voting about the redistribution of income

Is there an electoral equilibrium redistribution of income when each person votes self-interestedly rather than for what is seen as best for the community as a whole? Is redistribution a single-peaked issue with a well-defined equilibrium comparable to the equilibrium in ideal competitive markets, or must one look beyond voters' self-interest, to a sense of duty or a willingness to compromise, for an explanation of how redistribution is determined? There is such an equilibrium in a simple model of self-interested voting, and the presence of equilibrium in the model suggests that conflict over the redistribution of income may be mitigated as political parties are induced to adopt similar policies on redistribution, reducing what people stand to lose when their preferred political parties lose elections. Equilibrium tends to disintegrate when strong assumptions in the model are altered to take account of omitted aspects of the economy and society.

This chapter begins with a formal model where everything works well. Imagine a society with a typically skewed distribution of gross incomes where average income exceeds the income of the median person on the scale of rich and poor, a population of voters motivated by self-interest alone, a negative income tax as representative of all redistribution, and costly but undetectable tax evasion as representative of all sources of deadweight loss. For such a society, the formal model yields an electoral equilibrium redistribution comparable to the general equilibrium of prices and quantities in a competitive market.[1] It is proved that government by majority rule voting redistributes income from rich to poor without removing inequality altogether or changing the order of people on the scale of rich and poor, and that the amount of redistribution, measured by the rate of tax to finance it, is an increasing function of the efficiency of tax collection and the original disparity of income between rich and poor.

The proposition that more inequality promotes more redistribution is especially interesting because, though proved conclusively within the formal model, it may very well be wrong.[2] Over the last 30 years, there has been a widening of the distribution of income in the United States and many other countries, but top marginal tax rates have declined and other redistributive measures have not on balance been expanded. This is not a conclusive refutation because distribution and redistribution may have both been pushed along by forces not accounted for in the formal model, but it warrants a close look at the assumptions.

Implications of relaxing the assumptions are examined once the formal model is presented. The assumption that people vote self-interestedly takes no account of compassion or fear. Voters may support policies deemed best for the community as a whole or may favour redistribution to deter rebellion by the poor. Confinement of redistribution to the negative income tax takes no account of progressivity or of the range of social programmes – the old age pension, unemployment insurance, welfare and so on – protecting people from the ups and downs of fortune and improving the circumstances of the poor. Progressive taxation may be more efficient than the negative income tax but at the cost of losing the neat electoral equilibrium of redistribution. Confinement of tax avoidance to costly but undetectable tax evasion ignores the diversion of time from paid work to do-it-yourself activities or leisure, and migration from high-tax to low-tax jurisdictions. The formal model takes no account of abstention or political parties, the implicit assumption being that rival political parties include the median voter's preferred redistribution in their platforms because the party failing to do so must lose the election. Nor is there any recognition of the possibility that, by facilitating campaign advertising by the party of the rich, a widening of the distribution of income may lead to less, rather than more, redistribution. To postulate a given distribution of pre-tax, pre-transfer income is to ignore a wide range of policies – tariffs, investment grants, environmental rules, rights of corporations, patent law, ownership of natural resources, and so on – that have no less influence than the formal redistribution of income on the circumstances of rich and poor. Nor is there any recognition of income – oil revenue being the leading example – accruing in the first instance to the nation as a whole and needing to be allocated politically. Modification of these assumptions may alter the equilibrium distribution or may undermine the equilibrium altogether, causing the outcome of majority rule voting to depend in part on people's willingness to bargain and compromise. Varieties of campaign advertising, the Pareto distribution and the marginal cost of public funds are discussed in appendices.

## A simple model of electoral equilibrium redistribution

Imagine a society where the only role of government is to redistribute income. Whether or not to redistribute and, if so, how much are determined by majority rule voting. Assume:

1   There is a given and immutable distribution of gross (pre-tax, pre-transfer) incomes.
2   Like virtually every distribution of income that has ever been observed, the distribution of gross income in this society is skewed, with low incomes bunched together and high incomes spread out, so that the median income is less than the average income.[3] The ratio of median to average income will serve as a measure of equality. The Pareto distribution will be used in a numerical example.
3   Public decisions are made by majority rule voting.

4    Redistribution is constitutionally confined to a negative income tax, with an equal payment (called the demogrant) per person, rich or poor, financed by a proportional income tax. The rate of the negative income tax serves as the measure of redistribution.

5    There is no public expenditure other than the payment per person under the negative income tax.

6    People respond to taxation not by working less, but by concealing income from the tax collector, where concealment is undetectable once the required expenditure to avoid detection has been borne. To ensure that not all gross income is concealed from the tax collector and that the proportion concealed is an increasing function of the tax rate, the taxpayer's marginal cost of evasion must be an increasing function of the proportion of gross income evaded. A person's cost of tax evasion is a deadweight loss to society as a whole, for tax evader's gain is at the expense of the rest of the population.

7    Everybody is unreservedly greedy. In voting about the amount of redistribution or about whether to redistribute income at all, one seeks to maximize one's own post-tax, post-transfer income.

8    The model is atemporal. No account is taken of the future or the past.

The crux of the model is that i) at any given tax rate, everybody's chosen proportion of income concealed from the tax collector is the same, regardless of whether one's gross, pre-tax income is large or small, but ii) recognizing this, people with different incomes prefer different tax rates, and iii) the preferred tax rate of the median voter prevails.

Imagine a society with a given distribution of people's gross, pre-tax, pre-transfer incomes, $Y$, determined in the market independently of all tax and transfer policy, where all public revenue is acquired by a proportional tax at a rate $t$ and where people evade tax insofar as it is advantageous to do so. A person conceals a proportion $\tau$ of gross income to minimize the sum of tax paid and the cost of tax evasion. Observed income $y$ and is dependent on the tax rate, but gross income $Y$ is not. By definition, the tax base of a person who conceals a portion $\tau$ of gross income from the tax collector is

$$y = (1 - \tau)Y \tag{3.1}$$

Suppose i) tax evasion is costly but completely undetectable once the appropriate cost of concealment is borne and ii) the marginal cost of concealment is proportional to the share, $\tau$, of income concealed. Specifically the marginal cost as a proportion of gross income of concealing a share $\tau$ is $\beta\tau$ where $\beta$ is a technically given parameter interpretable as the efficiency of tax collection'. The full cost per dollar of gross income[4] of concealing a portion $\tau$ of one's income, $Y$, becomes $\beta\tau^2/2$.

On these assumptions, a person confronted with a tax rate $t$ conceals a portion $\tau$ of income $Y$ to minimize the total burden of taxation, equal to the sum of

$$\text{tax paid and cost of tax evasion} = t(1 - \tau)Y + \beta\tau^2 Y/2 \tag{3.2}$$

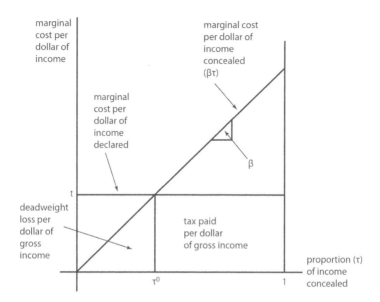

*Figure 3.1* The tax payer's decision about how much tax to evade by concealing income from the tax collector.

from which it follows – by minimizing this expression with respect to $\tau$ – that regardless of $Y$ and for any given $t$ and $\beta$, the taxpayer chooses $\tau$ such that

$$t = \beta\tau \qquad\qquad (3.3)$$

as illustrated in Figure 3.1 where the height of the flat line is the constant marginal cost of not concealing one's income and paying tax instead, while the height of the diagonal line is the increasing marginal cost of concealing income from the tax collector. The taxpayer's choice, $\tau^0$, of the proportion of income to conceal is where marginal costs are equalized as indicated in Equation (3.3). The area of the box at the bottom right-hand side of the figure is tax revenue as a proportion of income, the triangular area to the right of the box is the corresponding deadweight loss, and their sum is the full cost of taxation to the taxpayer per dollar of gross income. Absence of $Y$ in Equation (3.3) means that, for any given $\beta$, everybody's chosen value of $\tau$ must be the same.

The tax base, $y$, becomes

$$y = (1 - \tau)Y = (1 - t/\beta)Y \qquad\qquad (3.4)$$

and tax revenue as a proportion of gross income becomes

$$R = ty/Y = t(1 - \tau) = t(1 - t/\beta) \qquad\qquad (3.5)$$

A function such as Equation (3.5) connecting tax revenue to tax rate is called a Laffer curve. The Laffer curve is normally defined as showing how the tax rate affects total tax revenue in the nation as a whole. Equation (3.5) may be thought of as a miniature Laffer curve, describing the behaviour of a person rather than of the entire population. Tax revenue acquired from a person with income $Y$ is $RY$. Tax revenue acquired from the nation as a whole is $RY$ where $Y$ is the national income. When all public revenue is redistributed in a negative income tax, the demogrant in the negative income tax must be $RY^{av}$ where $Y^{av}$ is average income in the entire population.

It follows at once from Equation (3.5) that the slope of the miniature Laffer curve is

$$\delta R/\delta t = (1 - \tau) - t\delta\tau/\delta t = 1 - 2t/\beta \tag{3.6}$$

that $\varepsilon_{r,t}$ the elasticity of tax revenue $R$ with respect to the tax rate $t$ along the Laffer curve is

$$\varepsilon_{R,t} = (t/R)(\delta R/\delta t) = (1 - 2t/\beta)/(1 - t/\beta) = (\beta - 2t)/(\beta - t) \tag{3.7}$$

and that the revenue-maximizing tax rate, $t^*$, becomes

$$t^* = \beta/2 \tag{3.8}$$

because $\delta R/\delta t = 0$ implies that $2t/\beta = 1$. No higher rate could ever be advantageous to anybody because tax revenue would be diminished, but, as is evident from inspection of Figure 3.1, the greater the efficiency of tax collection, the higher the revenue-maximizing tax rate would be. Note that the revenue-maximizing tax rate of the miniature Laffer curve and the full Laffer curve must be the same.

For four curves in Figure 3.2 are miniature Laffer curves for four values of the efficiency of tax collection. The four values of $\beta$ are ½, 1, 2 and $\infty$. For any given value of $\beta$, total revenue, $R$, as a proportion of national income begins 0 when $t = 0$, rises to a maximum of $\beta/4$ when $t = \beta/2$ and declines thereafter. If $\beta = $ ½, total revenue is maximized at a tax rate of 25 per cent. If $\beta = 1$, total revenue is maximized at a rate of 50 per cent. If $\beta = 2$, total revenue is maximized at a rate of 100 per cent. The greater the efficiency of tax collection, the higher the tax rate at which revenue is maximized and the larger maximal revenue must be. If $\beta = 2$ and $t$ is set equal to 1, tax revenue becomes half the national income, wastage resources in concealing income from the tax collector becomes a quarter of the national income and the remaining quarter is left with the tax payer to be consumed. Note also, that if $\beta = $ infinity, tax evasion is always prohibitively expensive so that the Laffer curve becomes an upward-sloping straight line and the entire gross, pre-tax income can be appropriated by the tax collector with a tax rate of 100 per cent.

A feature of this economy is that, depending on the efficiency of tax collection, the Laffer curve need not peak at a tax rate of less than 100 per cent. It is commonly

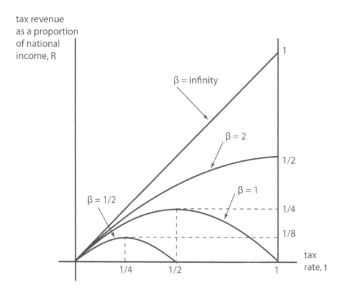

*Figure 3.2* How the location of the Laffer curve depends upon the efficiency of tax collection.

supposed that tax revenue is maximized at some rate well short of 100 per cent because the tax base shrinks as the tax rate is increased. The example shows that this need not be so. The base does shrink as the rate increases, but not necessarily by enough to reduce the revenue acquired. Any value of $\beta$ equal to or greater than 2 yields a steadily upward-sloping Laffer curve. To be sure, the value of $\beta$ – or, more generally, the cost of diminishing one's observed tax base no matter how it is done – is an empirical matter. Perhaps the truth is that the revenue-maximizing tax rate is well short of 100 per cent. Perhaps, as has been alleged, it is in the order of 50 per cent, in which case there is little room for redistribution once ordinary public goods have been acquired. The most that can be said on the strength of this model is that an entirely upward-sloping Laffer curve cannot be ruled out a priori. On the other hand, to say that society can maximize tax revenue at very high tax rates is not to say that it would wish to do so. Evidence and inferences about the shape of the Laffer curve will be discussed in the next chapter.

Now consider the redistribution of income by means of a negative income tax in an economy where all tax revenue is devoted to the redistribution of income so that average revenue acquired and the demogrant are one and the same. Though everybody conceals the same proportion of income in response to any given tax rate, each person has his own preferred degree of redistribution which can be represented unambiguously by his preferred tax rate. One's preferred tax rate is the rate at which one's net income, $I$, is as large as possible, where net income under a negative income tax takes account not just of tax paid and demogrant received, but of expenditure to hide a part of one's income from the tax collector and of one's estimate of other people's tax evasion. On the assumptions made so far, everybody's chosen $\tau$ as a function of $t$ is the same. One's preferred tax rate, $t(Y)$, depends on one's own gross income, $Y$, the average gross income, $Y^{av}$, the efficiency of tax collection, $\beta$, and the common rate of tax evasion $\tau$. Specifically, one's preferred tax rate maximizes one's net post-tax, post-transfer income, $I$, where[5]

$$\text{net income} = \text{gross income} - \text{tax paid} - \text{cost of tax evasion} + \text{demogrant}$$

$$(3.9)$$

As illustrated in Figure 3.1, 'tax paid' is $t(1-\tau)Y$, 'cost of tax evasion' is $\beta\tau^2 Y/2$ and 'the demogrant' is $t(1-\tau)Y^{av}$ so that net income, $I$, becomes a function of $t$, $Y$, $Y^{av}$ and $\beta$. Specifically, using Equation (3.3),

$$I(t, Y, Y^{av}, \beta) = Y - t(1 - t/\beta)Y + t(1 - t/\beta)Y^{av} - t^2 Y/2\beta \qquad (3.10)$$

Now think of a person as voter rather than as taxpayer. His preferred rate is whatever rate serves to maximize his net income for the given values of $Y$, $Y^{av}$ and $\beta$.

$$\delta I/\delta t = -Y + (t/\beta)Y + Y^{av} - (2t/\beta)Y^{av} = 0 \qquad (3.11)$$

Thus, as long as $Y < Y^{av}$, the preferred tax rate of a person with a gross income $Y$ becomes

$$t(Y) = \beta\{Y^{av} - Y\}/\{2Y^{av} - Y\} \qquad (3.12)$$

from which it follows that that the median voter's preferred tax rate is

$$t(Y^{med}) = \beta\{Y^{av} - Y^{med}\}/\{2Y^{av} - Y^{med}\} \qquad (3.13)$$

Several things follow from Equations (3.12) and (3.13). The higher one's income, the smaller tax rate and the less redistribution one prefers there to be. A person with no income at all wants a tax rate of $\beta/2$ as already shown in Equation (3.8). A person with half the average income wants a tax rate of $\beta/3$. A person with average income prefers no tax and no redistribution at all. Strictly speaking, person with above average income would prefer a negative tax rate financed by a lump sum tax, but, where that is not feasible, would settle for a tax rate of 0. The median voter's preferred tax rate falls steadily from a high of $\beta/2$ when $Y^{med} = 0$ to 0 when $Y^{med} = Y^{av}$.

The median voter's preferred tax rate depends on the efficiency of tax collection and the inequality in the distribution of income. The latter is represented in Equation (3.13) by the ratio of average to median income, but it can also be represented by a more direct measure of inequality such as the parameter $\alpha$ in the Pareto distribution of income, defined by the property that

$$n(Y) = (Y^{min}/Y)^{\alpha} \qquad\qquad (3.14)$$

or equivalently,

$$Y(n) = (1/n)^{1/\alpha} Y^{min} \qquad\qquad (3.15)$$

where $n(Y)$ is the proportion of the population with incomes greater than $Y$, where $Y^{min}$ – equal to $Y(1)$ – is the lowest income and where the parameter $\alpha$ is an indicator of *equality*, varying from a minimum of 1 when the distribution of income is as unequal as it can ever be to a maximum of infinity when everybody's income is the same. A key property of the Pareto distribution is that $\alpha$ is also a measure of the skewness of the distribution, for it is the skewness rather the width of the distribution of income that accounts for people's willingness to vote for redistribution.[6]

It is shown in an Appendix 3B that median and average incomes are

$$Y^{med} = Y(\tfrac{1}{2})^{1/\alpha} = (2)^{1/\alpha} Y^{min} \qquad\qquad (3.16)$$

and

$$Y^{av} = [\alpha/(\alpha - 1)]Y^{min} \qquad\qquad (3.17)$$

so that the ratio of mean income to median income becomes

$$Y^{av}/Y^{med} = \{\alpha/(\alpha - 1)\}(2)^{-1/\alpha} \qquad\qquad (3.18)$$

which decreases steadily from $\infty$ to 1 when equality, as represented by the parameter $\alpha$, rises from a minimum of 1 to a maximum of $\infty$, so that the ratio of mean to median income is an indicator of inequality in the distribution of income. Specifically,

$$\delta(Y^{av}/Y^{med})/\delta\alpha < 0 \qquad\qquad (3.19)$$

because both $2^{-1/\alpha}$ and $\alpha/(\alpha - 1)$ are decreasing functions of $\alpha$.

Since the median income is always less than the average, the median voter must have something to gain from a degree of redistribution of income.

From Equations (3.6) and (3.12), society's chosen tax rate can be computed for any given degree of equality, $\alpha$, in the distribution of income and for any given efficiency of tax collection, $\beta$. A selection of rates, increasing with $\beta$ and decreasing with $\alpha$, is shown in Table 3.1.

*Table 3.1* The median voter's preferred tax rate (*t* expressed as a per cent) dependent on the equality in the distribution of income ($\alpha$) and the efficiency of tax collection ($\beta$)

|  | $\beta = 3$ | $\beta = 2$ | $\beta = 1$ | $\beta = 1/2$ |
|---|---|---|---|---|
| $\alpha = 2$ | 68.1 | 45.3 | 22.7 | 11.3 |
| $\alpha = 3$ | 41.4 | 27.6 | 13.8 | 6.4 |
| $\alpha = 4$ | 29.4 | 19.5 | 9.8 | 4.9 |

Majority rule voting leads to the adoption of the preferred tax rate of the median voter because that rate beats any other rate in a head-to-head vote. With $\beta$ set equal to 3/2, Equation (3.12) shows society's chosen tax rate to be 34 per cent because

$$t(Y^{med}) = \beta(Y^{av} - Y^{med})/(2Y^{av} - Y^{med}) = (3/2)(2 - 1.4)/(4 - 1.4) = 0.34$$

$$(3.20)$$

It then follows at once from Equation (3.1) that, in a society with $\alpha = 2$ and $Y^{min} = 1$, the introduction of a negative income tax at a rate of 34 per cent:

- raises the income of the very poorest person by 20 per cent from 1 to 1.20;
- raises the median income by 7 per cent from 1.4 to 1.5;
- lowers average disposable income by 4 per cent from 2 to 1.92;[7]
- lowers the income of a person with a pre-tax pre-transfer income of 10 by 25 per cent to 7.51.

Majority rule voting leads to an incomplete redistribution of income by, in effect, assigning the choice of the tax rate to the median voter whose pre-tax, pre-transfer income is less than average income but still well above the income of the poorest person and whose best option is a rate at which the distribution of income is partially, but far from entirely, equalized. With the tax rate chosen in the interest of the median voter, the poor become better off, the rich become worse off, but a gap between rich and poor remains.

A curious feature of self-interested voting about redistribution has been recognized but not sufficiently emphasized. It is, to put it dramatically, that deadweight loss is the saviour of democracy. Without deadweight loss in taxation – from tax evasion as has been assumed or from some other source – it would be in the interest of any person whose income is less than the average to vote for a tax rate of 100 per cent, creating a situation where the rich have everything to lose from majority rule voting and would either impose some other form of government or lose all incentive to prosper. Admittedly, such a response is itself a form of deadweight loss, but it is far less palatable than a situation where ordinary deadweight loss confines redistribution within bounds that most people, rich and poor alike, can tolerate.

# Modifying the assumptions

## Motives for the redistribution of income

Pushing the analogy between elections and markets, it is assumed in the core model of this chapter that each person votes self-interestedly, favouring redistribution for no other reason than that he has more to gain as a recipient than he has to lose as a taxpayer, and with no concern for the welfare of anybody else. That may not be so. Voting about redistribution may also depend on compassion and on fear.

Even the portrayal of self-interest is limited. Being strictly atemporal, the core model of voting about redistribution takes no account of risk aversion and insurance. In practice, laws about the redistribution of income are expected to remain in force for a long enough time that people who are net contributors to redistribution today may see some chance of their becoming, or of their children or grandchildren becoming, beneficiaries tomorrow. One may willingly pay a high price today when one is rich to avert a small risk of starvation in years to come.

Compassion in this context is a willingness to give up part of one's income for the benefit of other people who are relatively worse off than oneself. In the context of the model, it is a willingness to vote for a negative income tax even though one's net income, $I$ in Equation (3.9), would be less than if there were no redistribution at all.

Compare two possible distributions of income in a three person society. In the first distribution, incomes are 3, 4 and 6. In the second, incomes are 1, 6 and 6. If people vote self-interestedly and as long as the deadweight loss in taxation is not too large, there is some redistribution in the first case because the median income, 4, is less than the average income, 13/3, but there is no redistribution in the second case because the distribution of income is skewed in the wrong way so that the median income, 6, is greater than the average, 13/3. By contrast, if people were altruistic, there would be more redistribution in the second case where the variance of incomes is larger and there is a wider gap between rich and poor.

Similarly, an increase in the number of wealthy people can be expected to generate more redistribution when people are altruistic but not when they vote in their own interest exclusively. Consider once again the three person society with incomes of 3, 4 and 6. The addition of two extra people, each with an incomes of 6, has opposite effects on redistribution depending on whether people are altruistic or self-interested. If people are altruistic, one would expect the two poorer people to become better off because any given transfer can be procured at a lower cost to each of the three richer people. If people are strictly self-interested, all redistribution would be stopped because the median income (6) has become greater than the average (5). A widening of the distribution of income as represented by a lower value of the parameter $\alpha$ in the Pareto distribution induces the median voter to favour more redistribution, not because the variance of the income distribution has increased but because the distribution has become even more skewed.

Compassion can take many forms. It may be utilitarian. A person may vote for redistribution, regardless of whether he or she personally is a net beneficiary or a net benefactor, to maximize the sum of the utilities of each and every person in society. Put aside the median voter and suppose instead that there is a moral consensus in favour of redistribution to maximize social welfare, $W$,

$$W = W(u_1, u_2, \ldots, u_N) \tag{3.21}$$

where each $u_1$ is the utility of person $i$ and $N$ is the population. Suppose also that

$$u_i = (I_i)^\varphi \tag{3.22}$$

where $I_i$ is the net post-tax, post-transfer income of person $i$, and where $\varphi$ is a parameter specifying the concavity of the utility of income function. Suppose finally that the social welfare function is utilitarian but with $W$ graduated to be commensurate with ordinary income; $W$ is the income such that, if everybody had precisely that income, no more, no less, social welfare would be exactly the same as with the given distribution of income. On these assumptions, social welfare, $W$, is such that

$$W^\varphi = (1/N)\{(I_1)^\varphi + (I_2)^\varphi + (I_3)^\varphi + \cdots + (I_N)^\varphi\} \tag{3.23}$$

So defined, social welfare is the moral equivalent of the existing distribution of income.[8]

The parameter $\varphi$ can be thought of as showing the importance of equality as compared with efficiency in social welfare. The *smaller* $\varphi$, the greater the weighting of equality must be. In principle, the parameter $\varphi$ might be anywhere from $-\infty$ to $+\infty$, but values above 1 may be ruled out because they would convert equality from a virtue to a vice, so that, for any given average income, an unequal allocation of income would be deemed morally superior to an equal allocation of income.[9] Negative values of $\varphi$ as low as $-\infty$ are still meaningful.[10]

At one extreme where $\varphi = 1$, the social welfare function becomes

$$W = (1/N)\{(I_1) + (I_2) + (I_3) + \cdots + (I_N)\} \tag{3.24}$$

meaning that the distribution of income is morally irrelevant and the best outcome is where the national income is maximized. When $\varphi = 0$, the social welfare function becomes Cobb–Douglas.[11] At the other extreme where $\varphi = -\infty$, the social welfare function becomes

$$W = I^{min} \tag{3.25}$$

where $I^{min}$ is the lowest of all post-tax, post transfer incomes. This criterion, called maximin, is to maximize the net income of the very poorest person in society.[12] It does not necessarily lead to the full equalization of income because the common income under full equality may be less than the lowest income when a degree of inequality remains.

A virtue of the social welfare function as a source of redistribution is that coalitions and bargaining are banished altogether. Once a social welfare function is acknowledged, once some given value of $\varphi$ is recognized as morally valid, there must be some socially optimal tax system, however difficult it may be in practice to say what the best tax system might be. The locus classicus of the problem is Mirlees (1971) where a complete tax structure is derived on the assumption that the impediment to redistribution is the tax-induced flight from labour to leisure rather than tax evasion.

Determination of the optimal tax structure for the maximization of social welfare rather than in accordance with the first preference of the median voter can be quite complex, but a socially optimal tax rate is easily constructed for a two-person economy. Imagine an economy with one rich person and one poor person whose pre-tax incomes are $Y_R$ and $Y_P$ where, of course, $Y_R > Y_P$. Suppose a benevolent dictator is taxing the rich person at a rate $t$ for the benefit of the poor person, and suppose the deadweight loss in taxation – there must be some such deadweight loss, for total income would, otherwise, be divided equally – is that only a fraction $\lambda$ of what is collected from the rich person is ultimately transferred to the poor person. Somehow a proportion $(1 - \lambda)$ is lost in transition. Post-tax, post transfer incomes of rich and poor become

$$I_R = Y_R(1 - t) \tag{3.26}$$

and

$$I_P = Y_P + \lambda t Y_R \tag{3.27}$$

subject to the constraint that

$$Y_P \leq I_P \leq I_R \tag{3.28}$$

The tax rate, $t$, must lie between $t^{min}$ and $t^{max}$ where

$$t^{min} = 0 \quad \text{when} \quad I_P = Y_P \tag{3.29}$$

and

$$t^{max} = [Y_R - Y_P]/[Y_R(1 + \lambda)] \quad \text{when} \quad I_P = I_R \tag{3.30}$$

Social welfare as defined in Equation (3.23) reduces to

$$W = (1/2)^{1/\varphi}[(I_R)^\varphi + (I_P)^\varphi]^{1/\varphi} = (1/2)^{1/\varphi}[\{Y_R(1 - t)\}^\varphi + \{y_P + \lambda t Y_R\}^\varphi]^{1/\varphi} \tag{3.31}$$

For any values of $Y_R$, $Y_P$ and $\varphi$, the welfare maximizing tax rate is such that

$$\delta W/\delta t = 0 \tag{3.32}$$

implying that

$$I_R/I_P = [Y_R(1-t)]/[Y_P + \lambda t Y_R] = (1/\lambda)^{1/(1-\varphi)} \qquad (3.33)$$

with the property that, as long as $\varphi < 1$, net incomes are equalized when either $\lambda = 1$ or $\varphi = -\infty$. Also, within the limits prescribed by Equations (3.30) and (3.31), the welfare-maximizing tax rate increases as $\lambda$ rises and as $\varphi$ falls,

$$\delta t/\delta \lambda > 0 \quad \text{and} \quad \delta t/\delta \varphi > 0 \qquad (3.34)$$

The income of the worst off person is maximized whenever equality takes absolute precedence over efficiency or whenever redistribution is costless in the sense that money can be transferred dollar-for-dollar from rich to poor.

Much of the literature of public finance treats redistribution as a moral question. An imaginary benevolent dictator designs redistributive policy and establishes progressive taxation to maximize social welfare interpreted as the sum of the utilities of everybody in the land. The purpose of public finance is then to figure out what exactly the benevolent dictator would do and to pass on that information to the government.[13] An implicit premise of this line of analysis is that people are prepared to accept peacefully whatever the benevolent dictator would prescribe. Citizens are presumed to have split personalities, acting selfishly in markets but to promote the common good as they see it when voting or participating in the public sphere.

A major difficulty with the social welfare function as a criterion for redistributive taxation is that there is no true God-given balance between efficiency and equality. Each person may have his own value of $\varphi$ reflecting his moral sense of what the trade-off should be. People may disagree profoundly about the value $\varphi$ and the implied shape of the social welfare function. People who see $\varphi$ as very high would oppose redistribution, people who see $\varphi$ as very low would favour redistribution. There is no obvious way to persuade anybody that his valuation of $\varphi$ is incorrect, and it is too easy to persuade oneself that the value of $\varphi$ with implications most beneficial to oneself is morally valid.

Compassion is not confined to utilitarianism. In voting, one may seek to maximize a weighted average of one's own income and some measure of the common good or a variant of social welfare in which some people's utilities count more than others'. Distaste for inequality may give rise to the redistribution of income even when social welfare as defined earlier is decreased. One may favour a reduction in the incomes of the very wealthy in circumstances where incomes in the rest of the population are unchanged.

> The case for drastic progression in taxation must be rested on the case against inequality – on the ethical or aesthetic judgement that the prevailing distribution of wealth and income reveals a degree ... of inequality which is distinctly evil or unlovely.
>
> Henry Simons (1938:15)[14]

The median voter theorem could be reconstructed in accordance with people's assessments of social welfare rather than with self-interest alone. People could be lined up according to their values of $\varphi$, with the median voter's preferred $t$ dependent on $\varphi$ rather than $Y$. The difficulty with this escape route is that society's preferred tax rate becomes unpredictable. A rich person may vote for a high tax rate because he is altruistic. A poor person may vote for a low tax rate because he identifies with the rich. It is no longer possible to infer society's preferred tax rate from the parameters of the distribution of income.

The final motive is fear. The very rich person who, in the formal model, would vote against any and all redistribution might vote differently in practice because he is afraid that, without some redistribution, the rules of the game would not be respected. A key assumption in the model was a given distribution of gross pre-tax, pre-transfer incomes. Implicit in that assumption was that the poor would not rise up to take what the rich would not give voluntarily or that large public expenditure would not be required to suppress rebellion. Coupled with a model of redistribution may be a model of revolution with its own costs to rich and poor alike and with the possibility that revolution might pay if and only if redistribution is denied.

Regardless of social welfare, redistribution of income may be seen as emerging gradually as, little by little, the privileged classes abandoning their privileges in fear of what might happen if they do not. Redistribution may arise from fear of disorder, of gradual disrespect for established property rights or of outright revolution if the standard of living of the poor falls or if the gap between rich and poor is not confined within some tolerable limit. 'Look at our own time and country and mention any single great change ... not carried by force, that is to say, ultimately by the fear of revolution' (Stephen, 1873 quoted in Cannon, 1973).[15] Stephen was speaking about the growth of franchise, but franchise may be seen as a guarantor of redistribution, which in turn may be seen as a way to make the present political and economic system tolerable to relatively poor people who might otherwise vote to overturn the system entirely.

> Plato felt that no one in a society should be more than four times richer than the poorest member of society for 'a society which is to be immune from the most fatal disorders which might more properly be called distraction than faction, there must be no place for penury in any section of the population, nor yet for opulence, as both breed either consequence'.
>
> Fair (1971: 552), quoting Plato (trans. Taylor, 1960: 127)

These motives for redistribution – self-interest, compassion and fear – are complementary and additive. The rate of the negative income tax might be high because all three motives are operative at once.

### The negative income tax as the paradigm for all redistribution

Ever since it was advocated by Milton Friedman in *Capitalism and Freedom* (1960), the negative income tax has served as the paradigmatic example of redistribution. It has many virtues. Unlike agricultural price supports, it is equally beneficial to all equally poor people, regardless of occupation. Though not strictly progressive, its greatest benefit is to the very poorest people with no income other than the demogrant, and its net benefit diminishes as income rises, turning into a steadily increasing net cost once income exceeds a certain level. It is self-limiting because deadweight loss in taxation causes people's preferred tax rate to decline steadily with income, ensuring that the preferred tax rate of the median voter beats any other tax rate in a pairwise vote. It minimizes government intervention in the economy and the enhancement of the authority of the bureaucracy, for, unlike industrial subsidies or price control, it requires no more than that a single number be chosen by the legislature and has virtually no impact on the determination of prices and wages in the competitive market.

The two constituents of the negative income tax – the demogrant and proportional taxation – may be examined separately because either could be adopted without the other. The negative income tax has been discussed in a context where everything happens in the current year, with no past or future, no disasters, no aging and no recognition that a person's low income this year may be an anomaly preceded and followed by higher incomes in other years. The natural extension of the demogrant to a world with education, sickness, unemployment, aging and death is a menu of social programmes to deal with a range of misfortunes. Welfare is demogrant for the long-term poor. Unemployment insurance is a demogrant for people whose incomes are temporarily and unexpectedly stopped. The publicly supplied old age pension is a demogrant for the old, financed, at least in part, by old people who happen to be prosperous. Socialized medical care is a demogrant for the sick who require a substantial gross income to maintain a reasonable standard of living. Public education is a demogrant to all children supplied in a manner most likely to be beneficial over their entire lives.

Advocates of a pure negative income tax might argue in its defence that misfortune may be covered by insurance. As long as the demogrant is sufficient, people can buy insurance, and, if they choose not to do so, their choices should be respected.

There are several arguments to the contrary. Not all risk can be insured against. There can be no private market for insurance against unemployment because of the moral hazard when such insurance creates an incentive to become unemployed and because of adverse selection when people with secure jobs are less likely than others to take out private unemployment insurance. Unemployment insurance must be for everybody, whether one wants to be insured or not. Private health insurance penalizes applicants with pre-existing conditions. A person already sickly when applying for insurance – for instance, a person born with a weak heart – would pay a higher than average premium if insurance could be purchased at all. The only way for the state to put everybody on the same footing would be to provide health care to anybody who needs it. There is also a risk of malfeasance by insurance companies. When an insured person falls ill, it is in the interest of the insurance company to find reasons for denying coverage, perhaps by claiming that the patient failed to inform the insurance company of all pre-existing conditions when applying for insurance. In the extreme, it is in the interest of the insurance company to let especially sick patients die, in expectation that the revenue from future premiums will fall short of the cost of care. Recognition of the possibility of malfeasance by insurance companies does not imply that insurance companies are less honourable than other firms or people. It does suggest that there may be a significant conflict between insurance companies seeking to pay out as little as possible and patients claiming their compensation is insufficient. Publicly supplied medical care may avoid such conflict. The government would need to decide how well doctors are to be paid, how much to invest in hospitals and which sick people are to be left to die for want of medical care because treatment too expensive.[16]

To be sure, public provision of specific services, notably education and health care, require greater supervision by the bureaucracy than the provision of a fixed sum of money to each person or family, but it does not require a massive bureaucratization of the rest of the economy. Prices in the rest of the market would still set autonomously, and the tax rate would be depend on total public expenditure regardless of whether that expenditure is for a demogrant or for specific services.

Replacement of the proportional taxation by progressive taxation raises a different set of problems. The postulated constitutional requirement restricting the redistribution of income to a negative income tax has the great virtue that there is a unique electoral equilibrium. The preference of the median voter prevails, leaving nothing to bargain or squabble or fight about. There are, however, two connected defects. Redistribution by a negative income tax is more expensive than other feasible methods of redistribution, and the constitutional requirement is not self-enforcing. Majority coalitions of voters have an incentive to replace the proportionality in the negative income tax with progressive taxation where the marginal rate is an increasing function of income.

An example shows what may be at stake. Drop the Pareto distribution of income, and suppose instead that there are just three people, or three groups of identical people, a poor person, a middle person and a rich person with pre-tax, pre-transfer incomes of $Y^P$, $Y^M$ and $Y^R$ respectively. Suppose $Y^P = 2$, $Y^M = 3$ and $Y^R = 7$. The numbers are chosen so that average income, $Y^{av} = 4$, is greater than median income, $Y^{med} = 3$, ensuring that redistribution through a negative income tax is advantageous to the median voter. The efficiency of tax collection, $\beta$, is set equal to 1, so that the revenue-maximizing tax rate – the rate for which $t(1 - t/\beta)$ is maximized – is 50 per cent.

From Equation (3.13), it follows that the electoral equilibrium tax rate, the preferred tax rate of the median voter, is

$$t(Y^{med}) = \beta\{Y^{av} - Y^{med}\}/\{2Y^{av} - Y^{med}\} = \{4 - 3\}/\{8 - 3\} = 1/5 = 20 \text{ per cent}$$

(3.35)

sufficient to finance a demogrant equal to

$$t(1 - t)Y^{av} = (1/5)(4/5)4 = 16/25 = 0.64$$

(3.36)

In accordance with Equation (3.11), each person's post-tax, post-transfer income equals gross income, minus tax paid, plus demogrant, minus expenditure to conceal tax evasion, so that, when $t = 20$ per cent, the three persons' post-tax, post-transfer incomes are

$$I(Y^P) = 2 - (1/5)(4/5)2 + (1/5)(4/5)4 - (1/5)^2 2/2 = 2.28 \qquad (3.37)$$

$$I(Y^M) = 3 - (1/5)(4/5)3 + (1/5)(4/5)4 - (1/5)^2 3/2 = 3.1 \qquad (3.38)$$

$$I(Y^R) = 7 - (1/5)(4/5)7 + (1/5)(4/5)4 - (1/5)^2 7/2 = 6.38 \qquad (3.39)$$

Redistribution of income by the electoral equilibrium negative income tax raises the income of the poor person from 2 to 2.28, raises the income of the middle person from 3 to 3.1 and lowers the income of the rich person from 7 to 6.38.

Redistribution is always costly. Combined post-tax, post-transfer income is always less than the combined total pre-tax, pre-transfer income in the population as a whole. In the example, the combined pre-tax, pre-transfer income is 12 (the sum of 2, 3 and 7), the combined post-tax, post-transfer income is 11.76 (the sum of 2.28, 3.1 and 6.38), and the gap between them – the deadweight loss – is 0.24. The rich person's cost of the negative income tax, 0.62, exceeds the other two people's benefits, $0.28 + 0.1$, by 0.24, which is the sum of all expenditures on concealing income from the tax collector. Each person's gain from manoeuvres to reduce tax paid is, in effect, a pure transfer to that person from the rest of society, but each person's cost of such manoeuvres is genuine waste of resources.

Part of the wastage of resources in the negative income tax can be avoided by a more progressive form of redistribution, but, abandonment of the constitutional rule restricting redistribution to the negative income tax gives rise to a classic exploitation problem where any two of the three people – or, more generally, any majority of voters – can combine to exploit the third.

Everybody, net beneficiaries as well as net contributors, can be made better off by a combination of progressive taxation and focused redistribution. Specifically, the negative income tax at a rate of 20 per cent might be replaced by i) a tax schedule with a rate of 0 per cent on all income up to 4 (so that only the rich person is taxed) and 18 per cent on all income above 4, and ii) a demogrant restricted to people with less than average income, paid two-thirds to the poor person and one third to the middle person. As the incentive to evade tax depends upon marginal, rather than average, tax rate, the tax paid by the rich person yields revenue of $t(1 - t)(Y^R - 4) = (0.18)(1 - 0.18)(3) = 0.4428$, of which two-thirds, or 0.2952, is paid as a demogrant to the poor person and the remaining third, or 0.1476, is paid to the middle person. As they pay no tax and bear no cost of tax evasion, the net incomes of the poor person and the middle person, $I(Y^P)$ and $I(Y^M)$, become 2.2952 and 3.1467 respectively, both larger than they would be under the negative income tax. The rich person receives no demorgant, but post-tax, post transfer income becomes

$$I(Y^R) = 7 - (0.18)(1 - 0.18)(3) - (0.18)^2(7/2) = 7 - 0.4428 - 0.1134 = 6.4438$$

$$(3.40)$$

which is also larger than under the negative income tax. The reduction in total deadweight loss in the switch from the negative income tax to a more focused progressive income tax has made all three people better off. This is, of course, only one of many progressive tax schedules that would make everybody better off than under a negative income tax.

The downside of the replacement of the negative income tax by progressive taxation with a focused demogrant is the loss of electoral equilibrium. The negative income tax yields a unique but inefficient electoral equilibrium. There are many efficient combinations of progressivity and a focused demogrant, none of which beats all the others in a pairwise vote. Any two-person coalition can use the power of the vote to exploit the third.

A coalition of the poor person and the middle person might vote for the imposition of the revenue-maximizing tax on the rich person only and for splitting the tax revenue between themselves. The revenue-maximizing tax rate is 50 per cent. At that rate, the rich person conceals half his income from the tax collector, pays a tax of $(0.5)(0.5)(7) = 1.75$, bears a deadweight loss of $(0.5)(0.5)(7)/2 = 0.875$ and keeps a net income of 4.375, considerably less than under a negative income tax. By sharing the tax revenue equally, the poor and middle persons raise their incomes to from 2.28 and 3.1 to 2.875 and 3.875 respectively. A coalition of the rich person and the poor person might agree upon a somewhat lower tax on the rich person and the middle person with a demogrant restricted to the poor person. A coalition of the rich person and the middle person might agree upon an allocation of the demogrant in proportion to the pre-tax incomes of the middle and poor persons. Once the negative income tax is abandoned, there is no telling which of the three possible coalitions will form or how they will share the benefits that the coalition provides.

There is, in short, no voting equilibrium in progressive taxation, comparable to the voting equilibrium in the negative income tax. With progressive taxation, the determination of the full tax structure must inevitably be the outcome of a large complex bargain among legislatures, with no assurance that any such bargain will actually be struck. People often bargain successfully but, as discussed in other chapters, there is no satisfactory explanation of when and how they do so. The choice between the negative income tax and genuine progressive taxation is a trade-off between equilibrium and efficiency. In the formal model with a constitutionally prescribed negative income tax, self-interest alone is sufficient to generate a narrowing of the distribution of income, though altruism or fear may be needed to keep the constitutional requirement in place. Nevertheless, beneath all welfare programmes and progressivity may be a general sense of how redistributive public policy should be, a distribution of people's preferences for redistribution dependent in part on their incomes, and a process by which redistribution is determined in accordance with something vaguely analogous to the first preference of the median voter setting the rate of the negative income tax.

### Tax evasion as the paradigm for all tax-induced contraction of the tax base

Deadweight loss has so far been assumed to arise from costly but undetectable concealment of income from the tax collector. The assumption is simple, adequate as an explanation of electoral equilibrium redistribution, but only one of several impediments to redistribution, including the switch from paid work to do-it-yourself activities, the out-migration of wealthy people,[17] the labour–leisure choice and the discouragement of enterprise. Tax evasion itself is modelled conveniently but unrealistically as costly but undetectable once the appropriate cost of tax evasion has been borne. The phrase 'underground economy' is taken literally. Part of one's income is hidden underground where the tax collector cannot find it, and the marginal cost of concealment increases with the proportion of income already concealed. Abstracted away in this description are the risk of detection, the expected cost to the tax evader of punishment if tax evasion is discovered, and the cost to the government of seeking out and punishing tax evaders. Incorporation of these considerations would require the expected cost of punishment to be added to the taxpayer's cost of concealment and the measure of tax revenue to be net of whatever portion of that revenue is devoted to detection and punishment of tax evasion.[18]

Costly but undetectable tax evasion can be justified not as realistic, but as representative of tax avoidance of many kinds. Recall the maximization of net income in Equation (3.10). The cost of tax evasion in that equation, $\beta \tau^2 Y/2$, can be replaced by a more general function, $D(\tau, t, Y)$, representing the cost to the taxpayer of diminishing his tax base. Suppose, for example, one responds to a tax increase by working fewer hours each day. The term $D(\tau, t, Y)$ might then be defined as the amount of money one would be prepared to pay in return for being enabled to contract the observable tax base by a proportion $\tau$ without diminishing one's supply of labour. It is hard to say what exactly the function $D(\tau, t, Y)$ would be, but it is reasonable to suppose that $D$ would be more than proportional to $\tau$ for any given value of $t$. In principle, a person's function $D(\tau, t, Y)$ could be determined from answers to a long series of questions of the form 'do you prefer this to that'. In practice, estimation of the 'elasticity of taxable income' in Equation (3.7) would cover all sources of tax avoidance.

An advantage of costly but undetectable tax evasion as the representative of all sources of deadweight loss in taxation is its simplicity. Unlike the labour–leisure choice, everything is in a single dimension, dollars, and strong results are very easily derived. Representation of the general function $D(\tau, t, Y)$ by the specific function $\beta \tau^2 Y/2$ does not change the story significantly.

An odd, almost paradoxical aspect of tax evasion as an impediment to redistribution is that democracy would seem to depend upon people's willingness to break the law. Without tax evasion, there would be complete equalization of income.

With complete equalization of income, all incentive to earn income would be removed. Understanding this, an impoverished people would be unwilling to put up with majority rule voting.

## The Laffer curve for the individual and for the nation

These are identical in the formal model as long as revenue is graduated as a proportion of gross income. In practice, they differ for two reasons. First, the value of $\beta$ need not be the same for everybody because people's opportunities for hiding income from the tax collector need not be the same. The value of $\beta$ may be much larger for a factory worker on a fixed salary than for a self-employed grocer. On average, the value of $\beta$ may be lower for the rich than for the poor because the rich tend to earn incomes in ways with greater opportunities for legal and illegal tax avoidance. Right or wrong, a standard argument against progressivity in the tax code is that the rich reach the peaks of their Laffer curves at relatively low tax rates. Where people's $\beta$ differ, the Laffer curve for the nation is a complex average of people's Laffer curves.

Second, even if everybody's value of $\beta$ were the same, the demogrant acquired at any given tax rate depends not just on people's capacity to contract taxable income, but on tax revenue net of the cost to the government of enforcing compliance. In the formal model, all cost associated with concealment of income from the tax collector is borne by the taxpayers themselves. In practice, concealment of income cannot be costly to the taxpayer without considerable public expenditure to impose that cost, public expenditure which can be expected to increase more than proportionally to the rate of tax imposed. Excluded altogether from the formal model, are the costs of the ministry of finance, the prosecution of tax evaders and imprisonment for tax fraud. The Laffer curve to the individual is his tax paid as a function of the tax rate; the Laffer curve to the nation is total tax paid less the cost of collection as a function of the tax rate. The higher the cost of collection, the lower the median voter's preferred tax rate will be.

## Political parties

There is so far no place in the story for political parties. Politics is confined to the choice of a rate for the negative income tax. Every person has a preferred rate and, in a contest between any two rates both above or below his preferred rate, votes for the rate that is closest to his preferred rate, ensuring that the preferred rate of the median voter beats any other rate in a pair-wise vote. That being so, it would seem that both of two competing political parties would choose the median voter's most preferred tax rate as their platforms, for, if one political party did so and the other did not, the party that did not would surely lose the election. In practice, there may be a tendency in this direction, but platforms of competing political parties are surely not identical. Modifications of the median voter story may be introduced to circumvent this implication.

With the narrowing of the distribution of income as the only matter about which people differ, it is not unreasonable to imagine electoral contests between a 'right' party tending to favour the rich and a 'left' party tending favour the poor, with relatively low and high tax rates respectively as their political platforms, but that is not the implication of the model as developed so far. The model yields an equilibrium tax rate, $t^{med}$ as shown in Equation (3.13), that wins in a pairwise vote with any other rate, implying, in a two party contest, that the party with the preferred tax rate of the median voter as its platform would win the election or that there would be a tie if both parties chose that rate as its platform. The introduction of uncertainty could push rates apart.

Consider a stripped down version of a model by Coate (2004a,b). Suppose voting is about a policy, $x$, within the range from 0 to 1, in a society with three voters and two political parties. There is a left-leaning voter whose first preference for $x$ is 0, a right-leaning voter whose first preference for $x$ is 1, and a swing voter whose first preference for $x$ is a random variable with equal chances of lying anywhere between 0 and 1. The utility function of any person $i$ is

$$u_i(x) = 1 - (x - x_i)^2 \qquad (3.41)$$

where $x_i$ is the first preference of person $i$ and $x$ is society's chosen value of the policy in question. Having to vote for one of two values of $x$, the swing voter will always choose the value of $x$ closest to his first preference, wherever that turns out to be.

The left party chooses platform $x_L$ to maximize the *expected* utility of the left voter, balancing the utility of the left voter in the event that the left party wins the election against the left party's chance of being elected. The right party chooses $x_R$ accordingly. The left party would like to set $x_L = 0$, but it cannot do so because that would surely lose it the election. The right party would like to set $x_R = 1$, but it cannot do so for the same reason.

The outcome is a Nash equilibrium where each party chooses its platform on the assumption that the platform of the other party is given. For any choice of $x_R$ by the right party, the left party chooses $x_L$ to maximize expected utility defined as

$$[1 - x_L^2][(x_L + x_R)/2] + [1 - x_R^2][1 - (x_L + x_R)/2] \qquad (3.42)$$

where $[1 - x_L^2]$ and $[1 - x_R^2]$ are the utilities of the left party in the event of a win for the left and right parties respectively, and $[(x_L + x_R)/2]$ is the probability that the swing voter votes for the left party. Maximizing the utility of the left party with respect to $x_L$, yields the first order condition

$$3x_L^2 + 2x_L x_R - x_R^2 = 0 \qquad (3.43)$$

Values of $x_L$ and $x_R$ are derivable from this equation together with the symmetry condition

$$x_L = 1 - x_R \qquad (3.44)$$

that both parties' platforms to be equidistant, to the left and to the right, from the parties' first preferences, 0 and 1. Together, Equations (3.43) and (3.44) imply that $x_L = 1/4$ and $x_R = 3/4$, on either side of the expected first preference (equal to ½) of the swing voter.

Here the swing voter and the median voter are one and the same. It is characteristic of this pattern of uncertainty for party platforms to lie on opposite sides of the first preference of the median voter so that, if the median voter's first preference moves spontaneously one way or another or if it can be pushed by advertising, the platforms of both competing political parties can be expected to move in that direction too, a phenomenon discussed in some detail in Austin-Smith (1987). Anything that pushes the median voter's first preference to the left or to the right can be expected to push both $x_L$ and $x_R$ accordingly. One can imagine how uncertainty about voters' preferences might be incorporated into the model of campaign advertising in the body of this chapter to account for differences in party platforms without removing the parties' incentives to persuade voters that their preferred policies are best for the expected median voter and for the country as a whole.

Divergent platforms can be explained in other ways as well. They can be explained by the presence of party activists who work to persuade citizens of the virtues of their preferred party and to get out and vote. Ulander (1989) and Morton (1991) have developed models in which platforms differ to provide incentives for activists who would not bother to work for a party if its platform were no different from that of its opponent. Divergent platforms can be explained by the multiplication of issues under the headings of left and right. If the party favouring low taxation is also in favour of permitting abortion while the party favouring high taxes is against permitting abortion, then the tax rates in the parties' platforms can differ without either party giving up all hope of winning the election.[19] Divergent platforms can also be explained as a response to voters' perceptions of the competence of politicians, an aspect of politics that has so far been assumed away in this chapter. Competence here refers to differences between politicians in their ability to deal with matters of common concern when supporters of both political parties tend to agree about what is to be done. If politicians in, for example, the left party are generally believed to be the more competent and as long as there is uncertainty about the policy preference – the choice of $x$ on a scale from 0 to 1 – of the median voter, then the left party can risk choosing a relatively low value of $x$ as its platform, trading off policy for competence. Both parties will, of course, seek to persuade voters that its politicians are the more competent.[20]

### *Biased abstention*

So far, everybody votes. Abstention would change nothing if rates of abstention were uncorrelated with income. The ratio of median to mean income would be the same among *voters* as among people eligible to vote, and the electoral equilibrium rate of the negative income tax would be the same as well. Abstention matters when rates of abstention vary with income. If the poor are less likely to vote, as seems to be the case in most countries, then the median income among voters becomes higher than the median income in the population as a whole, and the electoral equilibrium redistribution falls.

To establish this proposition, people are once again spread out evenly according to their incomes on a scale from *0* to *1*. A person with income *Y* is placed at a point *n* on the scale when a proportion *n* of the population have incomes equal to or greater than *Y*. The highest income is designated as *Y*(0), the lowest income is designated as *Y*(1), *Y*(n) is a decreasing function of *n* in between, and the median income is *Y*(½). If everybody voted or if everybody, regardless of income, were equally likely to abstain, the median voter and the person with the median income would be one and the same. Redistribution of income would then be in accordance with that person's preference as described in Equation (3.13) above.

Now suppose instead that the propensity to vote rather than abstain is systematically higher for the rich than for the poor. With such biassed abstention, a distinction must be drawn for people lined up according to their incomes between i) the proportion, *n*, with incomes greater than *Y*(n) among the entire population of people eligible to vote and ii) the proportion, *v*(n), of people with incomes greater than *Y*(n) among people who choose to vote rather than abstain. If nobody abstains, then *v*(n) and *n* are the same. If rich people are less likely to abstain, then *v*(n) > *n* for all *n* greater than 0 and less than 1 as illustrated in Figures 3.3 and 3.4.

To connect *v*(n) with *n*, define *P*(n) as the proportion of people with income *Y*(n) choosing to vote rather than abstain. To assume that the propensity to vote is higher among the rich than among the poor is to assume that *P*(n) decreases steadily with *n* as illustrated in Figure 3.3 with the proportion, *n*, of people eligible to vote on the horizontal axis and the proportion, *P*, of people who vote rather than

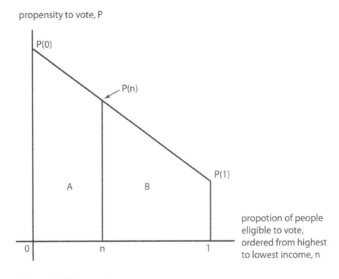

*Figure 3.3* Propensity to vote.

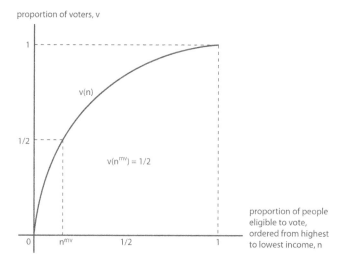

*Figure 3.4* Proportions of voters, $v$, and people eligible to vote, $n$.

abstain on the vertical axis. Suppose for convenience that $P(n)$ is a downward-sloping straight line.

$$P(n) = P(0) - n[P(0) - P(1)] \qquad (3.45)$$

For any given $n$, designate A and B as the areas to the left and to the right of $n$ below the diagonal line, reflecting numbers of votes cast by people with incomes greater than $Y(n)$ and by people with incomes less than $Y(n)$ respectively. As shares of the total population eligible to vote, the number of votes cast by people with incomes greater than $Y(n)$ is

$$A = n[P(0) + P(n)]/2 \qquad (3.46)$$

and the number of votes cast in the population as a whole is

$$A + B = [P(0) + P(1)]/2. \qquad (3.47)$$

Thus, the proportion, $v(n)$, of votes cast by the wealthiest portion, $n$, of the population – by people with incomes greater than $Y(n)$ – is

$$
\begin{aligned}
v(n) &= A/(A + B) \\
&= \{n[P(0) + P(n)]/2\} \div [P(0) + P(1)]/2 \\
&= \{n[P(0) + P(0) - n[P(0) - P(1)]\} \div [P(0) + P(1)] \\
&= n(1 + (1 - n)x) \quad \text{where } x \equiv [P(0) - P(1)]/[P(0) + P(1)] > 0
\end{aligned}
$$

$$= 0 \quad \text{when } n = 0$$

$$= 1 \quad \text{when } n = 1 \quad \text{and}$$

$$> n \quad \text{in between where } 0 < n < 1 \tag{3.48}$$

as illustrated by the concave function, $v(n)$, in Figure 3.4 with proportions, $n$, of people eligible to vote on the horizontal axis and proportions of voters, $v$, on the vertical axis. The inequality – that $v(n) > n$ – in last line of Equation (3.48) is a reflection of the discrepancy, $x$, between $P(0)$ and $P(1)$, the greater the discrepancy, the larger the gap between $v(x)$ and $x$ must be.

The location of the median voter, as distinct from the median person, on the scale of rich and poor is $n^{mv}$ defined by the property that $v(n^{mv}) = \frac{1}{2}$ at which the areas A and B in Figure 3.3 are the same. Since $v(n) > n$ for all $n$ between 0 and 1, it must be the case that $n^{mv} < \frac{1}{2}$ as illustrated in Figure 3.4 or, equivalently, that $Y(n^{mv}) > Y(\frac{1}{2})$.

It was shown at the beginning of this chapter that, the lower one's income, the more redistribution one prefers and that the electoral equilibrium redistribution of income, as represented by the rate of the negative income tax, is in accordance with the preference of the median voter. Hence, the rise in the income of the median voter generated by a disparity between rich and poor in their propensities to vote must lead to a reduction in the electoral equilibrium redistribution of income. Extreme bias could eliminate redistribution altogether.

There is another possibility. When monarchy first gave way to a form of majority rule voting, franchise was restricted by property qualifications. The rich were entitled to vote, but the poor were not. There would be a cut-off income, $Y^*$, such that one was entitled to vote if and only if $Y \geq Y^*$. Accordingly, there would be some proportion of the population, $n^*$ for which $Y(n^*) = Y^*$, such that only people for whom $n \leq n^*$ on the scale of rich and poor would be entitled to vote. With this restriction and with no abstentions among the enfranchised, the median voter would be the person with rank $n^*/2$ rather than $\frac{1}{2}$, and the rate, $t(n^*/2)$, of the negative income tax chosen by majority rule voting would be less than $t(\frac{1}{2})$ which would have been chosen had franchise not been restricted.

## Campaign advertising

An implication of the core model of redistribution in this chapter does not appear to be borne out by recent historical evidence. The model implies that, the wider the distribution of income, the greater the electoral equilibrium redistribution will be. A widening of the distribution of income in many countries over the last 30 years does not seem to have had that effect.[21] A possible explanation is campaign advertising.

So far, there has been nothing to advertise about. Voters know what they need to know in deciding how much redistribution to vote for. Now suppose instead that voters are open to persuasion, by the party of the rich attempting to convince voters that a bogeyman will do everybody harm if redistribution is carried too far, and by the party of the poor attempting to convince voters that there is no such bogeyman or that the bogeyman punishes society for too little rather than too much redistribution.

Who might the bogeyman be? There must be some significant impact of redistribution about which there are genuine grounds for dispute. There must be some relevant parameter not measured beyond any reasonable doubt, such that the rich are drawn by self-interest to argue that it is one thing and the poor are drawn by self-interest to argue that it is something else. The popular bogeyman today seems to be jobs. In a time of recession, it is convenient for the party of the rich to claim that high taxes destroy jobs and for the party of the poor to claim that programmes financed by high taxes create them. The bogeyman in this chapter is the location of the peak of the Laffer curve. Nobody doubts that there is some such curve, but there is enough uncertainty about the matter for people to be persuaded by campaign advertising that the maximal tax is high or low as the case may be. 'The Laffer curve peaks at a low tax rate', says the right-winger who, incidentally, tends to gain from low tax rates. 'The Laffer curve peaks at a high tax rate', says the left-winger who, incidentally, tends to gain from the redistribution financed by high tax rates. Both political parties advertise to persuade voters that their, real or contrived, views are correct.

Since the shape of the Laffer curve within the core model depends upon the efficiency of tax collection, $\beta$, as illustrated in Figure 3.2, it is reasonable to suppose that the magnitude of $\beta$ is what political parties advertise about, the party of the rich claiming $\beta$ to be low and the party of the poor claiming $\beta$ to be high. There is, however, a difficulty with that procedure. In the core model at the beginning of this chapter, the efficiency of tax collection is a technologically given fact of life allowing voters to know the cost of tax evasion exactly. Uncertainty about the size of $\beta$ would open the door to campaign advertising, but would leave tax payers confused about how much of their true incomes to declare.

To get around this ambiguity, reinterpret $\beta$ not as the actual efficiency of tax collection, but as voters' *anticipated* efficiency. Imagine a sequence in which the tax rate is determined in accordance with the median voter's anticipated efficiency of tax collection, then, once the tax rate has been chosen, the true efficiency of tax collection revealed, and, finally, actual tax paid is in accordance with the true efficiency of tax collection. Campaign advertising becomes influential at the beginning of the sequence in influencing voters' anticipations about the efficiency of tax collection.

The question at hand is whether campaign advertising can alter the impact of inequality on redistribution in the core model in this chapter. There, greater inequality led to an increase in the median voter's preferred tax rate to finance additional redistribution. The question is whether campaign advertising might reverse the process, greater inequality leading to less redistribution instead. The proposed answer here is that it might, though this is by no means inevitable.

When a true efficiency of tax collection, $\beta$, is universally recognized and the electoral equilibrium tax rate chosen accordingly, it must be the case that the wealthier half of the population would prefer less redistribution and the poorer half would prefer more. That being so, it is not unreasonable to adopt the working assumption that campaign advertising by the wealthier half of the population would try to persuade voters that $\beta$ is low (to persuade voters to support a lower tax rate) and that advertising by the poorer half of the population would try to persuade people that $\beta$ is high. Then, if expenditures on campaign advertising by both halves of the population are approximately proportional to their total incomes and if all dollars of advertising are equally influential, a widening of the distribution of income, by raising the disproportion in advertising, might possibly induce voters to adopt a lower tax rate and less redistribution.

There are three steps to the argument: First, as shown in Appendix 3B, greater inequality as represented by a fall in $\alpha$ in the Pareto distribution, leads to an increase in the ratio, $s$, of the total income, $S^{top}$, of the richer half of the population to the total income, $S^{bottom}$, of the poorer half.

$$\delta s / \delta \alpha < 0 \tag{3.49}$$

Second, it is assumed that the ratio, $c$, of campaign expenditure by the richer half of the population to persuade voters that $\beta$ is low to campaign expenditure by the poorer half to persuade voters that $\beta$ is high is an increasing function of the disproportion, $s$, in their total incomes.[22]

$$\delta c / \delta s > 0 \tag{3.50}$$

Third, it is assumed that campaign advertising is influential so that the higher $c$, the lower the anticipated efficiency of tax collection must be[23]

$$\delta \beta / \delta c < 0 \tag{3.51}$$

Assumptions about advertising are connected to the behaviour of the median voter through a generalization of Equation (3.12). The median voter's preferred tax rate is

$$t(Y^{med}) = f(m, \beta) \tag{3.52}$$

where $\beta$ is now the anticipated efficiency of tax collection and $m$ is the ratio $Y^{med} / Y^{av}$. As in Equation (3.13),

$$\delta f / \delta m < 0 \tag{3.53}$$

meaning that the higher the median income as a proportion of the average, the lower the preferred tax rate, and

$$\delta f / \delta \beta > 0 \tag{3.54}$$

meaning that the greater the anticipated efficiency of tax collection the higher the median voter's preferred tax rate must be. Corresponding to the two variables in this function are two distinct routes from inequality to redistribution, the direct route through m as described in connection with Equation (3.12) and the indirect route from inequality through campaign advertising to the voters' anticipation of $\beta$.

Pulling all this together, the effect of widening of the distribution of income on the median voter's preferred tax rate becomes $-\delta t^{med}/\delta(\alpha)$ where

$$-\delta t^{med}/\delta(\alpha) = -[\delta t^{med}/\delta m][\delta m/\delta(\alpha)] - [\delta t^{med}/\delta\beta][\delta\beta/\delta(\alpha)]$$

$$= -\underset{(-)}{[\delta t^{med}/\delta m]} \underset{(+)}{[\delta m/\delta(\alpha)]} - \underset{(+)}{[\delta t^{med}/\delta\beta]} \underset{(-)}{[\delta\beta/\delta c]} \underset{(+)}{[\delta c/\delta s]} \underset{(-)}{[\delta s/\delta(\alpha)]}$$

$$(3.55)$$

Think of the two expressions in Equation (3.55) as representing two routes from inequality to redistribution. The first expression is the direct route through the median voter's preference as it would be if the perceived efficiency of tax collection were invariant; it is positive showing greater inequality leading to a higher tax rate. The second expression is the indirect route through the influence of wealth upon advertising and of advertising upon anticipated efficiency of tax collection; it is negative showing greater inequality leading to a lower tax rate. The final outcome is ambiguous, but sufficient as a refutation of the proposition that increased in equality *must* lead to more redistribution. It may or may not do so. The two routes are illustrated in Figure 3.5.

As discussed in Appendix B, campaign advertising may influence perceptions in many complex ways. Advertising may be informative or persuasive. Advertising may supply scraps of information favourable to one's own cause or unfavourable to the cause of one's opponents. Advertising may emphasize some facts at the expense of others. Advertising expenditure may serve to verify information which the advertiser knows but the viewer, in the absence of advertising, would not. Advertising is confined here to influencing voters' opinions about the government's efficiency in tax collection and the location of the Laffer curve which, as shown in Figure 3.2, depends entirely on the perceived value of $\beta$.

An indispensable step in the path from the initial distribution of income to the equilibrium tax rate, as shown in Equation (3.55), is the assumption that, the greater the disparity of pre-tax incomes between rich and poor, the greater the disparity in their campaign contributions would be. Plausible as this assumption may be, no explanation is provided of why it might be so. On the contrary, campaign advertising may be a 'public good' for all beneficiaries of a win by any given political party, and, like all public goods, may be such that it is in no beneficiary's interest to contribute voluntarily. A person who is one among a million beneficiaries of a win for some party has no incentive to contribute to that party as long as the behaviour of other beneficiaries is independent of that person's behaviour. There would seem to be a 'paradox of not contributing' that is parallel to the 'paradox of not voting' discussed in Chapter 2. When public policy is about nothing

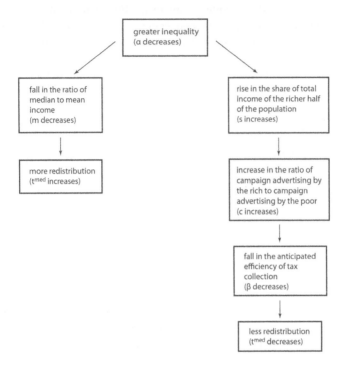

*Figure 3.5* From distribution to redistribution.

other than the rate of the negative income tax, there may be too many beneficia-ries of high rates, and too many beneficiaries of low rates to justify contributions by members of either group on purely self-interested grounds. More generally, rent-seeking requires a concentration of interests. The larger the group with inter-ests in common, the more difficult it becomes to induce contributions in support of a common cause.

Since the interests of the poor are widespread and common while the interests of the rich are narrowly focused, campaign contributions are more likely to be provided by the rich than by the poor. A monopoly may have every incentive to hire lobbyists and make campaign contributions to influence legislators and political parties to supply tariffs and other favourable policies. There may be no comparable incentive for each of the vast numbers of people who may be harmed by such policies to make campaign contributions to legislators and political parties that might oppose them.

Campaign contributions are themselves regulated by rules affecting the balance between rich and poor. Limits on the dollar value of contributions promote the interest of the poor. Interpretation of 'free speech' to allow unlimited contributions by people, corporations and political action committees promote the interest of the rich. There is a continuum from campaign contributions to outright bribery, as when politicians on leaving office may expect to be offered lucrative employment.

### Public goods

So far, except for the redistribution of income, the government has nothing to do. No police, no roads, no army, no public administration. Such abstraction is be useful for some purposes, but it may nonetheless be helpful to suggest how ordinary public expenditure might change the story. In general, public goods are such that the total supply conveys benefits to everybody at once, but within that definition several distinct usages may be distinguished.

Expenditure on pubic goods may be a fixed overhead cost of protecting life and property. The simplest version of this assumption is that, without some fixed expenditure, $Q$, per person, nothing could be produced and all incomes would be zero, but no additional expenditure would be of any use at all. As long as revenue per person is larger than $Q$, a tax rate $t$ supplies a demogrant of only $[t(1 - t/\beta)Y^{av} - Q]$ rather than $[t(1 - t/\beta)Y^{av}]$ as shown in Equation (3.10).

When $Q$ is necessary but invariant, the post-tax, post transfer income of a person with a pre-tax, pre-transfer income of $Y$ becomes

$$I = Y - t(1 - t/\beta)Y + [t(1 - t/\beta)Y^{av} - Q] - t^2 Y/2\beta \tag{3.56}$$

Comparing Equations (3.56) and (3.10), it becomes evident that people's preferred taxes and the identity of the median voter are unchanged as long as the required expenditure on public goods is less than tax revenue as it would be if no public goods were required. Everybody's net post-tax–post-transfer income is reduced by $Q$, as though the public good had been financed by a fixed, uniform tax per head.

Otherwise, if the required $Q$ is greater than tax revenue as it would be if no public goods were required, there is no longer any redistribution and everybody's preferred tax rate is whatever is needed to finance the required $Q$. With redistribution determined by self-interested voting, expenditure to finance public goods is either borne equally by everybody, rich or poor, or borne by people in proportion to their incomes, depending on whether the required expenditure is less than or greater than the demogrant as it would be if no public goods were required. When redistribution is displaced altogether, the tax rate, $t^*$, must be just high enough to pay for the required public goods, so that

$$t^*(1 - t^*/\beta)Y^{av} = Q \tag{3.57}$$

and the net income of a person with a gross income of $Y$ becomes

$$I = Y - t^*(1 - t^*/\beta)Y - t^{*2}Y/2\beta \tag{3.58}$$

This very restrictive description of the role of public goods as social overhead cost may be modified by the assumption that the utility, $W^j$, of person $j$ is buoyed up by a function of the nation's expenditure on public goods, specifically that

$$W^j = h(Q)I^j \tag{3.59}$$

where $I^j$ is the post-tax, post-transfer income of person $j$ and the function $h(Q)$ is concave. As voters, people choose $Q$ collectively, but each person responds to taxation as though $Q$ were invariant, so that one's proportion of gross income concealed from the tax collector is chosen to maximize $I^j$ regardless of the value of $Q$.

Alternatively, an expenditure of $Q^*$ per person may enhance the efficiency of tax collection. It has so far been assumed that the efficiency of tax collection, $\beta$, is invariant. It may be assumed instead that

$$\beta = \beta(Q^*) \tag{3.60}$$

where the efficiency of tax collection is now dependent on public expenditure per person, $Q^*$, devoted to enforcement. It is reasonable to assume that the function is concave and that, without expenditure to enforce tax collection, no revenue would be collected at all, i.e.

$$\beta(0) = 0, \beta'(Q^*) > 0 \quad \text{and} \quad \beta''(Q^*) < 0 \tag{3.61}$$

If all public revenue were devoted to nothing other than redistribution and the enhancement of the efficiency of tax collection, the post-tax, post-transfer income of a person with a gross income of $Y$ would be

$$I = Y - t(1 - t/\beta(Q^*))Y + [t(1 - t/\beta(Q^*))Y^{av} - Q^*] - t^2 Y/2\beta(Q^*) \tag{3.62}$$

which is maximized when

$$\delta I/\delta t = 0 \quad \text{and} \quad \delta I/\delta Q^* = 0 \tag{3.63}$$

The first of these requirements is a repetition of Equation (3.13) when $\beta$ is a function of $G$

$$t(Y) = \beta(Q^*)\{Y^{av} - Y\}/\{2Y^{av} - Y\} \tag{3.64}$$

The second requirement is

$$[\beta'(Q^*)/\beta(Q^*)^2][t^2/2][2Y^{av} - Y] = 1 \tag{3.65}$$

Together, these equations signify that each person has a preferred combination of $t$ and $Q^*$. People's preferences for $t$ and $Q^*$ are likely to be correlated as long as public expenditure is confined to redistribution and to the enforcement of tax collection. The higher your income, the lower your preferred tax rate when public revenue is redistributed, and the less you want the government to spend on bolstering the efficiency of tax collection because inefficiency in tax collection is likely to lower the median voter's preferred tax rate and to reduce the tax you pay. When people's preferences for $t$ and $Q^*$ are correlated, a median voter can still be identified and there would be an electoral equilibrium pair of $t$ and $Q^*$ as illustrated in Figure 2.9 of Chapter 2.

This clean result tends to disintegrate when the efficiency of tax collection varies not just with total revenue, but with the pre-tax, pre-transfer income of the taxpayer. It is at least possible that rich people have methods of tax avoidance that are closed to poor people, and vice versa. For example, poor people have little opportunity to minimize tax paid through the timing of the realization of capital gains. Since the most revenue that can be collected from any given person is at a rate of $\beta/2$, income-related differences in people's values of $\beta$ may influence the chosen progressivity of taxation.

Provision of nationwide overhead cost and enforcement of tax collection are not the only public goods. Public goods may be goods in their own right, contributing directly to the utility of the taxpayer. Public parks and public education are desirable in themselves and not just as multipliers of the benefits of ordinary goods and services. The utility function, $u^j$, of person $j$ would then be

$$u^j = u^j(I^j, Q^{**}) \tag{3.66}$$

where $Q^{**}$ is expenditure per person on this variant of public goods. An implication of Equation (3.66) is that each person's utility can be reconstructed as a function of both $Q^{**}$ and $t$ as long as tax revenue is apportioned between redistribution and the public good. The utility function becomes

$$u^j = u^j(t, Q^{**}) \tag{3.67}$$

Voting is now over two variables at once, which may give rise to a paradox of voting as illustrated in Figure 2.7 of Chapter 2 where no median voter can be identified. Preserved when a fixed overhead cost is required, the electoral equilibrium begins to break down when there are several varieties of public goods and voters' preferences among them are not perfectly correlated.

The simple story at the beginning of this chapter is that self-interested voting yields an electoral equilibrium redistribution of income without altering people's places on the scale of rich and poor and that impediments to taxation create a natural stopping place to redistribution well short of complete dispossession of the wealthy. Among the voting patterns discussed in Chapter 2 are two very different accounts of how voting works: the median voter theorem with a unique equilibrium when everybody votes self-interestedly, and the exploitation problem with no voting equilibrium at all and where majority rule voting becomes a recipe for chaos. Unlike the arbitrary reassignment of people's incomes one by one, the simple story at the beginning of this chapter places voting about the redistribution of income within the domain of the median voter theorem, with outcomes acceptable to a large portion of the population and no threat whatsoever to government by majority rule voting. The story is then modified by the recognition of altruism and fear as motives for redistribution, biased abstention, progressivity of the income tax, political parties, campaign advertising and public expenditure beyond mere redistribution. Yet enough of the simple story persists to justify a degree of confidence in the existence of an electoral equilibrium redistribution of income more or less in accordance with the preference of the median voter.

Not discussed in this chapter is the question of whether impediments to taxation, though necessary to avoid the complete expropriation of the rich by the poor, may be so large that there is a maximal tax revenue barely sufficient to finance necessary public goods, with little or nothing left over for redistribution. Whether that is so is the subject of the next chapter.

This chapter and the next are about a world where compromise is unnecessary, people's duty to vote is an unexplained fact of nature and property is secure. These constraints are relaxed in subsequent chapters. A need for compromise is recognized, the duty to vote is examined in detail, and the ever-present threat of exploitation becomes a major consideration in the organization of government and the economy.

## Appendix 3A: Campaign advertising

Advertising is sometimes classified as either informative or persuasive, but a more detailed classification is appropriate here because the selection of facts and emphasis upon facts placing one's party in a favourable light can be informative and persuasive at the same time. Effects of campaign advertising will be discussed under the headings: the black box, verification, truth telling, warm glow, mendacity, enthusiasm and scraps of information.

### A black box

For some purposes, it is reasonable to assume that campaign expenditures affect voting behaviour with no specification of how or why. That is route taken in models of 'protection for sale' (Grossman and Helpman, 1994, 1996) with emphasis on which industries buy protection and on how the price of protection is determined. Governments in office maximize the chance of re-election, balancing the gain in votes from campaign expenditure financed by the beneficiaries of tariffs against the loss of votes from the higher prices of protected goods. Specifically, the government chooses a vector of tariffs, $T$, to maximize its chance, $G$, of re-election, balancing the gain, $C(T)$, from tariff-induced campaign contributions against the loss in popularity, $W(T)$, from the tariffs themselves in accordance with a function such as

$$G = \theta C(T) + (1 - \theta) W(T) \tag{3A.1}$$

where $\theta$ is a weighting of these two considerations.[24] Grossman and Helpman's full model has much to say about the behaviour of lobbies and governments, but contains no explanation of why campaign advertising works, no explanation of the implicit trade-off in the mind of the voter between campaign advertising praising the virtues of the incumbent government or of a party seeking office and the diminution in welfare brought about by the tariffs imposed.

### *Verification*

For commercial advertising, Nelson (1974) draws a distinction between *search* qualities and *experience* qualities of information supplied by advertising. Advertising with search qualities supplies information that is true and that viewers of ads believe to be true because the sponsor of the ad would have no incentive to supply false information. 'Joe's shoe store is to be found at such-and-such a place.' Joe would have no incentive to falsify such information, no incentive to direct potential buyers of shoes to a grocery store instead. Viewers might be less willing to believe an ad claiming Joe's shoes to be the best in town because every shoe store has an incentive to make such claims.

Claims about quality are ubiquitous. Milgrom and Roberts (1986) suggest an ingenious reason why such claims might be believed. Consider cookies rather than shoes. Suppose there are two qualities of cookies with different market prices. Every person buys one box of cookies, each week forever. The cookies may be either high quality or low quality. Some people buy high quality cookies because they believe the higher quality is worth the higher cost. Others are content with the low quality but less expensive cookies.

Advertising enables a person who wants high quality cookies, and is prepared to pay the extra cost, to discover which brands of cookies are high quality and which are not. Trial and error would eventually be successful but might be expensive, especially if there are many more low quality brands than high quality brands. Costless advertising would be no help at all because every cookie maker would have an incentive to claim its brand to be high quality. Costly advertising makes a true claims believable by causing advertisers to lose money when claims are false. If an advertiser's claim is true, the buyer having experienced one box of high quality cookies continues to buy that brand cookies from then on, yielding the cookie seller a surplus from the sale of one extra box of cookies per week forever. If the claim is false, the cookie seller makes an extra profit on just one box of cookies, but the buyer seeking high quality cookies will never buy that brand again. The claim is verified when expenditure on advertising is high enough that the advertiser gains from advertising if and only is the claim is true. 'Try it. You'll like it,' says the ad-man. 'If you like it, you will buy more, becoming better off in the process, and I'll make more than enough money to cover the cost of the ad. If you don't like it, you'll become worse off, but I'll lose money too. It would never pay me to claim anything but the truth.'

The distinction between experience and search qualities can be carried over from commercial advertising to campaign advertising. Experience qualities are invoked by Prat (2002) in a model of elections where voters are primarily, but not exclusively, concerned about the competence of politicians, where parties know whether a candidate is competent, where voters initially do not, but where there is some chance that – quite apart from campaign advertising – voters will discover candidates' competence before voting takes place. But politicians are not cookies. 'Try it. You'll like it,' makes sense for cookies, or even for cars where the ad is intended to direct the potential customer to a car dealer who can supply some 'experience' of the car. The analogy is imperfect because, unlike cookies, politicians are chosen infrequently (once every few years rather than once a week), there is no universally recognized standard for evaluating politicians, and politicians' true qualities are often obscured in the ebb and flow of events.

### Truth telling

Search qualities are invoked by Coate (2004a) in a model of elections where voters are primarily concerned about the policies that parties would adopt if elected and where each party's choice of policies can be communicated to voters truthfully and believably but at some cost. Campaign advertising is the communication of a promise by a political party to the electorate, where the proportion of the electorate that learns about the promise is an increasing function of party's advertising expenditure, where the promise is about the party's platform and where, never mind why, the party is bound to keep its promise if elected. The promise is made to increase a party's chance of winning the election. The promise is kept to preserve the voters' trust in future elections. Coate (2004a) postulates truth telling in campaign advertising not because he supposes all such advertising to be true but to draw out certain less-than-obvious implications of the postulate for public policy.

Suppose that all politics is about the redistribution of income by means of a negative income tax, that the stalwarts of the left party favour a very high tax rate, $t^H$, and that the stalwarts of the right party favour a very low tax rate, $t^L$. But for campaign advertising, all voters would assume that those are the rates which the parties, if elected, would impose. Campaign advertising is a believable promise to be more moderate. Viewers of the left party's ads believe its promises to levy tax at a rate less than $t^H$. Viewers of the right party's ads believe its promise to levy tax at a rate more than $t^L$. Campaign advertising informs voters about the parties' promises, and, in doing so, induces parties to choose more moderate policies – with lower taxes in the left platform and higher taxes in the right platform – than the parties would choose if they were sure to be elected regardless.

Prat and Coate's models have an interesting difference in policy implications. In Prat's (2002) model, public funding and legal restrictions on amounts of campaign advertising are harmful on balance because advertising verifies nothing unless the advertiser bears the cost. In Coate's model, public funding and legal restrictions on amounts of campaign advertising can be socially beneficial because ads supply true information helping voters to decide which party they prefer, regardless of how that information is financed.

### False information

Campaign advertising may be false, or it may create a false impression without actually lying. Oil companies tout their green credentials or their support for small business. Within campaign advertising, lies are difficult to refute, especially after the *Citizens United* decision of the US Supreme Court allowing political action committees to conceal the sources of their funds. How does a candidate defend himself against the accusation by a political action committee that, as a soldier, he was cowardly, protecting himself against danger while endangering his comrades in arms? One can deny such charges or even sue the political action committee, but the case is unlikely to be resolved until well after the election. The accusation may have done its work if a few undecided voters are turned against the candidate or if a few people who might otherwise vote for the candidate are persuaded to abstain.

### Warm glow

'I'd like to teach the world to sing in perfect harmony. I'd like to buy the world a Coke and keep it company. It's the real thing ...' What is that all about? It is not false. It cannot be inviting the customer to try a new product because everybody has tasted Coca-cola already. It is intended to make people feel good about drinking Coca-cola, quite apart from how it tastes or its effects on people's health. Becker and Murphy (1993) have developed a model of advertising suggesting that Coke ads and the actual bottle of Coca-cola are like inputs into a larger product which is the entire experience of drinking Coca-cola. The term 'warm glow' has been used as part of an explanation of why people give to charity (Andreoni, 1989). You get a warm glow by helping others. Similarly, you may get a warm glow from the association of a memorable ad with the product you consume.

### Enthusiasm

Campaign expenditures may be to advertise or to get out the vote. In an environment where as much as half of the eligible voters abstain, persuasion of a party's supporters to vote may be no less important than persuasion of people who might not otherwise vote for one's party to change their minds. The two roles of money in elections are logically distinct, but not entirely distinct in practice. The person who would vote left if he votes at all may be induced by campaign advertising to vote rather than to abstain. Preaching to the converted makes sense in this context. Advertising in support of the left party may increase the number of votes for the left party by churning up enthusiasm rather than by changing anybody's views.

### Scraps of information

Advertising may persuade by mere assertion or by the provision of scraps of information supporting whatever the advertiser wishes to promote. 'This brand of aspirin is better than that brand of aspirin' or 'Our nation's prosperity is guaranteed by the genius and magnanimity of our great leader' or 'I can create jobs but he cannot' are mere assertion, perhaps made credible by repetition. Scraps of information may be persuasive in circumstances where nobody is absolutely sure of the truth and where there is likely to be more information scattered here and there than any one person is aware of. Advertising about the marginal cost of concealing income from the tax collector or about the location of the Laffer curve may be persuasive not just due to repetition, but by supplying genuine if incomplete information.

More generally, imagine an election between a left party and a right party where there is a great sea of information about the relative merits of the two parties, where each voter is aware of some, but not all, of the relevant information and where each party's campaign advertising is intended to supply as many voters as possible with extra bits of information favourable to that party and unfavourable to its opponent.

Think of all information relevant to the choice between political parties as a large number, $N$, of facts – more than any voter can be aware of – with all facts, $n$, labelled from 1 to $N$. Designate person $i$'s preference between the left and right parties as $v_i$, where $v_i > 0$ signifies that person $i$ prefers the left party, where $v_i < 0$ signifies that person $i$ prefers the right party and where person $i$'s strength of preference is indicated by the absolute value of $v_i$. Party preference, $v_i$, depends upon the set of facts of which the voter $i$ is aware and upon the weighting of each known fact in person $i$'s assessment of the relative merits of the two parties. Specifically, suppose

$$v_i = \sum_{n=1}^{N} \delta_{in} w_{in} \tag{3A.2}$$

where $\delta_{in}$ is equal to 1 or 0 depending on whether or not person $i$ is aware of fact $n$, and where $w_{in} > 0$ when knowledge of fact $n$ makes person $i$ more favourable to the *left* party, $w_{in} < 0$ when knowledge of fact $n$ makes person $i$ more favourable to the *right* party, and the importance of fact $n$ to person $i$ is indicated by the absolute value of $w_{in}$. No distinction is drawn here between what is commonly called 'positive' and 'negative' campaign advertising. A positive $w_{in}$ means that the fact $n$ is either a virtue of the left party or a defect of the right party, and vice versa if $w_{in}$ is negative.

There are two versions of the story. In the simpler version, campaign advertising influences $\delta_{in}$ but not $w_{in}$. Campaign advertising can make voters are aware of certain facts, but cannot affect the importance of facts in the voters' assessments of the relative merits of the two parties. Advertising by the left party would then be directed to changing $\delta_{in}$ from 0 to 1 if and only if $w_{in} > 0$, and advertising by the right party would be directed to changing $\delta_{in}$ from 0 to 1 if and only if $w_{in} < 0$. Presumably, the more is spent on advertising, the more voters are influenced in accordance with some mechanism discussed in connection with Equation (A3.2).

In the more complex version, campaign advertising affects both $\delta_{in}$ and $w_{in}$, on the assumption that facts become more important through repetition or through presentation in the appropriate light. Campaign advertising becomes especially complicated when facts have different effects upon different people. If $w_{in} > 0$ for some people and $w_{in} < 0$ for others, the left party has an incentive to reveal or to emphasize fact $n$ if and only if the former group is larger or, perhaps if people in the latter group would not vote for the left party regardless. A crafty politician might reveal certain facts to some people but not to others, as when campaign donors are told that their preferences will be respected, but ordinary voters are not. Nevertheless, the more money a party spends on advertising a given fact $n$, the more people will become aware of it (the larger will be the group for which $\delta_{in} = 1$ rather than 0) and the larger the absolute value of $w_{in}$ becomes.[25]

A well-endowed party can lie without actually lying. By supplying enough scraps of favourable information and by raising their apparent importance through repetition and spin, campaign advertising can create a false impression of the relative merits of two competing parties without supplying false information at all, influencing the outcome of an election in what most people would see as an undesirable way. All that is required is for campaign expenditure to be very much larger for one party than for the other. Outright deception is possible but not necessary for advertising to be effective.

Aspects of campaign advertising discussed here – costly transmission of information, verification of claims, outright mendacity, warm glow, generation enthusiasm and selective presentation of scraps of information – are complements rather than substitutes. One aspect of campaign advertising may be dominant in some particular case, but, typically, all have their places in campaign advertising as a whole. Ideally, all of these aspects of campaign advertising would be combined in one large model through which their relative importance can be assessed.[26] In practice, recognition of the many different routes from advertising to votes may be seen as justification for the black box notion of campaign advertising where each party's advertising augments its attractiveness in the eyes of the voter with no single explanation of why that is so.

## Appendix 3B: Using the Pareto distribution to illustrate how a widening of the distribution of income increases both the ratio of mean to median income and the ratio of the total income of the richer half to the total income of the poorer half of the population

The Pareto distribution is a convenient representation of the distribution of income for the purposes of this chapter. Like virtually every actual distribution of income that has ever been observed, it is skewed with large numbers of relatively poor people and small numbers of relatively rich people, so that the median income – the income of the person exactly half way along the scale from the poorest to the richest person, with as many people richer as there are people poorer – is always less than the average income and the gap between them widens as the distribution of income becomes less equal.

Equality is measured unambiguously by a parameter $\alpha$ varying from a minimum of 1 when the distribution of income is as unequal as it can ever be to a maximum of infinity at which everybody's income is the same.[27] There is assumed to be a minimal income, $Y^{min}$, the income of the very poorest person. Associated with every income, $Y$, is a number $n(Y)$ signifying the proportion of the population with incomes larger than $Y$. The Pareto distribution is

$$n(Y) = (Y^{min}/Y)^\alpha \qquad (3B.1)$$

It is characterized by the properties that $n(Y^{min}) = 1$, meaning that everybody's income exceeds the minimum income; that, for any $Y^{min}$, $n(Y)$ is a decreasing function of $\alpha$, meaning that the more equal the distribution the smaller is the proportion of people with incomes in excess of any given income $Y$; and that, regardless of $Y$, $n(Y) = 1$ when $\alpha$ rises to infinity at which all incomes are equal.

For $\alpha = 2$ which is not too far off estimated values in many countries, the Pareto distribution of income is illustrated in Figure 3B.1. Since, as will be shown, the median income, $Y^{med}$, and the average income, $Y^{av}$, are both multiples of the minimum income, $Y^{min}$, there is no harm in supposing that $Y^{min} = 1$. The median income – for which $n = \frac{1}{2}$ – is 1.414, the average income is 2 and the location on the scale from rich to poor of the person with the average income is 1/4, implying that three-quarters of the population have less than average income.

Median income, $Y^{med}$, is the income of the person half way along the scale from the poorest to the richest person. It is the income of the person for whom

$$n(Y^{med}) = (Y^{min}/Y^{med})^\alpha = \frac{1}{2}$$

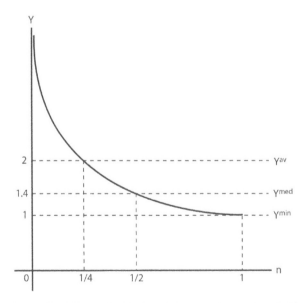

*Figure 3B.1* Pareto distribution of income with $\alpha = 2$ and $Y^{min} = 1$.

or, equivalently

$$Y^{med} = 2^{1/\alpha} Y^{min} \qquad (3B.2)$$

Average income, $Y^{av}$, is the ratio of total income to population or, equivalently, the sum of incomes weighted by the density of income along the line from 0 to 1.

$$Y^{av} = \int_{Y^{min}}^{\infty} Yf(Y)dY \qquad (3B.3)$$

where $f(Y) = -dn/dY = \alpha(Y^{min})^{\alpha} Y^{-\alpha-1}$ so that

$$Y^{av} = \int_{Y^{min}}^{\infty} Yf(Y)dY = \alpha \left(Y^{min}\right)^{\alpha} \int_{Y^{min}}^{\infty} Y^{-\alpha}dY = [\alpha/(\alpha-1)](Y^{min}) \qquad (3B.4)$$

The ratio of median to mean income is

$$Y^{med}/Y^{av} = 2^{1/\alpha}(\alpha-1)/\alpha \qquad (3B.5)$$

which is an increasing function of $\alpha$ because both $2^{1/\alpha}$ and $(\alpha-1)/\alpha$ are increasing functions of $\alpha$

$$d[2^{1/\alpha}(\alpha-1)/\alpha]/d\alpha = (2^{1/\alpha})d[(\alpha-1)/\alpha]/d\alpha + [(\alpha-1)/\alpha]\delta[2^{1/\alpha}]/d\alpha$$
$$= (2^{1/\alpha})[1/\alpha^2] + [(\alpha-1)/\alpha][2^{1-\alpha)/\alpha}]/\alpha > 0 \qquad (3B.6)$$

The ratio of total income in the wealthiest half of the population, $S^{top}$, to total income in the poorest half of the population, $S^{bottom}$, is

$$S^{top}/S^{bottom} = \int_{Y^{med}}^{\infty} Yf(Y)dY / \int_{Y^{min}}^{Y^{med}} Yf(Y)dY$$

$$= \int_{Y^{med}}^{\infty} f(Y)dY / \left\{ \int_{Y^{min}}^{\infty} Yf(Y)dY - \int_{Y^{med}}^{\infty} Yf(Y)dY \right\} \qquad (3B.7)$$

so that

$$S^{top}/S^{bottom} = \{(Y^{med})^{-\alpha+1}\}/\{(Y^{min})^{-\alpha+1} - (Y^{med})^{-\alpha+1}\}$$
$$= \{(2^{1/\alpha})^{-\alpha+1}\}/\{1 - (2^{1/\alpha})^{-\alpha+1}\} = \{1/2^{(\alpha-1)/\alpha}\}/\{1 - 1/2^{(\alpha-1)/\alpha}\}$$
$$= 1/(2^{(\alpha-1)/\alpha} - 1) \qquad (3B.8)$$

and

$$\delta\{S^{top}/S^{bottom}\}/\delta\alpha = \delta[(2^{(\alpha-1)/\alpha} - 1)^{-1}]/\delta\alpha$$
$$= (-1)[(2^{(\alpha-1)/\alpha} - 1)^{-2}][(\alpha - 1)/\alpha][2^{-1/\alpha}] < 0 \qquad (3B.9)$$

Equations 3B.8 and 3B.9 show the ratio $S^{top}/S^{bottom}$ of the shares of income acruing to the top and bottom halves of the population to be a decreasing function of $\alpha$, falling from infinity to 1 as $\alpha$ increases from 1 to infinity, that is, from the least to the greatest possible equality of income.

## Appendix 3C: The marginal cost of public funds

The government is considering the construction of a new road. The cost of the road to the government is $1 million. The present value of the benefit of the road to citizens is $1.1 million. Should the road be built? Not necessarily, for cost and benefit are not commensurate, one is borne by the government and the other accrues to citizens. They are not commensurate because the full cost of the road to citizens is not just the extra tax paid, but the sum of the extra tax paid and the extra cost of tax avoidance induced by whatever increase in the tax rate is required to finance the new road. When tax avoidance is by outright tax evasion as described in the discussion surrounding Equation (3.9) in the text of this chapter, a comparison of benefit and cost to the citizen requires the cost to the government, which is equal to the extra tax paid, to be scaled up by the marginal cost of public funds (*MCPF*) where

$$MCPF = [\Delta(\text{tax paid}) + \Delta(\text{cost of tax evasion})]/\Delta(\text{tax paid}) \qquad (3C.1)$$

where $\Delta(\text{tax paid})$ is the extra revenue required to finance the new road and $\Delta(\text{cost of tax evasion})$ is the corresponding increase in the cost of tax evasion, as described in Figure 3.1 in the text, induced by the required increase, $\Delta t$, in the tax rate to generate the extra tax revenue.[28] With costs and benefits as specified above, the new road is beneficial on balance if and only if

$$1.05 > MCPF \qquad (3C.2)$$

The marginal cost of public funds can be defined for a person or for the nation as a whole, but the two turn out to be the same in the simple model of tax evasion at the beginning of this chapter. Specifically, as shown in the discussion surrounding Equation (3.9),

$$\Delta(\text{tax paid}) = (1 - 2t/\beta)Y \qquad (3C.3)$$
$$\Delta(\text{cost of tax evasion}) = (t/\beta)Y \qquad (3C.4)$$

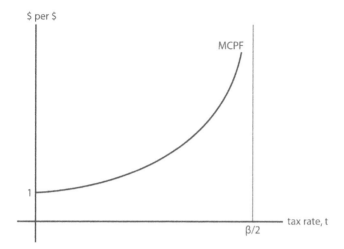

$ per $

MCPF

1

β/2

tax rate, t

*Figure 3C.1* The marginal cost of public funds as a function of the tax rate.

and

$$MCPF = [(1 - 2t/\beta)Y + (t/\beta)Y]/[(1 - 2t/\beta)Y]$$
$$= [(1 - t/\beta)Y]/[(1 - 2t/\beta)Y] = (\beta - t)/(\beta - 2t) \qquad (3C.5)$$

which is independent of $Y$ but dependent on $t$. From Equation (3.7), it follows that the marginal cost of public funds is the inverse of the elasticity of tax revenue to tax rate.

$$MCPF = 1/\varepsilon_{R,t} \qquad (3C.6)$$

The marginal cost of funds is illustrated in Figure 3C.1 with the tax rate on the horizontal axis and with '$ per $', meaning cost to the taxpayer per dollar of revenue to the government, on the vertical axis. The figure is derived from Equation (3C.5). The marginal cost of public funds begins at 1 when $t = 0$ and rises more than proportionally with $t$ until it reaches infinity whent $t = \beta/2$ at the top of the Laffer curve as shown in Figure 3.2.

The marginal cost of public funds is constant in one sense and variable in another. It is constant for any given tax rate. Once the tax rate is established and ignoring distributive considerations, a project is only worth doing if the benefit–cost ratio exceeds the marginal cost of public funds. It is variable in that it depends upon the the tax rate as shown in Figure 3C.1.

In the simple model of redistribution in this chapter – where all public revenue is redistributed, where there are no ordinary public goods and where tax evasion accounts for the shrinkage of the tax base in response to an increase in the tax rate – each person, along with his preferred tax rate, has a preferred marginal cost of public funds. To see why this is so, consider once again the derivation of a person's post-tax, post-transfer income, $I$, in Equation (3.9). As already discussed in connection with the equation, the person's preferred tax rate is whatever serves to maximize $I$, in which case

$$\Delta(\text{tax paid}) + \Delta(\text{cost of tax evasion}) = \Delta(\text{demogrant}) \tag{3C.7}$$

or

$$[\Delta(\text{tax paid}) + \Delta(\text{cost of tax evasion})]/\Delta(\text{tax paid}) = \Delta(\text{demogrant})/\Delta(\text{tax paid}) \tag{3C.8}$$

The right hand side of Equation (3C.8) reduces to $Y^{av}/Y$, the left hand side is the marginal cost of public funds at the preferred tax rate, $t$, of a person with gross income, $Y$, and the equation itself becomes

$$MCPF(t) = Y^{av}/Y \tag{3C.9}$$

When the actual tax rate is the preferred rate of the median voter, Equation (3C.9) becomes

$$MCPF = Y^{av}/Y^{med} \tag{3C.10}$$

where $MCPF$ is the actual marginal cost of public funds at society's chosen tax rate.[29]

Figure 3C.2 shows the marginal cost of public funds as a function of the tax rate, together with tax rates and corresponding marginal costs of public funds for the person with the median income, $Y^{med}$, and for a person with a smaller income, $Y$.

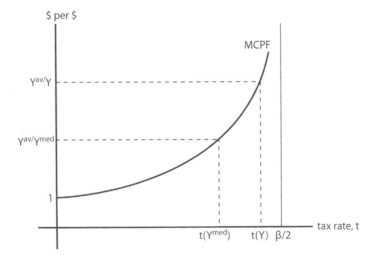

*Figure 3C.2* The electoral equilibrium marginal cost of public funds.

The story can be extended to account for public expenditure on roads, police, schools and so on. Think of all non-redistributory public expenditure as a sequence of projects lined up according to their benefit–cost ratios, where benefit is *to the citizen* and cost is *to the government*. Abstracting from distributional considerations and on the principle of cost–benefit analysis that 'a dollar is a dollar is a dollar to whomsoever it may accrue', a welfare-maximizing government can be expected to undertake only those projects for which benefit exceeds cost or to supply public goods up to the point where marginal benefit equals marginal cost. But marginal cost in this context must be to the citizen rather than to the government and, as such, must include the extra cost of tax evasion or other manoeuvres by the tax payer to minimize his extra tax bill that additional public expenditure requires. As is evident from the discussion surrounding Equation (3.9), the marginal cost to the taxpayer per dollar of public revenue is the same no matter how public revenue is spent, whether on redistribution or on ordinary public goods. In short, as illustrated in Figure 3C.3, public projects and public goods are supplied up to the point where the ratio of marginal benefit to marginal cost equals the marginal cost of public funds.

Two possibilities are illustrated on the two sides of Figure 3C.3, an extension of Figures 3C.1 and 3C.2, with the marginal cost per dollar of public expenditure shown as a function of the tax rate required to finance that expenditure rather than of the expenditure itself. Equilibrium on both sides of the figure is in accordance with the preference of the median voter. The two sides differ according to whether public goods block out redistribution altogether. With the marginal benefit–cost schedule as shown on the left-hand side, the demogrant is reduced by the demand for public goods but not eliminated altogether. Without public goods, the equilibrium tax rate would be $t(Y^{med})$ and the demogrant would be determined accordingly. With the benefit–cost schedule as shown in the figure, society acquires as much public goods as can be purchased at a tax rate of $t_1$, and only the additional revenue from the higher tax rate, $t(Y^{med})$, is redistributed as a demogrant. Projects or public goods with benefit–cost ratios above $Y^{av}/Y^{med}$ are acquired. Projects or public goods with benefit–cost ratios below $Y^{av}/Y^{med}$ are not. The right side of Figure 3C.3 illustrates conditions where the demogrant is eliminated. The benefit–cost schedule is now higher, crossing the schedule of

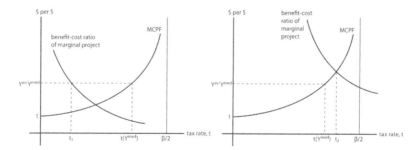

*Figure 3C.3* Public projects and public goods ordered by their benefit–cost ratios.

the marginal cost of public funds above $Y^{av}/Y^{med}$, at a tax rate $t_2$ which is higher than $t(Y^{med})$.

Note finally that the sharp distinction between redistribution and other public expenditure is just a convenient simplification to emphasize an important feature of the marginal cost of public funds. Public goods are not perfect substitutes for redistribution as the model implies. A wonderful new highway is little consolation to someone who does not have enough to eat. The story is just to emphasize that there may be a complex trade-off in use between redistribution and some forms of public goods.

## Notes

1 The model in this chapter covers much of the same ground as Meltzer and Richards (1981) except that the contraction of the tax base in response to an increase in the tax rate is due to tax evasion rather than the labour–leisure choice.

2 Proving something does not make it true. Proofs require axioms. Axioms may be self-evident truths as in high school geometry, they may be accurate enough of to make propositions trustworthy, or they may be abstractions focussing on important considerations that may not always be decisive.

3 Imagine a society of five people with incomes of 1, 2, 4, 7 and 11. The median income is 4 because the number of people with incomes less than 4 equals the number of people with incomes of more than 4. The average income is 5. If the distribution of income became more unequal – for example, by increasing the income of the richest person from 11 to 16 – the average income would rise to 6 but the median income would remain the same.

4 When the full cost of concealing a proportion $\tau$ of one's gross income $Y$ is $\beta\tau^2 Y/2$, the marginal cost becomes $\delta(\beta\tau^2 Y/2)/\delta t$ which is equal to $\beta\tau Y$.

5 Three distinct measures of income are employed: $Y$ is a person's true gross pre-tax, pre-transfer income regardless of how much of it is declared, $y$ is the person's income as observed by the tax collector, and $I$ is the person's net post-tax, post-transfer income.

6 Suppose $n = 1/10$ indicating that the income of the person $n$ exceeds the incomes of 90 per cent of the population. From Equation (3.18) it follows that $Y(n)/Y^{min} = 1$ when $\alpha = $ infinity, rises to 1.56 when $\alpha = 5$, rises to 2.15 when $\alpha = 3$, rises to 3.16 when $\alpha = 2$ and rises to 10 when $\alpha = 1$.

7 Summed over the entire population, the second and third expressions on the right-hand side of Equation (3.10) cancel out, leaving an average net loss (the deadweight loss) of $t^2 Y^{av}/2\beta$. With $\beta$ assumed equal to 3/2 and with $t$ estimated to be 0.34, the value of the expression becomes $0.0385Y^{av}$ (that is $[(0.34)^2/(2(3/2))]Y^{av}$), or approximately 4 per cent of average pre-tax, pre-transfer income.

8 There is another interpretation of $\varphi$ and $W$. The parameter $\varphi$ may be interpreted as a person's degree of risk aversion, and the term $W$ in Equation (3.23) may be interpreted as the person's valuation of a risky prospect with equal chances of each income, $I_i$. Sometimes moral and personal valuations are fused, so that a person who is relatively risk averse places a relatively high moral valuation of equality relative to total national income, but this is not necessarily so. A person who is not at all risk averse may still be concerned about the distribution of income in society as a whole. On utility of income as an indicator of risk aversion, see von Neumann and Morgenstern (1953, Appendix).

9 Consider a two-person economy where the total income is 6 and where the parameter $\varphi$ is equal to 2. With a completely equal distribution of income, social welfare in accordance with Equation (3.23) is equal to $(\frac{1}{2})^{\frac{1}{2}}[3^2 + 3^2]^{1/2} = (\frac{1}{2})^{\frac{1}{2}} [18]^{1/2} = (0.707)(4.243) = 3$. With an unequal distribution of 4 to one person and 2 to the other,

social welfare in accordance with Equation (3.23) rises to $(½)^{½}[4^2 + 2^2]^{1/2} = (½)^{½}$ $[20]^{1/2} = (0.707)(4.472) = 3.16$. In this case, inequality is morally superior to equality, even though average income is the same. Hence the ruling out of values of $\varphi$ greater than 1.

10  Suppose for example that $\varphi = -2$. With incomes of 3 and 3, social welfare becomes $(½)^{-1/2}\,[3^{-2} + 3^{-2}]^{-1/2} = (½)^{-1/2}\,[2/9]^{-1/2} = (1.414)(2.121) = 3$. With incomes of 2 and 4, social welfare falls to $(½)^{-1/2}\,[4^{-2} + 2^{-2}]^{-1/2} = (½)^{-1/2}\,[1/16 + 1/4]^{-1/2} = (1.414)(1.789) = 2.529$. Equality is a virtue once again.

11  For the proof, see Chiang (1974: 419).

12  From Equation (3.23), it follows at once that, for any $i$,

$$W = [I_i](1/n)^{1/\varphi}\{(I_1/I_i)^\varphi + (I_2/I_i)^\varphi + (I_3/I_i)^\varphi + \cdots + (I_n/I_i)^\varphi\}^{1/\varphi}$$

Let $i$ be the person with the very lowest value of $I$ so that all ratios $I_j/I_i$ are greater than 1 except where persons $i$ and $j$ are the same, and let $\varphi = -\infty$. It follows that

$$W = [I_i](1/n)^0\{(I_i/I_1)^\infty + (I_i/I_2)^\infty + (I_i/I_3)^\infty + \cdots + (I_i/I_n)^\infty\}^0 = I_i = I^{min}$$

because, except when $i = j$, all of the ratios within the curly brackets are less than 1. This indicator is looked upon as the standard of justice in Rawls (1971).

13  The comprehensive studies of optimal taxation in Tuomala (1990) and Boadway (2012) conform to this pattern. Neither discusses the possibility that voters might want something other than what the benevolent dictator would prescribe. Implicitly, voters are seen as favouring what is best for society rather than for themselves alone.

14  Cited in Stern (1976).

15  James Fitzjames Stephen, *Liberty, Equality and Fraternity* (1873) as quoted in Cannon (1973).

16  'What we now know as public assistance or relief, which is in various forms provided in all countries, is merely the old poor law adapted to modern conditions. The necessity of some such arrangements in an industrial society is unquestioned – be it only in the interest of those who require protection against acts of desperation on the part of the needy ... Once it becomes the recognized duty of the public to provide for the extreme needs of old age, unemployment, sickness, etc., ... it seems an obvious corollary to compel them to insure (or otherwise provide) against those common hazards of life' Hayek (1960: 285–6).

17  Boix (2003: 10 and 12) looks upon economic equality and capital mobility as the two main defences of democratic government. Economic equality refers to the width of the initial distribution of income. Capital mobility refers to wealthy people migrating to other jurisdictions with lower tax rates. The threat of migration constrains exploitative taxation, keeping government by majority rule tolerable to the wealthy elite.

18  On tax evasion, see Cowell (2003).

19  Redistribution is not exempt from the spoiler problem. Suppose there are three political parties rather than just two, a party of the rich, $R$, a party of the middle class, $M$, and a party of the poor, $P$, with platforms of tax rates of 0 per cent, 20 per cent and 50 per cent respectively. Suppose also that the electorate consists of three groups, the wealthiest 40 per cent with preferences $R, M, P$, a middle 30 per cent with preferences $M, P, R$, and a poorest 30 per cent with preferences $P, M, R$. In a first-past-the-post electoral regime, the party of the rich wins despite the fact that it would lose to the party of the middle class or the party of the poor if the other dropped out of the race. A majority (60 per cent) of voters would be better off if the party of the middle class and the party of the poor amalgamated in support of a tax rate between 20 per cent and 50 per cent, but politicians' egos might stand in the way. Proportional representation would require

compromise too. The party of the middle class would win under a regime of the single transferrable vote.

20  On the economics of competence, see Majumdar and Mukand (2004).

21  On the 'inequality-of-redistribution puzzle', see Docquier and Tarbalouti (2001) and Georgiadis and Manning (2012).

22  On the correlation between wealth and campaign contributions, see Ansolabehere, de Figueiredo, and Snyder (2003).

23  The influence of campaign expenditures on the anticipated efficiency of tax collection can be thought of as representative of the many ways, some but not all described in Appendix 3A, for money to influence votes. That there is such influence can and has been demonstrated. Palda (1973), Palda (1993), Stratmann (2009) and many others have estimated the elasticities of the vote share to campaign contributions. Bombardini and Trebbi (2011) have estimated the price in the form of campaign advertising for candidates in elections for the US House of Representatives to be $145 per additional vote. As these authors explain, such estimates are necessarily vague because the price per vote is likely to be a sharply increasing function of the amount of campaign advertising and can be expected to vary greatly from one constituency to the next. However, a self-interested contributor of campaign funds would be concerned not with the price per vote, but with the cost of – say – an extra 1 per cent chance of winning the election which would depend in part, as will be discussed in Chapter 7, on the probability that of an additional vote is pivotal, swinging the outcome of an election from one party to another.

24  Equation (3A.1) is a modification of Equation (5) in Grossman and Helpman (1994).

25  There is no bright line between campaign advertising and ordinary news. Supporters of all parties are inclined to see media bias on the other side. Introduction of Fox News in many American towns in the years before the 2000 presidential election has been estimated by Vigna, Stefano and Kaplan (2006) to have raised the Republican vote in those towns by about half of one per cent.

26  There is some problem in generalizing the verification model from one fact to many facts. In Pratt's model, there was only one fact – whether the quality of a candidate is high or low – and the voter had a chance of getting to know the fact prior to the election. It is unclear what inference the voter can draw from campaign advertising when there are many facts to be verified, that is, when a party makes many claims to virtue and many allegations about the vices of its opponent. Regardless of a party's total expenditure on campaign advertising, how is the voter to be sure that all the party's claims are true?

27  For estimates of $\alpha$ at various times and places, see Bronfenbrenner, 1971.

28  For fuller expositions of the marginal cost of public funds, see Browning (1976) and Dahlby (2008).

29  For a more extensive discussion of Equation (3C.9), see Usher (2006). In the year 2013, the ratio of mean to median household income in the United States was about 1.4 (United States Census, Historical Income Tables, 2013, Table H-11). This number is well within the range of estimates of the marginal cost of public funds at various times and places provided by Dahlby (2008), table 5.3.

## References

Andreoni, James (1989) Giving with impure altruism: applications to charity and ricardian equivalence, *Journal of Political Economy*, 97(6), 1447–58.

Ansolabehere, S, de Figueiredo, J. M. and Snyder, J. M. Jr. (2003) Why is there so little money in US politics?, *The Journal of Economic Perspectives*, 17(1), 105–30.

Austin-Smith, David (1987) Interest groups, campaign contributions and probabilistic voting, *Public Choice*, 54(2), 123–39.

Becker, Gary and Murphy, Kevin (1993) A simple theory of advertising as good or bad, *Quarterly Journal of Economics*, 108(4), 941–64.

Boadway, R. (2012) *From Optimal Tax Theory to Tax Policy: Retrospective and Prospective Views*, Cambridge, MA: MIT Press.

Boix, Charles (2003) *Democracy and Redistribution*, Cambridge: Cambridge University Press.

Bombardini, Matilde and Trebbi, Francesco (2011) Votes or money? Theory and evidence from the US Congress, *Journal of Public Economics*, 95(7–8), 587–611.

Bronfenbrenner, Martin (1971) *Income Distribution Theory*, Chicago: Aldine Atherton Press.

Browning, Edgar, K. (1976) The marginal cost of public funds, *Journal of Political Economy*, 84(2), 283–98.

Cannon, J. (1973) *Parliamentary Reform, 1640–1832*, Cambridge: Cambridge University Press.

Chiang, A. (1974) *Fundamental Methods of Mathematical Economics*, 2nd edn, New York: McGraw-Hill.

Coate, Stephen (2004a) Pareto-improving campaign finance policy, *American Economic Review*, 94(3), 628–55.

Coate, Stephen (2004b) Political competition with campaign contributions and informative advertising, *Journal of the European Economic Association*, 2(5), 772–804.

Cowell, F. A. (2003) *Cheating the Government: The Economics of Evasion*, Cambridge, MA: MIT Press.

Dahlby, Bev (2008) *The Marginal Cost of Public Funds: Theory and Applications*, Cambridge, MA: MIT Press.

Docquier, Frederic and Tarbalouti, Essaid (2001) Bribing votes: a new explanation of the inequality-redistribution puzzle in LDCs, *Public Choice*, 108(3–4), 259–72.

Fair, R. (1971) The optimal distribution of income, *Quarterly Journal of Economics*, 85, 551–79.

Friedman, M. (1960) *Capitalism and Freedom*, Chicago: University of Chicago Press.

Georgiadis, Andreas and Manning, Alan (2012) Spend it like Beckham? Inequality and redistribution in the UK, 1983–2004, *Public Choice*, 151, 537–63.

Grossman, Gene and Helpman, Elhanan (1994) Protection for sale, *American Economic Review*, 84(4), 833–50.

Grossman, Gene and Helpman, Elhanan (1996) Electoral competition and special interest politics, *Review of Economic Studies*, 63(2), 265–86.

Hayek, F. A. (1960) *The Constitution of Liberty*, Chicago: University of Chicago Press.

Majumdar, Sumon and Mukand, Sharun (2004) Policy gambles, *American Economic Review*, 94(4),1207–22.

Meltzer, Allan and Richards, Scott (1981) A rational theory of the size of government, *Journal of Political Economy*, 89(5), 914–27.

Milgrom, P. and Roberts, J. (1986) Price and advertising signals of product quality, *Journal of Political Economy*, 94(4), 796–821.

Mirlees, James (1971) An exploration of the theory of optimal income taxation, *The Review of Economic Studies*, 38(2), 175–208.

Morton, Rebecca (1991) Groups in rational turnout models, *American Journal of Political Science*, 35(3), 758–76.

Nelson, Philip (1974) Advertising as information, *Journal of Political Economy*, 82(4), 729–54.

Palda, Filip (1993) The desirability and effects of campaign spending limits, *Crime, Law and Social Change*, 21, 295–317.

Palda, Kristian (1973), Does advertising influence votes?, *Canadian Journal of Political Science*, 6(4), 638–55.

Plato, trans. Taylor, A. E. (1960) *The Laws*, London: Dent.

Prat, Andrea (2002) Campaign advertising and voter welfare, *Review of Economic Studies*, 69(4), 999–1018.

Rawls, John (1971) *A Theory of Justice*, Cambridge, MA: Harvard University Press.

Simons, Henry (1938) *Personal Income Taxation*, Chicago: University of Chicago Press.

Stern, N. (1976) On the specification of models of optimal income taxation, *Journal of Public Economics*, 6, 123–62.

Stratmann, Thomas (2009) How prices matter in politics: the returns to campaign advertising, *Public Choice*, 40(3/4), 359–77.

Tuomala, M. (1990) *Optimal Income Tax and Redistribution*, Oxford: Clarendon Press.

Ulander, Carole (1989) Rational turnout: the neglected role of groups, *American Journal of Political Science*, 33(2), 390–422.

United States Census (2013) Size of household by median and mean income, Historical Income Tables, Table H-11, Washington DC: US Census Bureau.

Usher, Dan (2006) The marginal cost of public funds is the ratio of mean to median income, *Public Finance Review*, 34(6), 687–711.

Vigna, Stefano, D. and Ethan Kaplan (2006) The Fox News effect: media bias and voting, national bureau of economic research, NBER Working Paper No. 12169, April.

von Neumann, J. and Morgenstern, O. (1953) *Theory of Games and Economic Behaviour*, 2nd edn. Princeton: Princeton University Press.

# 4 How high might the revenue-maximizing tax rate be?[1]

> In so far as men act rationally, they will at a higher (wage) rate divide their time between wage-earning and non-industrial uses in such a way as to earn *more money* but to work *fewer hours*.
>
> Frank Knight as quoted by Robbins (1930: 123–9)

The most dramatic argument against extensive redistribution of income is that it is impossible. No matter how compassionate we may be, if the revenue-maximizing tax rate is, for example, 60 per cent, so that no higher tax rate yields any extra tax revenue, then expenditure on redistribution cannot exceed the proceeds of a tax of 60 per cent less whatever portion of revenue is required to finance ordinary public goods, the army, the police and so on. There is a whiff of hypocrisy to the argument. People opposing redistribution would rather claim it to be impossible than to admit to a want of sympathy toward the poor. People favouring redistribution for selfish or altruistic reasons persuade themselves that the revenue-maximizing tax rate is high enough to accommodate policies they support. But there is a real issue here, and much effort has been devoted to the difficult task of figuring out what the revenue-maximizing tax rate might actually be. The purpose of this chapter is not to provide a definitive estimate of the revenue-maximizing tax rate, but to say in a general way what might be possible and to serve as a critique of the 'new tax responsiveness' literature in which the rate is estimated.[2]

The debate can be framed as about the shape of the Laffer curve connecting tax revenue and tax rate, in particular about the tax rate, $t^*$, at the top of the curve where tax revenue is maximized. Two possible shapes of the Laffer curve are illustrated in Figure 4.1. The higher curve (curve 1) has a higher revenue-maximizing tax rate, $t^{*1}$. The lower curve (curve 2) has a lower revenue-maximizing tax rate, $t^{*2}$. Large public expenditure may be possible if the Laffer curve is like curve 1 but not if the Laffer curve is like curve 2. Liberals know that the shape is more like curve 1 than curve 2. Conservatives know the opposite. The general problem is to determine which is which, or, to be more precise, to determine the size of the revenue-maximizing tax rate, $t^*$.

These are not the only conceivable shapes of the Laffer curve. Both curves in Figure 4.1 are humped, with no tax revenue at tax rates of 0 per cent and

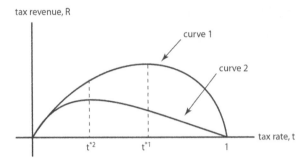

*Figure 4.1* Two possible shapes of the Laffer curve.

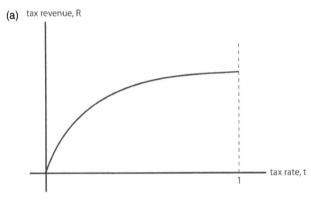

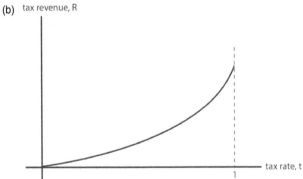

*Figure 4.2* Two other shapes for the Laffer curve.

100 per cent and with a revenue-maximizing tax rate of less than 100 per cent. It is at least conceivable that the Laffer curve is uniformly upward-sloping, either concave as in Figure 4.2(a) or convex as in Figure 4.2(b). It turns out that all three shapes are possible.

## From the supply curve of taxable income to the revenue-maximizing tax rate

Taxation is impeded by the taxpayer's incentive to reduce his tax bill, contracting his observable tax base through outright tax evasion, by working less or by other means. Contraction of the tax base is expensive, for, if that were not so, nobody would pay tax at all. Since taxpayers naturally choose the least expensive way of concealing any given share of the tax base, the marginal cost of contracting the tax base must increase with the proportion of tax base already concealed.

Imagine a supply curve of taxable income as illustrated in Figure 4.3 with taxable income as perceived by the tax collector, $y$, on the vertical axis and the 'price' of taxable income, $(1 - t)$, on the horizontal axis. The price of taxable income is like a market price in response to which taxable income is supplied by adjusting the amount of actual income concealed from the tax collector, by changing the supply of labour or by some other means. Regardless of why declared income is affected by the tax rate, Figure 4.3 shows an increase $\Delta t$ in the tax rate reducing the supply price of taxable income from $(1 - t)$ to $(1 - t - \Delta t)$ and causing taxable income to change from $y$ to $y - \Delta y$. This supply curve is shown as upward-sloping, but, as will be shown below, that need not always be so.

As the revenue-maximizing tax rate can never be observed directly, it must be inferred from some observable aspect of taxation at actual rates. The standard procedure in 'the new tax responsiveness' literature is to infer the revenue-maximizing tax rate from the estimated 'elasticity of taxable income' defined as the percentage change in the observable tax base in response to a given percentage change in the share of income that the taxpayer retains. Specifically,

$$\varepsilon = [\delta y/y]/[\delta(1 - t)/(1 - t)] = [(1 - t)/y]\delta y/\delta(1 - t) \qquad (4.1)$$

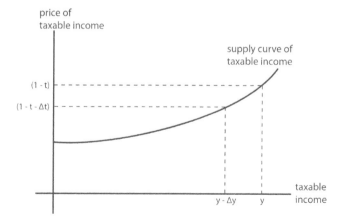

*Figure 4.3* The supply curve of taxable income.

where $\varepsilon$ is the elasticity of taxable income, $y$ is taxable income as observed by the tax collector and $t$ is the tax rate. The elasticity of taxable income is analogous to the elasticity of supply of labour, with $y$ playing the role of labour supply and $(1 - t)$ playing the role of the after tax wage of labour. Tax revenue, $R$, is

$$R = ty \tag{4.2}$$

and the elasticity of tax revenue with respect to the tax rate becomes

$$\varepsilon_{R,t} = (t/R)\delta R/\delta t = (1/y)[y + t\delta y/\delta t]$$
$$= 1 - (t/y)(\delta y/\delta(1 - t) = 1 - [t/(1 - t)]\varepsilon \tag{4.3}$$

As long as the Laffer curve is humped as in Figure 4.1, tax revenue, $R$, is maximized at the top of the Laffer curve where, by definition, $\varepsilon_{R,t} = 0$. The revenue-maximizing tax rate, $t^*$, is the rate for which

$$1 - [t^*/(1 - t^*)]\varepsilon = 0 \tag{4.4}$$

Thus, as long as $\varepsilon$ is invariant – the same regardless of the value of $t$ – the revenue-maximizing tax rate must be

$$t^* = 1/(1 + \varepsilon) \tag{4.5}$$

The revenue-maximizing tax rate, $t^*$, equals 100 per cent when $\varepsilon = 0$ meaning that $y$ is invariant and the supply curve of taxable income is vertical. It equals 50 per cent when $\varepsilon = 1$, it is 33⅓ per cent when $\varepsilon = 2$ and it is 0 per cent when $\varepsilon = $ infinity meaning that the supply curve is flat. If we can observe the elasticity of taxable income and can be confident that it is invariant, we can resolve the conflict between left and right over the location of the peak of the Laffer curve.

The revenue-maximizing tax rate can be estimated from Equation (4.5) if and only if $\varepsilon$ can be observed. For example, if a rise in the tax rate from 30 per cent to 34 per cent causes the tax base to shrink from $100 billion to $95 billion, the elasticity of taxable income would be 0.875, equal to $[5/100]/[0.04/(1 - 0.3)]$, and, assuming $\varepsilon$ to be invariant, the estimated revenue-maximizing tax rate would be about 53 per cent, equal to $1/(1 + 0.875)$.

From the definition of the elasticity of taxable income in Equation (4.1), it follows that the elasticity can only be invariant when $y$, $t$ and $\varepsilon$ are connected by a function

$$y = K(1 - t)^\varepsilon \tag{4.6}$$

where $K$ is a a positive constant, so that

$$R = Kt(1 - t)^\varepsilon \tag{4.7}$$

which is maximized at $t^*$ in accordance with Equation (4.5). Equation (4.7) requires that $R = 0$ when either $t = 0$ or $t = 1$, implying that the Laffer curve is humped as shown in Figure 4.1 rather than uniformly upward-sloping as shown in Figures 4.2(a) and 4.2(b).

Estimation of the revenue-maximizing tax rate in 'new tax responsiveness' literature has several critical features. It makes no reference to the mechanism by which taxable income responds to changes in the tax rate. It is equally valid when the supply curve of taxable income is due to tax evasion, to the labour–leisure choice or to any of the other ways that taxpayers respond to tax rates. It may refer to people in a particular tax bracket, typically the top bracket so that $t$ and $y$ are the tax rate and the average tax base among people in that bracket, or it may refer to averages in the economy as a whole. It takes no account of the progressivity of the tax structure. The new tax responsiveness literature cuts through a whole slew of difficulties, but only if its assumptions are correct.

Two questions immediately arise:

1   Given that taxable income changes over time for a variety of reasons – ordinary economic growth, the unemployment rate, fiscal policy and so on – how can one separate changes in $\Delta y$ due to changes in the tax rate as shown in Figure 4.1 from changes due to other considerations?
2   Can one be confident that the elasticity of taxable income observed today will be the same as the elasticity of taxable income at a different tax rate tomorrow?

Discussion of the first of these questions is just a brief review of literature on the new tax responsiveness literature. The focus of this chapter is on the second question, a question that can only be answered with reference to the mechanism presumed to be generating the Laffer curve. Whether the elasticity of taxable income remains unchanged when the tax rate rises or falls will be investigated when the elasticity of taxable income is generated by tax evasion and when it is generated by the labour–leisure choice.

The significance of the second question is illustrated in Figure 4.4, which shows two very different Laffer curves with the same values of $R$, $t$ and $dR/dt$ – and the same elasticity of taxable income – at the point $x$. The question becomes whether there is a way to determine which of these curves – or what other curve with the same elasticity of taxable income at the point $x$ – shows the true revenue-maximizing tax rate. The matter is settled immediately if the elasticity of taxable income is invariant throughout the true Laffer curve. The new tax responsiveness literature assumes that it is. Whether that is so is to be investigated in this chapter.

## Estimating the elasticity of taxable income and the revenue-maximizing tax rate

The principal difficulty in constructing this estimation is in distinguishing between changes in the tax base in response to changes in the tax rate and changes in the tax base reflecting other changes in the economy destined to occur regardless. It is not

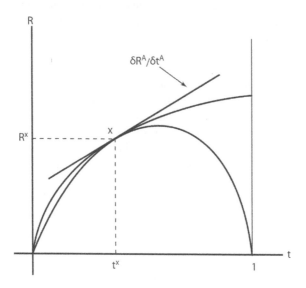

*Figure 4.4* Two possible Laffer curves with the same elasticity of taxable income.

sufficient just to observe the tax base before and after a change in the tax rate. To deal with this problem, estimates of the elasticity of taxable income are based upon the comparison of proportional changes in tax bases of two essentially similar groups, one confronted with a tax increase and the other not. Call the groups $J$ and $K$. Suppose that, initially, the two groups are taxed at the same rate, $t$, but that, as part of a general change in the tax structure, the tax rate on people in group $J$ is increased to $t + \Delta t$, while the tax rate on people in group $K$ remains unchanged at $t$. (Alternatively, $\Delta t$ may be the difference in the changes in their tax rates.) Both groups' tax bases may change over time, but the two groups are presumed to be sufficiently alike that their tax bases would have changed proportionally if the tax increase on people in group $J$ had not occurred. With percentage changes in the observed tax bases of groups $J$ and $K$ of $x$ and $y$, the percentage change in the tax base of group $J$ attributable to the increase in its tax rate becomes $x - y$.

A selection of estimates of the revenue-maximizing tax rate is presented in Table 4.1.

Suppose that, initially, both groups are taxed at a rate of 40 per cent, that the tax rate on group $J$ alone is increased from 40 per cent to 44 per cent while the tax rate on group $K$ remains unchanged at 40 per cent, and that, over a period spanning the change in the tax rate, the tax base of group $J$ is observed to rise by 9 per cent while the tax base of group $K$ is observed to rise by 12 per cent. From this information, the estimated elasticity of taxable income becomes

$$\varepsilon = [\Delta y/y]/[\Delta(1-t)/(1-t)] = [0.09 - 0.12]/[-0.04/(1-0.40)]$$
$$= [0.03]/[0.04/0.6] = 0.45 \qquad (4.8)$$

*Table 4.1* Estimates of the revenue-maximizing tax rate

| Author | Revenue-maximizing tax rate | |
|---|---|---|
| Clark (1945: 380) | 25% | Postulated a different mechanism constraining the tax rate |
| Stuart (1981: 1020) | 70% | Estimate for Sweden based up on elasticity of labour supply |
| Feige and McGee (1983: 511, table 1) | 32% to 91% | Depending upon estimated elasticities of supply in the observed and unobserved economy and upon the trade-off between sectors |
| Lindsey (1987: 202, table 8) | 40% | Introduces 'new tax response' estimation |
| Feldstein (1995: 565, table 2) | 25% to 50% | Elasticity of taxable income estimated to be between 1 and 3 |
| Diamond and Saez (2011: 171) | 73% | Estimate for top income bracket based upon the 'new tax response' |
| Goolsbee (2000: 375) | 70% to 100% | Elasticity of taxable income estimated to be between 0 and 0.4 |

Note: These estimates are not really comparable because they are based upon different assumptions about the response of tax base to tax rate.

and the estimated revenue-maximizing tax rate becomes

$$t^* = 1/[1 + 0.45] = 69 \text{ per cent} \tag{4.9}$$

There are many complications in this estimation procedure which account for the differences in the measures of the revenue-maximizing tax rate in Table 4.1. Typically, groups $J$ and $K$ are people in two adjacent tax brackets observed at times before and after the moment when tax rates on incomes in these brackets are changed. Both components – $[\delta y/y]$ and $[\delta(1 - t)/(1 - t)]$ – of the definition of $\varepsilon$ in Equation (4.1) present complications. These must be approximated by $[\Delta y/y]$ and $[\Delta(1 - t)/(1 - t)]$ where $\Delta y$ and $\Delta t$ are actual changes in the data. In measuring $\Delta(1 - t)/(1 - t)]$, it must be decided which taxes to take into account. In measuring $[\Delta y/y]$, a time period must be chosen over which the change in the tax base is observed. Specify the date of the tax chance as 0, and suppose the tax rate is observed $i$ years before and $i$ years after the change in the tax rate. With group $K$ as the control group, the estimate of $\Delta y$ for group $J$ becomes

$$\Delta y_J = y_{J,i} - y_{J,-i}[y_{K,i}/y_{K,-i}] \tag{4.10}$$

where $y_{J,i}$ is the observed tax base of group $J$ in year $i$, $y_{J,-i}$ is the observed tax base of group $J$ in year $-i$, $y_{K,i}$ is the observed tax base of group $K$ in year $i$ and $y_{K,-i}$ is the observed tax base of group $K$ in year $-i$.

The choice of $i$ matters because the timing of the impact of tax rate on tax base can occur in several ways with very different impacts upon estimates of $\Delta y_J$. Some possibilities are illustrated in Table 4.2. The table is constructed on the assumption that, initially, groups $J$ and $K$ are taxed at the same rate and that their tax bases would have changed proportionally over time in response to economic conditions in society as a whole – specifically, that the tax base in group $J$ would always be twice the tax base of group $K$ – if their tax rates remained the same. Then, on January 1 of year 1, the tax rate on group $J$ is raised, while the tax rate on group $K$ remains the same as before.

Ignore for the moment the last two rows of the table which will be explained later. The first column of the table identifies years before ($-i$) or after ($i$) the tax increase on people in group $J$. The second column shows the postulated tax base of the control group $K$ in each of these years. Numbers in this column are chosen arbitrarily. The remaining four columns show four alternative responses of the tax base of group $J$ to the tax increase: As shown in column (3), there may be no response, in which case the tax base of group $J$ remains at twice the tax base of group $K$. As shown in column (4), there may be a sudden and permanent decrease in tax base of group $J$ starting immediately after the tax increase; specifically, beginning in year 1, the tax base of group $J$ is assumed to become 2 less than it would otherwise be. As shown in column (5), the tax base of group $J$ may decrease gradually because it is costs less to make changes slowly than to make changes all at once. And as shown in the last column (6), if the tax increase is anticipated, there may be an increase in the observable tax base before the tax increase followed by a decrease afterwards, as taxpayers divert declared taxable income from a time when the tax rate is relatively high to a time when the tax rate is relatively low.

This final possibility is illustrated on the supposition that the tax increase has no effect upon the tax base except in the years immediately before and immediately after the tax increase. In year $-1$, the observable tax base rises from 20 to 23. Then, in year 1, tax base falls from 24 to 21, bringing it back to what it would be with no tax increase at all. Movement of part of the observable tax base from one year to another may be undertaken in several ways, among them by realizing capital gains or by cashing in stock options before rather than after a tax increase. Such opportunities are likely to be greater for the wealthy than for the poor.

The last two rows in the table show how the estimate in Equation (4.10) of the change, $\Delta y_J$, in the tax base of group $J$ is affected by the duration of the span over which the tax bases in groups $J$ and $K$ are observed. In the second to last row, the observations are over adjacent years, $-1$ and 1. In the last row, the observations are over six years from year $-3$ to year 3. By definition, $\Delta y_J$ is 0 whenever the tax increase has no impact on the tax base. A immediate and permanent reduction in the tax base causes the estimated reduction in the tax base ($-2$) to be the same regardless of the time span over which it is observed. A gradually increasing

Table 4.2 Alternative estimates of the effect upon the tax base of group $J$ of a tax increase at time 0 on group $J$ but not group $K$

| (1) years (i) before (−) or after (+) the tax increase | (2) tax base of group K | Implications of alternative assumptions about the effect of the tax increase at time 0 upon the tax base of group $J$ | | | |
|---|---|---|---|---|---|
| | | (3) no impact of taxation | (4) immediate and permanent contraction of tax base | (5) gradual contraction of the tax base after the year 0 | (6) switching part of the tax base from from year 1 to year −1 |
| −3 | 9 | 18 | 18 | 18 | 18 |
| −2 | 8 | 16 | 16 | 16 | 16 |
| −1 | 10 | 20 | 20 | 20 | 23 |
| 1 | 12 | 24 | 22 | 23 | 21 |
| 2 | 11 | 22 | 20 | 20 | 22 |
| 3 | 10 | 20 | 18 | 17 | 20 |
| $\Delta y_J$ {−1 to +1} | − | 0 | −2 | −1 | −6 |
| $\Delta y_J$ {−3 to +3} | − | 0 | −2 | −3 | 0 |

impact of the tax increase causes the estimated reduction in the tax base to be less when observed from year −1 to year 1 than when observed from year −3 to year 3. Substitution of the declared tax base from a year when tax is high to a year when tax is low is just the opposite. Observed from year −1 to year 1, the declared tax base of group $J$ falls by 6, i.e. $\Delta Y_J = -6$. Observed over a six year period from year −3 to year 3, there is no change in the declared tax base at all. The difference between Goolsbee's (2000) high estimate of the revenue-maximizing tax rate in the last row of Table 4.1 and the lower estimates in the rest of the table is due to this phenomenon.[3] Additional complications in the estimation of $\Delta Y_J$ arise from the possibility that, even without the tax increase, forces in the economy might have caused the tax bases of groups $J$ and $K$ to change at different rates.

The new tax responsiveness literature is a black box generating estimates ungrounded in any specific mechanism connecting tax base to tax rate. The estimates are what they are without specific reference to the reason why the base responds to rate. The tax-induced contraction of the tax base may be by the labour–leisure choice, increased do-it-yourself activity, illegal tax evasion, legal tax avoidance, out-migration of highly-taxed people, or some combination of these. Only the total outcome matters.

This is a considerable advantage, but there are disadvantages too. Appropriate public policy may depend on why taxable income is responds to changes in the tax rate. Tougher enforcement of the tax code might be especially warranted when tax evasion is the major influence on the elasticity of taxable income. An understanding of the innards of the black box might be helpful in deciding which of the estimates of the revenue-maximizing tax rate in Table 4.1 is more nearly correct. Also, as the sample of tax changes is small and as several arbitrary assumptions are required in the estimation of the elasticity of taxable income, it would be helpful to know whether the direction of the influence of tax rate on tax base is a necessary consequence of rational behaviour or just an observed fact at some given time and place.

The next two sections of this chapter deal with the constancy or variability of $\varepsilon$ as a reflection of tax evasion and of the labour–leisure choice. It will be shown that a) when the mechanism connecting base to rate is tax evasion, Equation (4.5) might be misleading because the elasticity of taxable income, $\varepsilon$, is not independent of the tax rate, and b) when the mechanism connecting base to rate is the labour–leisure choice, an increase in the tax rate need not induce taxpayers to diminish their tax base.

## Tax evasion

Recall the model of redistribution in the presence of tax evasion in Chapter 3 with taxable income, $y$, dependent on the a fixed pre-tax income, $Y$, the efficiency of tax collection, $\beta$, and the rate of tax, $t$,

$$y = (1 - \tau)Y = (1 - t/\beta)Y \qquad (4.11)$$

The Laffer curve connecting total tax revenue, $R$, and the tax rate, $t$, becomes

$$R = ty = t(1 - t/\beta)Y \tag{4.12}$$

and the derived revenue-maximizing tax rate becomes

$$t^{**} = \beta/2 \tag{4.13}$$

so that, for example, the revenue-maximizing tax rate is 25 per cent when $\beta = \frac{1}{2}$ but 50 per cent when $\beta = 1$ and 100 per cent when $\beta = 2$, as illustrated in Figure 3.2. It follows from Equation (4.11) that the elasticity of taxable income is

$$\varepsilon = [(1-t)/y][\delta y/\delta(1-t)] = [(1-t)/\{(1-t/\beta)Y\}][Y/\beta] = (1-t)/(\beta-t) \tag{4.14}$$

which is clearly dependent on $t$ and which falls to 0 as $t$ approaches 100 per cent.

There is here a marked discrepancy between the *inferred* dependence on the tax rate of the elasticity of taxable income in the tax evasion story and the *assumed* constancy of the elasticity of taxable income in the new tax responsiveness literature. Revenue-maximizing tax rates differ accordingly. In the tax evasion story, $t^{**} = \beta/2$ as shown in Equation (4.13). In the new tax responsiveness literature, $t^* = 1/(1+\varepsilon)$ as shown in Equation (4.5). Suppose, for example, that $\beta = 2$ so that the revenue-maximizing tax rate is 100 per cent, as implied by Equation (4.13) and may be read off Figure 3.3 in Chapter 3, and suppose the economy is observed when the actual tax rate is 20 per cent. In accordance with Equation (4.14), the observed value of $\varepsilon$ would have to be 0.44 (equal to $(1 - 0.2)/(2 - 0.2)$) implying, if $\varepsilon$ were invariant, a revenue-maximizing tax rate of about 70 per cent (equal to $1/(1+0.44)$). In an economy where deadweight loss is due to tax evasion, the new tax responsive literature would mistakenly infer that the revenue-maximizing tax rate is 70 per cent when, in fact, tax increases would generate additional revenue all the way up to 100 per cent.

Bear in mind that the revenue-maximizing tax rate is significantly higher than anybody with any income at all would actually favour. Recall the example surrounding Equation (3.22) of the Chapter 3 where $\beta$ is assumed to be 3/2 implying a revenue-maximizing tax rate of 75 per cent, but where the median voter's preferred tax rate is only 34 per cent. The impression that the revenue-maximizing tax rate is lower than is actually the case may influence the public's choice of tax rates.

Three features of the tax evasion story should be emphasized before the labour–leisure story is introduced. First, the elasticity of taxable income is necessarily positive, for the tax base always contracts when the tax rate is increased. Second, the Laffer curve may, but need not, be humped. Depending on the efficiency of tax collection, the Laffer curve may instead rise gradually all the way to a tax rate of 100 per cent as illustrated in Figure 4.2a. Third, as long as $\beta$ is invariant, the impact of tax rate on tax revenue is independent of how tax revenue is spent. Whether tax revenue is redistributed as assumed in Chapter 3 or spent on public goods such as the army and the police, has no impact at all on the shape of the Laffer curve. All this changes in the world of the labour–leisure choice.

## The labour–leisure choice

When the Laffer curve is a reflection of the labour–leisure choice rather than tax evasion, the elasticity of taxable income as defined in Equation (4.1) and the elasticity of supply of labour are one and the same, and the Laffer curve is humped with a revenue-maximizing tax rate of less than 100 per cent if and only if the supply curve of labour is upward sloping.

Suppose taxable income, $y$, is a function of the supply of labour, $H$,

$$y = wH \tag{4.15}$$

where $w$ is the wage rate, assumed to be invariant, and $H$, mnemonic for hours of labour, is a function of the net, post-tax wage, $w(1 - t)$. The worker responds to net wage and, if net wage is reduced, does not care whether it is because $w$ has fallen or $t$ has increased. Starting with the elasticity of taxable income, $\varepsilon$, in Equation (4.1), it follows that

$$\varepsilon = [(1 - t)/y]\delta y/\delta(1 - t) = [(1 - t)/wH]\delta wH/\delta(1 - t)$$
$$= [w(1 - t)/H]\delta H/\delta w(1 - t) = \varepsilon_{H,(1-t)} \tag{4.16}$$

where, since $w$ is assumed to be invariant, $\varepsilon_{H,(1-t)}$ is the elasticity of supply of labour. It follows at once from Equation (4.3) that the elasticity of tax revenue to the tax rate is

$$\varepsilon_{R,t} = 1 - [t/(1 - t)]\varepsilon_{H,(1-t)} \tag{4.17}$$

Since $t/(1 - t)$ goes from 0 to infinity as $t$ goes from 0 to 1, the elasticity of tax revenue with respect to the tax rate is necessarily positive when $\varepsilon_{H,(1-t)}$ is negative, but if $\varepsilon_{H,(1-t)}$ is positive, signifying that the supply curve of labour is upward sloping, then the elasticity of tax revenue to tax rate must remain positive when $t$ is low but turn negative at some $t$ less than 1. The Laffer curve is only humped when the supply curve of labour is upward sloping; the Laffer curve is uniformly upward sloping when the supply curve of labour is backward bending.

To illustrate this proposition, consider the upward-sloping and backward-bending supply curves in Figures 4.5a and 4.5b with the supply of labour, $H$, on the horizontal axis and the net wage, $w(1 - t)$, on the vertical axis. In both figures, it is understood that $\Delta t$ is positive so that $\Delta(1 - t)$ is automatically negative and $w(1 - t) > w(1 - t - \Delta t)$. Hours of work, $H$ is a function of $t$ and $\Delta H$ is defined as $H(t + \Delta t) - H(t)$. In Figure 4.5a, $\Delta H < 0$ meaning that hours of work decline

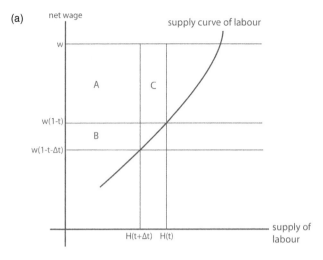

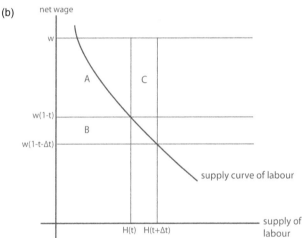

*Figure 4.5* Upward-sloping and backward-bending supply curves of labour.

as the tax rate is increased. In Figure 4.5b, $\Delta H > 0$ meaning that hours of work increase as the tax rate is increased.

In both versions of Figure 4.5, the elasticity of supply of labour is

$$\varepsilon_{H,(1-t)} = [\Delta H/H]/[\Delta(1-t)/(1-t)] \tag{4.18}$$

where $[\Delta(1 - t)/(1 - t)] < 0$ because the net wage falls in response to a tax increase, but $[\Delta H/H] < 0$ when the supply curve is upward sloping and $[\Delta H/H] > 0$ when the supply curve is backward bending. In other words,

$\varepsilon_{H,(1-t)} > 0$ when the supply curve is upward-sloping, and $\varepsilon_{H,(1-t)} < 0$ when the supply curve is backward bending.

With the upward-sloping supply curve as shown on Figure 4.5a,

$$R(t) = wtH(t) = \text{area } A + \text{area } B \tag{4.19}$$

and

$$R(t + \Delta t) = w(t + \Delta t)H(t + \Delta t) = \text{area } A + \text{area } C \tag{4.20}$$

where $H(t + \Delta t)$ and $R(t + \Delta t)$ are to be understood as the values of $H$ and $R$ when the tax rate is $t + \Delta t$. Hence,

$$\begin{aligned} \Delta R &= R(t + \Delta t) - R(t) = \text{area } B - \text{area } C \\ &= wH\Delta t - wt|\Delta H| = wH\Delta t + wt\Delta H \end{aligned} \tag{4.21}$$

where $\Delta H < 0$ and

$$\begin{aligned} \varepsilon_{R,t} &= [\Delta R/R]/[\Delta t/t] = \{(wH\Delta t + wt\Delta H)/(wHt)\}\{t/\Delta t\} \\ &= \{wHt + wt^2\Delta H/\Delta t\}/\{wHt\} = 1 - [t/(1-t)]\varepsilon_{H,(1-t)} \end{aligned} \tag{4.22}$$

which is Equation (4.17) once again where $\varepsilon_{H,(1-t)} > 0$ so that the Laffer curve must be humped.

Except for a reversal in the sign of $\varepsilon_{H,(1-t)}$, the story is the same for the backward-bending supply curve in Figure 4.5b. Now, since $\Delta H > 0$,

$$\begin{aligned} \Delta R &= R(t + \Delta t) - R(t) = \text{area } B + \text{area } C \\ &= wH\Delta t + wt\Delta H \end{aligned} \tag{4.23}$$

from which Equation (4.22) follows immediately with the exception that now $\varepsilon_{H,(1-t)} < 0$ because $\Delta H$ is positive whenever $\Delta t$ is positive. When the supply curve of labour is upward sloping, there is a revenue-maximizing tax rate for which area $B = \text{area } C$, and $\Delta R = 0$. When the supply curve of labour is backward-bending, the elasticity of tax revenue to tax rate is always positive and there is no revenue-maximizing tax rate of less than 100 per cent.[4]

### *Land and labour*

The model of labour–leisure choice is a contraction of a more general model. The derivation of the elasticity of tax revenue to tax rate in Equation (4.17) is based on the assumption, expressed in Equation (4.15), that output is produced with labour alone and that the marginal product of labour, $w$, is invariant. By contrast, if output depends exclusively on the availability of land, then

$$R = tmD \tag{4.24}$$

where $m$ is a technical parameter and $D$ is the supply of land which is assumed to be invariant. Then

$$\varepsilon_{Rt} = 1 \qquad (4.25)$$

and the Laffer curve must be an upward sloping straight line with tax revenue maximized at 100 per cent.

An intermediate case is where output depends on both land and labour but only labour varies in response to the tax rate. Suppose the production function is Cobb–Douglas.

$$Y = kL^\alpha D^{1-\alpha} \qquad (4.26)$$

where $k$ and $\alpha$ are technical parameters and where $\alpha$ is labour's share of income in equilibrium. If so, then[5]

$$\varepsilon_{Rt} = 1 - \alpha[t/(1-t)]\varepsilon_{H(1-t)} \qquad (4.27)$$

which is the same as Equation (4.17) except for the addition of $\alpha$. The Laffer curve is still humped as long as the supply curve of labour is upward sloping because $\varepsilon_{Rt}$ falls to 0 when $t$ rises to 1, but the peak of the curve is at a higher tax rate than when output is produced with labour alone.

The term $D$ in Equation (4.26) might refer to the capital stock rather than to land, but with an important qualification. The capital stock might be affected by the tax rate, especially in the long run through the intermediary of the rate of saving. To deal with this matter properly, it would be necessary to replace the atemporal model in this chapter with a model where past, present and future are all taken into account. Other aspects of the economy might also be important. The production function need not be Cobb–Douglas. As mentioned elsewhere in this chapter, the taxpayer's trade-off in use between goods and leisure may depend upon how tax revenue is spent. Regardless, the more complicated the story, the more difficult it becomes to infer the revenue-maximizing tax rate from the observed elasticity of taxable income at any time and place.[6]

Summarizing the argument so far, when the tax base is influenced by the tax rate through the labour–leisure choice rather than as a result of tax evasion, the shape of the Laffer curve depends critically on the elasticity of supply of labour, whether the worker's response to an increase in the tax rate is to work less for pay, diverting time to less expensive leisure or do-it-yourself activities or, as Frank Knight suggested in the quotation at the beginning of this chapter, to work more hours in order to maintain the consumption of goods. To look more closely at this question, the focus of this chapter now turns from the elasticity of the supply of labour to the elasticity of substitution between goods and leisure at the foundation of the supply curve. This is done in two stages: first on the assumption that indifference curves for goods and leisure are L-shaped, then with allowance for the possible range of the elasticity from 0 to infinity.

### Perfect complementarity between goods and leisure

A person has a fixed supply of time, designated as 1, to be allocated between work, $H$, and leisure, $L$, so that

$$L(t) + H(t) = 1 \qquad (4.28)$$

Perfect complementarity between goods and leisure means that indifference curves are L-shaped as illustrated in Figure 4.6, with goods, $G$, on the vertical axis and leisure, $L$, on the horizontal axis. The path of the vertices of indifference curves, called the 'wasteless combinations' curve, is upward sloping. The wasteless combinations curve shows all combinations of goods and leisure for which neither more goods nor more leisure would increase the person's utility unless combined with more of the other.

The response to taxation is illustrated in Figure 4.7, an extension of Figure 4.6 with the same 'wasteless combinations' curve but with the addition of the person's budget constraints in the absence of taxation and when a tax rate of $t$ is imposed. To avoid cluttering the diagram, the indifference curves are not shown. In the absence of taxation, the budget constraint of a person with a wage $w$ is the diagonal line with slope $w$ originating at the point 1 on the horizontal axis. The highest attainable indifference curve is at the crossing of the budget constraint and the wasteless combinations curve, yielding a combination, $G(0)$ and $L(0)$, of goods and leisure as indicated by the point $a$. It is immediately evident that one's allocation of time between labour and leisure is dependent on the tax rate. When a tax $t$ is imposed, the taxpayer's net wage falls from $w$ to $w(1-t)$ causing a counterclockwise swing in the budget constraint. Once again, the taxpayer, seeking

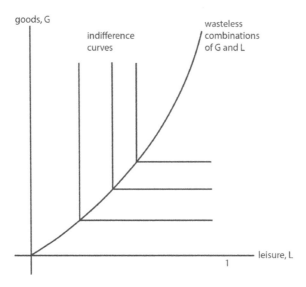

*Figure 4.6* Indifference curves with no substitution between goods and leisure.

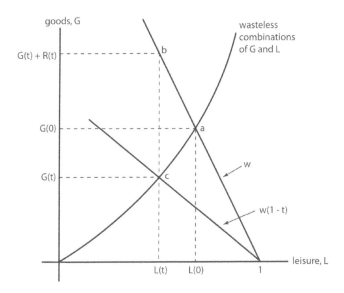

*Figure 4.7* A person's response to taxation.

to maximize utility, chooses a combination of goods and leisure at the crossing of the (new) budget constraint and the wasteless combination curve, yielding a combination, $G(t)$ and $L(t)$, of goods and leisure as shown by the point $c$.

An increase in the tax rate, $t$, represented by a counterclockwise rotation of the budget constraint, leads to a decrease in leisure, $L(t)$ and a corresponding increase in work, $H(t)$, ensuring that $\delta H/\delta t > 0$. Since revenue acquired from this person is

$$R(t) = twH(t) \tag{4.29}$$

The Laffer curve becomes steadily upward sloping as shown in a variant of Equation (4.3).

$$\varepsilon_{R,t} = 1 - (t/(1-t))[(w(1-t)/H)\delta H/\delta w(1-t)] > 0 \tag{4.30}$$

regardless of the value of $t$. Tax rate and tax base rise or fall together, guaranteeing that tax revenue increases with the tax rate all the way to 100 per cent.

Consider the special case where the wasteless combinations curve is an upward-sloping straight line with slope $\theta$. Along any such line,

$$\theta L = (1-t)(1-L)w \tag{4.31a}$$

because $G = \theta L$ along the wasteless combinations curve, and $G = (1-t)(1-L)w$ where $(1-L)$ is the hours of work required to procure an amount of goods $G$ when tax at a rate $t$ is imposed.

Equivalently,

$$L = (1-t)w/[\theta + (1-t)w) \tag{4.31b}$$

so that the Laffer curve becomes

$$R = t(1-L)w = \theta tw/[\theta + (1-t)w] \tag{4.32}$$

This Laffer curve is not humped. It starts at $R = 0$ at $t = 0$ and then rises steadily as $t$ increases, reaching a maximum of $w$ – which is as large as output can ever be when the endowment of time is set equal to $1$ – at $t = 1$.

This result is subject to an important qualification. Tax revenue is shown to increases steadily with the tax rate on the assumption that the taxpayer's labour–leisure choice is unaffected by how tax revenue is spent, as might be the case when revenue is to finance foreign aid, the army and the police. There is a very different outcome when tax revenue is redistributed.

Without abandoning the assumption that goods and leisure are perfect complements, suppose all public revenue is redistributed, increasing consumption of goods without affecting consumption of leisure except in so far as the taxpayer chooses to work more, or to work less, in response to a tax-financed transfer of goods. A distinction is required here between a person's tax paid, $R$, and subsidy received, $S$, where the two may be but are not necessarily the same.

With tax revenue completely redistributed and with perfect complementarity between goods and leisure, the supply of labour becomes invariant as illustrated in Figure 4.8. In the absence of any tax or subsidy, a person with a pre-tax wage $w$ consumes $\underline{L}$ units of leisure and $\underline{G}$ units of goods as represented by the point $a$. Provision of a subsidy, $S$, raises the initial endowment from 1 unit of labour and no goods to 1 unit of labour and $S$ goods as represented by the point $b$ placed a distance $S$ above the horizontal axis. Now suppose that there is imposed a tax at a rate just high enough to pay for the subsidy. Tax revenue, $R$, must be such that $R = S$. Being no better off and no worse off on account of the tax and subsidy together, the person's behaviour is unchanged. The upward shift in the person's budget constraint brought about the subsidy is exactly matched by the downward shift brought about by the imposition of the tax to finance it.

For any subsidy, $S$, there is some tax rate – call it $t(S)$ – that leaves leisure, goods, labour, $L$, $G$ and $(1-L)$, exactly as they would be in the absence of all tax and subsidy. The required tax rate is such that the slope of the post-subsidy budget constraint – the line starting at $B$ and with slope $w(1-t)$ – passes through the point $a$. When goods and leisure are prefect complements, tax-financed redistribution has no effect upon the welfare of the taxpayer for whom the subsidy is just equal to the tax paid. Otherwise, with some substitutability in use between goods and leisure, a tax-financed subsidy in a society of identical people makes everybody worse off because everybody bears the cost of actions – working less or hiding income from the tax collector – to reduce one's tax bill.

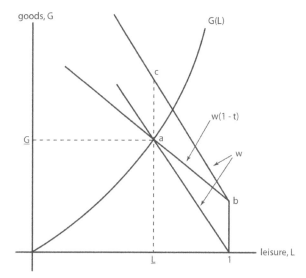

*Figure 4.8* Taxation and redistribution leave labour supply unchanged.

Note: $R = ca$ = the height of the point $b$ above the horizontal axis.

In a society where people's wages differ, where total tax revenue is redistributed equally as in a negative income tax and where goods and leisure are perfect complements, the net beneficiaries of redistribution – people with less than average wage – are induced by the system to work less, and the net contributors are induced to work more. If, in addition, the income distribution is skewed in the usual way so that the median wage is less than the average wage, the median voter (the person with the median wage) favours a tax rate of 100 per cent.

A uniform tax rate of 100 per cent may be impossible without redistribution when a minimal consumption of goods and leisure is required, but a top marginal rate of as much as 100 per cent remains feasible as illustrated in Figure 4.9. The figure compares the effects of a simple form of progressive taxation upon two taxpayers with identical L-shaped indifference curves but with different wages. One taxpayer has a high wage, $w^2$, and the other has a low wage, $w^1$. The tax schedule has three components: a uniform subsidy, $S$, a uniform tax rate $t$ on all income less than some specified amount and a tax rate of 100 per cent on all income above that amount. The figure is drawn on the assumption that only the person with the high wage ever earns enough for any of his income to be subject to the higher tax rate, but that the entire income of the person with the low wage is taxed at the low rate $t$. Thus, each person has two budget constraints, a pre-tax constraint represented by the upward-sloping straight lines through the point 1 on the horizontal axis, and a post-tax budget constraint represented by the kinked heavy lines. Each person's chosen supply of labour is where the post-tax budget

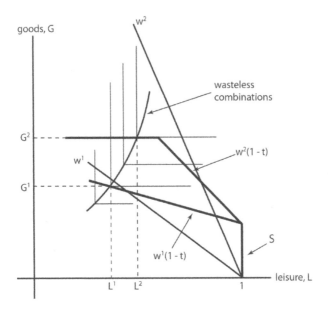

*Figure 4.9* Progressive taxation with a top marginal tax rate of 100 per cent.

constraints cuts the wasteless combinations curve, placing them on the highest attainable indifference curve.

The figure could easily have been drawn with more than two tax brackets and with a top rate of less than 100 per cent. The reason for the special assumption about the top bracket is to demonstrate that, though a tax rate of 100 per cent is virtually impossible when all income is taxed at one flat rate, a top rate of 100 per cent becomes possible when goods and leisure are perfect complements.[7] In fact, a top rate of more than 100 per cent could be revenue-maximizing on the extreme assumptions that have been made so far. The rationale for these assumptions is not that they are likely to be valid in practice, but to add weight to the argument that the revenue-maximizing top rate may be higher than is often supposed and to serve as preface to the discussion of the substitutability between goods and leisure.

Before proceeding to the more general case with substitutability in use between goods and leisure, note that the tax evasion story and the simple labour–leisure story as told so far have completely opposite implications about the elasticity of taxable income. In the tax evasion story, the elasticity of taxable income is necessarily positive; $\varepsilon > 0$ almost by definition. In the labour–leisure story with perfect complementarity, the elasticity of taxable income is necessarily negative; $\varepsilon < 0$ as people work more to preserve their desired balance between goods and leisure. The contrast may have empirical implications. Any observed value of the elasticity of taxable income pertains to a group of people within which the elasticity might be positive for some and negative for others. The observed $\varepsilon$ can only be an average which may or may not be independent of the tax rate.

## The elasticity of substitution in use between goods and leisure

The question then arises of how large the substitutability between goods and leisure can be before the revenue-maximizing tax rate falls below 100 per cent. Substitutability is introduced by means of a utility function with a constant elasticity of substitution (CES) in use between goods and leisure.

$$u = u(G, L) = \{mG^{\rho} + nL^{\rho}\}^{1/\rho} \tag{4.33}$$

where, to keep matters simple, $m$ and $n$ are both set equal to 1, where $\rho$ is a transformation of the elasticity of substitution in use, $\sigma$,[8] between goods and leisure and where, with no redistribution of income, the attainable $G$ depends on the wage rate, $w$, the tax rate, $t$, and the supply of labour, $H$,

$$G = wH(1 - t) = w(1 - L)(1 - t) \tag{4.34}$$

Maximizing utility with respect to the budget constraint yields a first order condition

$$(G/L)^{\rho-1} = 1/w(1 - t) \tag{4.35}$$

Replacing $G$ with $wH(1 - t)$ from Equation (4.34), replacing $L$ with $1 - H$, and recognizing that $\sigma = 1/(1 - \rho)$ as shown in note 8, Equation (4.35) is converted to

$$[H/(1 - H)]^{\rho-1}[w(1 - t)]^{\rho} = 1 \tag{4.36}$$

from which, recognizing that $\sigma = 1/(1 - \rho)$, it follows that

$$H = 1/[w(1 - t)]^{1-\sigma} + 1] \tag{4.37}$$

so that

$$\delta H/\delta(1 - t) = (\sigma - 1)H^2 w^{1-\sigma}(1 - t)^{-\sigma} \tag{4.38}$$

which is positive or negative depending on whether $\sigma > 1$ or $\sigma < 1$. The same is true of the elasticity of taxable income.

$$\varepsilon = [(1 - t)/H][\delta H/\delta(1 - t)] = (\sigma - 1)Hw^{1-\sigma}(1 - t)^{1-\sigma} \tag{4.39}$$

If $\sigma > 1$ indicating that goods and leisure are quite substitutable in use, then $\delta H/\delta(1 - t) > 0$ and $\varepsilon > 0$ as well so that the response to a tax increase is to *decrease* the supply of labour, substituting leisure for goods because goods have become more expensive. If $\sigma < 1$, indicating that goods and leisure are less substitutable in use, then $\delta H/\delta(1 - t) < 0$ and $\varepsilon < 0$ as well, so that the response to a tax increase is to *increase* the supply of labour, working more to make up the lost income as Knight claimed (as quoted in Robbins, 1930), generating a convex Laffer curve as was the case with perfect complementarity between goods and leisure. In either case, as shown in Equation (4.39), the elasticity of taxable income depends on $t$ so that revenue-maximizing tax rate cannot be predicted from $\varepsilon$ in accordance with Equation (4.4). If $\sigma = 1$, then $\varepsilon = 0$ meaning that the tax base is independent of the tax rate so that the Laffer curve is an upward-sloping straight line. The CES production function in Equation (4.33) reduces to a Cobb–Douglas function in that case.[9]

Equation (4.28) shows $\varepsilon$ as a function of $t$ regardless of whether tax revenue is maximized, but it follows immediately from Equation (4.4) that

$$\varepsilon = (1-t)/t \tag{4.40}$$

when tax revenue is maximized. Thus, from Equation (4.39) and (4.40) together, it follows that tax revenue is maximized when

$$(1-t)/t = (\sigma - 1)Hw^{1-\sigma}(1-t)^{1-\sigma} \tag{4.41}$$

which holds for some $t$ less than 100 per cent as long as $\sigma > 1$. Other things equal, the greater the elasticity of substitution, the lower the revenue-maximizing $t$ must be.

From Equation (4.37), it follows that the taxpayer's Laffer curve – tax payment denominated in goods as a function of the tax rate – becomes

$$R = Htw = tw/[w(1-t)^{1-\sigma} + 1] \tag{4.42}$$

from which tax paid may be computed as a function of the tax rate, the elasticity of substitution and the wage rate.

Table 4.3 shows tax paid as a proportion of a person's income as computed from Equation (4.42) for a selection of tax rates, $t$, from 0 to 100 per cent, for a selection

*Table 4.3* Tax revenue as a function of the elasticity of substitution and the tax rate

| | $\sigma = 0$ | $\sigma = 0.5$ | $\sigma = 1$ | $\sigma = 1.5$ | $\sigma = 2$ | $\sigma = 3$ | $\sigma = 5$ |
|---|---|---|---|---|---|---|---|
| $t = 0$ | 0 | 0 | 0 | 0 | 0 | 0 | 0 |
| $t = 0.1$ | 0.0526 | 0.0513 | 0.05 | 0.0487 | 0.0474 | 0.0448 | 0.0396 |
| $t = 0.2$ | 0.1111 | 0.1056 | 0.1 | 0.0944 | 0.0889 | 0.0780 | 0.05812* |
| $t = 0.3$ | 0.1765 | 0.1633 | 0.15 | 0.1367 | 0.1235 | 0.0987 | 0.05808 |
| $t = 0.4$ | 0.25 | 0.2254 | 0.2 | 0.1746 | 0.15 | 0.1059* | 0.0459 |
| $t = 0.5$ | 0.3333 | 0.2929 | 0.25 | 0.2071 | 0.1667 | 0.1 | 0.2071 |
| $t = 0.6$ | 0.4286 | 0.3675 | 0.3 | 0.2325 | 0.1714* | 0.0828 | 0.0150 |
| $t = 0.7$ | 0.5385 | 0.4523 | 0.35 | 0.2477* | 0.1615 | 0.0578 | 0.0056 |
| $t = 0.8$ | 0.6667 | 0.5528 | 0.4 | 0.2472 | 0.1333 | 0.0308 | 0.0013 |
| $t = 0.9$ | 0.8182 | 0.6838 | 0.45 | 0.2162 | 0.0818 | 0.0089 | 0.0001 |
| $t = 1$ | 1* | 1* | 0.5* | 0 | 0 | 0 | 0 |

Note: The revenue-maximizing tax rate for each elasticity of substitution is indicated by *.

of elasticities of substitution, $\sigma$, from 0 to 5 and for the special case where $w = 1$. Combinations of $t$ and $\sigma$ indicated by * indicate the revenue-maximizing tax rates for each $\sigma$.

Several features of the table should be noted.

- The numbers in the table show the Laffer curve to be humped – maximizing tax revenue at a rate of less than 100 per cent – if and only if the elasticity of substitution in use between goods and leisure is greater than 1.
- From Equation (4.42), it follows immediately that, regardless of the tax rate, exactly half of the taxpayer's available time is devoted to labour when the elasticity of substitution between goods and leisure is exactly 1, so that $R = Ht = t/2$. The Laffer curve is an upward-sloping straight line with a maximal revenue of ½.
- When the elasticity of substitution is greater than 1, tax revenue is always maximized at a tax rate of less than 100 per cent, a rate beyond which the revenue loss from the diversion from labour to leisure caused by an increase in the tax rate exceeds the revenue gain from the higher tax on what is left of the original base. For each value of $\sigma$, the maximal revenue is indicated by *.
- The higher the elasticity of substitution, the lower the revenue-maximizing tax rate. At $\sigma = 1$, the revenue-maximizing tax rate is 100 per cent. At $\sigma = 1.5$, the revenue-maximizing tax rate falls to 70 per cent. At $\sigma = 2$, the revenue-maximizing tax rate falls to 60 per cent. At $\sigma = 3$, the revenue-maximizing tax rate falls to 40 per cent. At $\sigma = 5$, the revenue-maximizing tax rate falls to 20 per cent.
- There is an imposed symmetry in the utility function of Equation (4.33); the rate of substitution between goods and leisure is assumed to depend on their ratio alone and is unaffected by a proportional increase or decrease in both together. That restriction does not apply to the L-shaped indifference curves in Figure 4.6.

## Choosing the Laffer curve

An implicit assumption in all of the models discussed so far is that the Laffer curve is given rather than chosen, a feature of technology and markets not subject to influence by public policy. A point on the Laffer curve may be chosen, but the curve itself may not. The assumption is false.

Consider tax evasion. As illustrated in Figure 3.2, the shape of the Laffer curve has been assumed to depend on the efficiency of tax collection, $\beta$, looked upon as an unalterable fact of nature. This depiction of tax evasion is adopted for simplicity, allowing tax revenue to be easily derived from the tax rate.

In reality, there is no simple relation between the cost of tax evasion and the amount of income concealed. There is always some chance that tax evasion will be detected, causing the expected cost of tax evasion to depend not just upon the amount of income concealed, but upon public expenditure to detect tax evasion and upon the severity of punishment when tax evasion is detected.[10] It is as though $\beta$ were an increasing function of the severity of punishment, so that, by choosing the severity of punishment, the government is choosing one among the Laffer curves displayed in Figure 3.2. It is arguable, paraphrasing a well-known saying by Gary Becker, that we should hang people for tax violations, driving $\beta$ (or its counterpart in a more realistic model of taxation) to infinity, causing the Laffer curve to be an upward-sloping straight line and enabling society to choose whatever tax rate it prefers without having to worry about the effect of tax rate on tax base.[11]

There is a conflict here between rich and poor, the rich opposing severity of punishment for tax evasion not just to avoid punishment when tax evasion is detected, but to generate a Laffer curve with a low revenue-maximizing tax rate. Tax loopholes, designation of some income as capital gains, and tolerance of off-shore accounts tend to be of special benefit to the rich, and are all comparable to a lessening of the efficiency of tax collection, causing the elasticity of taxable income, $\varepsilon$ in Equation (4.1) to be higher for the rich than for the poor. The argument adds weight to the case for closing loopholes as well as to the case for moderate top tax rates.

A different ambiguity in the Laffer curve emerges when the elasticity of taxable income is a reflection of the labour–leisure choice. In that case, tax revenue comes to depend not just on the tax rate but on how public revenue is spent and how public expenditure affects the supply of labour. An implicit assumption in the model of the labour–leisure choice as set out above, a variation of Equation (3.63) in Chapter 3, is that

$$W = W(u(G, L), R) \qquad (4.43)$$

where $W$ is the taxpayer's welfare as a function of private utility, $u$, and public goods, $R$, where private utility depends on private goods and leisure, and where public expenditure per person and tax revenue per person are one and the same. Think of public expenditure as devoted exclusively to the purchase of public goods, such as the army, the police and foreign aid, with no influence on how the taxpayer allocates his time between labour and leisure. The taxpayer chooses $G$ and $L$ to maximize $u$ subject to a budget constraint $G = w(1 - t)(1 - L)$, causing the Laffer curve to be independent of how tax revenue is spent.

That is not the only possibility. Suppose instead that part of public revenue is redistributed so that

$$W = W(u(G, L), R - S) \qquad (4.44)$$

where $S$ is redistribution per person and $G = w((1 - t)(1 - L) + S$, so that per capita expenditure on public goods is reduced from $R$ to $R - S$. The increase in $G$ over and above what it would be without the subsidy causes the taxpayer to supply somewhat less labour, reducing the slope of the Laffer curve as illustrated in Figure 4.10 which is an extension of Figure 4.8.

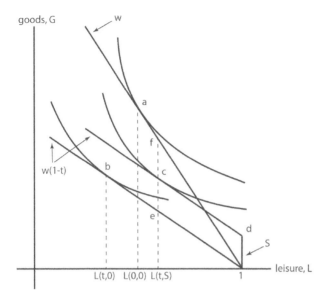

*Figure 4.10* Redistribution and labour supply.

Now leisure becomes $L(t, S)$, a function of the tax rate and the subsidy. With neither tax nor subsidy, the person's chosen combination of goods and leisure is at the point $a$ and the corresponding the supply of labour is $[1 - L(0, 0)]$. When taxation at a rate $t$ is imposed but none of tax revenue is redistributed, the person's chosen combination of goods and leisure is at the point $b$ and the supply of labour increases to $[1 - L(t, 0)]$ meaning that the Laffer curve is convex rather than humped as illustrated in Figure 4.2. The subsidy, $S$, is shown in the figure as changing the taxpayer's initial endowment from 1 unit of time and no goods to 1 unit of time and $S$ goods, as indicated by the point $d$. From that starting point, the taxpayer chooses a combination of goods and leisure is at the point c, reducing the supply of labour from $[1 - L(t, 0)]$ to $[1 - L(t, S]$, lowering the Laffer curve and increasing its curvature. Other public expenditures may have the opposite effect. By increasing the demand for cars, expenditure on roads may divert time from leisure to goods.

In short, the Laffer curve and the revenue-maximizing tax rate are chosen rather than found. Tax revenue depends not just on the tax rate, but on the severity of punishment for tax evasion and on the composition of public expenditure.

## Starvation

It has been argued so far that the revenue-maximizing tax rate may well rise to 100 per cent, due in the tax evasion story to the efficiency of tax collection or in the labour–leisure story to the backward-bending supply curve of labour. One may well protest that this cannot be so. At a tax rate of 100 per cent, all of one's income is appropriated by the tax collector with nothing left over for the taxpayer at all. There would be nothing to eat. There would be no point in working. The Laffer curve must surely be humped after all.

Suppose, to take an extreme example, that the efficiency of tax collection is infinite as illustrated in the top curve of Figure 3.2. Then, at a tax rate of 100 per cent and as long as tax revenue is not redistributed, tax revenue uses up the entire national income, with nothing left over for food, housing or clothing. An unambiguous implication of the model, this in nonetheless impossible. The culprit here is the assumption that pre-tax income $Y$ is invariant. If instead a subsistence income were required, so that $Y$ falls unless post-tax, post-transfer income, $I$, exceeds some given amount, the Laffer curve would decline at very high tax rates and a tax rate of 100 per cent would no longer possible. Similarly in the labour–leisure model, the wage, $w$, which was assumed to be constant, may decline sharply unless some subsistence combination of $G$ and $L$ is attained.

On the other hand, a top marginal tax rate of as high as 100 per cent may be sometimes be possible. It may be possible in the circumstances of Figure 4.9 where tax rates of less than 100 per cent on income in lower tax brackets leave the wealthy tax payer with post-tax income above the subsistence level. It may also be possible in the tax evasion model when $\beta$ is low enough that the required subsistence income is provided by the difference between income concealed from the tax collector and the cost of concealment. Hiding income from the tax collector and diverting time from work for pay to do-it-yourself activities are alike in that a residue of consumption may preserved no matter how high the tax rate happens to be.

Talk of tax rates of 100 per cent may be a deliberate exaggeration of the general principle that the Laffer curve may remain upward sloping even at rates higher than anybody would be inclined to impose. Imagine a tax schedule of 50 per cent on income up to $100,000 a year and 95 per cent on income above that limit. A person who would work hard enough to earn $300,000 if income were untaxed may work just as hard when income is taxed at these rates. With declining marginal utility of income, an extra income of $10,000 (i.e. 5 per cent of $200,000) may provide as much of an incentive when one's income would otherwise be $50,000 as an extra income of $200,000 when one's income would otherwise be $100,000.

Influence on entrepreneurship can go either way. High taxation may deter innovation. Better take a safe and steady job if most of the benefit of successful innovation will be taxed away. On the other hand, inherently risky innovation may be encouraged by the infrastructure and social safety net financed by taxation, placing a floor on what the innovator stands to lose if his business fails. Imagine an entrepreneur with some chance of making a great fortune and some chance of bankruptcy and destitution, where the probabilities depend on the entrepreneur's diligence and inventiveness, so that hard work today reduces the risk of bankruptcy tomorrow. It may be too late to slack off by the time the entrepreneur knows whether earnings are high enough to the subject to the top marginal tax rate. Or consider the incentives of highly paid executives whose incomes may reflect productivity, but may be no more than trust wages, set to ensure the executive's loyalty, or a return on speculation where the gainer's win is at the expense of other people. A top marginal tax rate of 100 per cent on income above, say, a million dollars, would fix top incomes at that amount, leaving more money left over for shareholders. The executive may even be induced to work harder than when his income in any year is enough to support him for the rest of his life.[12]

There may be migrational externalities. High and progressive taxation in one jurisdiction may drive wealthy people to other jurisdictions where taxes are lower and less progressive. A distinction may be drawn in this context between the Laffer curve as it would be in the absence of migration and as it would be for the remaining residents of a jurisdiction where high taxation drives out many of the principal contributors to a system of redistribution. High taxation alone need have no such effect if combined with desirable and expensive public services, but rich people may be driven away when taxation is to finance a transfer from rich to poor. That is the standard argument for assigning redistributive powers to high levels of government, to provincial governments rather than to municipalities, to the federal government rather than to the provinces.

## A final word

A great virtue of the new tax responsive literature is that it identifies the revenue-maximizing tax rate regardless of why tax base responds to tax rate, inferring the revenue-maximizing tax rate from the observed elasticity of taxable income. But the inference is only valid when elasticity of taxable income invariant, remaining unchanged regardless of the tax rate. Why tax base responds to tax rate becomes important because only with reference to a particular mechanism connecting the one to the other can it be determined whether the elasticity of taxable income is really constant or not. Two mechanisms are examined in this chapter, and in neither is the elasticity constant. Neither tax evasion nor the labour-leisure choice supplies the foundation that the new tax responsiveness literature requires. The Laffer curve need not be humped, a revenue-maximizing tax rate of 100 per cent is not impossible and whole concept of the Laffer curve is blurred because tax revenue at any given tax rate depends on laws, regulations and how tax revenue is spent.

The moral of the story is that the revenue-maximizing tax rate ought not to be taken too seriously. There may be such a rate out there, but it is likely to be far higher than any majority of voters would be inclined to favour. Redistribution is constrained because it is expensive rather than impossible.

## Notes

1  Thanks to John Hartwick for several helpful comments and suggestions.
2  For a detailed description the new tax responsiveness literature, see Feldstein (1995), Diamond and Saez (2011) and Saez, Slemrod and Giertz (2012).
3  By contrast, Buchanan and Lee (1982) argue that the tax induced contraction in the tax base is likely to occur gradually, as shown here in column (6) of Table 4.2, so that the revenue-maximizing tax rate at the top of the Laffer curve diminishes over time.

4 Scraps of evidence suggest that the supply curve of labour is backward bending. The shape of the supply curve should be reflected in historical statistics of hours of work and the real wage. Between 1909 and 1999, the real wage per hour (expressed in 1999 dollars) in the United States *rose* from $3.80 to $13.90, but work per week *fell* from 53 to 42 hours. See Fisk (2001)

5   $\varepsilon_{Rt} = (t/R)\delta R/\delta t = (t/tY)\delta(tkH^\alpha D^{1-\alpha})/\delta t = (1/Y)(Y + (t\alpha Y/H)\delta H/\delta t)$

$= 1 - \alpha(t/H)\delta H/\delta(1-t) = 1 - \alpha[t/(1-t)][H/(1-t)]\delta H/\delta(1-t)$

$= 1 - \alpha[t/(1-t)]\varepsilon_{H(1-t)}$

6 The effect of land and capital on the shape of the Laffer curve was worked out in discussions with my colleague John Hartwick.

7 This result is in sharp contrast to the proposition, derived on very different assumptions, that the appropriate top marginal tax rate is 0 per cent. The proposition is derived on the assumption that the top rate is only imposed on income so high that it would be earned by the very richest person if and only if that income is not subject to tax. Diamond and Saez (2011: 173) dismiss this result as irrelevant in practice.

8 The elasticity of substitution, $\sigma$, is defined as

$$\sigma = [\% \text{ change in } G/L]/[\% \text{ change in } -\delta G/\delta L]$$

$$= \{d(G/L)/(G/L)\}/\{d(u_L/u_G)/(u_L/u_G)\}$$

where $u_G = \{mG^\rho + nL^\rho\}^{1/\rho-1}\{a\rho G^{\rho-1}\}$ and $u_L = \{mG^\rho + nL^\rho\}^{1/\rho-1}\{b\rho L^{\rho-1}\}$ so that $u_L/u_G = (n/m)(G/L)^{1-\rho}$ and $d(u_L/u_G)/d(G/L) = (n/m)(1-\rho)(G/L)^{-\rho}$
Rearranging the components of the definition of the elasticity, we see that

$$\sigma = \{1/d(u_L/u_G)/d(G/L)\}\{(u_L/u_G)/(G/L)\} = \{1/[(n/m)(1-\rho)(G/L)^{-\rho}]\}$$

$$\times \{(n/m)(G/L)^{1-\rho}/(G, L)\} = 1/(1-\rho)$$

9 See Allen (1967: 51).
10 On the appropriate severity of punishment, see Yitzaki (1987).
11 'We should hang people for parking violations' does not mean we should hang people for parking violations. It is a rhetorical device in the search for the appropriate severity of punishment. For tax evasion as for parking violations, breaking the paradox shows what the appropriate severity should be.
12 Back in 1975, a would-be entrepreneur was considering whether to start a firm to be called Microsoft. Deterred by the top marginal tax rate of 75 per cent at that time, he decided against it and took an ordinary job instead.

# References

Allen, R. D. G. (1967) *Macro-Economic Theory a Mathematical Treatment*, London: Macmillan.

Buchanan, J. M. and Lee, D. R. (1982) Politics, time and the Laffer curve, *Journal of Political Economy*, 90(4), 816–819.

Clark, Colin (1945) Public finance and changes in the value of money, *The Economic Journal*, 55, 371–89.

Diamond, P. And Saez, E. (2011) The case for progressive tax: from basic research to policy recommendations, *The Journal of Economic Perspectives*, 25, 165–90.

Feige, E. L. and McGee, R.T. (1983) Sweden's Laffer curve: taxation and the unobserved economy, *Scandinavian Journal of Economics*, 85(4), 499–519.

Feldstein, M (1995) The effects of marginal tax rates on marginal income: a panel study of the 1986 Tax Reform Act, *Journal of Political Economy*, 103, 351–72.

Fisk, Donald, M. (2001) American labor in the twentieth century, *Compensation and Working Conditions*, US Bureau of Labour Statistics.

Goolsbee, A. (2000) What happens when you tax the rich? Evidence from executive compensation, *Journal of Political Economy*, 108(2), 352–78.

Knight, F. H. (1921) *Risk, Uncertainty and Profit*, Boston, MA: Hart, Schaffner & Marx; Houghton Mifflin Co.

Lindsey, L. (1987) Individual taxpayer response to tax cuts, 1982–1984, with implications for the revenue-maximizing tax rate, *Journal of Political Economy*, 33, 173–206.

Robbins, L. (1930) On the elasticity of demand for income in terms of effort, *Economica*, 29, 123–9.

Saez, E., Slemrod, J. and Giertz, S. (2012) The elasticity of taxable income with respect to marginal tax rates, *Journal of Economic Literature*, 50(1), 3–50.

Stuart, C.E. (1981) Swedish tax rates, labour supply and tax revenue *Journal of Political Economy*, 89, 1020–38.

Yitzaki, S. (1987) On the excess burden of tax evasion, *Public Finance Review*, 15(2), 123–37.

# 5 Bargaining and voting[1]

In the nineteenth century, economics was often called the 'dismal science' largely because the equilibria predicted from price theory were not palatable to those who called it dismal. In what seems to me a deeper sense, however, politics is *the* dismal science because there are no fundamental equilibria to predict.

William Riker (1980a: 443)

A state cannot be constituted from any chance body of persons ... Most of the states that have admitted persons of another stock ... have been troubled by sedition ...

Aristotle (Barker, 1946: I, 210)

a pure democracy, by which I mean a society consisting of a small number of citizens who assemble and administer the government in person, can admit no cure from the mischiefs of faction. A common passion or interest will, in almost every case be felt by a majority of the whole; a communication and concert, results from the form of government itself; and there is nothing to check the inducements to sacrifice the weaker party, or an obnoxious individual. Hence it is that such democracies have ever been spectacles of turbulence and contention; have ever been found incompatible with personal security or the rights of property; and have, in general, been as short in their lives as they have been violent in their deaths ... The remedy for this inconveniency is, to divide the legislature into different branches; and to render them by different modes of election, and different principles of action, as little connected with each other, as the nature of their common functions, and their common dependence on the society, will admit.

James Madison, *The Federalist Papers #10*
(Hacker, 1964: 20)

Voting carries society part way to a unique political outcome. Bargaining is required to complete the journey. One cannot say where the journey will end, and there is risk of breakdown along the way. Bargaining had no place in the simple world in Chapter 3 of voting and redistribution, where politics could be reduced to the choice of a single number, the rate of the negative income tax, and the first preference of the median voter could be expected to prevail. Bargaining comes into its own as soon as two or more issues have to be resolved simultaneously or when a pie must be divided among two or more claimants.

Bargaining is at once necessary and corruptive. It is necessary because legislators must strike deals in the formulation of public policy. It is corruptive as an ingredient of the process by which majority rule voting allows majorities to exploit the corresponding minorities, lessening the people's willingness to abide by the rules of democratic government. These two sides of bargaining will be discussed in turn. This chapter begins with a list of circumstances where bargaining is an indispensable part of majority rule voting. There follows an examination of the exploitation problem and of rules and institutions to deal with it.

## Indispensable bargains

Ideally, political markets should work like commercial markets. Political outcomes would emerge through voting from the distribution of citizens' preferences, just as economic outcomes emerge through pricing from the distribution of people's property and tastes, with nothing left over to bargain about. Even in commercial markets there are exceptions such as bilateral monopoly where bargaining is indispensable, but the role of bargaining in democratic politics is far greater.

There are a few simple cases where bargaining is dispensed with altogether. Voting alone is sufficient to choose between two distinct options. Nor is there anything to bargain about when preferences conform to the assumptions of the median voter theorem, that is, when options can be ordered on a scale from left to right, each voter has a preferred option, and, between any two options both to the right or both to the left of one's preferred option, one always votes for the option closest to one's preferred option. The theorem itself is that the first preference of the person in the middle (with as many people to the right as to the left when people are lined up according to their preferences on the left–right scale) beats any other option in a pairwise vote and is the sole survivor in *any* sequence of pairwise votes as long as the first preference of the median voter is included somewhere in the sequence. The median voter theorem applies to the choice of platforms of political parties as long as people's preferences on different issues can be lined up on one and the same scale, so that, for example, people's views about the severity of punishment are perfectly correlated with, and entirely predictable from, their views about the redistribution of income.[2] There are many circumstances where that is not so.

### *Choosing platforms of political parties*

Voting must be supported by bargaining when two issues have to be resolved simultaneously and when voters' preferences on the two issues can no longer be lined up on one and the same scale. Consider the recent health care debate in the US Congress. Ultimately, a health care bill had to be voted up or down. Before that could happen, it had to be decided, among other things (see Farhana and Tse, 2009):

- whether there is to be a public option
- the size of the tax, if any, on very expensive private health care plans

- whether insurance companies may refuse to cover pre-existing conditions
- how much to subsidize health care for poor people
- whether to tax people who choose not to take out health insurance
- whether to levy an excise tax on the very wealthy to cover the extra cost of insuring the poor

The important consideration here is that an agreement on these matters must be reached before voting takes place, for there must be something definite to vote about. A health care bill must be preceded by a bargain among a majority of legislators who agree that some such bill should be passed, but who have somewhat different preferences about the specifics of the bill. Compromise is inescapable if any bill is to be passed. Bargaining and voting are inextricably joined together.

Consider a party caucus with three participants, persons $A$, $B$ and $C$, who favour the adoption of a health bill but must agree on the content of a bill before any such bill can be passed. A health bill is assumed to be two-dimensional, specifying the 'quality of care', $q$, and the 'progressivity of tax to finance medical care', $t$, as illustrated in Figure 5.1 with $q$ on the vertical axis and $t$ on the horizontal axis. First preferences of persons $A$, $B$ and $C$ are labelled accordingly, and their indifference curves are shown as loops around first preferences.

Figure 5.1 is an extension of Figure 2.6 in Chapter 2 with a different emphasis. There it was shown that no combination of $q$ and $t$ beats every other combination in a pairwise vote. The emphasis in Figure 5.1 is on compromise without which no health care bill can be adopted. Passage of a health care bill requires the formation of a majority coalition (of at least two but possibly of all three people) and a

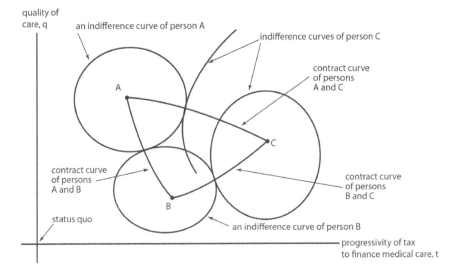

*Figure 5.1* Preferences of three voters about a two-dimensional platform.

resolution of the inevitable conflict of interest among the members of the coalition. One of three coalitions might be formed depending on who can cooperate with whom. Any two people is a majority and can dictate the terms of a bill if they can agree about what those terms are to be, but there is no telling a priori which pair – *A* and *B*, *B* and *C* or *A* and *C* – will strike a deal or what deal each of the three pairs would strike.

A deal between persons *A* and *B* would establish a combination $(q, t)$ somewhere along their contract curve, shown on the figure as the locus of tangencies of their indifference curves between the points *A* and *B*, for any combination off the contract curve would be worse for both *A* and *B* than some point on the curve. There remains a conflict of interest between person *A* and person *B* over which point to choose, person *A* becoming progressively better off and person *B* becoming progressively worse off the closer the agreed-upon combination is to point *A* along the contract curve. The same is true for a deal between person *A* and person *C* or between person *B* and person *C*. Nor can one rule our three-way agreement, presumably on some point within the approximately triangular area bound by the three contract curves. If one person is stubborn, a deal might be struck between the other two. If two people are stubborn, both demanding combinations close to their first preferences, then no deal is struck and no bill is passed despite the fact that a deal could make all three people better off.

Without compromise, no platforms could be agreed upon, no bills could be passed and the status quo would be preserved. Bargaining is indispensable for public decision-making by majority rule voting, but there is no equilibrium bargain comparable to the equilibrium in a competitive market. Democracy requires a modicum of good will and compromise.[3]

### *Parliamentary procedure*

Within the legislature, unique decisions on complex issues can sometimes be reached through parliamentary procedure in which one person proposes a bill, others propose amendments and there is a prescribed sequence of pairwise votes. First, amendments are voted up or down in the reverse of the order in which they are presented. Then, the second-to-last vote is between the original bill and the bill as amended, and the final vote is between the winner of the in that vote and the status quo.

This process automatically yields the Condorcet winner if there is one. Otherwise, parliamentary procedure supplies an advantage to the status quo over the original bill and to the original bill over amendments. Consider the choice among the status quo, *Q*, a bill to replace the status quo, *X*, and an amended bill, *Y* in a legislature with three voters whose orders of preference, from most preferred to least preferred, are *XYQ*, *YQX* and *QXY*. This generates a standard 'paradox of voting' where each option is defeated by some other option in a pairwise vote. Parliamentary procedure prescribes two pairwise votes, the first between *X* and *Y* (the original bill and the amended bill) and the second between the winner in the first vote and *Q* (the status quo). Despite the paradox of voting, the status quo emerges victorious because $X$ beats $Y$ in the first vote and is beaten by $Q$ in the second. No bill is passed without a reasonably strong preference for it.[4]

But bargaining is not eliminated completely. Two of the three voters – the person with preferences $XYQ$ and the person with preferences $YQX$ – prefer the amended bill, $Y$, to the status quo, $Q$. Both become better off if the person with preferences $XYQ$ acts strategically in the initial vote, opting not for his first preference $X$, but for the amended bill, $Y$, which then beats $Q$ in the final vote. The remaining person, with preferences $QXY$, is harmed by the manoeuvre, for the outcome is shifted from his most preferred, $Q$, to his least preferred, $Y$, alternative.

That is not the end of the story. To make the best of a bad situation, the person with preference $QXY$, who but for strategic voting would have attained his first preference, may offer this deal to the person with preference ordering $XYQ$: 'Don't act strategically. Vote for $X$ over $Y$ in the first round, and I in turn promise to vote for $X$ instead of $Q$ in the second, for outcome $X$ is better for both of us than outcome $Y$.' Both parties to the deal become better off as long as all promises are kept.

Bargaining in this context is an exchange of promises. Sincere voting yields a determinate outcome, but a majority of the voters can still make themselves better off by a side deal in which a different outcome emerges.

### Delegation

Formal parliamentary procedure is only part of the network of subsidiary rules that render voting, if not fully determinate, more likely to be so. The paradox of voting, strategy and manipulation can sometimes be circumvented by delegation, as illustrated in a simple an example where a majority of voters prefers some bill to no bill, but, within that majority, there is a paradox of voting about which version of the bill to adopt. Imagine five people, $A$, $B$, $C$, $D$ and $E$, voting among four options, the status quo, $Q$, and one of three variants of a bill, $X$, $Y$ and $Z$. Two people, $A$ and $B$, oppose any variant of the bill. The remaining three people, $C$, $D$ and $E$, all prefer some bill to no bill, but differ about which bill to adopt. Orders of preference, where '=' means indifference, are:

person $A$:   $Q, X = Y = Z$
person $B$:   $Q, X = Y = Z$
person $C$:   $X, Y, Z, Q$
person $D$:   $Y, Z, X, Q$
person $E$:   $Z, X, Y, Q$

Here the paradox of voting is especially destructive. In the original paradox of voting, compromise between any two supporters of the bill would be sufficient to assure passage. Now, unanimity among the bill's supporters is required because, for example, if persons $C$ and $D$ refuse to support option $Z$, person $E$ can block the bill altogether by joining with person $A$ and person $B$ in voting against it. This is an instance of 'many-sided public policy' where all alternatives are on an equal footing and where there is no obvious rule for deciding which variant of the bill should be supported. Delegation in this context is the appointment of a representative of all the bill's supporters to choose whichever variant the representative thinks best.

Delegation may take many forms: In times of war, the ancient Romans would appoint a dictator, typically for six months, with absolute power during his tenure, and only held responsible for his actions when his tenure was up. A more modest delegation allows the prime minister to propose a version of a bill that is at least tolerable to the great majority of its supporters. A committee of Parliament, the Senate and the House of Representatives may be instructed to work out the details of a bill when it would be cumbersome or excessively time-consuming for the entire legislature to do so.[5] The risk in delegation is that the delegate may refuse to relinquish authority when it is time to do so. Both Margaret Thatcher and Tony Blair were easily divested of authority by their party caucus. The appointment of Hitler as Chancellor of Germany in 1933 is the classic example of delegation gone wrong. The ideal in delegation is to circumvent bargaining, but the main objective of delegation may be obtained if bargaining is confined within a manageable scope.

There is little doubt that parliamentary procedure and delegation can be helpful or even necessary for the maintenance of government by majority rule voting which might otherwise break down in dissension and chaos. The question here is whether, between them, they are sufficient to dispense with bargaining altogether. The claim here is that they are not, that a core requirement for bargaining remains.

Rules and delegates must themselves be chosen. Bargains circumvented by rules or delegation re-emerge when rules or delegates are selected. To circumvent the paradox of voting, rules or delegates must in the end lead to the selection of $X$, $Y$ or $Z$. Once this is recognized, the choice of rules or delegates becomes tantamount to the choice among options $X$, $Y$ and $Z$. But there is a difference in timing. Delegates are typically appointed for specific periods of time. Once chosen, the rules of the legislature are typically in force for a long time during which many different bills are considered. Legislators who may be unhappy with the effect of rules on some particular bill may be reluctant to change the rules because they want the rules to remain in force for many other bills to come. A particular rule might be advantageous over the long haul even though it is disadvantageous today.

### Vote trading

Similar problems arise when groups of legislators with different preferences must vote up or down on two or more bills. Consider the case illustrated in Figure 5.2 with two bills and three distinct groups of legislators. One bill is to ban abortion. The other bill is to deregulate the economy. Represent passage of the bill to ban abortion by $X$, and its rejection by $R_X$. Represent passage of the bill to deregulate the economy by $Y$, and its rejection by $R_Y$. There are four possible outcomes on both bills together: $(X, Y)$, $(R_X, R_Y)$, $(X, R_Y)$ and $(R_X, Y)$. The legislature consists

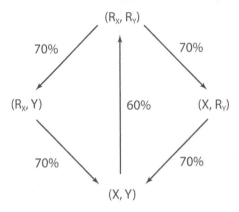

*Figure 5.2* Contests between combinations of outcomes.

of three groups of people, 30 per cent religious, 30 per cent free marketeers and 40 per cent moderates.

Moderates want neither bill passed, but, if just one bill is to be passed, they do not care which bill it is. Their order of preference among pairs of outcomes is

$$(R_X, \ R_Y), (X, \ R_Y) = (R_X, \ Y), (X, \ Y)$$

Free-marketeers are passionately in favour of deregulation, but, other things being equal, oppose the prohibition of abortion. Their order of preference is

$$(R_X, \ Y), (X, \ Y), (R_X, \ R_Y), (X, \ R_Y)$$

Religious folks are passionately in favour of the prohibition of abortion, but, other things being equal, oppose deregulation. Their order of preference is

$$(X, \ R_Y), (X, \ Y), (R_X, \ R_Y), (R_X, \ Y)$$

Suppose that the two bills, to prohibit abortion and to deregulate the economy, are voted upon separately and that everybody votes sincerely. When preferences are as postulated above, both bills are destined to fail, with 30 per cent of the legislature in favour and 70 per cent opposed. The outcome is $(R_X, \ R_Y)$ which is the first preference of the moderates but is the next to last preference of both the free marketeers and the religious folk.

A better result for both religious folk and free marketeers (though much worse for the moderates) can be obtained by a bargain between them. The religious folk pledge to vote for deregulation, and, in return, the free marketeers pledge to vote to prohibit abortion. The deal causes both bills to pass with 60 per cent of the vote, changing the overall result of voting from $(R_X, \ R_Y)$ which is third on both group's ordering to $(X, \ Y)$ which is second. Such deals are implicit in the formation of the platforms of political parties. The current alliance between God and money on what is commonly called 'the right' may have more to do with elections than with any natural affinity between them.

The alliance between religious folk and free marketeers is not the only possible alliance. A better deal for both moderates and the free marketeers can be had by the former pledging to vote for deregulation in return for the latter voting against abortion, yielding the outcome $(R_X, Y)$. A similar deal is possible between religious folk and moderates. Outcomes of all pairwise votes are shown by the directed arrows in Figure 5.2. There are two paradoxes of voting, and society's choice among the four two-dimensional outcomes depends on who cooperates with whom and which among several possible bargains is struck.

## Countervailing power as an encouragement to compromise

Imagine a society somewhat like that in Chapter 3 where politics is about the redistribution and nothing else and where redistribution is undertaken by a negative income tax at a rate $t$ somewhere between a a minimum of 0 at which there is no redistribution at all and a maximum of $t^{max}$ at which the income of the poorest person is as high as possible. If voters' preferences varied steadily within these limits, one would expect the first preference of the median voter to prevail. The outcome would be some $t^*$ strictly between 0 and $t^{max}$. But voters' preferences need not vary continuously as was assumed in Chapter 3. Instead, citizens may divide into two distinct factions: libertarians who oppose redistribution altogether, and socialists who favour maximal redistribution in the sense of making recipients as well off as possible. Libertarians favour $t = 0$. Socialists favour a rate $t^{max}$ which may be well short of 100 per cent depending on the shape of the Laffer curve. It might be supposed that preferences are ideological, or it might be supposed that the population consists of a wealthy class and a poor class where everybody's income within each class is exactly the same and everybody votes self-interestedly.[6]

This is illustrated in Figure 5.3 with libertarians' utility as a function of the tax rate, $u^L(t)$, on the vertical axis, socialists' utility as a function of the tax rate, $u^S(t)$, on the horizontal axis, and all combinations of utilities for different values of $t$ from 0 to $t^{max}$ indicated by points on the heavy downward-sloping curved line. The point $G$ will be discussed later.

The outcome of simple majority rule voting is evident. With more socialist votes than libertarian votes, the outcome is $t = 0$. With more libertarian votes than socialist votes, the outcome is $t = t^{max}$. Nothing in between is possible. The median voter is solidly within one faction or solidly within the other; not even a tie broken by the flip of a coin yields an outcome in between.

The situation is unsatisfactory for three reasons: First, huge changes in policy may arise from tiny shifts in public opinion. In a close election, one socialist persuaded about the virtues of libertarianism may be enough to overturn the entire welfare state, and one libertarian persuaded about the virtues of socialism may be enough to bring it back again. Campaign advertising, personalities of politicians

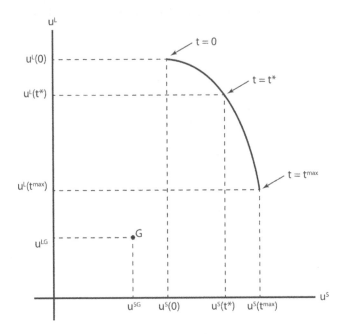

*Figure 5.3* Bargaining between legislatures.

or peculiarities of party organization may swing outcomes from one extreme to the other. Second, voters are worse off in expectation where one of two extremes may emerge almost at random than they would become if compromise could be struck. Everybody, socialists and libertarians alike, may be better off in expectation with a tax rate of – say – $t^{max}/2$ than with equal chances of $t = 0$ and $t = t^{max}$. Third, swings between extremes may be corruptive to democracy. People may be less willing to live with the outcome of elections and government in office may be less willing to step down on losing an election when policy changes are massive than when policy changes are relatively small.

A defence against such extremism is the bicameral legislature where laws can only be passed with the assent of both houses. There would presumably be a status quo that would be maintained unless both houses come to an agreement on some new law or policy. Whether the legislature consists of one house or two houses would make no difference if preference in the electorate were overwhelmingly on one side or the other, for, were that so, the larger faction could be expected to win in both houses. But if the sides are closely balanced, there is a good chance that one house votes for $t = 0$, the other votes for $t = t^{max}$, and nothing changes unless the two sides come together. Compromise may be encouraged, as James Madison claimed in the quotation at the beginning of this chapter, when the legislative branch is split into the Senate and the House of Representatives 'to render them by different modes of election, and different principles of action, as little connected with each other, as the nature of their common functions, and their common dependence on the society, will admit'.

The point $t^*$ on the heavy line may be interpreted in several ways. It has been interpreted as the median voter's preferred tax rate. It can be reinterpreted as the status quo which would be maintained unless both houses vote for something else. On this interpretation, the role of the bicameral legislature is to block innovation that does not have substantial support among the electorate. It can also be interpreted as a compromise between the two houses, a compromise that would be better for everybody in expectation than the outcome in a unicameral legislature where one of the two extremes prevails.

There is another, less satisfactory, possibility. The status quo may be more than just a pre-existing tax rate. It may be a pre-existing set of regulations, represented by the point $G$, mnemonic for gridlock, which are no longer satisfactory to anybody but cannot be replace unless both houses agree on an alternative which may be thought as a point on the heavy line in Figure 5.3. With $G$ as the alternative, both houses are pressured to strike a deal, though there is no telling where between $t = 0$ and $t = t^{max}$ the deal would be. In practice, deals are often struck, but one can never be sure. Gridlock may be the outcome if one or both factions is stubborn. The classic bargaining problem in Figure 5.3 is the subject of the next chapter.

The bicameral legislature is not the minority's only protection. The President of the United States has a veto over legislation. The filibuster has evolved to the point where a 60 per cent majority is, in effect, required to pass legislation, so that, to take an extreme case, a bill with 100 per cent of the votes in the House and 59 per cent of the votes in the Senate would still not pass into law, even with presidential approval. A complex network of subsidiary rules can be seen as placing government by majority rule voting on a continuum between the extremes of 'disfunctional government' and the 'elected dictator'. Fear of exploitation of minorities by majorities warrants the choice of rules allowing minorities to delay or block legislation not favoured by significantly more than 50 per cent of the legislature, making democratic government less efficient and limiting the capacity of the government in office to get things done. Too much emphasis on protection of minorities provides incentives for any and every interest group to hold up legislation unless it gets its way. Too little emphasis provides the elected government with the means to do as it pleases until the next election, helping its friends, harming its enemies and influencing the flow of information.[7]

## Blocking predatory bargains

Bargains discussed so far are not always attainable, but, when attainable, are generally advantageous. Other bargains are corrosive, and can only be avoided by strict limits on what people vote about. Recall the *exploitation problem* from Chapter 2 where five people vote about the apportionment of $750,000. A 'fair' allocation would supply each of the five people with $150,000. The allocation may not be fair because majority rule voting enables any three of the five people to appropriate the entire sum for themselves, raising incomes of each of the three members of the majority coalition from $150,000, as they would be under a 'fair' allocation, to $250,000, with nothing left over for the excluded minority. The example generalizes immediately to the allocation by voting of the entire national income and to any number of people eligible to vote.

Several aspects of this ploy are noteworthy.

- There is no telling a priori who the three members of the majority coalition will turn out to be. Any majority that can agree to act in unison will do.
- A person who would vote for a fair allocation if his vote were decisive, might nonetheless join a predatory coalition for fear that some other coalition will be formed from which he is excluded. Better to exploit than to be exploited.
- A coalition, once formed, may be undermined by a suitable offer from one or both of the remaining two people. People excluded from the original majority coalition might seek out one member of the coalition, offering him, say, $350,000 to join them instead. A new majority coalition would then be formed in support of a new allocation of the national income, supplying $350,000 to the 'traitor' and $200,000 to each of the two people who were excluded from the original coalition, with nothing left over for the remaining two people who had been members of the original coalition. In fact, any coalition can be undermined by some other coalition with a new allocation of the national income supplying more income to a few members of the original coalition and some income to people excluded from the original coalition.
- A person asked to defect from a majority coalition may refuse to do so not because he is loyal, but in fear that the new coalition will itself will be undermined by yet another coalition from which he is excluded. The defector with an income of $350,000 in the new coalition is automatically a target for exclusion from subsequent coalitions, for appropriation of his income yields $175,000 to each of two other people. Better to exclude the traitor than some other person whose income yields less.
- In view of the difficulties in forming and maintaining a predatory coalition, one would expect such coalitions to emerge out of pre-existing divisions in society, allowing members of a coalition to recognize one another and to vote accordingly. In principle, any majority will do, but in practice a badge is needed to indicate who belongs and who does not. Race is a badge. Wealth itself is a badge, as when a majority of the poor votes to expropriate a minority of the rich. Religion is an excellent badge, which is why the constitutional division of church and state plays such an important role in the defence of the democracy in America.

Exploitation in voting requires members of the majority coalition to *recognize* one another, to *allocate* the spoils among themselves and to *resist* the entreaties of the members of the excluded minority who could otherwise take advantage of the paradox of voting to lure away members of the majority coalition. The required bargain may be difficult but not impossible to construct. The moral of the story is that nobody will accept the outcome of majority rule voting peacefully, and no government will risk loss of office in an election unless such bargains can somehow be blocked. This five person example seems to be what James Madison described as a 'pure democracy' in the quotation at the beginning of this chapter, democracy that would indeed be 'as short in their lives as they have been violent in their deaths'.

Replacement of the pure democracy by representative government, with elected legislators and political parties, changes the story considerably, but the exploitation problem persists in a different form. Majority coalitions may re-emerge as political parties dedicated to serving one segment of the population at the expense of the rest. With the majority assembled on religious lines, all government posts can be assigned to members of the majority religion and industrial policy can be designed accordingly, subsidizing some firms at the expense of others. If majorities are permanent, parties favouring such majorities may be expected to last indefinitely, becoming increasingly corrupt with the passage of time. If rewards of office are high enough and with some risk of the government in office today being turned out at the next election, the personnel of the government and their supporters in the population at large may abandon democracy altogether to preserve their advantages indefinitely, for loss of office may be descent from the top to the bottom of society. Knowing this, the minority might rebel if it can, establishing a dictatorship of its own. Even with representative government, the exploitation problem could render democracy unworkable. Whether prospects of actual democratic governments are really so dismal depends upon three considerations that can be classified under the headings of society, government and equity.

### Society

Predatory coalitions of voters are more likely to form, and to hold together, when society is already divided into well-defined and clearly identifiable groups – into different stocks as Aristotle said – based upon race, religion, geography or even wealth, serving as badges showing who belongs to the majority coalition and who does not. Sub-divisions of society can always be identified, but their suitability as glue holding coalitions together depends upon their distinctiveness and upon intra-group loyalty. Race and religion are more likely to serve as a basis for faction when people of different races or religions live entirely separate lives with little contact and no inter-marriage than when a person's grandchildren are quite likely to be of mixed race or to belong to a different religion. A country with a great diversity of religious belief is safer than a country with just two competing religions.[8] Coalitions of rich or poor are less likely to form when there is substantial inter-generational mobility up and down the income scale. Any badge separating people into two distinct factions is potentially dangerous.[9]

### Government

Constitutions of democratic countries are designed to reduce exploitation of minorities by majorities through the division of powers into executive, legislative and judiciary, with overlapping domains of authority. The president of the United

States may veto legislation. The legislature must confirm presidential appointments. The supreme court may nullify legislation not in accordance with the constitution. Arbitrary actions by a narrow and perhaps unrepresentative majority in the legislature are also contained by the establishment of two legislative chambers with different representations in the population as a whole, the House of Commons and Senate in Canada, and the Senate and the House of Representatives in the United States. With two chambers, a predatory majority in one may be thwarted by a different predatory majority in the other. To exploit their minorities, the two factions would need to compromise. That in itself may be difficult. If successful, it would be tantamount to the formation of a larger majority in society as a whole with a correspondingly smaller minority and correspondingly smaller gains from exploitation. When each chamber represents the will of the people imperfectly and when a bare majority is sufficient to pass bills, a double majority is thought to be safer than a majority in one chamber alone.[10] In the words of Thomas Jefferson, quoted by James Madison in *The Federalist Papers* #48 (Hacker, 1964: 114),

> An elective despotism was not the government we fought for, but one which should not only be founded on free principles but in which the power of government should be so divided and balanced among the several bodies of magistracy, as so no one could transcend their legal limits, without being effectively checked and restrained by the others.

In a sense, democratic government is designed to be inefficient, with bargaining as an impediment to predatory actions. This would be of little use if bargaining were easy and determinate, if, for example, the two branches of the legislature could always resolve differences with little fuss. Exploitation becomes difficult and less of a threat to minorities when acquiescence of several branches of government is required and when that acquiescence is difficult to negotiate.

### Equity

Government by majority rule voting is protected by cordoning off aspects of the economy and society that cannot be safely voted about. People are willing to live with the ups and downs of democratic politics and the government is prepared to relinquish office peacefully, when the majority rule voting is combined with laws and customs placing a floor under what defeated leaders and their supporters stand to lose in an election. Government by majority rule voting persists because, and only because, of a general understanding that there is what might be called a *system of equity* defending enough of people's income and standing in society from predation by the government in office to make an electorally mandated change of government tolerable.[11] A system of equity makes democracy workable by setting a lower limit to what leaders and their supporters stand to lose in an election.

Majority rule voting is protected by civil rights.[12] Free speech, privacy and freedom from arbitrary imprisonment are surely valuable in themselves, but they are also valuable because democracy could not be sustained – no minority acquiescing peacefully to the decisions of the majority and no government in office willing to risk loss of office in an election – if a majority in parliament could terrorize or punish the minority at will. The rule of law plays a similar role. A ban on ad hominem legislation and on unequal treatment by the courts places a limit upon what one stands to lose if one's party fails to win the election. Laws must not reward the supporters of the party in power or punish its enemies. Governments do violate this principle to some extent, but gross violation places democracy in jeopardy.

Majority rule voting is also protected by property rights. The national income is very much larger, and citizens are very much more prosperous, when at least a significant proportion of the nation's property is privately owned than when the entire means of production is directed by the state. But efficiency is not the only virtue. Constitutional protection of property rights preserves people's willingness to respect the results of an election by limiting what one stands to lose at the ballot box. Without secure property rights, predatory bargains would be too lucrative for the majority and too devastating for the minority. A majority in the legislature could impoverish the minority completely. No government would be prepared to risk loss of office in an election if its successor could not be trusted to respect the property of its supporters. The exploitation problem would prove insurmountable and democracy would soon self-destruct. Not all capitalist societies are democracies, but all democracies are capitalist, maintaining private ownership of a significant portion of the means of production.

The great threat to majority rule voting is that there might be too much at stake in the election, so that losers would prefer to rebel or abandon majority rule altogether than to acquiesce to the outcome of the vote. Democracy is a recipe for chaos unless defended by a great substratum of laws and customs rendering predatory bargaining more difficult and less profitable. People respect such rules and customs in the belief that democracy itself may be at stake. Ideally, people's respect for rules and customs would be sufficient to dissolve the bonds of obedience when the rules and customs are violated by the government of the day. The policeman, the soldier and the bureaucrat, accustomed to obey the commands of their superiors, must cease to do so when the rules of equity are violated. As a last resort, there must be a mechanism or process – resort to independent courts, whistle-blowing, civil disobedience or outright rebellion – to deter governments from inequitable actions.

Risk of exploitation of minorities can never be eliminated altogether, but it can be reduced not just through the design of government so that the passage of legislation requires what is in effect a super-majority, but by insulating aspects of society and the economy from the domain of politics. Untouchable civil rights and property rights place a floor under what governments voted out of office and minorities in the population at large have to lose from an adverse vote. Equity and property rights are the subject of Chapters 9 and 10.

Much would seem to depend upon whether bargaining itself is determinate, whether there is a bargaining equilibrium assigning shares to bargainers, just as competitive markets assign incomes to people. In the next chapter, it is argued that there is not. It is argued that bargaining is indeterminate in the sense that, though many bargains are struck more or less costlessly, there is no predicting from initial conditions what exactly the bargain will be and no guarantee that any bargain will be struck at all.

## Appendix 5A: The escape from bargaining to equilibrium

It is assumed in this chapter that bargaining is fundamentally indeterminate. It is argued in detail in the next chapter that there is no known mechanism comparable to the general equilibrium in a competitive economy to render bargaining determinate, avoiding the risk of chaos if bargains are not struck. We must live with the indeterminacy of bargaining, though laws and customs can be designed to minimize the potential harm. Alternatively, a bargaining solution may be introduced as an axiom in theorems explaining observed political outcomes, or politics may be described in a way that renders bargaining unnecessary or determinate.

The first route is taken by Alesina and Rosenthal (1995) who treat all politics as the choice among outcomes on a left–right scale – the choice of a single variable $x$ between 0 and 1 – where outcomes depend on deals within the legislature and between the legislature and the president, and (the major premise) where bargains reflect weighted averages of the preferences of the bargainers. These assumptions explain observable aspects of politics that are difficult to explain any other way.

Bargaining is circumvented by delegation in the *citizen-candidate* models by Osborne and Slivinski (1996) and by Besley and Coate (1997). All citizens participate in the legislature, anybody can run for office, everybody's preference is common knowledge and whoever wins the election is expected to act in accordance with his own preference exclusively because no promise to act otherwise would be credible. The models differ in their specifications of what people vote about. In the Osborne and Slivinski model, voting is about the choice of a parameter such as the rate in a negative income tax. In Besley and Coate's model, a wider range of options is allowed, including the allocation among voters of the entire national income. These models are discussed in Chapter 11.

A unique political outcome is guaranteed by the *probabilistic voting theorem* under much less promising circumstances. The probabilistic voting theorem circumvents the exploitation problem, guaranteeing a unique outcome, represented in the platforms of both of two competing political parties. The source of equilibrium is a set of concave votes-to-offers functions for each interest group in society, allowing political parties to maximize votes in the allocation of the national income among interest groups and leaving nothing whatsoever to bargain about (Mueller (2003): chapter 12). Chapter 12 below is a critique of the theorem on the grounds that the concave votes-to-offers function is implausible and the theorem breaks down, restoring the paradox of voting, when because the exploitation of minorities is not ruled out altogether. For a critical analysis of the theorem, see also Kirchgassner (2000).

Containment of bargaining through the design of government is carried to its logical extreme in Shepsle and Weingast's model (1981) of *structure-induced equilibrium*, the principal example being the committee system in the US Congress designed to restrict the range of options facing the House and Senate as a whole. A distinction needs to be drawn in this context between structural constraints that reduce the range of bargaining and structural constraints that remove the need for bargaining altogether. The title of Shepsle and Weingast's paper is 'Structure-induced equilibrium and legislative choice.' The word 'equilibrium' might be replaced by the clumsy but more accurate phrase 'reduction in the range over which bargaining is required for political outcomes to emerge', but the moral of the story would be preserved. See also Riker (1980a).

Voting over the allocation of allocation of total income can be made determinate by the imposition of appropriate rules of procedure. In the extreme, the entire income can be assigned to one randomly chosen voter, or, equivalently, an agenda setter can be selected at random on the understanding that all income vanishes (that nobody gets anything) unless the agenda setter's proposal is accepted in an up-or-down vote. The agenda setter would then offer a penny to just over half the voters and keep the rest of the income for him- or herself. A more plausible procedure has been examined by Baron and Frerejohn (1989). A randomly chosen agenda-setter is entitled to propose a bill. If that bill fails to pass, another randomly chosen agenda setter would be entitled to propose a new bill the following year, raising every voter's reservation value of a bill this year to the present value of an equal share of total income next year. The process may continue forever, or until such time as a bill is passed. Equilibrium in such models depends critically upon the exclusion of credible promises. One cannot promise to behave tomorrow in a way that may not be in one's interest when tomorrow comes. Otherwise, in an electorate consisting of a majority of blue people and a minority of red people where people of each color are fiercely loyal to one another, there is nothing to stop the blue people from grabbing the entire income for themselves by promising one another to vote against any bill with a different allocation. The exploitation problem is circumvented in this model by simply assuming it away.

## Notes

1  This chapter is a slightly modified version of an article in *Public Choice*, (Usher, 2012).
2  The median voter theorem is the source of the left–right distinction in contemporary politics. Desperate to imagine a political equilibrium, people talk as though preferences on all issues in an election can be spread out on one and the same scale, so that someone who is relatively right-leaning on any one issue is equally right-leaning on every other. The left–right distinction originated in the French National Assembly of 1789 where people were seated in accordance with their preferences about the fate of the monarchy, from restoration at the extreme right to execution at the extreme left.
3  Two interesting exceptions where discussed in Chapter 2. The first is where the most preferred platform of – say – person *C* just happens to lie on the contract curve between

*A* and *B*. In that case, the requirements of the median voter theorem are met, with *C* as the median voter whose preference prevails in any sequence of pairwise votes. The second is where 'indifference curves are all perfect circles and that the individual optima are evenly distributed over the issue space' (Tullock, 1967: 268). When the issue space is itself circular, the option represented by the point at the centre of the circle beats any other option in a pairwise vote, restoring the median voter theorem in two-dimensional space and rendering bargaining unnecessary. These, however, are very strong assumptions. Indeterminacy reappears if the electorate, no matter how large, consists of just three, or just a few, groups of identical people. Indeterminacy also reappears when the number of dimensions and the number of voters is the same.

4  For a brief introduction to parliamentary procedure, see Riker (1980b).
5  On delegation in the US Congress see Kiewiet and McCubbins (1991).
6  The distribution of income would be two spikes rather than a hump as was assumed in Chapter 3.
7  Critics of government in the United States and Canada have seen these governments as moving too far in opposite directions. Mann and Ornstein (2012) see the United States government as becoming increasingly disfunctional with minorities empowered to block legislation. Savoie (1999), Martin (2010) and Simpson (2001) see the Canadian federal government of as becoming increasingly centralized with dangerously little check on the personal authority of the prime minister. None or these critics are predicting the end of democratic government, but all see cause for concern.
8  'If there were only one religion in England, we should have no fear of despotism; if there were two, they would cut each other's throats; but there are thirty, and live in peace and happiness' Voltaire (quoted in Gordon, 1999: 230).
9  Rabushka and Shepsle (1972), Chua (2003) and Mann (2005) have extended this line of reasoning to the study of ethnic cleansing.
10  In a review of the history of democracy from ancient Athens until the present day, Gordon (1999) develops a case for the proposition that democracy can only be preserved by countervailing power within the legislature and among the different branches of government. Gordon's emphasis is on the descent into tyranny. The emphasis here is on the exploitation of minorities. The two are intimately connected because tyranny emerges automatically when government by majority rule voting cannot be sustained.
11  The word 'equity' is often used as a fancy synonym for equality. The usage here is different. It is a set of well-recognized and generally respected rules specifying who is entitled to what, rules that may, but need not, require equality in income or status. On this usage of equity, see Chapters 9 and 10 and Usher (1981).
12  'Insulation' as a requirement for democracy is discussed in Tilly (2007).

# References

Alesina, Alberto and Rosenthal, Howard (1995) *Partisan Politics, Divided Government and the Economy*, Cambridge: Cambridge University Press.

Barker, Ernest, (Ed. and Trans.) (1946) *The Politics of Aristotle*, Oxford: Clarendon Press.

Baron, D and Frerejohn, J. (1989) Bargaining in legislatures, *American Political Science Review*, 83(4), 1181–206.

Besley, T. and Coate, S. (1997) An economic model of representative democracy, *Quarterly Journal of Economics*, 112(1), 85–114.

Chua, Amy, (2003) *World on Fire: How Exporting Free Market Democracy Breeds Ethnic Hatred and Global Instability*, New York: Doubleday.

Farhana, H. and Tse, A. (2009) Comparing the house and senate health care proposals, *New York Times*, December 19.

Gordon, H. S. (1999) *Controlling the State: Constitutionalism from Ancient Athens to Today*, Cambridge, MA: Harvard University Press.

Hacker, A., (Ed.)(1964) *The Federalist Papers by Alexander Hamilton, John Jay and James Madison*, New York: Washington Square Press, nos. 10 and 48.

Kiewiet, D. and McCubbins, M. (1991) *The Logic of Delegation: Congressional Parties and the Appropriations Process*, Chicago: University of Chicago Press.

Kirchgassner, G. (2000) Probabilistic voting and equilibrium: an impossibility result, *Public Choice*, 103(1–2), 35–48.

Mann, Michael (2005) *The Dark Side of Democracy*, Cambridge: Cambridge University Press.

Mann, T. E. and Ornstein, N. J. (2012) *It's Even Worse than it Looks: How the American Constitutional System Collided with the New Politics of Extremism*, New York: Basic Books.

Martin, Lawrence (2010) *Harperland: The Politics of Control*, Toronto: Viking Canada.

Mueller, Dennis (2003) *Public Choice III*, Cambridge: Cambridge University Press.

Osborne, M. and Slivinski, A. (1996) A Model of Political Competition with Citizen-Candidates', *Quarterly Journal of Economics*, 111(1), 65–96.

Rabushka, Alvin and Shepsle, K. (1972) *Politics in Plural Societies: A Theory of Democratic Instability*, Belleveu: Merrill.

Riker, William (1980a) Implications from the disequilibrium of majority rule for the study of institutions, *American Political Science Review*, 74(2), 432–46.

Riker, William (1980b) *Liberalism versus Populism*, San Francisco: W. H. Freeman.

Savoie, Donald (1999) *Governing from the Centre: The Concentration of Power in Canadian Politics*, Toronto: University of Toronto Press.

Shepsle, K. and Weingast, B. (1981) Structure-induced equilibrium and legislative choice, *Public Choice*, 37(3), 503–19.

Simpson, Jeffrey (2001) *The Friendly Dictatorship*, Toronto: McClelland and Stewart.

Tullock, G. (1967) The general irrelevance of the general impossibility theorem, *Quarterly Journal of Economics*, 81(2), 256–70.

Tilly, C. (2007) *Democracy*, Cambridge: Cambridge University Press.

Usher, Dan (1981) *The Economic Prerequisite to Democracy*, Oxford: Blackwell.

Usher, Dan (2012) Bargaining and voting, *Public Choice*, 151(3–4), 739–55.

# 6   Bargaining unexplained[1]

There would arise a general demand for a *principle of arbitration.*

And this aspiration of the commercial world would be but one breath in the universal sigh for articles of peace. For almost every species of social and political contract is affected with an indeterminateness like that which has been described; an evil which is likely to be much more felt when, with the growth of intelligence and liberty, the principle of *contract* shall have replaced both the appeal to force and the acquiescence of custom. Throughout the whole region of in a wide sense *contract*, in the general absence of a mechanism like perfect competition, the same essential indeterminateness prevails; in international, in domestic politics; between nations, classes, sexes.

The whole creation groans and yearns, desiderating a principle of arbitration, an end of strifes.

Edgeworth (1881: 51)

In the standard model of the competitive economy, universal self-interest can be relied upon to generate prices, quantities and the distribution of income in response to initial conditions of ownership and to technical constraints. The model tells us when equilibrium is to be expected, when, and in what sense, outcomes are socially optimal and when public intervention might be warranted. One seeks for analogous results from models of bargaining: reliance on self-interest, proof of equilibrium in the core model and recognition of circumstances where the assumptions of the core model are violated. The claim in this chapter is that the analogy does not hold. Bargaining models yield determinate equilibria, but only on the strength of assumptions with too little distance from what is to be proved or because what is called bargaining in such models is very different from bargaining as commonly understood. Confidence in people's capacity for bargaining and compromise comes from experience rather than theory, but we also know that bargaining fails from time to time. Large sums are sometimes divided up painlessly; friendships or valuable partnerships may be destroyed in disputes over trifles. Bargaining models may be downright misleading by suggesting determinacy in circumstances where there is none. Bargaining and compromise cannot be subsumed under the heading of self-interest in response to external constraints. Bargaining remains unexplained.

Bargaining is everywhere: in wage setting between employers and employees, in allocating tasks and rewards between partners in business, in patent pools, in deals to avert costly litigation, in the formation of platforms of political parties, in allocating cabinet posts in coalition government, in reconciling of House and Senate versions of a bill, in deals between nations to avert the descent into war, in attempts by Sunnis and Shiites in Iraq to forge a viable government. If the argument in this chapter is correct, outcomes depend on something more than a mechanical resolution of competing interests.

This chapter begins with an exposition of the paradigmatic bargain where two people are jointly entitled to a pie if and only if they can agree about how large each person's slice is to be. The bargaining problem is to determine which among the many mutually advantageous bargains will actually be struck. Three bargaining solutions are then examined within the framework of the paradigmatic bargain: the Nash (1950) bargaining solution based upon a common sense of fairness, Hicks' (1932) and Zeuthen's (1930) models of concessions in proportion to harm from failure to agree and the Staahl–Rubinstein solution (Staahl (1972) and Rubinstein (1982)), based upon an imposed bargaining procedure. The models are described simply to highlight their implicit assumptions and to emphasize the contrast between bargaining as depicted in models and bargaining as it is commonly understood to be. There is finally a list of the critical simplifications in the paradigmatic bargain together with discussion of what happens when these simplifications are replaced. A simple proof of the Staahl–Rubinstein bargaining solution with emphasis on implications of variations in the assumptions is presented as an appendix.

## The paradigmatic bargain

A bargain is a division of the spoils. Two people are entitled to something collectively, but they cannot appropriate or make use of it until they agree about how it is to be shared. Bargaining may be over the allocation of things or of money. A bargain must make both participants better off than if no bargain were struck, but a conflict of interest remains, for a particular allocation must be chosen from the set of all possible allocations, some relatively advantageous to one party, some relatively advantageous to the other.

The paradigmatic bargain is illustrated in Figure 6.1. Two people, an engineer, $E$, and an ophthalmologist, $O$, (the mnemonics will change presently) have a plan for a joint venture that can only proceed once they agree about how the revenue from the venture is to be shared between them. Apart from the joint venture, they have 'outside' incomes of $\underline{Y}_E$ and $\underline{Y}_O$, represented on the figure as the 'no-agreement point' $\alpha$. The revenue from the venture is $P$ (the pie to be divided between them), and their combined income if the venture proceeds would be $Y$ where

$$\underline{Y}_E + \underline{Y}_O + P = Y \tag{6.1}$$

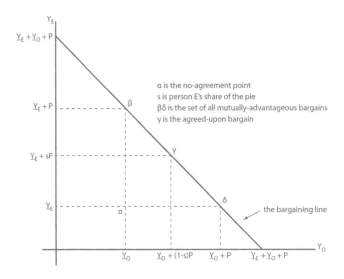

*Figure 6.1* The paradigmatic bargain.

The combined income, $Y$, is represented on the figure by the height of the diagonal 45° line, called the 'bargaining line'. All post-bargaining incomes – $Y_E$ to person $E$ and $Y_O$ to person $O$ – can be represented by points on the bargaining line. A bargain in this context is the choice by agreement of a value for a parameter $s$, representing person $E$'s share of the pie, where person $O$'s share would be $(1 - s)$ and where $s$ must lie between 0 and 1 to ensure that both parties become better off than they would be at the no-agreement point. Net gains from the venture are $\Delta Y_E$ and $\Delta Y_O$, such that

$$\Delta Y_E = (Y_E - \underline{Y}_E) = sP \qquad (6.2)$$

and

$$\Delta Y_O = (Y_O - \underline{Y}_O) = (1 - s)P \qquad (6.3)$$

All mutually advantageous bargains can be represented as points on the bargaining line between $\beta$ (for which $s = 1$ so that the entire surplus accrues to person $E$) and $\delta$ (for which $s = 0$ so that the entire surplus accrues to person $O$). A bargain is represented by the point $\gamma$ between these limits. An increase in $s$ moves $\gamma$ toward $\beta$, and a decrease in $s$ moves $\gamma$ toward $\delta$. Nothing so far suggests how such a bargain might be struck.

There are a number of what might be called trivial solutions to the bargaining problem: prior agreements to divide the pie equally, to assign the entire pie to one party or the other by the flip of a coin, or to allocate the pie in some prescribed proportion, a share $S$ to person $E$ with a share $(1 - S)$ left over for person $O$. These are genuine bargaining solutions in one sense, but no solution at all in another. They are genuine solutions in that the pie is completely allocated. They are no solutions at all in that they convert what might otherwise be true bargaining into an aspect of property rights. If, for instance, the pie is allocated by a flip of a coin, each bargainer's chance of acquiring the pie is possessed as exclusively as the house or the stocks this person owns. Bargaining only takes place when property rights are incomplete and allocation must be by mutual agreement. The trivial solutions are nonetheless interesting because they reappear as components of the seriously proposed bargaining solutions to be discussed below.

## Bargaining solutions

Ideally, confidence in the determinacy of bargaining would be bolstered by the existence of equilibrium in explicit models of bargaining. Three such models will be examined briefly in turn: models based upon a common sense of fairness, a sequence of concessions and a prescribed bargaining procedure. For each, it will be argued that the model, though interesting and instructive, does not in the end supply the confidence we seek.

### A shared sense of what is fair

Begin with the working assumption (to be modified presently) that, for the apportionment of a fixed sum of money between two people, a 'fair' bargain is a fifty-fifty split. Even so, the notion of fairness would be vague and perhaps of little use unless it could be extended in some natural way from bargaining over dollars to bargaining over the apportionment of things – like family heirlooms or authority over children in the event of divorce – for which there are no well-specified market prices. Sometimes gains from a bargain can only be represented as utilities. Utility supplants money as the object of bargaining when a sense of fairness leads bargainers to take account of disparities in their incomes.

The difficulty in bargaining about utilities is that utility is ordinal, defined up to a linear transformation, and not comparable from one person to the next. For bargaining over a sum of money, $P$, it is commonly supposed that a fair bargain is a fifty-fifty split, with $\Delta Y_E = \Delta Y_O$ and with person $E$'s share, $s$, equal to one half. Similarly, in bargaining over the assignment of utilities, we would like to equate $\Delta u^E$ and $\Delta u^O$ where $\Delta u^E$ is the impact of the bargain on the utility, $u^E(Y_E)$, of person $E$ and $\Delta u^O$ is the impact of the bargain on the utility, $u^O(Y_O)$, of person $O$. We would like to define a fair division of the pie as one for which $\Delta u^E = \Delta u^O$, where

$$\Delta u^E = [u^E(\underline{Y}_E + sP) - u^E(\underline{Y}_E)] \tag{6.4}$$

$$\Delta u^O = [u^O(\underline{Y}_O + (1-s)P) - u^O(\underline{Y}_O)] \tag{6.5}$$

and where $\underline{Y}_E$ and $\underline{Y}_E$ are incomes of persons $E$ and $O$ as they were prior to the bargain. That is not feasible because utilities are incommensurate. The resulting value of $s$ would be affected by a linear transformation of either utility function.

There is a way around this difficulty, leading to a rule called the Nash bargaining solution (Nash, 1950). Whenever $\Delta Y_E$ is equal to $\Delta Y_O$, the product $\Delta Y_E \Delta Y_O$ is automatically maximized subject to the constraint that $\Delta Y_E + \Delta Y_O = P$, and the product $s(1 - s)$ is maximized as well. This property of fair allocation can be extended from income to utility even though the simple equality of shares cannot. The Nash bargaining solution is to choose $s$ to maximize the product

$$\Delta u^E \Delta u^O = [u^E(\underline{Y}_E + sP) - u^E(\underline{Y}_E)][u^O(\underline{Y}_O + (1 - s)P) - u^O(\underline{Y}_O)] \quad (6.6)$$

yielding a value of $s$ that is independent of a linear transformation of either utility function and that equals ½ – a fifty-fifty split of the pie – whenever both utilities are linear functions of income.

The Nash bargaining solution is a theorem derived, like all theorems, from a set of axioms. Among Nash's axioms is this: 'If $S$ is symmetric and $u_1$ and $u_2$ display this, then $c(S)$ must lie on the line $u_1 = u_2$.' (Axiom 8 ), where $S$ is the set of all possible outcomes and $c(S)$ is the set of all outcomes that are deemed to be fair. All by itself, Nash's Axiom 8 mandates a fifty-fifty split of the pie in the simple paradigmatic bargain or whenever utility is proportional to income. Nash's programme is to extend the notion of fair allocation from money to utils, but not to justify the fair allocation itself. Bargainers who for one reason or another refuse to accept a fifty-fifty split as a fair allocation of the pie – bargainers who do not conform to Axiom 8 – would have no difficulty in refusing to accept the shares assigned in the Nash bargaining solution.[2]

There is some question as to whether the common understanding of what is fair in the Nash bargaining solution leaves room for bargaining as the term is usually understood. If people agreed about what is fair and if they acted accordingly, there would be nothing left to bargain about. When we speak of 'explaining' bargains, what we usually have in mind is a bargaining outcome comparable to the outcome in general equilibrium in competitive markets where people act in their own interest exclusively, responding to market-determined prices but not to one another. Nobody in perfect competition is 'fair'. Everybody is unremittingly greedy, cooperating with others if and only if it is personally advantageous to do so. To accept a fair bargain because it is fair is a different order of behaviour altogether. It is the incorporation of uncoerced good-will into the core of the market. It is an admission of failure in the great project of explaining outcomes in the economy by self-interest alone. Indeed, if people could be relied upon to be 'fair' voluntarily, the market itself might prove unnecessary except perhaps to identify each person's appropriate behaviour in any given situation.

Fairness as equality in the Nash bargaining solution takes no account of the bargainers' contributions to the common enterprise. It is conceivable, for example, that the ophthalmologist has contributed far more to the common project, in time and creativity, than has the engineer. A fair allocation of the revenue from the project might award the ophthalmologist the larger share. It is by no means obvious how these two aspects of fairness might be reconciled.

The Nash bargaining solution is redistributive – assigning the larger slice to the person with the smaller income – as long as the bargainers' utility of income functions are the same and the common utility of income function is concave.[3] There is some question as to whether redistribution is appropriate in this context. It is at least arguable that redistribution should be of peoples' total incomes rather than of the portion of income in dispute. Ignoring bargainers' contributions to the joint venture, a notion of fairness might suggest a simple fifty-fifty split on the understanding that each bargainer's share of the pie would be included in total income for tax purposes.

By the same token, the notion of a fair bargain is meaningless except in a context of well-established property rights, for, if disputes are to be resolved by a fifty-fifty split of the pie, it becomes in everybody's interest to create disputes at other people's expense. I assert that a third of what you claim to be your land is really mine, and we agree that I get one sixth. A state of affairs where what anybody chooses to call a dispute is resolved by a fifty-fifty split is untenable in the long run. A bargain to split what is initially jointly owned or collective property may be fair. A bargain to split what is initially your exclusive property is automatically unfair. The line between individually owned and collectively owned property is not always as sharp as we would like.

For bargains over the allocation of money, a fifty-fifty split might be acceptable not just because it is fair, but because it is a focal point, the only readily recognizable rule. If a fifty-fifty split were customary, then all bargainers would know exactly what to do. A general convention that people in a dispute ought to split the difference evenly would be relatively easy for everybody to follow. Other conventions would be difficult to maintain. For instance, a convention supplying two-thirds of the pie to person $E$ and the remaining third to person $O$ is meaningless without a prior understanding about who is to play the role of person $E$ and who is to play the role of person $O$. Perhaps such a convention might be founded on class structure, but that would require a substantial modification of the assumptions about the paradigmatic bargain in Figure 6.1. A convention to divide the pie equally might be enforced by an understanding that people who deviate from the convention will be punished by their fellow citizens who would refuse to deal with them again, but a convention enforced by sanction is the antithesis of what most people would think of as a bargain.[4] Bargaining only takes place in the absence of coercion.

Genuine bargaining is, almost by definition, indeterminate. A bargain is the resolution of a dispute. If bargainers can be relied upon to respect a notion of fairness, to agree on a fifty-fifty split of the pie, or to accept shares mandated by the Nash bargaining solution, then bargaining is just playacting, for there is no real dispute and nothing left to bargain about.

## Concessions in proportion to harm from failure to agree

In the early 1930s, Hicks (1932) and Zeuthen (1930) developed models of bargaining between companies and unions when both have a degree of monopoly power. Bargaining in these models consisted of a series of concessions dependent on the harm to each party from a failure to agree and upon each party's judgment of the likelihood that the other would concede instead. Hicks draws what he calls an 'employer's concession curve' and a 'union's resistance curve'. The crossing of these curves identifies the agreed-upon wage. In the Zeuthen model, the failure of employees and owners to agree leads to 'conflict', the exact meaning of which is not spelled out in detail. Zeuthen's principal assumption is that each bargainer's concession is proportional to his expected harm from conflict as it would be if antagonism between the bargainers rises to the point where the entire pie is wasted through a failure to agree.[5]

Both models allocate the surplus in proportion to harms that do not actually occur because they are averted by timely concessions. Strikes in Hicks's model are imagined strikes. Conflict in Zeuthen's model is imagined conflict. Neither model contains an explanation of when, if at all, bargaining breaks down and the unfortunate alternative to agreement is realized. Nor is it explained how bargaining in the midst of a strike or bargaining in the midst of conflict differs from bargaining in anticipation of these events. Neither party is bloody-minded, insisting on favourable terms come hell or high water. This consideration is especially problematic because, if one bargainer is really and truly adamant, it is usually in the interest of the other party to back down. More will be said about this presently. Bargaining is made determinate within these models, but only by ignoring essential features of the world where bargains are struck. There is no satisfactory explanation of the timing and the magnitude of concessions, and no allowance for the possibility that the final agreement is conditioned by the history of bidding as well as by the initial values of the bargainers' harms from conflict.

Genuine concessions are modeled by Cross (1965).[6] Both parties' concessions are rendered determinate by the principle that delay is costly so that, if you do not concede quickly, then I must. At least three kinds of harm might be identified:

1  loss by both parties of what would otherwise be their shares of the pie;
2  delay which may be more costly for one party than for another depending on their rates of discount; and
3  actual harm inflicted as when a labour union goes on strike or when the firm locks out its employees.

Cross derives the sequence of concessions as the outcome of rational, self-interested behaviour, transporting this aspect of bargaining from the domain of psychology – where people may act stubbornly, vindictively or irrationally – into the domain of economics – where each person does what is best for himself in the light of his best guess of what others will do. Yet the model contains no persuasive explanation of why bargainers do not proceed to the ultimate deal all at once if the ultimate deal is predictable from the initial conditions, as Cross assumes it to be.

In the light of subsequent literature, these models would seem to be open to the objection that the bargainers are neither entirely fair-minded, as in the Nash bargaining solution, nor entirely self-interested in any rational and calculating way. Bargainers are seen as making concessions, but their concessions do not arise naturally from the maximization of an objective function in response to given constraints. It is difficult to decide how much weight to attach to this objection. Want of strict rationality may account for the eclipse of these models in the economic literature, but, in their defence, it may be argued that bargaining is not really as rational a process as more recent models would suggest.

### Mutually agreed-upon procedures

A bargaining solution may arise not just from a common understanding of fairness or as the outcome of a sequence of concessions, but as the outcome of a prescribed sequence of alternating offers by one party to be accepted or rejected by the other.

Begin with the simplest possible case where the pie vanishes if the first and only offer is not accepted. Persons $E$ and $O$ (now mnemonic for even and odd) are bargaining over the allocation of a pie that emerges just for an instant and disappears if it is not shared at once. The pie appears for just long enough for one person say, 'I offer you such-and-such a share and I will take the rest.' and for the other person to reply either 'yes' or 'no'. No other speech is admitted. Suppose, no matter why, it is person $O$ who is entitled to make the offer. If the person $E$'s response is 'yes', the pie is shared accordingly. If person $E$'s response is 'no', the pie vanishes and nobody gets anything.

It is obvious what happens. As long as both parties are super-rational, person $O$ offers person $E$ a penny, keeping the rest of the pie for himself. Recognizing that a penny is better than nothing, person $E$ accepts the offer, and the pie is allocated accordingly. If the original pie was \$100, person $E$ ends up with one penny and person $O$ ends up with \$99.99. In effect, the person entitled to make the take-it-or-leave-it offer gets to keep the entire pie.

If that seems a bit harsh, and much too far from anything we would ordinarily call bargaining, we can even out the allocation by allowing the pie to disappear over two time periods rather than just one. Suppose

- the pie appears at sunrise of day 1 and disappears in two stages, half at sunset on day 1 and the other half at sunset on day 2,
- offers to share the pie (or what remains of it when the offer is made) are made at noon each day, by person $O$ on day 1 and, if person $O$'s offer is rejected, by person $E$ on day 2,
- every offer is an assignment of shares,
- the recipient of an offer must accept or reject it immediately,
- nothing else may be said by either person, and
- (an assumption soon to be relaxed) there is no discounting of future income.

Again it is obvious what must happen. At noon on day 1, person $O$ offers person $E$ *half* the pie, and person $E$ accepts. Why? If person $E$ rejected person $O$'s offer on day 1, the most person $E$ could expect would be half the original pie because nothing more would be left on day 2 when it is person $E$'s turn to make an offer. Except for the switch in roles and the size of the pie, both parties find themselves in the same situation at noon on day 2 as in the one period take-it-or-leave-it bargain, and they act accordingly. Since person $E$ can be assured of half of the pie (less a penny) by waiting until his turn to make an offer comes round, he would never accept less than half of the pie in any offer from person $O$ on day 1, and person $O$ has no incentive to offer more.

There is, of course, nothing inevitable about the equal sharing of the pie or about the restriction of bargaining to two periods. The pie may disappear over any number of days, and the disappearances each day need not be the same. Suppose the pie diminishes over four days: 1/10 at sunset on day 1; 2/10 at sunset on day 2; 3/10 at sunset on day 3; and the remaining 4/10 at sunset on day 4. If so, then at noon on day 1, person $O$ offers 3/5 of the pie (2/10 plus 4/10) to person $E$, leaving the remaining 2/5 of the pie (1/10 plus 3/10) for person $O$, and person $E$ accepts. Person $O$ would accept nothing less. Person $E$ need offer nothing more. The logic of this allocations is backward induction.

Begin by supposing that no deal has been struck by noon on day 4, the last day when any of the pie remains. Since the day 4 is an even day, it is person $E$'s turn to make an offer. As in the one period case, person $E$ offers just a penny to person $O$, keeping the remainder – which is only 4/10 of the original pie – for himself. Now step backward from the day 4 to day 3 when 7/10 of the pie remains and when person $O$ is entitled to make the offer. Person $O$ cannot expect person $E$ to accept anything less than 4/10 of the pie, for that is what *person* E could acquire by waiting for his turn to make an offer, but person $O$ need not offer more. Person $O$ offers 4/10 of the pie to person $E$, and keeps the remaining 3/10. Step backward one more day to day 2 when 9/10 of the pie remains and person $E$ is entitled to make the offer. Person $E$ cannot expect person $O$ to accept anything less than 3/10 of the pie, for that is what person $O$ could acquire by waiting, but person $E$ need not offer more. Person $E$ offers 3/10 of the pie to person $O$, and keeps the remaining 6/10 of the pie. Finally, person $O$ is entitled to make the offer on day 1 before any of the pie has vanished. Person $O$ cannot expect person $E$ to accept anything less than 6/10 of the pie which is what person $E$ could acquire by waiting, but person $O$ need not offer more. Person $O$ offers 6/10 of the pie to person E, and keeps the remaining 4/10.

When the pie diminishes over a number of days, each bargainer captures the sum of the diminutions of the pie on the evenings of all the days when he is entitled to make the offer. Person $E$ obtains a slice equal to the sum of the diminutions in all even-numbered days, and person $O$ obtains a slice equal to the sum of the diminutions on all odd-numbered days.

Generalizing slightly, when time is graduated in years rather than days, when a pie of size $P$ diminishes spontaneously over the course of $n$ years, when person $E$ is entitled to make an offer in all even years and when person $O$ is entitled to make an offer in all odd years, then an acceptable offer would be made in the very first year of bargaining with a slice $P_E$ to person $E$ and a slice $P_O$ to person $O$

where

$$P_E = \sum_{t \text{ even}} p_t \quad \text{and} \quad P_O = \sum_{t \text{ odd}} p_t \quad \text{and} \quad P_E + P_O = P \tag{6.7}$$

and where $p_t$ is the size of the slice of the pie that disappears on the year $t$. This is an equilibrium bargain because it is in the interest of each person to accept a share of the pie equal to the sum of the disappearances in all of the years when he would be entitled to make the take-it-or-leave-it offer. None of the pie is lost in the process of bargaining because the bargain is struck in the of the first year before any of the pie has disappeared.

An interesting extension of this model replaces disappearance by discounting. Suppose that i) the pie over which people bargain lasts undiminished forever, or would do so unless a bargain is struck, but ii) both bargainers value present income over future income, each in accordance with his own rate of discount, and iii) bargainers are entitled to make offers in alternative years. It is proved in the appendix to this chapter that, once again, a bargain is struck as soon as bargaining begins, but that now the equilibrium shares of the pie are inversely proportional to the bargainers' discount rates. Specifically, person $E$'s share becomes

$$s = r_O/(r_E + r_O) \tag{6.8a}$$

and person $O$'s share must be

$$(1 - s) = r_E/(r_E + r_O) \tag{6.8b}$$

where $r_E$ and $r_O$ are the discount rates of persons $E$ and $O$. If my discount rate is high, my share of the pie is correspondingly low. To have a high discount rate is analogous to sacrificing a large share of the pie if one refuses the other bargainer's offer, so that one's equilibrium share of the pie is correspondingly reduced. Equation (6.8) is called the Staahl–Rubinstein bargaining solution.[7]

To induce a deal as soon as bargaining begins, the present value of the pie must be made to shrink when the deal is delayed. Two equally effective processes have been discussed: physical contraction over time, and reduction in present value due to discounting. The processes are analytically similar, but the latter has the distinct advantage that it is based upon the characteristics of bargainers (their rates of discount) rather than upon the imposed conditions in which bargaining takes place. Rates of discount are attached to people. Physical shrinkage of the pie is not.

The explanation based upon bargainers' discount rates has serious problems of its own. As shown in the appendix, Equation (6.8) is strictly valid as a bargaining equilibrium if and only if the bargainers are immortal and the pie lasts forever in the event that no bargain is struck. The Staahl–Rubinstein bargaining solution requires that bargainers $E$ and $O$ be prepared to carry on making offer and counter-offer until the year 3016 if no agreement had been reached before that date. Without that assumption, Equation (6.8) is just an approximation, though it becomes more and more accurate the longer the time before the pie finally disappears.

Nothing so extreme is required for the explanation based on physical diminution of the pie. Bargaining opportunities arise from time to time, and then disappear. In business and politics, it is rare for today's opportunities to remain available in five years' time, and it is not unreasonable to suppose that physical shrinkage of the pie might have more impact on the outcome of bargaining than bargainers' rates of discount.

The relative importance of discounting and shrinkage of the pie can be assessed by incorporating both in a larger model. Suppose

- both parties discount future income,
- starting in the year 0, the parties are entitled to make offers in alternate years up to the time when an offer is accepted or the pie is arbitrarily assigned, and
- if no deal is struck by the year $T$, there is an imposed allocation of the pie with a share $S$ to person $E$ and a share $(1 - S)$ to person $O$.

It is shown in the appendix that a bargain is struck immediately in the very first year of bargaining, with a share $s(0)$ to person $E$, where (to a first approximation and abstracting from a small first-mover advantage)

$$s(0) = (1 - z)[r_O/(r_E + r_O)] + zS \tag{6.9}$$

and where

$$z = 1/[(1 + r_E)(1 + r_O)]^{(T-1)/2} \tag{6.10}$$

so that $z = 1$ when $T = 1$, $z = 0$ when $T$ approaches infinity, and person $E$'s share varies steadily from $S$ when $T = 1$ to $r_O/\{r_E + r_O\}$, which is the Staahl–Rubinstein bargaining solution, when $T$ approaches infinity.

Suppose, for example, that the pie is divided equally ($S = \frac{1}{2}$) in the eighth year unless a deal is struck beforehand (i.e. $T = 8$), that person $E$'s discount rate is 9 per cent ($r_E = 0.09$) and that person $O$'s discount rate is 1 per cent ($r_O = 0.01$). If so, the pie is allocated by common consent in the year 0, with a share of 37.2 per cent to person $E$ and the remaining 62.8 per cent to person $O$. In the year 0, person $E$ would offer person $O$ a share of 62.8 per cent and person $O$ would accept. By contrast, if the pie would remain undiminished forever, person $E$'s share would be only 10 per cent in accordance with the pure Staahl–Rubinstein bargaining solution in Equation (6.8) or, equivalently, in Equation (6.9) when $T$ approaches infinity. Person $E$'s share of 37.2 per cent in this deal is much closer to the 50 per cent he would obtain if the bargainers did not discount future income than the 10 per cent he would obtain if bargainers discounted future income but the pie lasted forever. One example proves nothing, but it does highlight the significance of the assumption in the Staahl–Rubinstein model that the pie remains undiminished, and ready to be allocated, forever unless some bargain is struck.

An equilibrium bargain can be computed for any arbitrarily assigned pattern of disappearance of the pie or apportionment of the pie between bargainers at an assigned time some years ahead. What cannot be altered if there is to be an equilibrium at all is the imposed sequence of offers to be accepted or rejected by the other party. Nothing works unless bargainers respect the required sequence of speech. The procedure itself may be agreed upon by bargainers or externally imposed. If the procedure originates from a prior agreement between the bargainers, and insofar as its outcome may be predicted from the characteristics of the bargainers and of the procedure itself, then the outcome of bargaining is foretold in the chosen procedure, and there is really nothing to bargain about. What we are calling bargaining would, once again, be play-acting, with no real give and take between bargainers and some question as to whether what is being called bargaining theory is really about bargaining at all. Nor would the procedure correspond to what we normally think of as bargaining if the procedure were externally imposed, for, once again, the outcome of bargaining would be predetermined before the bargainers ever meet.

### Conversations and threats

Whatever else it may be, bargaining is a conversation. Bargainers talk to one another, make offers, tell stories about why their offers ought to be accepted, appeal to one another's sense of fairness, reject offers, and so on. The model of bargaining as fair division ignores this aspect of bargaining altogether, for outcomes emerge directly from the initial conditions with no room for speech at all. The Staahl–Rubinstein solution acquires a certain plausibility from its resemblance to conversation, but the conversation is artificial in two respects: because, as discussed above, the equilibrium deal is struck before any actual conversation takes place, and because bargainers are severely restricted in what they can say and when they can say it. Speech is limited to three, and only three, utterances: 'I offer ...', 'Yes' and 'No', with a switch in the bargainers' roles at each stage of the conversation, until a deal is struck. There is a prescribed spacing between utterances and a prescribed order of speech, neither of which are to be found in actual conversation or negotiation between firms, between employer and employees or between the buyer and seller of a house.

Actual bargaining is far less orderly and coherent. There is no fixed order of speech. People interrupt one another. People try to persuade one another of their good faith and of their unwillingness to accept one penny less than some stipulated amount. *Ex post*, negotiation may have been a sequence of offers, first by one person, then by the other. *Ex ante*, there is no prescribed order of speech, no restriction on the content of speech and, most importantly, no prescribed time between utterances. And it is the *ex ante* sequence, or absence of sequence, that matters in actual bargaining. Nobody enforces the prescribed sequence of offers or the rule of silence in the intervals between one offer and the next. Talk is unrestricted. There are in practice no gags, and, without gags, it is virtually impossible to predict what the outcome of bargaining will be. The ordering of speech in the

Staahl–Rubinstein model is more than a convenient simplification. It is an essential part of the model without which the model falls apart completely.

Equally indispensable to the Staahl–Rubinstein bargaining solution is the assumption of 'sub-game perfection': that bargainers cannot promise today to act tomorrow in a way that will not be in their interest when tomorrow comes. What this amounts to is the total banishment from the model of promises and threats. Return to the example where $r_E = 9$ per cent, $r_O = 1$ per cent and the pie remains undiminished but unallocated forever unless some bargain is struck. In that case, the Staahl–Rubinstein bargaining solution supplies 10 per cent of the pie to person E and the remaining 90 per cent to person $O$. An entirely different outcome emerges if person E can commit himself but person $O$ cannot. Then, person $E$ can appropriate any share of the pie – say 60 per cent – by committing to accept nothing less. Person $E$ might make the commitment binding by means of a side contract to pay a third party a substantial sum if he accepts less than 60 per cent of the pie in his bargain with person $O$. Person $O$ must give way, for the alternative is to lose the entire pie and to acquire nothing. To be sure, person $E$ has no monopoly on threats. If person $E$ can make threats backed up by side contracts or by a need to preserve his reputation as a tough and astute bargainer, then so too can person $O$. If both parties can be stubborn and if their demands are incompatible, adding up to more than the value of the pie to be shared, there can be no agreement and both end up with nothing.

Risk of failure makes bargainers cautious but does not abolish threats altogether. Abandon the rigid sequence, and the outcome of bargaining comes to depend on who gets to make the first threat, on the credibility of threats, on the parties' concern for their reputations, and on how stubborn the bargainers choose to be. Abandon the rigid sequence, and the neat bargaining equilibrium disintegrates. The postulate of sub-game perfection preserves the sequence automatically. There may be times when this postulate is reasonable and accurate, but there are surely other times when it is not. Bargainers may have an incentive to hang tough, to 'make yourself into a force of nature'. Adolph Hitler is alleged to have said while bargaining that 'one of us has got to be reasonable, and it isn't going to be Hitler'.

The *locus classicus* on threats and blackmail is Schelling (1956). The article is not, strictly speaking, a theory of bargaining, for it supplies no formal prediction of how shares of a pie will actually be allocated among the claimants. It is an examination of relevant considerations, placing considerable stress on commitment and on the importance of binding oneself to refuse anything less than some large share of the pie. Perhaps, the lion's share of the pie goes to whoever is the first to commit himself and to communicate that commitment to the other bargainer, but it is virtually impossible to say a priori who that will turn out to be.

Concern for reputation may influence bargaining in two opposite ways. On the one hand, you want a reputation for being reasonable and accommodating to induce prospective partners to join with you in new ventures. Nobody wants to become your partner if you are expected to be too rigid whenever conflicts of interest arise. One the other hand, costly intransigence today may pay off tomorrow as a warning to partners that you can be tough. Your partners might be induced to concede to your demands if you have acquired a reputation for being stubborn enough to resist conceding to their's. You want to appear soft to prospective partners and hard afterwards. The postulate of sequential rationality, or sub-game perfection, abstracts such behaviour away. Seduced by the elegance of these assumptions – possibly even by the connotations of the words 'rationality' and 'perfection', for who can object to anything that is at once rational and perfect – a vast range of behaviour is swept out of sight. Schelling's essay remains as a corrective, even a reproach, to much of the more recent literature on bargaining.

## Reconsideration of the paradigmatic bargain

Useful as it is for the exposition of bargaining theory, the paradigmatic bargain is a great simplification of bargaining as it actually occurs. It is exemplified in Figure 6.1 by a deal between two inventors sharing the revenue from their invention. Other contexts might be kept in mind as the assumptions of the paradigmatic bargain are reviewed: firms bargaining to avoid a costly law suit, countries bargaining to avert war and politicians bargaining over the platform of a political party. Simplifications in the paradigmatic bargain can be classified as:

- surrounding property rights
- unique no-agreement point
- common perception of the no-agreement point
- bargaining over money rather than actions
- two bargainers
- no transaction cost
- no externalities

Assumptions about surrounding property rights draw a clear line between disputed and undisputed income, so that there is no question about which people are, and which are not, jointly entitled to the disputed income and the agreed-upon shares of the disputed income become a part of each bargainer's property rights. Once struck, a bargain must be secure, so that one can never return to the scene of the bargain demanding more. As depicted in Figure 6.1, bargaining is a completion of property rights, a voluntary transformation of unallocated jointly owned property into allocated private property, to be protected like all property by the state.

The unique no-agreement point may be a pair of expected rather than actual incomes. Consider once again the engineer, $E$, and the ophthalmologist, $O$, in the original paradigmatic bargain. They have an understanding about the allocation of the surplus from their invention, but a dispute has arisen about the meaning of their contract. The dispute is over an amount of money, $P$, which may be allocated between them by litigation or by agreement. Suppose allocation by litigation is costly, but allocation by agreement is not. Assume for convenience that the cost of litigation, $L$, is the same for both parties, that, instead of dividing the disputed sum between the two parties, the court would award the whole amount to one party or to the other, and that there is a probability, $\pi$, of the court awarding the disputed income to person $E$. In these circumstances, the no-agreement point becomes a pair of certainty equivalent incomes, $(Y_E, Y_O)$, such that

$$u^E(Y_E) = \pi u^E(\underline{Y}_E + P - L) + (1 - \pi)u^E(\underline{Y}_E - L) \tag{6.11}$$

and

$$u^O(Y_O) = \pi u^O(\underline{Y}_O - L) + (1 - \pi)u^O(\underline{Y}_O + P - L) \tag{6.12}$$

where $u^E$ and $u^O$ are utility of income functions of persons $E$ and $O$ respectively and where $\underline{Y}_E$ and $\underline{Y}_O$ are their outside incomes, incomes having nothing to do with the dispute between them. As long as each person is aware of the other's outside income and utility function, and as long as person $E$'s chance of success at litigation, $\pi$, is common knowledge, then the no-agreement point as a pair of certainty equivalent incomes is common knowledge as well. Actual incomes in the absence of an agreement are replaced by certainty equivalents, but otherwise Figure 6.1 remains the same.[8]

Common perceptions are different. Without common perceptions, the no-agreement point in Figure 6.1 must be replaced by two distinct points, one as seen by person $E$ and the other as seen by person $O$. Suppose, specifically, that person $E$ and person $O$, while continuing to perceive the same values of $P$ and $L$ in Equations (6.11) and (6.12), have different perceptions of the probability, $\pi$, that the court will decide in favour of person $E$. Person $E$ perceives a value of $\pi^E$ and person $O$ perceives a value of $\pi^O$, where $\pi^E > \pi^O$ when both persons are relatively optimistic about their prospects at litigation. Then, as illustrated in Figure 6.2, the no-agreement point as seen by person $E$ is $\alpha_E$ representing the certainty equivalent incomes – $Y_E$ and $Y_O$ in Equations (6.11) and (6.12) – corresponding to person $E$'s perception, $\pi^E$, of his chance of success at litigation, and the no-agreement point as seen by person $O$ is $\alpha_O$ representing the certainty equivalent incomes corresponding to person $O$'s perception of person $E$'s chance of success at litigation. Person $E$'s perceived no-agreement point, $\alpha_E$, must be to the northwest of person $O$'s perceived no-agreement point, $\alpha_O$, whenever $\pi^E > \pi^O$. Corresponding to the two perceived no-agreement points are two perceived ranges of mutually advantageous bargains, $\beta_E\delta_E$ and $\beta_O\delta_O$. These ranges may or may not overlap. They are shown as overlapping in Figure 6.2, but there would be no overlap and no prospect whatsoever of a deal to circumvent litigation if $\pi^E$ were very much larger than $\pi^O$. Even with a common range, $\beta_O\delta_E$, of perceived mutually advantageous bargains, each person would see the deal as occupying a relatively unattractive portion of the bargaining range.[9]

Countries bargain as an alternative to war, but bargains between countries differ from bargains between people in several ways. Disputes between countries are typically about territory rather than money, one country's gain is the other's loss

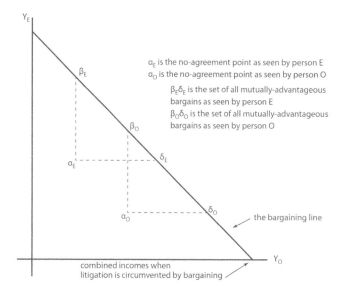

*Figure 6.2* Discordant optimism.

and, unlike the paradigmatic bargain where failure to agree is the loss of potential benefit to both bargainers, failure of countries to agree is an aggregate loss
of life and income. Disputes between countries also differ from disputes between
people in the absence of secure property rights to whatever the bargainers agree
upon. Resolution disputes between people, whether by bargaining or by litigation,
creates new property rights that are protected by the state. Resolution of disputes between countries do not, except to the extent that agreements are enforced
by international law. Typically, countries cannot credibly commit themselves to
remain peaceful, and what a country gives up in a bargain today may influence
its ability to wage war tomorrow. Locations of the no-agreement points, $\alpha_E$ and
$\alpha_O$, may be affected by military expenditure,[10] by random events and by which
country strikes first. Four distinct no-agreement points may be identified, associated with different expectations about each country's chance of winning the war
and about first strike advantages. One country may go to war today in fear that the
other will go to war tomorrow.[11]

Bargaining over actions – I'll do this as long as you do that – would be essentially the same as bargaining over the apportionment of money if the costs of
actions could be identified and, more importantly, if promised actions could be
observed and enforced by the state. This requirement may be missing in deals
between firms to cooperate in common ventures.[12] It may also be missing in bargaining within groups of voters who can make themselves better off at the expense
of the rest of the electorate if and only if they can credibly agree to support some
policy through thick and thin whatever else may be proposed.[13]

Restriction of the paradigmatic bargain to two bargainers may or may not be important depending on whose consent is required for a deal to be struck. Extra bargainers may complicate the situation but do not change the paradigmatic bargain fundamentally as long as unanimous agreement among all bargainers, no matter how many, is required for the allocation of the pie to proceed. Extra bargainers change things fundamentally when unanimity is replaced by plurality, transferring bargaining into majority rule voting and introducing the prospect of bargaining among members of the majority coalition over the apportionment of whatever monetary or policy advantages participation in a majority coalition provides.

Bargaining may impose transaction cost. Ambiguity of the entitlement to $P$ may lead bargainers to actions causing their combined allocation, $\Delta Y_E + \Delta Y_O$ in Equations (6.2) and (6.3), to fall below, $P$, as it would be if bargaining were costless. Transaction cost has been described as cost 'that cannot be conceived in a Robinson Crusoe economy' (Cheung, 1987: 56), of 'executing contracts effectively, attenuating opportunism' (Williamson, 1979: 233–61) and of 'establishing and maintaining property rights' (Allen, 1991: 1–18).[14] Minimization of transaction cost is commonly advocated as a criterion for choosing among alternative laws, the premise being that the best law for any given purpose is whatever requires the lowest transaction cost. Transaction cost is an elastic expression. The cost of litigation or war may be interpreted as transaction cost. It was assumed in the exposition of the paradigmatic bargain that bargaining is costless. Strictly speaking, that need not be so because bargaining is time consuming and may involve legal expenses. What is important here is that the cost, if any, of bargaining be very much less than the cost of what bargaining is intended to circumvent.

Bargaining externalities are gains, or losses as the case may be, to people other than the bargainers themselves. Such gains or losses may be of no interest to the bargainers, but they are surely relevant when bargains can be encouraged or discouraged by public policy. Externalities may be positive or negative. Positive externalities are likely to arise from patent pools facilitating the development of new products. Negative externalities are likely to arise from cartels. Both externalities are also present in majority rule voting. Bargaining yields a positive externality when, for example, most legislators favour some type of health-care reform, legislators differ about what exactly the reform should be, and a deal must be struck if any health-care bill is to be passed. A major negative externality arises from the 'exploitation problem' in majority rule voting, but the externality here is more than the waste of money; it is the risk of the dissolution of democratic government. Constitutional rules and parliamentary procedure are designed in part to keep such predatory bargaining in check.

A common theme in much of the literature on bargaining is the reconciliation of the bargaining equilibrium in the paradigmatic bargain – based upon the Nash bargaining solution or the Staahl–Rubinstein bargaining solution – with the fact that bargaining often fails in practice, so that people do resort to litigation and countries do go to war. Relaxing some of the implicit assumptions in the paradigmatic bargain supplies reasons why mutually advantageous bargains might not be struck. People may be just plain stubborn, unable to agree on the selection of one particular allocation of the pie from among a set of all mutually advantageous allocations, some relatively advantageous to one party, some relatively advantageous to the other.

*** 

In high school geometry, we derived far from self-evident theorems – such as that the square on the hypotenuse equals the sum of the squares on the other two sides – from axioms seen as self-evidently correct. In the social sciences, we have no such luxury. Axioms are no longer self-evidently correct, but must instead be sufficiently representative of what the theorems are about to render theorems interesting and useful: not so close as to convert theorems into tautologies, but not so distant as to raise doubts about whether the terms in the theorems correspond to what they are claimed to depict. '$X$ implies $X'$ is as valid as a theorem can be, but it doesn't inspire much confidence in the truth of $X$. A theorem about, for example, prices would not really be about prices if what are called prices in the assumptions had wings or were announced, arbitrarily and permanently, from on high.

The Nash bargaining solution is not a tautology, but it is open to misuse. It is proved that, if bargainers are prepared to split the difference in certain simple situations and on several other quite plausible assumptions, then a mutually acceptable bargain is struck in more complex situations such as the allocation of things rather than money, a bargain characterized by the maximization of the expression on the left-hand side of Equation (6.6). The misuse is to suppose that the theorem supplies reason to believe that a fair bargain will actually be struck. That is an assumption rather than an implication of the theorem.

By contrast, the Staahl–Rubinstein bargaining solution requires assumptions that are very far from the circumstances of bargaining as we know it. The fixed sequence of speech, the preservation of the pie forever unless a bargain is struck and the blocking of commitments by the postulate of sub-game perfection are so far from bargaining as we know it as to raise questions about whether what is called bargaining in the model is really bargaining at all.

As mentioned at the beginning of this chapter, bargaining solutions acquire plausibility from an implicit comparison with perfect competition. At the core of economics is the proposition that there is a domain of society where outcomes are not just determinate but desirable when everybody does as exactly they please without regard for anybody else. There are of course many qualifications and exceptions which are the responsibility of economists to recognize. What is astonishing about the proposition, or would be if the proposition were not so universally recognized, is that it is ever true at all. The proof of the existence and optimality of the competitive equilibrium passes the two-part test that the assumptions are in themselves reasonable but not so close to the conclusion as the render the conclusion uninformative.

Bargaining theory can be seen as the search for a comparable equilibrium. Universal self-interest in the Staahl–Rubinstein solution or a shared sense of fairness in the Nash solution are thought to render bargaining equally determinate. The thesis in this chapter is that bargaining and markets are fundamentally different.

There may be empirical regularities in bargaining, but that is all. It is of course impossible to prove that no satisfactory bargaining equilibrium will ever be discovered. It is argued here that none has been discovered yet and that the prospects do not look favourable. Society runs on a mixture of self-interest and compromise, not self-interest alone.

This story in this chapter reinforces the economist's traditional suspicion of bargaining and rejection of the common belief that people 'sitting around the table' can always be expected to resolve disputes. The moral of the story is to restrict the scope of bargaining. Laws, rules and institutions should be designed to consign as much as possible of the world's work to the domain where self-interest can be recruited for the common good, conserving our limited capacity to bargain and compromise for those domains where bargaining and compromise are really indispensable because nothing else will do.

## Appendix 6A: Derivation of the Staahl–Rubinstein bargaining solution

A pie is to be shared by agreement between two people, $E$ and $O$, both completely rational and unreservedly greedy, through a prescribed sequence of alternating offers, terminating when an offer is accepted. There is one, and only one, offer per year. In the first minute of every year $t$, one person – person $E$ in even years and person $O$ in odd years – makes an offer assigning a share $s(t)$ to person $E$ and a share $1 - s(t)$ to person $O$. In the second minute, the other person says either 'yes' or 'no'. If 'yes', the pie is immediately divided accordingly. If 'no', nothing happens until the following year when the process is repeated with the roles reversed. The pie remains undiminished and unallocated forever or until somebody's offer is accepted.

The Staahl–Rubinstein bargaining solution is an equilibrium determination of shares depending on the persons' rates of interest, $r_E$ for person $E$ and $r_O$ for person $O$. Although bargaining could go on indefinitely, the very opposite occurs. Whichever person is entitled to make the first offer proposes a share $r_O/(r_O + r_E)$ for person $E$, leaving a share $r_E/(r_O + r_E)$ for person $O$. The other party accepts.

The derivation of the Staahl–Rubinstein bargaining solution makes use of the intermediate assumption that, if no deal is struck by some year $T$, the pie is then allocated arbitrarily with a share $S$ assigned to person $E$ and the remaining share $(1 - S)$ assigned to person $O$. The solution itself is then derived by raising $T$ to infinity. A key assumption in the proof is sub-game perfection: neither party can promise to refuse any offer of less than some given share if that offer is the best available at the time it is made. Suppose for convenience that the process begins in the year 0 and that $T$ is even, so that person $E$ makes the first offer and the final offer as well.

The proof is by reverse induction. In the year $T$, person $E$ offers to take a share $S$, leaving person $O$ with a share $(1 - S)$. Person $O$ will not take less because $(1 - S)$ is his arbitrarily assigned share in the year $T$, and person $E$ need not offer more. Thus,

$$S(T) = S \tag{6A.1}$$

Go back one year to the year $T - 1$ when it is person $O$'s turn to make the offer. Person $O$'s offer, $s(T - 1)$, to person $E$ must leave person $E$ no worse off than person $E$ would be by waiting one year for his assigned share, $S$, of the pie, but person $O$ need not offer more. The present value in the year $T - 1$ of a share $S$ in the year $T$ is $S/(1 + r_E)$, and that is what person $E$ is offered.

$$s(T - 1) = S/(1 + r_E) \tag{6A.2}$$

leaving a share $1 - S/(1 + r_E)$ for person $O$.

Now step back an additional year to $T - 2$ when person $E$ is again entitled to make the offer. The most that person $E$ need offer person $O$ is $[1 - S/(1 + r_E)]/(1 + r_O)$ which is the present value of what person $O$ could obtain by waiting a year for his turn to make an offer. Person $E$'s share is the remainder

$$s(T - 2) = 1 - [1 - S/(1 + r_E)]/(1 + r_O) = x + zS \tag{6A.3}$$

where $x = r_O/(1 + r_O)$ and $z = 1/(1 + r_O)(1 + r_E)$.

The derivation of person $E$'s offer in the year when bargaining begins makes use of the fact that person $E$'s share in the year $T - 4$ bears precisely the relation to his share in the year $T - 2$ that his share in the year $T - 2$ bore to his share in the year $T$, and so on all the way back to the year 0. Specifically,

$$s(T - 4) = x + zs(T - 2) = x + z[x + zS] = x[1 + z] + z^2 S \tag{6A.4}$$

$$s(T - 6) = x + zs(T - 4) = x[1 + z + z^2] + z^3 S \tag{6A.5}$$

and so on, each pair of years adding an extra term to the time series in square brackets and an extra power of $z$ in the second expression, until

$$s(0) = x[1 + z + z^2 + \cdots + z^{(T/2)-1}] + z^{T/2} S = (1 - z^{T/2})[x/(1 - z)] + z^{T/2} S \tag{6A.6}$$

which is a weighted average of $[x/(1 - z)]$ and $S$, equal to the former when $T$ approaches infinity and to the latter when $T = 0$. Note finally that

$$x/(1 - z) = (r_O + r_O r_E)/(r_O + r_E + r_O r_E) \cong r_O/(r_O + r_E) \tag{6A.7}$$

where the approximation holds exactly when the 'years' are short enough to remove person $E$'s first mover advantage. Ignoring $r_O r_E$, the equilibrium share, $s(0)$, of person $E$ is

$$s(0) = (1 - z^{T/2})[r_O/(r_O + r_E)] + (z^{T/2})S \tag{6A.8}$$

which is Equation (6.9) in the text. As soon as bargaining begins, person $E$ offers a share $1 - s(0)$ to person $O$, leaving a share $s(0)$ for himself. Person $O$ accepts, and the bargain is struck. From Equation (6A.8), it follows that $s(0) = r_O/(r_O + r_E)$ when $T$ approaches infinity and that $s(0) = S$ when $T = 1$.

Suppose $r_O = 1$ per cent and $r_E = 9$ per cent. Person $E$'s share in the Staahl–Rubinstein bargaining solution is $1/10$. Person $E$'s share rises to 37.2 per cent, in accordance to Equation (6A.8), when an arbitrary distribution with $S = \frac{1}{2}$ would be imposed in the year 8 (i.e., $T = 8$) if a deal has not already been reached. A similar formula could be derived from the assumption that the pie disintegrates if not already allocated by agreement in some year $T$.

# Notes

1 Earlier versions of this chapter appeared as Usher (2001) and Usher (2012).
2 The notion of fairness can be expanded from mere equality, as in Nash's model, to include the absence of envy with an appeal to efficiency when equality and the absence of envy cannot be attained except by trimming the pie. For a thorough analysis of these considerations see Brams and Taylor (1996).
3 The Nash bargaining solution need not be redistributive if utility functions differ. Suppose i) that persons $E$ and $O$ are bargaining over the allocation of $P$ dollars, ii) that their utility functions are $U_E = (Y_E)^{\frac{1}{2}}$ and $U_O = Y_O$ where $Y_E$ and $Y_O$ are their incomes, and iii) that, to keep the arithmetic simple, the initial income of person $E$ is zero. On these assumptions, the value of $\Delta u^E \Delta u^O$ in Equation (6.6) reduces to $[(sP)^{\frac{1}{2}}][(1 - s)P]$ which is maximized when $s = 1/3$. The fair share of person $E$ is either one half or one third depending on whether fairness is defined with reference to dollars or to utils. This is true despite the fact that person $E$ could well be very much less well off than person $O$.
4 Such a mechanism is analysed by Axelrod (1984).
5 For a critical review of these models, see Harsanyi (1956).
6 See also Ellingsen (1999).
7 The earliest bargaining solution of this type was proposed by Ingolf Staahl (1972). A more tractable form of the model was proposed by Ariel Rubinstein (1982). For a short and simple demonstration of the Staahl–Rubinstein bargaining model, see Sutton (1986). For a thorough treatment of the subject, see Osborne and Rubinstein (1990) and Muthoo (1999).
8 A more realistic account of the cost of litigation might employ a model of conflict where each party's expenditure on litigation is chosen to generate the most advantageous no-agreement point, taking account of how the other party is expected to behave. On conflict models, see Hirshleifer (1991).
9 Priest and Klein (1984) explain the resort to litigation by the failure to strike mutually advantageous bargains when parties to a dispute see different no-agreement points, each relatively favourable to oneself.
10 See Garfinkel (1990).
11 Fearon (1995) classifies 'rational explanations for war' under the headings of 'rational miscalculation' (referred to here as 'discordant optimism'), the 'commitment problem' and 'indivisibilities' (i.e. who shall be king).
12 Hart (1995) shows how close working relations between firms could be preferable to amalgamation into one large firm if and only if the firms' agreed-upon actions could be observed and, therefore, enforced by the state.

13 Otherwise, such deals can be undermined by an agenda setter who can, in some circumstances, manipulate the legislature to adopt whatever policy he prefers. See Riker (1980).
14 Transaction cost is defined as the sum of certain types of cost to all participants in a transaction. As such, it implicitly subsumes all impediments to bargaining under the heading of cost, and it treats the distribution of income as irrelevant for the choice of laws. For an explanation of how the concept is employed, see Posner (1998).

# References

Allen, Douglas (1991) What are transactions costs?, *Research in Law and Economics*, 14, 1–18.

Axelrod, Robert (1984) *The Evolution of Cooperation*, New York: Basic Books.

Brams, Steven, J. and Taylor, Alan, D. (1996) *Fair Division: From Cake-cutting to Dispute Resolution*, Cambridge: Cambridge University Press.

Cheung, Steven (1987) Economic organization and transaction cost, In John Eatwell, Murray Milgate and Peter Newman, (Eds), *The New Palgrave: A Dictionary of Economics*. London: Palgrave Macmillan.

Cross, John, G. (1965) A theory of the bargaining process, *American Economic Review*, 55(1–2), 67–94.

Edgeworth, F. Y. (1961[1881]) *Mathematical Psychics*, New York: Augustus M. Kelley.

Ellingsen, Tore (1999) The evolution of bargaining behaviour, *Quarterly Journal of Economics*, 112(2), 581–601.

Fearon, James (1995) Rational explanations for war, *International Organization*, 49(3), 379–414.

Garfinkel, Michelle (1990) Arming as strategic investment in cooperative equilibrium, *American Economic Review*, 80(1), 50–68.

Harsanyi, John (1956) Approaches to the bargaining problem before and after the theory of games: a critical discussion of Zeuthen's, Hicks's and Nash's Theories, *Econometrica*, 24(2),144–57.

Hart, Oliver (1995) *Firms, Contracts and Financial Structure*, Oxford: Clarendon Press.

Hicks, John, R. (1932) *The Theory of Wages*, London: Macmillan, chapter vii.

Hirshleifer, Jack (1991) The technology of conflict as an economic activity, *American Economic Review*, 81(2), 130–4.

Muthoo, Abhinay (1999) *Bargaining Theory with Applications*, Cambridge: Cambridge University Press.

Nash, John (1950) The bargaining problem, *Econometrica*, 18(2), 155–62.

Osborne, Martin and Rubinstein, Ariel (1990) *Bargaining and Markets*, New York: Academic Press.

Posner, Richard (1998) *Economic Analysis of Law*, Boston: Little Brown.

Priest, George and Klein, Benjamin (1984) The selection of disputes for litigation, *Journal of Legal Studies*, 13(1), 1–55.

Riker, William (1980) *Liberalism versus Populism*, San Francisco: W. H. Freeman.

Rubinstein, Ariel (1982) Perfect equilibrium in a bargaining model, *Econometrica*, 50(1), 97–109.

Schelling, Thomas (1956) An essay on bargaining, *American Economic Review*, 46(3), 281–306.

Staahl, Ingolf (1972) *Bargaining Theory*, Stockholm: EFI.

Sutton, J. (1986) Non-cooperative bargaining theory: an introduction, *Review of Economic Studies*, 53(5), 709–24.

Usher, Dan (2001) *Mysterious Bargaining*, QED Queen's Economics Department Working Paper, no. 1001.

Usher, Dan (2012) Bargaining unexplained, *Public Choice*, 151(1–2), 23–41.

Williamson, Oliver (1979) Transaction cost economics: the governance of contractual relations, *Journal of Law and Economics*, 22(2), 233–61.

Zeuthen, F. (1930), *Problems of Monopoly and Economic Warfare*, London: G. Routledge & Sons.

# 7   What exactly is a duty to vote?

A duty to vote may be nothing more than a minimal obligation to show up at the ballot box, or it may also prescribe rules about how to choose among competing political parties or candidates for office. This chapter is a defence of the narrower interpretation. The claim is that what citizens see – and ought to see – as a duty to vote is the minimal obligation alone. As long as one does not vote frivolously or cruelly, a duty to vote contains no prescription for choosing among candidates or political parties. A duty to vote is not primarily to procure the socially preferred outcome in today's election. It is to protect government by majority rule voting.

Duty has no place in conventional economic analysis where a clear line is typically drawn between the private sector within which people are assumed to be unreservedly greedy and the public sector within which actions are taken in accordance with some notion of the common good. Citizens' obligations to pay taxes and obey the law are enforced by the threat of punishment. Nobody is assumed to do what is right for no other reason than that it is the right thing to do.

Voting conforms badly to this pattern. On the one hand, it is essential for the preservation of what we all see as a good society that large numbers of people choose to vote rather than to abstain. On the other hand, it is somewhere between difficult and impossible to compel one another do vote appropriately. No voice from on high tells us what exactly a duty to vote requires of us, how to weigh public and private good and how one person's obligation is affected by another's refusal to recognize any such obligation.

In general, duty is a moral requirement upon the citizen to act in accordance with a rule where:

1   There must be something important at stake. Citizens must expect to be significantly better off on average when they all (or an appropriately large proportion of them) comply with the rule than when a large proportion refuses to do so.
2   Self-interest alone must be insufficient to procure compliance. Each person must be better off by not acting dutifully as long as enough others act dutifully.
3   Sufficient compliance is not secured by law. No action is said to be dutiful when it is adequately enforced by the law. Risk of detection and punishment must be insufficient to procure full compliance.

There is some ambiguity about the proportion of the population required for the common benefit from dutiful behaviour to emerge. Duty arises in situations lying somewhere between a multi-person prisoners' dilemma where the sought-after benefit to society as a whole is only obtained when everybody acts dutifully and a multi-person chicken game where one dutiful person is sufficient. Required proportions vary from case to case.

We begin with an attempt to specify what is at stake. For there to be a duty to vote, society as a whole must be significantly better off when everybody, or almost everybody, votes than when a large portion of the eligible voters abstains. A critique of arguments to the contrary – that abstention may sometimes be harmless or socially advantageous on balance – is a vehicle for showing where exactly the harm from abstention lies. A distinction is then drawn between what will be called wide and narrow duties to vote. A wide duty to vote is an obligation to vote for the party that seems best for society as a whole. A narrow duty to vote is an obligation to vote rather than to abstain, with no additional obligation about who or what to vote for. A case will be made for the narrow interpretation. There are also brief discussions of expressive voting and the avoidance vicarious cruelty.

In the classic formulation (Riker and Ordeshook, 1968) of the role of duty in voting, a person votes or abstains according to whether

$$\pi B + D > C \qquad\qquad (7.1)$$

where $B$ is one's personal benefit if one's preferred party wins the election, $D$ is the value one places upon voting as a duty to the rest of the community, $C$ is one's cost of voting and $\pi$ is the probability of casting a pivotal vote, of swinging the outcome of an election from the political party one opposes to the political party one favours.

This representation of the cost and expected benefit of voting highlights two important aspects of a person's decision whether to vote or abstain. The first called the *paradox of not voting* is that, though everybody is better off when everybody votes, it is in nobody's immediate self-interest to do so. Voting rather than abstaining is beneficial to the voter himself if and only if one's vote is pivotal, swinging the outcome of the election from one party to another. One's chance of casting a pivotal vote is generally believed to be so small that, to the purely self-interested voter for whom $D = 0$, voting does not pay. Imagine yourself as an eligible voter in an election between a left party and a right party where exactly 100,000 other people are expected to vote and where, among these people, the left party is equally likely to win anywhere between 49,000 and 55,000 votes, giving it a five-to-one chance $[(55 - 50)/(50 - 49)]$ of winning the election, but, as will be discussed in detail in the next chapter, only a one-in-six thousand chance $[1/(55,000 - 49,000)]$ of casting a pivotal vote.[1] Suppose, finally, that a person's cost of voting, $C$, is $20. Thus, for voting to be advantageous to a purely self-interested voter, that voter's benefit, $B$, from a win by the party he votes for must be at least $120,000, which is substantially more than a win for one's preferred candidate is normally thought to be worth. (When $D = 0$, voting becomes advantageous if and only if $\pi B > C$, or $B > C/\pi = 20/(1/6,000) = 120,000$.)

The other aspect of voting highlighted in Equation (7.1) is what might be called *opposing externalities*. There is not much chance of a person's vote determining the outcome of an election, but, if it does, it becomes more or less equally beneficial to all of the thousands (or perhaps hundreds of thousands) of other people who favour the same candidate or party while, at the same time, harming the thousands of other people who oppose that candidate or party. Returning to our example, a tie means that 50,000 people favour each of the two political parties. Suppose everybody places a value of, say, $6,000 on a win for his preferred candidate. If so, a person's expected gain from voting is only $1 ($6,000 $\times$ 1/6,000), but the expected gain to all like-minded voters is $50,000 (50,000 $\times$ $6,000 $\times$ 1/6,000), and the expected loss to all opposing voters is $50,000 as well. The assumed cost of voting, $20, is 20 times the expected benefit to the voter, but is only a tiny fraction (20 $\div$ 50,000) of the expected gain to all like-minded voters.

Purely self-interested voting means that $D = 0$ and that people vote or abstain according to whether or not $\pi B > C$. A duty to vote arises because the probability of casting a pivotal vote is believed to be too small to make voting worthwhile. The paradox of not voting and the presence of opposing externalities are important elements in the rationale for a duty to vote and carry suggestions about what exactly that duty should be.

## The social cost of widespread abstention

As there can be no duty to vote unless widespread abstention is harmful to society as a whole, the content of the duty to vote can only be identified in the light of what that harm might be. There is some question as to whether abstention is harmful at all. It has been argued that abstention is innocuous or even socially beneficial on balance. It has also been argued that the harm from abstention is genuine and substantial. These arguments – based upon different assumptions about what voters know, how voters behave and the mechanics of majority rule voting – must be confronted in deciding what exactly a duty to vote requires. In this section, six propositions are discussed in turn, three about circumstances where abstention may be harmless followed by three about why abstention may harmful enough to warrant a duty to vote:

1   Abstention may be unbiased, avoiding the cost of voting with little or no effect on the outcomes of elections.
2   Duties are substitutable; voting is just one of many good deeds people do for one another, and it is no violation of duty to abstain and do some other good deed instead.
3   People who choose to abstain should do so because they are less knowledgeable and less public-spirited than people who choose to vote.
4   Uncoordinated abstention is biased, typically though not necessarily, against the poor, with electoral results and subsequent policy distorted accordingly.

5   By creating the opportunity for voting pacts, widespread abstention causes outcomes of elections to depend relatively more on organization of the electorate (and on funds to finance such organization) than on the preferences of the electorate.

6   Widespread abstention facilitates explicit or implicit bribery and vote buying, with voters lured by tax dollars to support one party or another.

In weighing the pros and cons of abstention, it is important to distinguish between effects on the outcome of an election today and effects on the mechanism of government by majority rule voting, the preservation of which is a large part of the rationale for a duty to vote.

### Unbiased abstention

Abstention may be socially beneficial on balance by avoiding much of the cost of voting without at the same time having any significant effect upon the outcomes of elections. How this might happen is best explained by a modification of the previous example. Replace the assumption that 100,000 people vote with the assumption that there are 100,000 people eligible to vote, some of whom may choose to abstain. Originally, when nobody abstained, each voter had a 1-in-6,000 chance of casting a pivotal vote. Suppose instead that half of the eligible the eligible voters, 50,000 people, abstain and that, among the abstainers, exactly half, 25,000, would have voted for the left party and half, 25,000, would have voted for the right party. If, without any abstentions, the left party would have won between 49,000 and 55,000 out of 100,000 votes cast, then the left party must win between 24,000 and 30,000 of the 50,000 votes cast when 25,000 supporters of each party abstain. With equal numbers of abstentions, the parties' chances of wining the election remain unchanged at 5-to-1 $[(30-25)/(25-24)]$. Each person's cost of voting ($20) and probability of casting a pivotal vote (1/6,000) remain unchanged as well. The only effect of abstentions is to reduce the total cost of voting from $2,000,000 when everybody votes to $1,000,000 when half of the eligible voters abstain. Equal abstentions are like paired absences among members of parliament on opposite sides of the aisle. Abstention is socially advantageous because the total cost of voting is reduced without changing anybody's chance of casting a pivotal vote or the parties' chances of winning the election.

The crux of this argument is that there is no duty to vote because actual abstentions are enough like this extreme example for the total cost saving from abstentions when everybody votes or abstains as he pleases them to exceed the social cost of the expected change, if any, in the outcome of the vote. The key assumption in this argument is that abstentions are equal, random or independent of party preference. A close-enough approximation to equal abstentions among supporters of both parties can be generated by replacing the assumption that fixed numbers of eligible voters abstain with the assumption that the cost of voting is a random number between 0 and some maximal amount, with no correlation between people's costs of voting and their preferences between left and right parties. Ledyard (1984) employs such an assumption to derive an equilibrium when each person chooses whether to vote or abstain. Borgers (2004) uses the assumption to show that abstention need not entail social cost. When costs of voting are randomly distributed but uncorrelated with party preference, self-interested abstention introduces some uncertainty into the outcome of an election, but the main features of the simple numerical example are preserved.

Essentially the same argument can be made by fixing people's cost of voting and allowing the benefits from a win by one's preferred party to vary from person to person, so that the people who vote are those whose benefits from a win by their preferred parties are high, and the people who abstain are those whose benefits are low. As will be shown presently, a modification of this formulation supplies a simple explanation of why abstention may be harmful on balance.

Imagine a society with $N$ voters lined up from left to right in accordance with their valuations (positive or negative) of a win for the left party. Define $B(n)$ as the $n$th person's valuation of a win for the left party – the difference between the $n$th person's income in the event of a win for the left party and the $n$th person's income in the event of a win for the right party – so that, the larger $n$, the smaller $B(n)$ must be. Person $n$ favours the left party or the right party according to whether $B(n) > 0$ or $B(n) < 0$. If the 100th voter values a win for the left party at \$2,000, then $B(100) = 2,000$. If the 3,000th voter values a win for the right party at \$500, then $B(3,000) = -500$. A schedule of all voters' valuations can be illustrated as a downward-sloping curve on a graph with valuations, $B$, on the vertical axis and voters ordered by their valuations on the horizontal axis. Three possible schedules of voters' valuations are shown in Figure 7.1. To keep matters simple, these schedules are downward-sloping straight lines with a common slope $s$.

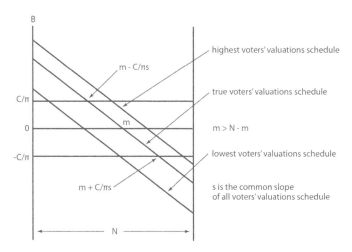

*Figure 7.1* Why abstention might be socially desirable.

Uncertainty about the outcome of an election, and the determination of every person's probability of casting a pivotal vote, are introduced here by the assumption that, through chance alone, the true voters' valuation schedule lies somewhere between the highest and the lowest schedule in the figure, and that all schedules between these limits are equally likely. The locations of the highest and lowest schedule are both common knowledge, and the true schedule is deemed equally likely to lie anywhere in between. Everybody knows that some people are left-leaning and other people are right-leaning, but nobody is quite sure which side will have the most votes on election day. Since all schedules between the highest and the lowest are equally likely, the probability, $\pi$, of a person's vote being pivotal is the inverse of the horizontal distance (the number of voters) between the highest and lowest voters' valuations schedules. Everybody's chance of casting a pivotal vote must, necessarily, be the same.[2]

Certainty about one's own value of $B$ is reconciled with uncertainty about the location of the true voters' valuations schedule by the assumption that nobody is quite sure about his own rank on the schedule; a high value of $B$ might signify a high ranking on the true schedule, or a high schedule, or a combination of the two.

With a cost of voting, $C$, and a chance of casting a pivotal vote, $\pi$, a strictly selfish person (for whom $D=0$), i) votes for the left party if and only if $B$ is greater than $C/\pi$, ii) votes for the right party (bearing in mind that $B$ would be negative) if and only if the absolute value of $B$ is greater than $C/\pi$, and iii) abstains when $B$ is in between $C/\pi$ and $-C/\pi$. The two horizontal lines in the figure are at a distance $C/\pi$ above and below the horizontal axis. People vote rather than abstain if and only if their values of $B$ lie above (when $B > 0$) or below (when $B < 0$) these lines.

Now suppose that, by chance, the in-between schedule crosses the horizontal axis at the point $m$. If voting were costless (that is, if $C = 0$), the left party would acquire m votes, and the right party would acquire $N - m$ votes. As the figure is drawn, $m > N - m$ so that left party wins the election. Self-interested abstentions reduce the number of votes for the left party from $m$ to $m - C/\pi s$ (where $s$ is the common slope of the voters' valuation curves), and reduce the number of votes for the right party from $N - m$ to $N - m - C/\pi s$. By comparison with a situation where nobody abstains, there is a total cost saving of $2(C/\pi)^2/s$, but the left party wins regardless. Once again, abstentions are unambiguously beneficial to society as a whole by reducing the cost of voting without affecting the outcome of the election.

The general principle in this example is that abstentions drawn equally from both political parties can do no harm because they have no effect upon the outcome of an election. If the left party would win by 10,000 votes when there are no abstentions and if abstentions reduce numbers of votes for both parties equally, then the left party must win by 10,000 votes regardless. If so, public policy should be directed to *increasing* the number of abstentions. Voluntary voting becomes preferable to compulsory voting. A tax or fee on voting would make everybody better off as long as the revenue from the tax is appropriately redistributed, for the total cost of voting would be reduced without affecting the outcome of elections.

The more abstentions the better, as long as abstentions are unbiased and there is some mechanism, like that in Figure 7.1, to apportion abstentions equally between political parties.

## Trading of one duty for another

Voting may be looked upon as one of a number of ethically equivalent ways of fulfilling one's obligation to be nice to one's fellow citizens. 'Citizens do not have a duty to vote. At most they have duties of beneficence and reciprocity that can be discharged in any number of ways besides voting.' (Brennan, 2011: 161). The question at hand is whether duty is singular or plural, whether there is a general obligation to assist one's fellow citizens, leaving the community no worse off when performance one duty is substituted for performance of another, or there are many specific obligations all necessary for the well-functioning of society. The answer depends on what can be expected to happen if large numbers of people abstain and do some other dutiful thing instead. Arguments below about the consequences of widespread abstention suggest that we would all be very much worse off. Different duties may be like different necessary conditions for a given end, where all such conditions must be met if the end is to be attained. One is equally charitable by contributing to the United Way as by contributing to Médecins Sans Frontières, but contributing to the United Way is no substitute for an willingness to vote. Maintenance of government by majority rule voting requires people to vote, regardless of how kind they are to one another in different ways.

## Deferential abstention

Abstention may be socially desirable when support for one party or the other originates from opinions rather than interests. By contrast with the situation considered throughout most of this chapter where each of two competing political parties is generally understood to be best for some portion of the population, voting may be about matters of common concern where one of two parties would turn out to be best for everybody, but people disagree about which party that would be.[3] Supporters of the right party believe that everybody would be better off if the right party is elected. Supporters of the left party believe that everybody would be better off if the left party is elected. People with no opinion either way or who are very unsure of their opinions might well abstain, leaving the choice between parties to others who are better informed, and it would be best for the community as a whole that they do so.[4] A distinction can be drawn between motives for abstention: self-interested abstention when the expected benefit of voting is less than the cost and deferential abstention when an eligible voter relies on other voters' judgments of what is best for everybody. Deferential abstention may be in the service of the common good.

Deferential abstention may remain socially beneficial even if nobody is absolutely certain which party is best. People who are relatively uninformed and who see a large chance they might be mistaken may choose to abstain in deference to their better informed fellow citizens.

The argument is valid on its premises, but the premises themselves are doubtful. The assumption that one of two parties will be best for everybody may be incorrect, though it is in the interest of political parties to claim this to be so. It is easy to imagine that what is best for oneself is best for everybody else as well, or perhaps the conceited vote and the modest abstain. Deferential abstention can bias the outcome of elections if people are inclined to vote for policies or parties tending to favour their own groups, regions, industries or social classes, especially if not all groups are equally informed. Nor is it clear how uncertain one must be to warrant deferential abstention

Complications arise when several motives operate at once. At any election, some people abstain to avoid the cost of voting, others in deference to their better informed fellow citizens and still others because ignorance about the policies of the political parties reduces the anticipated benefit from a pivotal vote. Want of information transforms the probability $\pi$ in Equation (7.1) from the chance of casting a pivotal vote to the chance of becoming better off as a consequence of the effect of one's vote on the outcome of the election. Nor can one be sure why one abstains. Deferential abstention may be no more than an excuse to avoid the trouble of voting. Problems arising from widespread abstention are much the same regardless of whether abstention is from deference or from self-interest.

### *Biased abstention*

Abstentions may be biased in favour of one of two competing parties. Biassed abstention can be socially desirable when, for example, a win by the right party would make everybody better off, a majority of eligible voters mistakenly believe they would be better off if the left party won instead, but, knowing themselves to be relatively uninformed, a great many supporters of the left party abstain. Bias may, of course, work in the opposite direction. The bias that worries many observers is that described in Chapter 3 where abstention by a large proportion of poor people causes public policy to shift away from the redistribution of income and toward policies of special benefit to the rich. Think of redistribution broadly defined as a single-peaked issue where the outcome of voting is a reflection of the first preference of the person with the median income not among the entire electorate, but among the portion of the electorate that actually votes. If a disproportion of the poor abstain, the median voter becomes wealthier, there is less redistribution and all poor people are made worse off than they would be if everybody chose to vote rather than to abstain. As discussed in Gilens (2012) and Bartels (2008),[5] the poor are more likely to abstain, less likely to contribute to political parties and less likely to volunteer in political campaigns, causing public policy to be more in conformity with the interests of the rich than with the interests of the poor.

The distributive consequences of biased abstention is of special concern in view of the widening distribution of income in Canada and the United States, with virtually none of the growth of income over the last 30 years accruing to the bottom half. Biased abstention may be both a consequence and a cause of the widening of the gap between rich and the poor, a consequence because, for whatever reason, abstention is correlated with income, and a cause because abstention by the poor tilts public policy in favour of the rich.

Biased abstention may be illustrated with a modification of Figure 7.1. The argument surrounding Figure 7.1 that abstention is unbiased depended critically on the assumption that the true voters' valuations schedule is linear. Otherwise, the party preferred by a majority of the population could easily fail to win the election. To show how abstention might swing an election from one party to another, it is sufficient to ignore uncertainty and to assume instead that a single voters' valuations schedule is recognized by all voters at once. The schedule in Figure 7.2 differs from the schedules in Figure 7.1 in that the slope is no longer constant throughout its length. Now the schedule is kinked at a distance $m$ along the horizontal axis, steeper to the right of the point $m$ than to the left. Think of the schedule in Figure 7.2 as one among a set of schedules bounded by upper and lower schedules so that the value of $\pi$ is the inverse of the average distance between them.

As the figure is drawn, $m > N - m$ signifying that a majority of voters favours the left party and would vote for the left party if voting were costless. The right party might win nevertheless when voting is costly. With a cost of voting $C$ and when every voter has a chance $\pi$ of casting a pivotal vote, the $n$th person votes if and only if $B(n)$ is either greater than $C/\pi$ or less than $-C/\pi$. The $n_L$ people for whom $B(n) \geq C/\pi$ vote for the left party, the $N - n_R$ people for whom $B(n) \leq -C/\pi$ vote for the right party, and the $n_R - n_L$ people for whom $C/\pi \geq B(n) \geq -C/\pi$ abstain. As Figure 7.2 is drawn, the right-hand slope is sufficiently

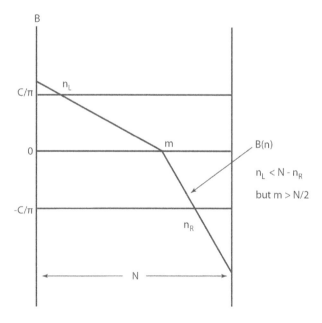

*Figure 7.2* The more popular party loses the election.

steeper than the left-hand slope so that $N - n_R > n_L$ despite the fact that $m > N - m$. Enough supporters of the left party abstain for the right party to win the election.

This is more than a theoretical curiosum. Think of the right party as the party of the rich, of the left party as the party of the poor, and of the distribution of income as skewed in the usual way with a few rich people and many poor people so that $m$ is larger than $N/2$ and the left party wins the election as long as voting is costless. The kink in the voters' valuations curve at $m$ means that rich people place relatively larger valuations on a win for the right party than poor people place on a win for the left party, so that, for any given $x$, the absolute value of $B(m + x)$ is larger than the absolute value of $B(m - x)$ and the minimal benefit $(C/\pi)$ required to make voting advantageous deters more poor people than rich people. As Figure 7.2 is drawn, sufficiently more poor people are deterred for the party of the rich minority to win the election. Abstentions provoked by the cost of voting are beneficial on average as long as there is no impact on the outcome of elections, but there are good reasons why that may not be so.[6]

It is arguable that this bias in favour of the rich is illusory because their cost of voting is higher too. If people's values of $B$ are inversely proportional to their incomes, if people's incomes per hour are proportional to their productivities of labour, and if the time required to vote is the same for everybody, then everybody's cost of voting should be proportional to income; $B/C$ would then be no larger on average for the rich than for the poor, and rich people would have no greater propensity to vote. However, this is not true of income derived from ownership of capital or where voting is sufficiently different from work that there is no one-to-one trade-off in hours devoted to each activity. The experience of working is very different from one person to the next. The experience of voting is not.

Two so far unemphasized assumptions should be mentioned. The first is that everybody knows his own value of $B$ to the penny. If not, resources can be devoted to informing or bamboozling people about the virtues of one party or the vices of the other. When everybody, or almost everybody, votes, political activity can be redirected to persuading people of the virtues of this or that political party, what it will do for particular groups of people and why it is best for the nation as a whole. When large numbers of eligible voters are expected to abstain, political activity may be concentrated on getting out the vote. The rich may vote vicariously by contributing to the cost of electioneering and campaign advertising. The other assumption is that is voters' actions are uncoordinated. Voters are assumed to do what is best for themselves (or for what they sees as best for society) in the light of what they believe the rest of the electorate may do but with no side deals among groups of eligible voters to act in unison. That need not be so.

## Voting pacts

An immediate implication of the voting externalities discussed above in connection with Equation (7.1) is that, at no extra cost, each two like-minded eligible voters can double the chance of casting a pivotal vote by a side deal in which each promises the other to vote rather than to abstain. Each of a thousand like-minded voters can multiply the chance by a thousand. Such deals may be called 'voting pacts'.

Among like-minded people, voting is the private provision of a public good. Nobody pays tax voluntarily because everybody's valuation of the extra services of the army or the police made possible by their tax alone is almost certainly less than the tax they pay. Everybody favours compulsory taxation because everybody's valuation of the entire services of the army and the police is almost certainly greater than the tax they pay. Similarly, everybody within a group of like-minded eligible voters, all pro-left or all pro-right, might promise one another to vote as long as the rest of the group does so too.[7]

Consider once again a person with a cost of voting of $20, a probability of casting a pivotal vote of 1/6,000 and, consequently, an expected cost of swinging the election of $120,000. Such a person abstains unless his benefit from a win by his preferred party exceeds $120,000. The required benefit can be cut in half by a deal between any two like-minded voters who might not otherwise vote at all. Consider two eligible voters – both supporters of the left party or both supporters of the right – each of whom values a win for his preferred party at, say, $100,000. Acting separately and self-interestedly, they would both abstain. Acting together, each voting on condition that the other does so too, they double the chance of being pivotal, from 1/6,000 to 1/3,000, cutting each of their expected costs of swinging the election from $120,000 to $60,000, at which it becomes individually advantageous for both of them to vote rather than to abstain. Acting together, 100 like-minded eligible voters can raise the probability of swinging the election from 1/6,000 to 1/60 at which voting becomes individually advantageous as long as one's benefit of a win for one's preferred party exceeds not $120,000, but only $1,200. If left-leaning voters are cooperative while right-leaning voters are not, the left party could win the election even though more than half of the eligible voters prefer the right party to the left.[8]

Voting pacts are like the production of public goods in that each participant benefits from the sum of all contributions, but voting pacts differ from ordinary public goods in important ways. Their benefits accrue not to society as a whole, but to a part of society, people favouring one of two political parties, at the expense of the rest. More importantly, there is no legally binding mechanism to ensure that all beneficiaries of voting pacts contribute their share of the cost. Agreements to share the cost of ordinary public goods are enforced by the state. Agreements to vote for one of two competing parties can only be enforced imperfectly and incompletely, through social pressure exerted by friends, neighbours, churches, labour unions and so on. Whether or not one votes can be observed. Whom one votes for cannot be observed at all. Voting pacts rely on nothing more than the exhortation to 'get out and vote' among people who recognize one another to be on the same side of the fence. That may be, but is not necessarily, sufficient depending on the degree of social cohesion.

Imperfect though they may be, voting pacts can have a profound effect upon the outcome of an election. Consider the extreme example summarized in Table 7.1 of

*Table 7.1* A two-class society

|  | Number of eligible voters favouring each party | Benefit per person of a win for the favoured party | Total surplus |
|---|---|---|---|
| Left | 900 | $100 | $90,000 |
| Right | 100 | $300 | $30,000 |

Note: The cost of voting, *C*, is $20.

a two-class society with 100 rich people each placing a value of $300 on a win for the right party, and with 900 poor people each placing $100 on a win for the left party. If everybody votes, the left party wins 9-to-1, and society would be better off too, because the dollar value of the gains from a win by the left party exceeds the dollar value of the gains from the right party.

In this society, 101 votes by left supporters is enough to ensure a win for the left party, and one extra vote, raising the total to 102, is enough to ensure that no voter, left or right, can be pivotal. With more than 101 votes for the left party, there is no chance of the right party winning the election, and additional supporters of the right party might as well abstain to save themselves the cost of voting in circumstances where their votes can have no effect.

Supporters of the left party are locked into a complex maze where each person is made better off by abstaining than by voting as long as some minimal number of other like-minded people are prepared to vote instead. Suppose once again that the cost of voting is $20. Among supporters of the left party, voters gain $80 but abstainers gain $100 as long as enough left-leaning people vote to ensure that the left party wins the election. How then are the voters selected? In a sense, the voters are suckers, bearing a burden that could very well be borne by somebody else instead. Each voter may well think to himself that, if he abstains, some other left-leaning person will be induced to vote in his place for fear of the emergence of a voting pact on the right. Perhaps supporters of one party or the other can devise a punishment for abstention. Exclusion from common activities or mere disapproval may be sufficient. Perhaps, if and when potential pact members can identify one another, they can devise a grim-trigger strategy of dissolving the entire pact if any member abstains. Pacts may be easier to enforce among all like-minded beneficiaries than among a proportion of them.

Despite the left's overwhelming majority, it remains possible for cooperation among left-leaning people to break down altogether, and for the right party to win instead. Failure is especially likely if voting is expensive. Suppose the cost of voting were $120 rather than $20. It would then be in no left supporter's interest to vote without an agreement among a number of left supporters to share the cost. The right party could easily win despite the fact that there is a net gain of $60,000 to society as a whole from a win for the left. There may be no equilibrium comparable to that illustrated in Figure 7.1, and the outcome of the election may turn on who can cooperate with whom. Voting becomes a multi-person chicken game in which a sacrifice, the cost of voting, is required on the part of some minimum number of people to procure a common reward accruing not just to those who sacrifice, but to those who refuse to do so as well.

With costly participation, a voting pact is advantageous to its members if and only if

$$\Pi B > C + K \qquad (7.2)$$

where $C$ is once again the cost of voting, $\Pi$ is the probability that the *pact* is pivotal and $K$ is the extra cost per participant of organizing and administering the pact. The value of $\Pi$ would be 1 if the pact were sure to generate a win for the party it supporters. The value of $\Pi$ would be less than 1 if there were just a chance of doing so. It is not unreasonable to suppose that the cost to each participant rises together with the size, $s$, of the pact

$$K = K(s) \qquad (7.3)$$

where $\delta K / \delta s > 0$ because it is more expensive per member to hold together a large pact than to hold together a small one.

With reference to the example in Table 7.1, it is at least possible that the right party wins the election because there is some pact of size, $s$, costing less than \$280 per member, i.e. for which

$$K(s) + 20 < 300 \qquad (7.4)$$

but none costing less than \$80 per person, no pact of size, $s$, such that

$$K(s) + 20 < 100 \qquad (7.5)$$

Despite the left's overwhelming majority, it is possible for the right party to win the election because an effective pact is feasible on the right side alone.[9]

For any given number of people eligible to vote, for any given proportions of left and right supporters in the population as a whole and as long as supporters of both parties are equally likely to abstain when there are no voting pacts, it follows at once that an increase in abstentions increases the chance of a majority being overturned by a voting pact, for abstentions automatically reduce the size of the majority that must be overcome.

Abstentions magnify the importance of mobilization as compared with persuasion. If everybody votes, then the most a party can do to increase its chance of being elected is to persuade people that it the better than its rival. Otherwise, if many people are prepared to abstain, there are likely to be substantial cadres of people on the edge of voting left or on the edge of voting right, who can be induced to vote for a party not just by arguments about its virtues, but by meetings, personal contact, transportation to the polling station and so on.

Voting pacts may be bands of fanatics – neo-Nazis being the obvious example but religion will do just as well – devoted exclusively to some cause and prepared to vote en mass for any party that will support it. The more people abstain, the stronger are such groups likely to be.

## Implicit bribery

The logic of implicit bribery by political parties is best introduced by example: There is an election to choose a leader who, once elected, has considerable authority over the finances of the community. The election is conducted by a show of hands, so that everybody knows how everybody else votes. There are two candidates, one honest and the other is dishonest. Voting is costless and everybody votes. Ignore ordinary public goods which are assumed to be the same regardless of which candidate is elected. Policies of the two candidates are the same except that, if elected, the dishonest candidate would impose a burden, $Z$, (like an extra tax with no extra benefit) on everybody, together with an additional tax $T$ on people who vote against the dishonest candidate, where the revenue from the additional tax is returned in equal amounts to all taxpayers. Suppose for the moment that everybody but a small band of righteous people votes self-interestedly and that the chance of anybody's vote being pivotal is small enough that it may be ignored. The numbers $Z$ and $T$ can be chosen so that nobody gains from the election of the dishonest candidate, but it is in each person's interest to vote for rather than against the dishonest candidate when everybody else does so too.

It is obvious what happens. Let $P$ be the expected chance of the dishonest candidate winning the election, $p$ be the proportion that votes for the honest candidate and $\pi$ be the chance that a person's vote is pivotal. If the honest candidate wins, it does not matter to anybody who voted for whom, and the magnitudes of $Z$ and $T$ become irrelevant. If the dishonest candidate wins, everybody who votes for the dishonest candidate bears a loss of $Z - pT$ where $p$ is the proportion of the electorate that votes for the honest candidate, while everybody who votes for the honest candidate bears a loss of $Z + T(1 - p)$. Since the loss from voting for the dishonest candidate is less than the loss from voting for the honest candidate, everybody but the few righteous people votes for the dishonest candidate, and the dishonest candidate wins the election. All voters would be better off if a majority voted for the honest candidate, but nobody has an incentive to do so. The dishonest candidate has trapped the electorate in a multi-person prisoners' dilemma. Voters are bribed with their own money to vote for the dishonest candidate.

The honest candidate cannot win unless righteous people constitute a majority of the electorate, the perceived probability of a win by the dishonest candidate is low or one's chance of casting a pivotal vote is exceedingly large. A vote for the honest candidate creates a chance $\pi$ of swinging the election from a win by the dishonest candidate to a win by the honest candidate coupled with a chance $(1 - \pi)$ of having no effect on the outcome of the election election. One's expected loss if one votes for the honest candidate is $(1 - \pi)P(Z + (1 - p)T$ which is the product of the chance one's vote is not pivotal, the perceived chance of a win by the dishonest candidate when one's vote is not pivotal, and the loss to a supporter of the honest candidate in that event. One's expected loss if one votes for the dishonest candidate is $[\pi + (1 - \pi)P](Z - pT)$ which is the product of the chance of a win by the dishonest candidate and the loss to a supporter of the dishonest candidate in that event.

A purely self-interested person never votes for the honest candidate unless

$$(1 - \pi)P(Z + (1 - P)T < [\pi + (1 - \pi)P](Z - pT) \tag{7.6}$$

or, equivalently,

$$\pi/(1 - \pi) > PT/(Z - pT) \tag{7.7}$$

a requirement that is never met unless the probability of casting a pivotal vote is much higher than it is generally believed to be.

Implicit bribery becomes more difficult, but not completely impossible, when voting is closed, so that nobody knows for sure how anybody else has voted. Consider the British and Canadian systems where people vote for members of parliament, where the party with the most members of parliament forms the government, where people's votes are confidential, but where the government in office, knowing how each constituency has voted, can find ways to reward some constituencies and punish others according to how they voted. Investment may be more generously subsidized in some constituencies than in others. Tariffs, public services or price supports may be selectively imposed. The story is told of the road paved up to but not beyond the ballot box. 'Pork' may be more or less equally distributed. Outright bribery of voters is illegal, but actions tantamount to bribery are not. Voting to avoid punishment by the ruling party may still be tempting when there are strong common interests within one's constituency.[10]

Voting to deter implicit bribery differs from voting to avoid biased outcomes or to reduce the influence of voting pacts. To avoid biased outcomes or reduce the influence of voting pacts, it is generally sufficient to vote rather than abstain. To block implicit bribery, it is less important how many people vote or abstain as long as people who do vote are prepared to vote against a party seen as corrupt. Nevertheless, the more abstentions, the easier and less costly does implicit bribery become.

## The content of a duty to vote

As mentioned at the beginning of this chapter, a duty to vote may be interpreted widely or narrowly, as an obligation to vote for the candidate or party thought best for society as a whole or an obligation to vote with no additional obligation about whom to vote for. The wide interpretation may be looked upon as a variant of rule utilitarianism prescribing behaviour to 'maximize social utility if it is followed by everybody' (Harsanyi, 1980: 116). It is subject to three large ambiguities: that people vary in their ascriptions of utility in circumstances where no single universally recognized correct ascription can be identified, that people differ in the 'other people' about whom they are concerned and that duty may only be binding on any one person when enough other people can be expected to act dutifully as well. The narrow interpretation prescribes one and the same duty to everybody, and, like a census of preference, reveals the will of the majority when everybody votes from self-interest alone. These interpretations will be discussed in turn.

### Duty to vote for the good of society as a whole

Imagine an election between a left party and a right party in a society of $N$ people where a win for the left party generates a distribution of post-tax, post-transfer incomes $(y_{1L}, y_{2L}, \ldots, y_{NL})$ and a win for the right party generates a distribution $(y_{1R}, y_{2R}, \ldots, y_{NR})$. The party with the most votes wins the election regardless of differences among voters' intensities of preferences or dollar values of what they stand to gain or lose in an elections. One person values a win by his preferred party at $10. Another person values a win for his preferred party at a million dollars. Their votes are counted the same. A person, $n$, who votes selfishly, with no regard for the interests of the rest of society, votes for the left party if and only if $y_{nL} > y_{nR}$.

Duty to vote in the interest of society as a whole might be interpreted as requiring one to vote for whichever party can be expected to generate the larger national income; voting for the left party if and only if

$$\sum_{n=1}^{N} y_{nL} > \sum_{n=1}^{N} y_{nR} \tag{7.8}$$

This interpretation of social welfare has the unfortunate property that it leaves no scope for redistribution. Typically, provision of a dollars' worth to the poor – through progressive income taxation, unemployment insurance, welfare and so on – costs more than a dollar in taxation to the rich, and society's willingness to make such transfers implies that something other than the plain national income is being maximized.

As discussed by Feddersen (2004), by Feddersen and Sandroni (2006) and by Edlin, Gelman and Kaplan (2008), a broader notion of social welfare may be employed. Social welfare may be interpreted as the sum of people's utilities. A duty to vote for whichever party is thought to maximize the welfare of society as a whole would then require one to vote for the left party if and only if

$$W_L > W_R \tag{7.9}$$

where $W_L$ and $W_L$ are the income equivalents of average utility in the event of wins by the left and right parties respectively, identified implicitly by the equations

$$Nu(W_L) = \sum_{n=1}^{N} u(y_{nL}) \tag{7.10a}$$

$$Nu(W_R) = \sum_{n=1}^{N} u(y_{nR}) \tag{7.10b}$$

and where the utility of income function $u(y)$ is constructed so that, in choosing between combinations of incomes, like $(y_{1L}, y_{2L}, \ldots, y_{NL})$ and $(y_{1R}, y_{2R}, \ldots, y_{NR})$, one selects the combination with the higher average utility regardless of whether average income is higher or not. The incomes, $W_L$ and $W_R$, are such that, if one had them for certain, one's utility would equal the expected utilities derived from the combinations of incomes $(y_{1L}, y_{2L}, \ldots, y_{NL})$ and $(y_{1R}, y_{2R}, \ldots, y_{NR})$ respectively. Imagine two societies, one with a higher average income and the other with a smaller dispersion of income. A person might prefer either society depending on the shape of his utility of income function. The larger the curvature of the utility of income function, the greater the weighting of equality would be. The utility of income function strikes a balance between average income and the dispersion of income.

Utility may be interpreted as representing risk aversion or dislike of inequality. Following von Neumann and Morgenstern (1947), the social welfare in any society or political outcome might be defined as the income which, if one had it for certain would make one as well off as one would be with equal chances of having the incomes of each and every person there. Alternatively, utility may reflect one's ranking of societies based not just upon average income, but upon the gap between the incomes of rich and poor.[11]

A serious difficulty with the utilitarian interpretation of the content of a duty to vote is that the utility of income function differs from one person to another, with significant implications for the choice of public policy but with no overarching criterion to determine whose utility of income function is appropriate. Intrinsic to the notion of duty is that two people in the same circumstances should have the same duty as well. That turns out not to be so. A utilitarian criterion may require one person to vote left and another person to vote right. A simple example shows what is at stake.

Suppose the general form of the utility of income function is

$$u(y) = y^\beta \tag{7.11}$$

where $\beta$ is a parameter that may differ from one person to the next, with no God-given rule determining where, between the limits of $-\infty$ and 1, society's true value of ought to be. The parameter may be interpreted as a person's degree of risk aversion or as an indicator of one's trade-off between average income per head and the distribution of income in society as a whole. A person for whom $\beta = 1$ votes for the party expected to generate the highest national income because utility and income are the same. A person for whom $\beta = -\infty$ votes for the party expected to provide the highest income for the poorest person in society. A person for whom $\alpha$ is between $-\infty$ and 1 places weight upon both total income and equality of income, depending on how close $\beta$ is to one or the other extreme.[12]

Consider a society with equal numbers of rich and poor people, where the left party favours some redistribution and the right party favours none, and where (as is almost always the case in practice) redistribution is expensive in that each dollar added to the income of the poor is at the cost of a reduction of more than one dollar in the income of the rich. Specifically, suppose that the pre-tax, pre-transfer incomes per head of rich and poor people are $100 and $10 respectively, that each dollar of redistribution to the poor costs $2 to the rich, that the right party opposes redistribution altogether and that the left party, if elected, would redistribute $10 to each poor person at a cost of $20 to each rich person. Thus, if the right party is elected, the incomes of rich and poor people remain at $100 and $10, while, if the left party is elected, the post-tax, post-transfer incomes of rich and poor people become $80 and $20 respectively, reducing the national income per head from $55 to $50.

Now compare measures of social welfare as seen by two voters, one for whom $\beta = 1$ and the other for whom $\beta = \frac{1}{2}$. To the voter for whom $\beta = 1$, social welfare in Equation (7.10) reduces to

$$W_L = (\frac{1}{2})[y_R + y_P] = (\frac{1}{2})[80 + 20] = 50 \tag{7.12a}$$

and

$$W_R = (\frac{1}{2})[y_R + y_P] = (\frac{1}{2})[100 + 10] = 55 \tag{7.12b}$$

where $y_R$ and $y_P$ are post-tax, post-transfer incomes of rich and poor people. Since $W_R > W_L$, it becomes the duty of this person to vote for the right party. By contrast, to the voter for whom $\beta = \frac{1}{2}$, social welfare in Equation (7.10) reduces to

$$W_L = (\frac{1}{2})^2[(y_R)^{\frac{1}{2}} + (y_P)^{\frac{1}{2}}]^2 = (1/4)[(80)^{\frac{1}{2}} + (20)^{1/2}]^2 = 44.0000 \tag{7.13a}$$

and

$$W_R = (\frac{1}{2})^2[(y_R)^{\frac{1}{2}} + (y_P)^{\frac{1}{2}}]^2 = (1/4)[(100)^{\frac{1}{2}} + (10)^{\frac{1}{2}}]^2 = 43.3115 \tag{7.13b}$$

Since $W_L$ has become larger than $W_R$, it becomes the duty of this person to vote for the left party instead.

One acquires a moral obligation to vote right or left depending on the curvature of one's utility of income function. It's worse than that. Considering the old saying that 'its hard to get a man to understand something when his salary depends on his not understanding it', it would not be at all surprising if many rich people sincerely believed $\beta$ to be close to 1 while many poor people sincerely believed $\beta$ to be substantially less than that, self-interest conditioning people's beliefs about what is best for society as a whole. The utilitarian criterion for voting crumbles on close inspection.

Another problem with the utilitarian notion of the duty to vote is that people differ in their degrees of concern for other people. A Canadian voting in a federal election might be expected take some account of the welfare of all Canadians, but not equally so. A person from the province of Alberta might, other things being equal, be inclined to vote for a party that pays more attention to the concerns of the people of Alberta than to the concerns of the people of Quebec, while a person from the province of Quebec might, other things being equal, be inclined to vote for a party that pays more attention to Quebec than to Alberta. Can either person be said to act undutifully, or should a duty to vote be defined broadly enough that all such behaviour is counted as dutiful as long as one is concerned about other people at all? And how much weight does a broadly defined duty to vote place upon the utility of non-Canadians when parties differ in their willingness to provide foreign aid? Each citizen may be somewhat concerned about all other citizens, but there is surely a tendency of workers to vote for the party most favourable to the working class, employers for the party most favourable to business, people in the east vote for the party most favourable to the east, people in the west vote for the party most favourable to the west, and people everywhere vote for the party with a foreign policy most sympathetic to the old country, whichever country that happens to be.

Social welfare, $W_1$, as seen by person 1, can then be defined as $W_1$ in the equation

$$u^1(W_1) = \sum_{n=1}^{N} f_n^1 u^1(y_n) \tag{7.14}$$

which differs from Equation (7.10) in that other people are weighted differently according to person 1's degree of concern, $f_n^1$, for each other person $n$. If person 1 is completely selfish, then $f_1^1 = 1$ and $f_n^1 = 0$ for any $n$ other than 1. If person 1 is completely unselfish person, all $f_n^1$ are the same. Most people are between these extremes. Alternatively, concern for other people may be confined to people who are worse off than oneself so that $f_n^1 = 0$ unless $y_n < y_1$. The problem is similar to the problem when people have different utility of income functions. To define a duty to vote as a requirement to vote in the interest of the community as a whole either counts most voters as at least partly undutiful or allows each person's duty to be dependent on that person's preferences, subordinating duty to what one likes or wants.

A third problem with the utilitarian notion of duty is that the call of duty may differ in a society where everybody can be expected to act dutifully from what it becomes in a society where some people act dutifully but others do not. Imagine a society with three people (or factions), $A$, $B$ and $C$, voting whether or not to undertake some or all of six projects, three efficient and three not, with different net beneficiaries. Each project costs \$300, and all public expenditure is financed by a head tax so that the cost to each person of each project undertaken is \$100. Benefits of each project to each person are shown in the Table 7.2.

The first three projects are efficient (because $150 + 90 + 90 > 300$) and the last three projects are not (because $115 + 90 + 90 < 300$), so that an ordinary cost–benefit rule would mandate that only the first three be undertaken, yielding a net benefit of \$30 to each of the three people.

Assume for simplicity that the value of $\beta$ in Equation (7.11) is equal to 1 so that income, $y$, and utility, $u$, are one and the same, and duty boils down to simple cost–benefit analysis. Assume also that the decision whether or not to undertake each

*Table 7.2* Benefits of each project to each person

|  | *Person A* | *Person B* | *Person C* |
|---|---|---|---|
| Project 1 | $150 | $90 | $90 |
| Project 2 | $90 | $150 | $90 |
| Project 3 | $90 | $90 | $150 |
| Project 4 | $115 | $90 | $90 |
| Project 5 | $90 | $115 | $90 |
| Project 6 | $90 | $90 | $115 |

project is by majority rule voting and that all three people vote ethically to max-imize the difference between the total benefit and total cost of whatever projects are undertaken. If so, they would all vote for the first three projects and against the last three, replicating the outcome of cost–benefit analysis. Alternatively, if all three people were strictly selfish but with no coordination or logrolling among pairs of voters, all six projects would be rejected two votes to one, only person *A* voting for projects 1 and 4, only person *B* voting for projects 2 and 5, and only person *C* voting for projects 3 and 6.

A different outcome emerges when person *A* alone is dutiful and persons *B* and *C* are strictly selfish. In that case, projects 2 and 3 are adopted by a two to one majority – persons *A* and *B* voting for project 2 and persons *A* and *C* voting for project 3 – yielding a net gain of $40 for each of persons *B* and *C* $(150 + 90 - 200)$ and a net loss of $20 for person *A* $(90 + 90 - 200)$.

When person *A* is dutiful and persons *B* and *C* are strictly selfish, the outcome of uncorrelated voting is exactly what it would be if all three people were strictly selfish but persons *B* and *C* had coordinated their votes on the first three projects to exploit person *A*. The plight of person *A* would be even worse if persons *B* and *C* actually coordinated their votes because the inefficient projects 4 and 5 would also be adopted. Rules appropriate when they are universally obeyed may be inappropriate otherwise.

The thorough-going dyed-in-the-wool utilitarian is a sucker who allows himself to be victimized by the rest of the electorate. Utilitarian behaviour confined to one of three voters may even be self-defeating because, if all three voters were strictly selfish, they might bargain their way to an efficient outcome where the first three projects are adopted and the last three are not. As long as person *A* is dutiful, persons *B* and *C* lose all incentive to accept such a deal. Similarly, the true utilitarian disapproves of all 'pork' but places no more weight on pork for his own constituency than for any other. Knowing this, political parties would be inclined to distribute pork to constituencies that can be expected to respond favourably at the ballot box.[13]

Even with a common utility of income function as in Equation (7.11), a rule is required specifying who must vote and who may abstain. Abstention might be harmful for the reasons discussed earlier in this chapter, but, in seeking to maximize social welfare, a balance must be drawn between the expected harm from a person's abstention and the cost of voting itself. The person for whom voting requires a 1000 mile trip by dog sled to the voting booth may well be excused. Utilitarian voting must permit abstentions when the cost of voting exceeds some limit. It is difficult to say a priori what the limit might be, especially as the limit would depend on how many people can be expected to vote dutifully. If almost everybody can be expected to vote dutifully in accordance with Equation (7.9) and if everybody's utility of income function is the same, than almost everybody – everybody whose cost of voting exceeds some very small amount – can be excused because the result of the election is almost certainly the same regardless. But, if dutiful voters constitute a bare majority of the electorate, then each and every dutiful person must vote, almost regardless of the cost.

### *A duty to vote with no additional requirement about who or what to vote for*

An interesting objection to the narrow interpretation of the duty to vote casts light on what is at stake. A duty to cast one's ballot with no additional obligation to vote for common good as opposed to what is best for oneself alone invokes two entirely different criteria for what are in effect two steps on one and the same path, coming to the ballot box an casting one's vote. It would seem to make no sense that 'an earlier member of the sequence is justified by a different ethical principle from that used to justify a later one' Meehl (1977: 23). The choice between voting and abstention would be rule-utilitarian while the choice of which party to vote for would be exclusively self-interested. Meehl (1977: 24) goes on to argue that if an ethical principle:

> is rationally active at the moment of his casting his ballot, it cannot become mysteriously irrelevant or be replaced by an act prospective, or a maxim of prudence-egocentric kind of principle as the basis of rational choice between the candidates.

An opposing argument is that, of the two rules 'You must vote' and 'In voting, you must choose between candidates on some ethical principle', the former is much more compelling because the adverse consequences for society as a whole of a widespread violation of the first rule are far worse than the adverse consequence of a widespread violation of the second. The preservation of democracy depends critically on the one but not the other. There are several reasons why this is so.

The requirement to vote with no additional requirement to vote for what one sees as the common good is clear and unambiguous. You either vote or you don't. By contrast, as discussed earlier in the chapter, the utilitarian requirement means different things to different people. People differ in the shapes of their utility of income functions and in their degrees of concern for their fellow citizens. The very same decision at the ballot box could be utilitarian for one person but not for another. Whether or not one votes is at least to some extent observable. Whether or not one votes on utilitarian principles is known only to oneself. Duty disintegrates in the absence of a clear specification of what duty requires one to do.

Widespread acceptance of a narrowly defined duty to vote avoids much of the bias in the outcome of elections, the influence of voting pacts, the advantage to the party that can afford to mobilize the electorate and the implicit bribery that may arise when a significant portion of the eligible voters abstain. Harm from absten-tion is largely independent on whether people vote selfishly or for what they see as the common good. Harm from disproportionate abstention – between rich and poor, educated and uneducated, or groups separated ethnically or geographically – accrues to groups as a whole, to all members of groups regardless of whether they vote or abstain. If a majority of poor people favours one particular party, a decision by some poor people to abstain injures all poor people, those who vote and those who abstain, because that party's chance of being elected is reduced.

Widespread acceptance of a duty to vote with no additional requirement to vote on utilitarian principles can, to some extent, bring utilitarian outcomes through the back door. This narrow conception of the duty to vote transforms the election into a census of preference. Even if everybody votes selfishly for the party that serves their interest best, with no thought for the welfare of the community as a whole, the aggregate effect of this narrowly conceived duty to vote is to elect the party that a majority of voters prefer. The greater the diversity of interpretations of what is best for society as a whole, the more likely it becomes that universal self-interested voting yields an outcome closer to some notion of the common good than if each person votes for what he believes the common good to be. Errors may be compounded by an almost inevitable tendency to hypocrisy, imaging that what is best for oneself is best for others as well, adopting the most advantageous curvature of the utility of income function or restricting the pool of people about whom one is concerned to those whose interests are the same as one's own. One knows one's own interest. The rest is guesswork. The best attainable outcome in this imperfect world may be a large turnout of people who vote as they do for a variety of reasons know only to themselves.[14] A person who votes against public support for the poor may be wanting in sympathy, but is not violating a duty to vote.[15]

Finally, a narrowly defined duty to vote may be sufficient to escape from the 'paradox of not voting' that no plausible measure of the chance, $\pi$, of casting a pivotal vote is large enough to induce people to vote on purely selfish grounds. As shown in Equation (7.1), voting is disadvantageous to the voter unless either $\pi B > C$ or the voter makes up the difference between $C$ and $\pi B$ by placing a sufficiently large value, $D$, on the performance of duty. The consensus based on evidence and logic is that $\pi$ is almost never large enough. On the other hand, treating the act of voting as a two-stage process – getting oneself to the ballot box, and deciding who or what to vote for once one is there – creates the possibility that pure self-interest is sufficient to induce thoughtful voting at the second, less expensive stage once a sense of duty, narrowly defined, has attended to the first. Divide $C$ in Equation (7.1) into $C_1$, the cost of getting to the ballot box, and $C_2$, the cost of voting carefully once you are there. Pure self-interest would be insufficient to bring you to the ballot box but sufficient to induce thoughtful voting once you are there if

$$C_2 < \pi B < C_1 + C_2 \tag{7.15}$$

Consider once again the example at the beginning of this chapter where the cost of voting is $20, a voter's benefit from a win by the preferred party is $6,000, but the chance of one's vote being pivotal is only 1/6,000, so that one's expected gain from voting is only $1 which is a twentieth of the cost. Interpret the cost of voting as using up one hour of time at an alternative cost of $20 per hour, but suppose that, of the hour required to vote, 59 minutes is occupied getting to the ballot box but only 1 extra minute is required to vote thoughtfully once you are there. If so, the cost of getting to the ballot box, $C_1$, is about $19.67 [$20(59/60)] and the extra cost of voting thoughtfully, $C_2$, is only 33¢ which is more than covered by the voter's expected gain of $1 from voting. Even the purely self-interested person who would not vote at all but for a narrowly defined duty to vote, does not hand in a blank ballot because the expected gain from voting carefully is worth the effort. In this little example, the duty to vote with no extra obligation about whom to vote for does the heavy lifting; self-interest can be counted upon to do the rest.

These considerations bear upon the pros and cons of compulsory voting. Compulsory voting automatically avoids the bias in electoral outcomes when, for example, an especially large proportion of poor people abstain, and it focuses political campaigns on persuading voters of the virtues of one's party rather than on organizing citizens to vote rather than abstain. Compulsory voting does not force one to vote thoughtfully, but it may be just what is required if, as in the example above, one's chance of casting a pivotal vote is high enough to justify thoughtful voting if one votes at all. On the other hand, citizens not sufficiently patriotic to vote voluntarily may not vote thoughtfully and may be dangerously susceptible to political propaganda.[16] Voting based on little more than slogans and sound bites may be far worse than not voting at all.

### Self-interest constrained

Consider these statements:

1   One has a duty to vote rather than abstain.
2   One has a duty to vote Republican rather than Democratic (or vice versa as the case may be).
3   One has a duty not to vote for the neo-Nazis.

The first of these statements is generally believed to be correct because the preservation of democracy depends on a willingness of at least a significant portion of the population to vote rather than to abstain, though exceptions are made for people in circumstances where it is especially costly to vote.

The second statement sounds more like party propaganda than like a serious moral injunction. Everybody understands that voting is, and should be, at least partially self-interested. It would be naive to suppose that everybody who votes Republican does so because a win for the Republicans is thought best for the nation as a whole regardless of the effect on the individual voter, especially when such high-minded behaviour cannot be expected from the rest of the electorate. A member of parliament is expected to serve the interests of the people in his constituency as well as in the nation as a whole. One party tilts in favour of the rich. Another party tilts in favour of the poor. People understand this and vote accordingly. There is no harm in that, no threat to democratic government.

One's duty not to vote for the neo-Nazis can be looked upon from two connected points of view. The principle that one may vote as self-interestedly or as dutifully as one pleases may be qualified by the requirement that one should not vote cruelly or prejudicially. Self-interest or class interest is to be expected, but there is a line that may not be crossed between permissible self-interest and contempt for other people. In so far as a duty to vote is for the protection and preservation of democratic government, a duty to vote may reasonably be said to exclude voting in a way that undermines democratic government. Nothing in the formal rules of majority rule voting blocks a majority of voters from granting dictatorial power to the glorious leader; to do so may nonetheless be a violation of one's duty to vote.

Alternatively, a duty to vote with no restrictions about whom or what to vote for may be seen as part of a larger web of duties that citizenship implies. A person who votes against all public assistance for the poor and sick, or who votes to banish, disenfranchise or enslave members of a religious or ethnic minority may be seen not as violating a duty to vote, but as violating duties to care for one's fellow citizens and to avoid vicarious cruelty. If it is wrong for governments to oppress minorities, it may be equally wrong for citizens to oppress minorities indirectly by voting for a party that will act oppressively once in office. Coupled with the duty to vote is a duty to keep oneself well enough informed about the politics of one's country that one's vote, be it selfish or utilitarian, is not for the party that is cruel or evil. A balance among duties may be required. Full utilitarian voting may be more than can reasonably demanded of the citizen. Some concern for other people may be required.

### *Expressive voting as a substitute for self-interest and duty*

An argument can be made that discussion of the content of the duty to vote is misdirected because voting need not be costly at all. The argument is that people may enjoy voting or may vote to express themselves rather than to influence the outcome of an election. Self-interest is deemed irrelevant because the chance of one's vote being decisive is much too small. Duty is deemed irrelevant because people are not dutiful, especially not in circumstances where nobody can count on anybody else to be dutiful. Enjoyment in voting and self-expression are deemed sufficient to explain why people vote rather than abstain.

People may enjoy voting as participation in the ceremony of democracy, voting for whomever they please in full knowledge that others do so too. It is joining the parade. If so, then $C$ in Equation (7.1) has been placed on the wrong side of the equation, and the paradox of not voting vanishes.

Voting for enjoyment pertains primarily to whether or not one votes. Expressive voting pertains primarily to whom or what one votes for.

> The expressive account begins from the observation that, given the negligible probability of any particular voter being decisive, the act of voting is effectively de-coupled from the causal consequences of voting for electoral outcomes. Individually rational voting behaviour cannot therefore be explained primarily in terms of those considerations that are relevant to the voters expressing a preference in and of itself. These considerations are termed expressive considerations. Voting is, on this account, much more like cheering at a football match than it is like purchasing an asset portfolio; and any direct analogy with market choice is inappropriate.
>
> Brennan and Hamlin (1998: 149–50)

> People behave rationally in seeking expressive utility from acts or decisions that confirm personal identity' where 'by confirming pleasing attributes of being generous, cooperative, trusting and trustworthy, or ethical and moral.
>
> Hillman (2010: 403)

Benefit from voting expressively is not weighted by the chance of casting a pivotal vote. Expressive voting transforms Riker and Ordeshook's (1968) criterion for voting in Equation (7.1) into

$$\pi B + D + E > C \tag{7.16}$$

where, once again, $\pi$, $B$, $C$ and $D$ are the chance of casting a pivotal vote, one's benefit from a win for the party one vote's for, one's cost of voting and the value one places on doing one's duty, and where $D$, which may be the value of the avoidance of guilt, would be 0 if one had no sense of duty at all. The new ingredient in the equation is $E$ defined as one's value of expressing oneself through the ballot box, the 'warm glow' one gets from identifying with something one admires or respects. The main feature of $E$ is that it is independent of the chance of casting a pivotal vote. My warm glow from voting for goodness is independent of the chance of goodness emerging as the outcome of the election. To me, it is my goodness of heart that matters. Expressive voting supplies a rationale for large numbers of people to vote rather than abstain.

Expressive voting has several curious features. First, one's warm glow from voting may arise from evil as well as from good. What could be more expressive than *The Triumph of the Will* (Riefenstahl, 1935)? Suppose one hates Jews, or hates Muslims, or hates Christians, or hates atheists. If one knew one's vote was to be decisive, a sense of decency might cause one to desist from voting for a policy or party inflicting harm on whatever group one hates, but, if voting is just expressive (and secret to boot), one might be willing to give the expression of one's prejudices full sway in the knowledge that nobody gets hurt in the end. A person with a deep hatred of murderers might vote for the death penalty when it is virtually impossible for his vote to be decisive, but that same person might vote against the death penalty if there is some non-negligible chance of his vote making a difference. People may well vote expressively, but expressive voting is a two-edged sword which may, but need not, shore up decent government.

For good or for evil, expressive voting may give rise to 'expressive-policy traps' making all voters worse off than if they voted 'instrumentally' instead. (Hillman, 2010). Consider a policy with a positive expressive benefit of $E$ and a negative private benefit of $B$. An expressive-policy trap may occur when $B < 0$, $E > 0$ but $B + E < 0$ meaning that the typical person is worse off if the policy is adopted, but $\pi B + E > 0$ meaning that one's expressive benefit, $E$, exceeds one's *expected* cost, $\pi B$, of voting for rather than against the policy. Everybody votes for the policy because everybody's expressive benefit exceeds expected harm from the policy itself, but everybody is harmed because the policy is adopted. Similarly, since $\pi$ diminishes with the size of the electorate, the likelihood of ethical policies being adopted is higher in societies with large electorates than in societies with small electorates (Feddersen, Gailmard and Sandroni, 2009).

There is some question about whether $E$ is really and truly independent of $\pi$. Surely whatever satisfaction one gets from voting for something is enhanced by the knowledge that there is some chance of one's vote being effectual. It is the difference between merely saying that one is sympathetic to the poor and actually doing something with a small chance of helping the poor a great deal. There is also something fishy about expressive voting in a secret ballot. Expression normally requires somebody who speaks and somebody who listens. Nobody listens to one's vote. Nobody else knows who one votes for. Voting when nobody knows what you vote for and regardless of the chance that your vote is pivotal is the weakest imaginable form of expression.

A distinction can be drawn between the motive for and the content of a duty to vote. Enjoyment of voting and of expressing oneself are reasons *why* citizens might vote rather than abstain. Alternative specifications of the duty to vote are about *what* that duty requires the citizen to do voluntarily in order that government by majority rule voting to works well today and will be maintained tomorrow. Yet, the why and the what are intertwined. The content of one's duty to vote may depend on whether other people can be expected to vote dutifully too. Enjoyment and a sense of expressing oneself through voting may originate in the belief that one is doing what one ought to do.

Expressive voting may be no more than a reason why the act of voting is pleasant rather than unpleasant (or less costly than it may at first appear), increasing turnout at the ballot box without at the same time influencing any voter's choice among the available options, regardless of whether one votes in one's own interest or in the interest of the community as a whole. Duty need not always be painful. Alternatively, expressive voting may have its own objectives quite apart from a voter's judgment of the relative merits of the available options, leading some people to vote for policies or parties they would vote against if they believed their votes to be influential. Among people who vote expressively, some may vote for good and others may vote for evil, some vote for one party and some vote for another. Expressive voting may or may not lead to outcomes in the interest of a majority of the electorate.

\*\*\*

Duty kicks in when self-interest fails. Duty is an elusive virtue, a scarce commodity, abstracted from ordinary economic analysis and not to be invoked unless there is no alternative in sight. A duty to vote arises because mass abstention jeopardizes democratic government and because neither pure self-interest nor fear of punishment is sufficient inducement not to abstain. The content of the duty to vote – what exactly a duty to vote requires – is determined accordingly.

In a critique of reasons why there may be a duty to vote, Lomasky and Brennan (2000: 78) argue that the decision to vote or abstain is 'self-stabilizing' in the sense that 'an equilibrium emerges that does not have any evidently morally unsatisfactory properties'. The claim in this chapter is that the equilibrium in the absence of a duty to vote is indeed unsatisfactory, but, as long as a significant proportion of the population chooses to vote, society can get by when people vote as self-interestedly or as altruistically as they please.

The self-sustaining equilibrium is unsatisfactory for several reasons. Without a widespread duty to vote, all but a tiny share of the population would abstain because the value of $\pi$ in Equation (7.1) would otherwise be too small to justify voting on purely self-interested grounds. The peculiar externalities in majority rule voting – that the small chance of one's vote being pivotal is accompanied by two massive externalities, positive to all like-minded voters and negative to all voters in favour of the party one votes against – can allow abstention to be biased against some group of voters, typically though not necessarily the poor, and may cause the machinery of majority rule voting to work less well than when everybody, or almost everybody, votes. The remaining voters are likely to be unrepresentative of the general population, and political outcomes are likely to differ greatly from outcomes as they would be if nobody abstained. Massive abstention would enhance the efficacy of voting pacts, handing elections to groups of people who can commit themselves to vote for the common cause. Small organized bands of fanatics may become more influential. Electoral bribery becomes easier and more dangerous as the proportion of the population that votes declines. Victory in elections goes to the better organized and financed party rather than to the party preferred by a majority of the electorate.

The main argument here is that a duty to vote brings the citizen to the ballot box but leaves the citizen relatively free in his choice of candidate or party to vote for. A narrowly conceived duty to vote supplies a clear and simple rule for citizens to follow. It avoids the biases and the scope for manipulation from widespread abstention. It may be sufficient to induce thoughtful behaviour at the ballot box. If respected by a significant proportion of the population, it supplies a census of preference which may be as close as one can come in this imperfect world to a measure of the common good.

A duty to vote is required because, with rare exceptions, $\pi B$ in Equation (7.1) falls short of $C$. Duty need not dictate whom to vote for because universal self-interested voting tends to promote a tolerable approximation to the common good. Purely ethical voting is heroism beyond the call of duty, and may even be self-defeating, as when people differ in their willingness to act ethically, their perceptions of what is best for other people, or the shapes of their utility of income functions. The common good to be secured by a general willingness to vote rather than to abstain is not just a victory for this or that party in today's election, but the preservation of the system of majority rule voting.

A widespread duty to vote creates a reasonable prospect of a win for the party preferred by a majority of the population, with no residual influence of voting pacts, no bias in favour of groups with especially high propensities to vote and no role for the mobilization of voters, as distinct from the provision of relevant information, in influencing the platforms of political parties and the outcomes of elections. But it is no breach of duty to vote for the party that is best for oneself in the knowledge that others will do so too. Duty extends no further than is necessary for the will of the majority to prevail and to keep the dictator away.

## Notes

1  The magnitude of $\pi$ is the subject of some controversy in the literature of voting. Many authors would consider the estimate here to be much, much too large, and would question whether the chance of casing a pivotal vote is ever large enough to have any impact on one's decision whether to vote or abstain. The matter is discussed in the next chapter.
2  If, for any $n$, the difference between $B(n)$ on the highest schedule and $B(n)$ on the lowest schedule is 10,000 votes, then the chance, $\pi$, that a person's vote is pivotal must be 1/10,000.
3  In the discussion of self-interested abstention surrounding Figure 7.1, every person, $n$, knows his own (positive or negative) value, $B(n)$, of a win for the left party, and knows that there is a schedule of such values for the rest of the electorate. Now it is supposed instead that $B$ is the same for everybody, but nobody is quite sure whether the common value of $B$ is positive or negative.
4  Such a society is envisioned by Caplan (2007), with economists in the role of philosopher kings. Three groups are recognized, the public, the enlightened public and the economists. Much is made of the evidence that the enlightened public tends to believe in and to favour many of the same things as the economists. Caplan argues that 'voters who know the most do not want to expropriate their less clear-headed countrymen. Like other voters, their goal is, by and large, to maximize social welfare. They just happen to know more about how to do it.' Caplan (2007: 197) would like to require voters 'to pass a test of economic literacy to vote'. Since wise and public-spirited people are relatively unlikely to abstain, such abstention as does occur is in practice desirable.
5  Information from the 2,000 Current Population Survey in the United States, shows turnout in senatorial elections increasing steadily with income from a low of about 25 per cent among the very poor to over 60 per cent among the rich. (Gilens, 2012: 240).
6  Figure 7.2 exemplifies the general principle in Campbell (1999: 1199) that 'the alternative preferred by more expected "zealous" voters, who have either larger stakes in the outcome of the election or small costs of participating, wins with high probability in any equilibrium, even if the expected proportion of the entire electorate that shares that preference is arbitrarily small'.
7  Voting pacts are first cousins, if not closer, to the voting behaviour of groups as modelled by Uhlaner (1989) and Morton (1991). Their emphasis is upon leaders and followers,

upon the interaction between candidates seeking office and citizens choosing whether and for whom to vote, but they must postulate some material or psychic private advantage in voting to overcome the free rider problem. Uhlaner discusses rewards from successful candidates to groups small enough to make each person's vote advantageous. There is also a family resemblance between voting behaviour of groups and the probabilistic voting theorem demonstrating an equilibrium when candidates distribute goodies to groups so as to maximize the probability of being elected. For a simple exposition of probabilistic voting, see Mueller (2003). Chapter 12 of this book is a critique of the concept of probabilistic voting.

8  Imagine a society where 100,000 people vote rather than abstain and where, among these people, there are equal chances of anywhere between 49,000 people and 55,000 people voting for the left party, so that the left party has a 5-to-1 chance (equal to 5/6 or 83⅓ per cent) of winning the election and an additional voter has a 1-in-6,000 chance of casting a pivotal vote. Now imagine an additional 100 people all of whom would vote for the left party if they voted at all. Any one of these people choosing to vote or abstain independently of how the other 99 behave has the original 1-in-6,000 chance of casting a pivotal vote, but, if all of the 100 additional people choose to vote, there are now equal chances of anywhere between 49,100 people and 55,100 people voting for the left party, raising its chance of winning the election from 5-to-1 to 5.1-to-0.9 (that is, from 5/6 to (5.1)/6 or 85 per cent). The hundred extra people voting for the left party, raises its chance of winning the election from 83⅓ per cent to 85 per cent, an increase of 1⅔ per cent or, equivalently, 1/60. As part of a voting pact, the chance one's vote is pivotal rises from 1/6,000 to 1/60. Strictly speaking, this calculation should make allowance for the chance of a tie, but that chance is very small.

9  Consider Myerson's (1998) example based upon Palfrey and Rosenthal's (1985) model where everybody's (absolute) values of $B$ and $C$ are the same, where equilibrium turnout is obtained by random voting and where everybody votes or abstains on the flip of a party-specific weighted coin. With a population of 1 million right supporters and 2 million left supporters, the expected number of votes is shown to be no more than 32 for each political party. A voting pact of as few as 33 voters would be virtually guaranteed to swing the election if supporters of the opposing party did not respond in kind.

10  'Implicit bribery' may be contrasted with 'special interest politics' as described in Grossman and Helpman (2001). In the former, the politician says to the constituency, 'You vote for me or I will punish you.' In the latter, the constituency says to the politician, 'You favour me and I will reward you with campaign advertising to influence the electorate.'

11  Think of a risky situation where a person acquire either of two incomes, a very big income, $y^B$, and a very small income, $y^S$. For any income, $y$ in between, there is some probability $\pi$ for which one indifferent between acquiring an income $y$ for sure and a gamble with a probabilities $\pi$ and $(1 - \pi)$ of acquiring the very big income and the very small income respectively. Define the utility of income function such that, for every $y$ and its corresponding $\pi$, $u(y)$ is just equal to $\pi$. Clearly, $u(y)$ is an increasing function of $y$ and $u(y)$ is concave if the person to whom the function refers is risk averse. Since $y^B$ and $y^S$ are chosen arbitrarily, utility of income can only be defined up to a linear transformation. Since people differ in aversion to risk, the utility of income function differs from one person to the next.

12  This is proved in an appendix to Chiang (1984).

13  In voting, the maxim 'Do unto others as you would have them do unto you,' may be a terrible mistake. You would have people vote altruistically for the common good as they see it, in which case your duty would be to vote altruistically too or perhaps to abstain when you believe others' assessments of the common good are better than your own. But if others can be expected to vote self-interestedly rather than in the interest

of the community as a whole, then no more can be reasonably be expected of you, for the outcome when everybody votes self-interestedly is likely to be better for you and probably for the community as a whole than the outcome when other people vote self-interestedly and you alone – or together with like-minded voters – do not. Your duty may depend not upon how others ought to behave, but upon how others can reasonably be expected to behave. A distinction is sometimes drawn between utilitarianism as a prescription for individual behaviour and utilitarianism as a criterion for the law and public policy. The latter is exempt from the objections raised here.

14  With reference to the distinction between 'whether to vote' and 'who to vote for', Fiorina (1976: 410) had this to say: 'Perhaps the citizen does decide to vote on the basis of such non-instrumental factors as citizen duty, but then chooses a candidate on relatively more instrumental grounds. Such a bifurcated decision process is less elegant theoretically than a unified one, but given the data we must keep an open mind.'

15  Curiously, if everybody placed the same absolute value, $B$, on a win for his preferred party, voting for the common good and voting selfishly would boil down to one and the same thing. Since a vote can only be pivotal when the rest of the electorate is tied, the total benefits to all right-leaning voters from a win by the right party and the total benefits to all left-leaning voters from a win by the left party would have to be the same. Expressed in dollars, benefits (or costs) to all left-leaning voters and costs (or benefits) to all right-leaning voters must cancel out, so that the utilitarian measure of the common good as seen by a pivotal voter and the pivotal voter's own benefit from voting must be one and the same. When everybody's absolute value of $B$ is the same, people cannot differ in their assessments of the common good unless they have different judgments about what parties in office will do or about other voters' intensities of preferences. On the other hand, if everybody preferred one party to the other, self-interested voting and utilitarian voting would, once again, yield the same result.

16  Compulsory voting is advocated by Lijphart (1997) who claims that turnout is declining in most countries, that the propensity to vote rather than to abstain increases with education and wealth, and that there is a corresponding bias in public policy against the uneducated and the poor. On the pros and cons of compulsory voting, see Birch (2009).

# References

Bartels, L. M. (2008) *Unequal Democracy: The Political Economy of the New Gilded Age*, Princeton: Princeton University Press.

Birch, Sarah (2009) *Full Participation: A Comparative Study of Compulsory Voting*, Manchester: Manchester University Press.

Borgers, T. (2004) Costly voting, *American Economic Review*, 94(1), 57–66.

Brennan, G. and Hamlin, A. (1998) Expressive voting and electoral equilibrium, *Public Choice*, 95, 149–75.

Brennan, J. (2011) *The Ethics of Voting*, Princeton: Princeton University Press.

Campbell, C. M. (1999) Large elections and decisive minorities, *Journal of Political Economy*, 107(6), 1199–217.

Caplan, B. (2007) *The Myth of the Rational Voter: Why Democracies Choose Bad Policies*, Princeton: Princeton University Press.

Chiang, A. C. (1984) *Fundamental Methods of Mathematical Economics*, 3rd edn, New York: McGraw-Hill.

Edlin, A. S., Gelman, A. and Kaplan, N. (2008) Vote for charity's sake, *Economists' Voice*, available online at http://works.bepress.com/cgi/viewcontent.cgi?article=1075& context=aaron_edlin [accessed 2 September, 2015].

Feddersen, T. (2004) Rational choice theory and the paradox of not voting, *Journal of Economic Perspectives*, 18(1), 99–112.

Feddersen, T. and Sandroni, A. (2006) A theory of participation in elections, *American Economic Review*, 96(4), 1271–83.

Feddersen, T., Gailmard, S. and Sandroni, A. (2009) Moral bias in large elections, *The American Political Science Review*, 103(2), 175–92.

Fiorina, M.P. (1976) The voting decision: instrumental and expressive aspects, *The Journal of Politics*, 38(2), 390–413.

Gilens, M. (2012) *Affluence and Influence: Economic Inequality and Political Power in America*, Princeton: Princeton University Press.

Grossman, G. M. and Helpman, E. (2001) *Special Interest Politics*, Cambridge, MA: The MIT Press.

Harsanyi, J. (1980) Rule utilitarianism, rights, obligations and the theory of rational behaviour, *Theory and Decision*, 12(2), 115–33.

Hillman, A. Y. (2010) Expressive behaviour in economics and politics, *European Journal of Political Economy*, 26(4), 403–18.

Ledyard, J. (1984) The pure theory of two candidate elections, *Public Choice*, 44(1), 7–41.

Lijphart, A. (1997) Unequal participation: democracy's unresolved dilemma, *The American Political Science Review*, 91(1), 1–14.

Lomasky, L. and Brennan, G. (2000) Is there a duty to vote?, *Social Philosophy and Policy*, 17(1), 62–86.

Meehl, Paul, E. (1977) The selfish voter paradox and the throw-away vote argument, *The American Political Science Review*, 71(1), 11–30.

Morton, R. (1991) Groups in rational turnout models, *American Journal of Political Science*, 35(3), 758–76.

Mueller, D. C. (2003) *Public Choice III*, Cambridge: Cambridge University Press.

Myerson, R. B. (1998) Population uncertainty and poison games, *International Journal of Game Theory*, 27, 375–92.

Palfrey, T. R. and Rosenthal, H. (1985) Voter participation and strategic uncertainty, *The American Political Science Review*, 79(1),62–78.

Riefenstahl, L. (1935) *The Triumph of the Will*, a film by Leni Riefenstahl-Produktion.

Riker, W. and Ordeshook, P. C. (1968) A theory of the calculus of voting, *The American Political Science Review*, 62(1), 25–42.

Uhlaner, C. J. (1989) Rational turnout: the neglected role of groups, *American Journal of Political Science*, 33(2), 390–422.

von Neumann, J. and Morgenstern, O. (1947) *Theory of Games and Economic Behaviour*, 2nd edn, Princeton: Princeton University Press.

# 8 An alternative explanation of the chance of casting a pivotal vote[1]

A person's vote may be inconsequential or pivotal. When one votes, there is a very large chance of one's vote having no effect on oneself or anybody else, together with a very small chance of pivoting the outcome of the election from a win by the party one votes against to win by the party one votes for, generating a modest benefit for oneself plus two massive externalities: a positive externality for the thousands, possibly even millions, of people who stand to gain from a win by the party one votes for, and a negative externality for the thousands, possibly even millions, of people who stand to gain from a win by the party one votes against.

This chapter is about a postulated mechanism by which people's chance of casting a pivotal vote and their decisions to vote or abstain are simultaneously determined. The chance of casting a pivotal vote is of interest because of its effect upon the relative importance of self-interest and duty as motives for voting rather than abstention, because estimates of that chance vary enormously depending on how they are constructed and because other aspects of voting are seen differently depending on how the chance of casting a pivotal vote is conceived.

Riker and Ordeshook (1968) formulated a person's decision to vote or abstain according to whether

$$\pi B + D > C \tag{8.1}$$

where $B$ is one's personal benefit if one's preferred party wins the election, $D$ is the value one places upon voting as a duty to the rest of the community, $C$ is one's cost of voting and $\pi$ is the probability of casting a pivotal vote.

The chance of casting a pivotal vote, $\pi$, could be defined as one's probability of swinging the outcome of an election i) by voting rather than abstaining or ii) by switching one's vote from one party to another. The former definition (i) is adopted here. The chance of casting a pivotal vote is the same for everybody in one sense, but different in another. It is the same in the sense that if I believe my chance to be 1-in-10,000, I would be illogical not to suppose that your chance is 1-in-10,000 as well. On the other hand, possessing different information about the election, you and I may have different estimates of our common chance of casting a pivotal vote. Consider an election with two competing parties and an electorate of $N + 1$ people, one person seen as choosing to vote or abstain and $N$ other people whose votes may or may not be tied. The distinction is not really among people but between the roles that people play. It is assumed for convenience that $N$ is an even number and that ties are broken by the flip of a coin, so that one's chance of casting a pivotal vote is half the probability that, but for one's vote, the election would be tied.[2]

The variables $B$ and $D$ are the voter's valuations of his own gain from a win by the party he votes for and of doing his bit for the rest of the nation. If, for example, the cost of voting, $C$, is \$20 and the voter's personal gain, $B$, from a win by the party he votes for is \$1,000, then the probability of casting a pivotal vote, $\pi$, required to justify voting on self-interested grounds alone must be at least 1/50. In this formulation $D$ is the satisfaction of doing one's duty regardless of whether or nor one's vote is pivotal. If $\pi$ were only 1/1,000, then a voter's valuation of $D$ of at least \$19 would be required. What one wants to know about $\pi$ is whether it is:

1  large enough to account for the decision to vote or abstain, so that $\pi B > C$;
2  large enough to be influential but insufficient to account, all by itself, for the decision to vote or abstain because $\pi B + D > C$ even though $C > \pi B$ and $C > D$; or
3  infinitesimal so that $D$ must exceed $C$ if a person is to vote at all.

Riker and Ordeshook  speak of a 'paradox of not voting' that any reasonable measure of the chance of casting a pivotal vote is too small to justify voting on self-interested grounds alone.

Measures of the chance of casting a pivotal vote may be historical or theoretical. Historical measures bypass the motives of voters, observing past variability of election results and estimating the chance of casting a pivotal vote accordingly. Theoretical measures take explicit account of how the chance of casting a pivotal vote and people's decisions to vote or abstain are at the same time influenced by voters' beliefs and by the uncertainty they face. Theoretical measures carry interesting implications about elections, but they become suspect if estimates of the chance of casting a pivotal vote differ too much from what the historical record would suggest.

The commonly used theoretical measure is based upon *person-by-person ran-domization*, while the proposed alternative in this chapter is based upon *nation-wide randomization*. Person-by-person randomization, draws upon an analogy between voting and sampling. Other people's votes for the left party and other people's votes for right party in a two-party contest are looked upon as analogous to the drawing of blue or red balls from an urn containing given proportions of each colour, so that one's chance of casting a pivotal vote becomes the chance that numbers of other people's draws of blue and red balls from the urn are the same. Nationwide randomization is the shifting, up or down, of a schedule of vot-ers' valuations of a win for the left party. The schedule is constructed by lining up all eligible voters according to their monetary valuations of a win for the left party, where a negative valuation signifies support for the right party. Shifts in the schedule of preferences alter the numbers of voters for each party, creating a chance that numbers of votes for each party are the same.

The models have markedly different implications about one's chance of casting a pivotal vote. With *person-by-person* randomization, the chance of casting a pivotal vote is 'infinitesimal'. With *nationwide* randomization, it is merely 'small', where the difference between infinitesimal and small affects the roles of duty and self-interest in one's decision to vote or abstain. If, as is often supposed,[3] the chance is infinitesimal, it can never be in anybody's self-interest to vote rather than abstain, and government by majority rule voting must rely entirely upon the citizen's sense of a duty to vote, a willingness to do the right thing because it is the right thing to do. A small chance of casting a pivotal vote leaves open the possibility that some people have enough to gain from a win by their preferred party, or can form voting pacts with other like-minded people, to make voting advantageous from an entirely self-interested point of view.

The chapter begins with a comparison of two estimates of the chance of casting a pivotal vote, one based upon the record of past elections and the other based upon a model of person-by-person randomization. There is a huge discrepancy in these estimates. An example is constructed where, in a constituency of 100,000 people, evidence of past elections suggests that the chance of casting a pivotal vote is about 1-in-5,000, while a comparable inference from person-by-person randomization suggests a chance of about 1-in-50 billion! Both estimates are based on somewhat arbitrary initial conditions, but a discrepancy that large can only be attributed to the difference in methods of computation. There follows a critical examination of two ways of accounting for the discrepancy, recognition that abstention increases the chance of casting a pivotal vote and correlation among voters' preferences between parties. The core of the chapter is a description and critique of the model of nationwide randomization: how it allows eligible voters to differ not just in their party preferences, but in their valuations of a win for the party they prefer, how it is broadly commensurate with the historical record, how abstention may bias the outcome of an election away from the preference of the majority of voters, how the party that wins the election may fail to provide the greater social welfare and how duty and self-interest interact. The chapter ends with a broader discussion of why people vote.

## The discrepancy

The gap between historical and theoretical measures may be illustrated in the comparison between estimates based upon Blais' (2000) record of Canadian elections and Beck's (1975) model of person-by-person randomization. What stands out in the comparison is that the historical estimate of the chance of casting a pivotal is small, but the estimate based upon the model of person-by-person randomization is utterly infinitesimal.

An historical estimate looks at the record of past elections, observes the distribution of the percentage of votes of one of two competing parties (somehow fudging for the presence of third parties), computes the probability of a tie and, since ties are broken by the flip of a coin, divides that in half to get the probability that an additional voter can swing the outcome of the vote from one party to the other. Blais observed that, among all of the 4,626 elections in Canadian federal constituencies between 1945 and 1997, only one was tied, suggesting as a very crude first approximation that the probability of casting a pivotal vote is about 1 in 4,626. Blais also noted that in only 5 out of the 295 constituencies in the 1997 election was the margin of victory less or equal to 100. Assuming the probability of a tied vote to be one hundredth of the probability of a margin of victory of 100, a person's chance of finding himself in a constituency where, but for his vote, the election would be tied becomes (1/100)(5/295) and one's chance of casting a pivotal vote would be (1/100)(5/295), equal to 0.0001695, or 1-in-5,900. Averaging the two numbers – 4,625 and 5,900 – we can say that the chance of casting a pivotal vote in a Canadian constituency is in the neighborhood of 1-in-5,000.

Blais' computation can be modified to account for additional information. In measuring the probability of a pivotal vote in the US House of Representatives and in US state legislatures – estimated as 1-in-89,000 and as 1-in-15,000 respectively – Mulligan and Hunter (2003) distinguish between the chance of a person's vote being pivotal in a randomly chosen *state* (essentially Blais' computation) and the chance of a randomly chosen person's vote being pivotal dependent on the population of the state where he resides. A more accurate estimation of the chance of casting a pivotal vote is constructed from a function connecting the incidence of votes within a given margin (Blais' margin was 100) and the width of the margin. Gelman, King and Boscardin (1998) employ information from opinion polls to estimate both the mean and the variance of the expected vote for one of two competing parties, where, the greater the deviation of the mean from 50 per cent and the smaller the variance, the smaller is a person's chance of casting a pivotal vote. Gelman, Silver and Edlin (2008) estimate a person's chance of casting the pivotal vote for the president of the United States to be about 1-in-60 million, where that chance must be computed as the product of the probability of one's vote being pivotal within one's state and the probability that one's state is pivotal within the nation.

If Blais' estimate of one's chance of casting a pivotal vote – approximately 1-in-5,000 – is correct and if the cost and trouble of casting one's ballot is, say, $20, it becomes individually advantageous to vote rather than to abstain when one's benefit of a win by the party one votes for is in excess of $100,000. That is surely more than most people would expect to gain and too high to induce voting on selfish grounds alone. On the other hand, a millionaire who expects the party he favours to levy an income tax at a rate of, say, 3 per cent less than would be imposed by the other party, would value a win by his preferred party at $30,000 per year which amounts to more than $100,000 over a five year period. The probability of casting a pivotal vote is small, but not so small as to deter every single voter or remove the chance of casting a pivotal vote from the list of considerations in determining whether one votes or abstains.

Records of past elections provide a rough idea of the chance that one's vote is pivotal, but there is some question as to whether outcomes in past elections are really predictive of the outcome in an election today. Regardless of the history of elections, the probability of a voter being pivotal may be relatively high in some elections and relatively low in others, high when an election is expected to be close, and low when one party is almost certain to win. Most importantly, the probability of a voter being pivotal is observed rather than derived from assumptions about voters' behaviour. The historical record is a black box generating numbers. It is most useful as a check on models to be discussed later in the chapter, raising suspicion whenever outcomes are too far from what common sense would suggest.

By contrast, person-by-person randomization, first used to the best of my knowledge in Beck (1975), draws upon an analogy between voting and sampling. Ignoring abstentions, imagine all voters lined up at the ballot box, and voting one by one. Before each person votes, the angel of chance assigns that person a preference, for the left party with a probability of $p$ and for the right party with a probability $(1 - p)$. With a total of $N$ votes cast, the number of votes for the left party is analogous to the number of blue balls in $N$ drawings from an urn containing blue and red balls in proportions $p$ and $(1 - p)$. The distribution of the number of blue balls is binomial with mean $pN$ and standard deviation $[p(1 - p)N]^{1/2}$. Suppose $N$ to be even. As explained in footnote 2, there is an analogous formula when $N$ is odd.

The election is tied when exactly $N/2$ blue balls are drawn. The probability, $T$, of a tie is 'the probability that the first $N/2$ balls are blue and the remaining $N/2$ balls are red' times 'the number of ways to place $N/2$ balls in $N$ slots'. Specifically,

$$T = \{(p)^{N/2}(1 - p)^{N/2}\}\{N!/[(N/2)!(N/2)!]\} \tag{8.2}$$

where the probability of any person's vote turning out to be pivotal is half the probability of a tie.

As the binomial distribution is bell shaped, the probability of any particular number of votes for the left party, $n$, depends on its distance from the mean, $pN$, highest when $n$ itself is the mean, and steadily lower the farther from the mean $n$ happens to be. The probability that $n = N/2$ is greatest when $p = \frac{1}{2}$.

To estimate the probability of a tied vote, $T$, in accordance with Equation (8.2), it is necessary to know the total population of voters, $N$, and the probability, $p$, that a randomly chosen person votes for the left party. To produce an estimate comparable to the historical estimate above, assume there to be 100,000 voters, a round figure roughly comparable to the number of voters in a Canadian constituency. It is less clear what to choose as the value of $p$. For this example, the value of $p$ is set equal to 0.49 which is a good deal closer to a fifty-fifty split than is observed in most elections. (For tables of the chance of a tied vote, $T$, dependent on alternative values of $N$ and $p$, see Beck (1975: 75) and Chamberlain and Rothschild (1981: 153).) On these assumptions, the chance of a tied vote in accordance with

Equation (8.2) turns out to be $(0.5)10^{-11}$ amounting to 1 chance in 50 billion. The chance of one's vote turning out to be pivotal is 1-in-50 billion.

Thus, with a cost of voting of $20, a person's required benefit from a win for that person's preferred party sufficient to make voting advantageous rises from $100,000 as estimated above to $21 trillion, two thirds of the national income of Canada. Or, to express the same point differently, if one's value of a win for one's preferred party is $100,000, a chance of no more than 1-in-50 billion of casting a pivotal vote would cover just one five thousandth of a percent of the cost of voting. Calculations like this have led many observers to treat the chance of casting a pivotal vote as infinitesimal and irrelevant.

Is the chance of casting a pivotal vote merely small or utterly infinitesimal? In an electorate of 100,000 voters, is the chance of casting a pivotal vote in the order of 1-in-5 thousand as the examination of past elections would suggest, or is it in the order of 1-in-50 billion as would seem to be implied by the randomization model? To be sure, these numbers are based upon arbitrary assumptions, but the difference between them is large enough to swamp all such considerations.

The question is of some importance. If the answer is 'small', then self-interest has some weight (along with other considerations) in a person's decision whether to vote or abstain. Self-interest may operate through voting pacts among groups of like-minded people who promise one another to vote for the party they all favour, raising the chance of casting a pivotal vote by the number of participants in the pact.[4] In rare cases where a person's value of a win for his preferred party is very high, a small chance of being pivotal may be sufficient all by itself to justify voting on purely selfish grounds. If the answer is 'infinitesimal', then none of these considerations can have a bearing on a person's decision whether to vote or abstain. Duty, and duty alone, must be invoked to explain why people vote at all.

## Escape routes

The discrepancy is disturbing because we are unwilling to live with two vastly discordant estimates of one and the same thing, and because it matters for the maintenance of democratic government whether self-interest is or is not relevant in the decision to vote or abstain. Two escape routes have been proposed: mass abstention raising each remaining voter's chance of casting a pivotal vote, and covariance of people's choices to vote or abstain. These will be considered in turn before proceeding to the alternative model which travels both routes to some extent and which is the main subject of this chapter.

The first of these routes is best introduced by the well-known paradox that if the chance of casting a pivotal vote is effectively zero, or too small to justify voting, then nobody votes, driving up the chance of casting a pivotal vote from 0 to 1, so that everybody votes. The paradox is resolved when just enough people abstain to drive up the chance of casting a pivotal vote to the point where voting becomes advantageous for people who vote and disadvantageous for eligible voters who abstain. But a process is required to determine who votes and who abstains when everybody acts as he does in his own interest alone. Owen and

Grofman (1984) and Palfrey and Rosenthal (1985) assume all eligible voters to adopt a mixed strategy, choosing to vote or abstain by the flip of a weighted coin, where weights attached to voting rather than abstention would depend on which party one votes for, but both weights, and the corresponding numbers of people voting for both parties, would be sufficient to make voting advantageous in accordance with Equation (8.1) with $D = 0$. Typically, though not invariably, estimated proportions of abstentions are very, very large and there is some possibility of multiple equilibria. Using a variant of this model, Myerson (1998) shows that, from a population of three million eligible voters of whom one million favour the left party and two million favour the right party, an average of as few as 32 supporters of each party can be expected to vote rather than abstain. Ledyard (1984) shrinks the number of voters by allowing people's cost of voting to vary from 0 to some maximal amount.

Random abstention does supply the missing equilibrium, but it introduces difficulties of its own. It requires an electorate of super-rational mathematicians who can figure out appropriate probabilities of voting in the light of what the rest of the electorate is expected to do. It implies far smaller proportions of the electorate to vote rather than abstain than is observed in actual elections. Most importantly, elections become intolerably at the mercy of voting pacts. The game-theoretic foundation of this equilibrium abstracts from the possibility of coordinated voting. In the example in the preceding paragraph, as few as 50 coordinated voters would be sufficient to supply a very high probability of swinging the election.

The other escape route is more promising and involves assumptions to be carried over to the model which is the main subject of this chapter. Implicit in person-by-person randomization as postulated by Beck (1975), is the complete independence, or absence of covariance, among votes: each person is presumed to have a probability $p$ of voting for the left party where the value of $p$ is not itself a variable. No matter how many people have already voted for the right party, if the value of $p$ is known to be 55 per cent, then the next voter is believed to have a 55 per cent chance of voting for the right party. This assumption can be modified. Instead of supposing each person to have a fixed probability of voting for the left party, Fischer (1999), following a procedure introduced by Good and Mayer (1975), inferred each voter's mean probability and standard deviation of voting for the left party from the number of people favouring the left party in a real or imaginary opinion poll, and then went on to infer the 'rational expectations' distribution of the proportion of votes for the left party in the entire population of voters, from which the chance of casting a pivotal vote could be derived. This variant of person-by-person randomization yields a distribution much wider than that in Beck's (1975) model and with a much higher chance of casting a pivotal vote, but without departing from assumption that all voters are essentially alike in that their choices are drawn from one and the same probability distribution. Chamberlain and Rothschild (1981) assume instead that $p$ itself is chosen from a probability distribution of possible values between 0 and 1. Their model is in effect a cross between the historical model and person-to-person randomization, replacing the black box in the estimate based upon the historical record with a mechanism that could generate similar outcomes with two angels of chance, the first choosing $p$ for the entire population, and the second choosing each person's vote for the given value of $p$.

There are difficulties with this escape route as well. The first angel of chance seems to do all the heavy lifting. Outcomes of elections depend upon the randomization of $p$ rather than upon the randomization of individual voting for some given value of $p$, but there is no apparent mechanism generating variations of $p$ in response to the circumstances of the economy. Nor are there recognized differences in voters' intensity of preference; no differentiation among died-in-the-wool lefties, died-in-the-wool righties and swing voters who might go either way. An additional problem is more apparent than real. To make $p$ into a random variable requires that one and only one random event – as distinct from person-by-person randomization where there are as many random events as there are voters – influences the outcome of the election as a whole. In a model of voting, this one event must affect all voters at once without at the same time switching all votes from one party to the other. This can only occur if voters differ from one another in some systematic way, as will be the case in the alternative model to be presented below.

Hidden within person-by-person randomization is a special assumption about sampling. Imagine a population of exactly one million voters with no abstentions, where exactly half a million people vote left and where the other half vote right. Clearly, on these assumptions, the outcome is a tie, and any additional voter must be pivotal despite the fact that the probability of a randomly chosen person voting for the left party remains equal to ½. With $p = $ ½, the probability of a tied election is 100 per cent in this case, as compared with a 0.25 percent in the calculation based upon person-by-person randomization (Chamberlain and Rothschild, 1981: 153). The discrepancy arises from the distinction between sampling with and without replacement. A ball picked randomly from an urn may or may not be returned to the urn before the next ball is drawn. Person-by-person randomization employs sampling with replacement. Voting may be more like sampling without replacement. Enormous in this example, the difference between estimated probabilities of a tie would be less pronounced when the proportion of population that votes is significantly less than 1.

As discussed so far, person-to-person randomization is of *interests*. Everybody knows what is best for himself, some people would be made better off with a win by the left party and other people would be made better off with a win by the right. Alternatively, randomization may be of *opinions*. One of two parties may be better for everybody, but people may differ in their judgments about which party that is. On this assumption, everybody gains the same fixed amount $B$ when the better party wins, but a proportion, $p$, of eligible voters thinks the left party is better and a proportion $(1 - p)$ thinks the right party is better. If people are correct on average – in the sense that $p > $ ½ if and only if the left party is preferable – and as long as the value of $p$ is not common knowledge, the probability of the better party winning the election is an increasing function of the number of people who vote

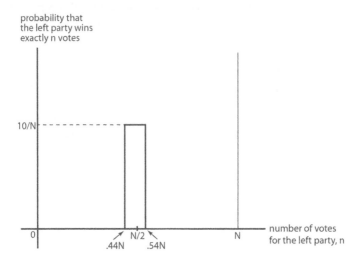

*Figure 8.1* The probability distribution of the number of votes for the left party when all outcomes between 44 per cent and 54 per cent are equally likely.

rather than abstain. The socially optimal proportion of voters in the population becomes that for which a person's cost of voting is just equal to the expected gain to society as a whole from the chance of swinging the election advantageously.

The discrepancy between the estimates based upon the record of past elections and upon person-by-person randomization is illustrated in the contrast between Figures 8.1 and 8.2. Both figures show distributions of votes in a left–right contest where the mean vote for the left party is set at 49 per cent. Figure 8.1 is a very stylized version of a supposed record of past elections where the left party has never won less than 44 per cent of the vote or more than 54 per cent and where the likelihood of every outcome in between is assumed to be the same, so that, with an assumed population of 100,000, the chance of a tie must be 1/10,000 and the left party's chance of winning the election today is 40 per cent [$(54 - 50)/(54 - 44)$]. Figure 8.2 illustrates a postulated binomial distribution in person-by-person randomization where each and every person has a 49 per cent chance of voting for the left party.

An interesting feature of the distribution of possible outcomes in Figure 8.1 is the complete separation of the chance of casting a pivotal vote from the chance of a win for the left party. As the figure is drawn, the chance of a person casting a pivotal vote is 1/10,000. With the same dispersion of expected votes, a 2 per cent increase in the chance of a win for the left party pushes the entire distribution the right – the left party now capturing between 46 per cent and 56 per cent of the votes – without changing the chance of casting a pivotal vote.[5] The probabilities of winning and of casting a pivotal vote cease to be independent under person-by-person randomization as illustrated in Figure 8.2.

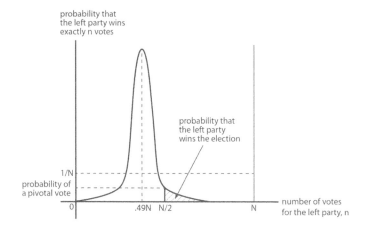

*Figure 8.2* The probability distribution of the number of votes for the left party when each voter has a 49 per cent chance of voting for the left party.

The essential difference between these distributions is in their standard deviations. In Figure 8.1, the standard deviation (the expected distance between a randomly chosen outcome and the mean) is 2,500. Since the expected vote for the left party is 49,000 and since the vote in the event of a tie is 50,000, a tied vote is only 0.4 standard deviations away from the mean (1,000/2,500). The standard deviation in Figure 8.2 is much smaller. It is about 150 (equal to $[Np(1 - p)]^{1/2}$ when $p = 0.49$ and $N = 100,000$) so that a tied vote – a distance of 1,000 votes from the mean – is about 6.7 standard deviations away (1,000/150). The chance of an observation being 6.7 standard deviations away from the mean is in the order of 1 in a billion. Technically a bell-shaped curve, the distribution of outcomes in Figure 8.2 is more like a needle than a bell with a relatively high probability at $n = 49,000$ and very low probabilities of all other outcomes. The reason for the discrepancy is that people's votes in Figure 8.1 are correlated while people's votes in Figure 8.2 are not. Distributions like that in Figure 8.1 emerge when random events cause everybody's chance of voting for the left party to be higher this year (or lower as the case may be) than in past elections. Swings in the entire pattern of voters' preferences are incorporated in the alternative model to be discussed next.

## The alternative: nationwide rather than person-by-person randomization

The main features of nationwide randomization are

- A recognition not just of whether one votes left or right, as the case may be, but *by how much* one values a win for the party of one's choice, allowing for a distinction between strong supporters of this or that party and swing voters.

- A schedule of voters' valuations of a win for the left party.
- Uncertainty about the location of the entire schedule rather than about what each voter, one by one, will do.
- A disconnect between majority and utility so that the party winning the most votes does not necessarily provide the greater social welfare.
- A *small but not infinitesimal* chance of casting a pivotal vote, reconciling the outcome of the model with the historical evidence.

The model is presented in three stages: description of a voters' valuation schedule in the absence of uncertainty, introduction of uncertainty as the random shift of the entire schedule, up or down, and incorporation of a cost of voting.

In the absence of uncertainty, people's incomes depend entirely on which party wins the election. Person $j$'s income is $y^L(j)$ in the event of a win for the left party and is $y^R(j)$ in the event of a win for the right party, and person $j$'s, positive or negative, valuation, $B(j)$, of a win for the left party is

$$B(j) = y^L(j) - y^R(j) \tag{8.3}$$

If Joan places a value of \$4,000 on a win for the left party, then, for Joan, $B = 4{,}000$. If Charles places a value of \$10,000 on a win for the right party, then, for Charles, $B = -10{,}000$. Any group of $N$ people may then be lined up on a schedule in accordance with their valuations of a win for the left party.

A voters' valuations schedule is illustrated in Figure 8.3 with benefits $B(n)$ on the vertical axis and with $N$ eligible voters lined up appropriately on the horizontal

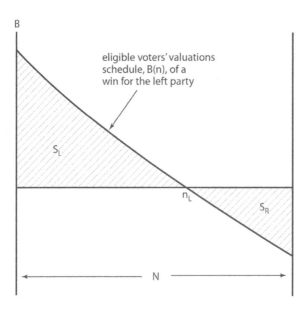

*Figure 8.3* The distribution of voters' valuations of a win for the left party.

axis, where $B(1)$ is the dollar value of a win for the left party to the person with the highest such valuation, $B(2)$ is the next highest valuation, and so on, until $B(N)$ which is the lowest of all valuations and which must be negative if the right party is to capture any votes at all. Assuming for convenience that there is nobody for whom $B(n) = 0$, let $n_L$ be the largest $n$ for which $B(n) > 0$. If everybody votes and as long as all votes are cast selfishly – for the left party when $B(n) > 0$ and for the right party when $B(n) < 0$ – then the left party wins whenever $n_L > N/2$ and the right party wins whenever $n_L < N/2$.

Now think about the voters' valuation schedule as pertaining to all but one person who is choosing whether to vote or abstain in the light of what he knows about the rest of the electorate. Thus, strictly speaking, the voters' valuation schedule differs from one person to the next, but suppose the difference is slight enough to be ignored. The voters' valuations schedule is drawn continuously, even though it is really confined to integral values of $n$ from 0 to $N$. Nationwide randomization allows for permanent pro-left voters, permanent pro-right voters and moderates in between, with chance shifting everybody's preference somewhat left or somewhat right as the case may be.

The areas designated as $S_L$ and $S_R$ respectively are the total of the valuations by all left-supporters of a win for the left party and the total of the valuations by all right-supporters of a win for the right party. Specifically,

$$S_L = \text{sum of all } B(n) \text{ for which } B(n) > 0 \qquad (8.4a)$$

and

$$S_R = \text{sum of the absolute values of all } B(n) \text{ for which } B(n) < 0 \qquad (8.4b)$$

As the figure is drawn, $n_L > N/2$ and $S_L > S_R$ signifying that the left party wins the election as long as everybody votes and that a win for the left party is best for the nation as a whole.[6] A different postulated shape of the voters' valuation curve – with the same value of $n_L$ but flatter to the left of $n_L$ and steeper to the right – could create a discrepancy between number of votes and aggregate benefits.

As long as the location of the voters' valuations schedule is common knowledge, the outcome of the election must be known with certainty – a win for the left party winning if $n_L > N/2$ and the right party winning otherwise – and there is no chance of any additional vote being pivotal unless $n_L = N/2$. Uncertainty about whether or not one's vote is pivotal can only arise from each voter's uncertainty about the electorate as a whole. In person-by-person randomization, that uncertainty was created by designating each and every voter, one by one, as a left-supporter or a right-supporter, in accordance with the flip of a weighted coin. In nationwide randomization, that uncertainty is about the location of the entire voters' valuations schedule. Each person looks upon the political preferences of the electorate as a whole as a voters' valuations schedule selected by the angel of chance from a set of feasible schedules within a range from highest to lowest as illustrated in Figure 8.4. Voters know the location of the highest and the

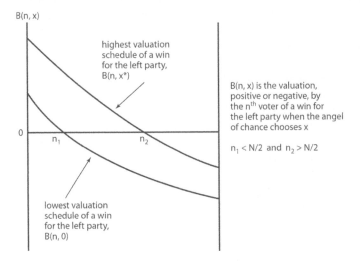

*Figure 8.4* Highest and lowest voters' valuations schedules.

lowest possible schedules. Voters do not know which schedule has been chosen in between. Knowing the locations of both schedules, voters must also know the minimal, $n_1$, and the maximal, $n_2$, numbers of votes for the left party. As the figure is drawn, $n_1 < N/2 < n_2$, giving both parties some chance of winning the election.

Selection by the angel of chance of one out of a range of possible voters' valuations schedules can be represented as the choice of a single parameter $x$. Imagine a 'basic' schedule $B(n)$ such as is illustrated in Figure 8.3 that is shifted up or down in accordance with a random variable $x$ selected by the angel of chance, converting the valuation schedule of a win for the left party from $B(n)$ to $B(n, x)$ where

$$B(n, x) = B(n) + x \qquad\qquad (8.5)$$

where $x$ varies from 0 to some maximal value, $x^*$. An increase in $x$ pushes the schedule up, raising all valuations of a win for the left party and lowering all valuations of a win for the right party accordingly. It is difficult to say a priori what the distribution of the random variable, $x$, might be, but, in the interest of simplicity, it is assumed here to be uniform, equally likely to take on any value from a minimum of 0 to a maximum of $x^*$.

On these assumptions, the voters' valuations schedule is equally likely to lie anywhere between the highest schedule, $B(n, x^*)$, generating, for each person n, the largest possible valuation of a win for the left party (or the smallest possible valuation of a win for the right party), and the lowest schedule, $B(n, 0)$, generating, for each person n, the largest possible valuation of a win for the right party.

It is important to emphasize what voters do and do not know. They must know their own preferences and, if they also knew their ranking on the voters' valuations schedule, they could not help knowing which schedule the angel of chance had chosen. It is therefore assumed that everybody knows his own value, $B$, of a win for the left party, but that nobody knows his rank on the schedule. A person with a high value of $B$ does not know whether that is because his own rank is high or because the community's $x$ is high. This person alone may be especially partial to the left party, or the entire community may have become so. For example, if Joan knows her own value of a win for the left party to be \$4,000, if $B(2, 172) = 4,000$ on the lowest voters' valuations schedule and if $B(10,956) = 4,000$ on the highest voters' valuations schedule, Joan could infer that she is between the 2,172th and 10,956th left-leaning person in the entire electorate, but she would have no idea where within these limits her ranking lies. Choice by the angel of chance of a voters' valuations schedule is no more than a rationalization of the general idea that voters have some imperfect perception about the preferences of the rest of the electorate.

To keep the model as simple as possible, a common stylized uncertainty is imposed. Everybody is alike in their perceptions of i) the shape of the voters' valuations schedule, ii) the location of the highest and lowest schedules and iii) the distribution of $x$, seen as uniform between 0 and $x^*$. A bell-shaped distribution of $x$ would be more realistic but less tractable. Voters may in practice have different pictures in their minds about how the rest of the electorate behaves, but that possibility is being assumed away to ensure that everybody's estimate of $\pi$ is the same.

On these assumptions, intervention by the angel of chance creates two distinct electoral probabilities, the probability, $\pi$, of any person's vote being pivotal and the probability, $P$, of the left party winning the election. With reference to Figure 8.4 and assuming all numbers of left supporters between $n_1$ and $n_2$ to be equally likely, the probability, $\pi$, of a person's vote becoming pivotal depends upon the *width* of the band between $n_1$ and $n_2$ and the probability, $P$, of a win for the left party depends upon the *location* of the band, whether it is mainly to the right or mainly to the left of the centre point, $N/2$.

Since all schedules within the band between $n_2$ and $n_1$ are equally likely, the chance of a tie must be $1/[n_2 - n_1]$, and a voter's chance of being pivotal must be

$$\pi = 1/[(n_2 - n_1)] \tag{8.6}$$

A slightly more complicated derivation of this formula is redundant in the present context where nobody abstains because voting is costless, but becomes useful for generalizing the formula once a cost of voting is introduced. Define a party's plurality of votes as its number of votes over and above half the number of votes cast, that is, over and above the number of votes required to tie the election. The probability of a tied vote is the inverse of the range of possible outcomes from the largest possible plurality for the left party to the largest possible plurality for the right party. The largest possible plurality for the left party is $n_2 - N/2$ on the highest voters' valuations schedule and the largest possible plurality for the right party is $(N - n_1) - N/2$, where $N/2$ is the number of votes for each party when there is a tie.

The range of possible outcomes

= maximal plurality for the left party + maximal plurality for the right party

$$= [n_2 - N/2] + [(N - n_1) - N/2] = n_2 - n_1 \qquad (8.7)$$

from which Equation (8.6) follows immediately. In the numerical example above where the left party is assumed to win anywhere between 44 per cent and 54 per cent of the votes, the maximal plurality for the left party is 4 per cent, the maximal plurality for the right party is 6 per cent, the range of possible outcomes is 10 per cent. With a population of 100,000 voters and with a range of possible outcomes of 10 per cent and the chance of one's vote being pivotal is 1/10,000.

The probability, $P$, of a win for the left party is the ratio of 'the maximal plurality for the left party' to 'the sum of both pluralities' as shown in Equation (8.8).

$$P = [n_2 - N/2]/[n_2 - n_1] \qquad (8.8)$$

which, as Figure 8.4 is drawn, is somewhat less than ½.

Probabilities of a win for the left party and of casting a pivotal vote can be adjusted to take account of people's decisions to vote or abstain once a cost of voting is introduced. With costly voting and as long as people are strictly self-interested, the decision to vote or abstain is in accordance with Equation (8.1) with $D$ set equal to 0. With a common cost of voting, $C$, and with a common probability, $\pi$, of casting a pivotal vote, a person votes for the left party when

$$B > C/\pi \qquad (8.9a)$$

for the right party when

$$-B > C/\pi \qquad (8.9b)$$

and abstains otherwise, i.e. when

$$C/\pi > |B| \qquad (8.9c)$$

Like market prices, $\pi$ is at once a signpost for each and every voter and a characteristic of the community of voters as a whole. A person votes or abstains in accordance with the electorate's value of $\pi$, but the electorate's value of $\pi$ depends on what voters choose to do.

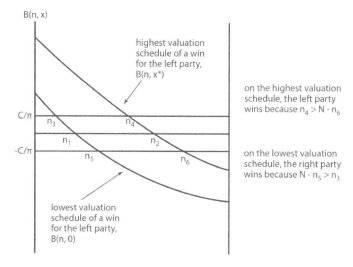

*Figure 8.5* Uncertainty about others' preferences, the cost of voting and the chance of casting a pivotal vote.

Numbers of voters and abstainers are illustrated in Figure 8.5, a reproduction of Figure 8.4 with the addition of two horizontal lines at distances $C/\pi$ above and below the horizontal axis. In accordance with Equation (8.9), one votes for the left party if one's value of $B$ is above the higher line, one votes for the right party if one's value of $B$ is below the lower line, and one abstains in between.

The highest valuation schedule is that for which the angel of chance has chosen $x = x^*$. The lowest valuation schedule is that for which the angel of chance has chosen $x = 0$. A situation could arise where one party is so much preferred to the other that it wins the election regardless of which valuation schedule is chosen. Assume instead that

$$n_4 > N - n_6 \text{ and } n_3 < N - n_5 \qquad (8.10)$$

so that left party wins when the highest valuation schedule is chosen, the right party wins when the lowest valuation schedule is chosen and everybody has some chance of casting a pivotal vote.

The range of possible outcomes is the sum of the maximal plurality for the left party and the maximal plurality for the right party, as illustrated in Figure 8.5. If the highest voters' valuations curve is selected, the number of votes cast for the left party is $n_4$, the number of votes cast for the right party is $(N - n_6)$, the total number of votes cast is $n_4 + (N - n_6)$, the required number of votes for each party for there to be a tie is $[n_4 + (N - n_6)]/2$ and the excess vote for the left party, over and above the minimum required to win the election, is $n_4 - [n_4 + (N - n_6)]/2$.

*Table 8.1* Numbers of votes and abstentions

|  | Highest valuation schedule: left party wins | Lowest valuation schedule: right party wins |
|---|---|---|
| Abstentions | $n_6 - n_4$ | $n_5 - n_3$ |
| Votes for the left party | $n_4$ | $n_3$ |
| Votes for the right party | $N - n_6$ | $N - n_5$ |
| Excess vote for the winning party | $n_4 - [n_4 + (N - n_6)]/2$ | $(N - n_5) - [n_3 + (N - n_5)]/2$ |

Note: On the assumption that each party has some chance of winning the election.

If the lowest voters' valuations curve is selected, the number of votes cast for the right party is $(N - n_5)$, the number of votes cast for the left party is $n_3$, the total number of votes cast is $n_3 + (N - n_5)$, the required number of votes for each party for there to be a tie is $[n_3 + (N - n_5)]/2$ and the excess vote for the right party is $(N - n_5) - [n_3 + (N - n_5)]/2$. This information is summarized in Table 8.1.

The range of possible outcomes between the largest number of excess votes for the right party and the largest number of excess votes for the left party is

$$= \{n_4 - [n_4 + (N - n_6)]/2\} + \{(N - n_5) - [n_3 + (N - n_5)]/2\}$$
$$= [n_4 + n_6 - n_5 - n_3]/2 \tag{8.11}$$

and the chance that a person's vote is pivotal becomes

$$\pi = 1/[\text{twice the range of possible outcomes}] = 1/[n_4 + n_6 - n_5 - n_3] \tag{8.12}$$

which boils down to Equation (8.6) when either $C = 0$ or the highest and the lowest voters' valuations schedules are parallel lines.

The probability, $P$, that the left party wins the election is the ratio of the maximal excess vote for the left party to the sum of both parties' maximal excess votes, i.e.

$$P = [n_4 + n_6 - N]/[n_4 + n_6 - n_3 - n_5] \tag{8.13}$$

Note finally the independence of $P$ and $\pi$. As illustrated in Figure 8.5, the highest and lowest voters' valuations schedules may both shift upward increasing the left party's chance of winning the election without at the same time changing anybody's chance of casting a pivotal vote. That is because $P$ depends on the average height of the two curves while $\pi$ depends on the distance between them. Person-by-person randomization has a very different implication. There, a change in the left party's chance of winning the election would normally be accompanied by a massive change in the probability of casting a decisive vote.

The information in Figure 8.5 can be looked upon from two points of view. It is, on the one hand, a picture of how the collectivity behaves, showing everybody's probability of being pivotal, the range of possible pluralities for each party, the number of abstentions, and the valuations of a win for one's preferred party required to induce a person to vote. It is, on the other hand, a guide for deciding whether to vote or to abstain, supplying the critical value of $\pi$ in Equation (8.1). These points of view are consistent as long as nobody can infer from his own value of $B$ what valuation schedule the angel of chance has selected.

## A numerical example

Figure 8.6 is a reconstruction of Figure 8.5 with numbers of voters and abstainers computed by the imposition of a specific voters' valuations schedule. The number of eligible voters, $N$, is 10,000. The postulated schedule is

$$B(n, x) = 90,000 - 20n + x \tag{8.14}$$

where $n$ is the ordering of people from left to right and where the angel of chance picks $x$ from a uniform distribution with a minimum of 0 and a maximum of 30,000.

As shown on Figure 8.6, the lowest schedule, for which $x = 0$, is

$$B = 90,000 - 20n \tag{8.15}$$

which is a downward-sloping straight line beginning at $B = 90,000$ when $n = 0$ at the left hand vertical axis, ending at $B = -110,000$ when $n = 10,000$ at the right hand vertical axis, and cutting the horizontal axis where $B = 0$ at $n_1 = 4,500$. The

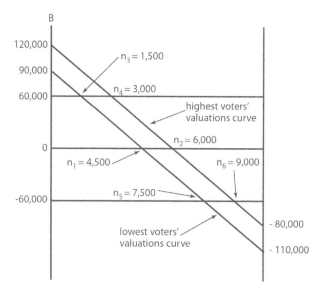

*Figure 8.6* Votes and abstentions when voting is costly.

highest schedule, for which $x = 30,000$ is

$$B = 90,000 - 20n + 30,000 \tag{8.16}$$

beginning at $B = 120,000$ when $n = 0$, ending at $B = -80,000$ when $n = 10,000$ and crossing the horizontal axis at $n_2 = 6,000$.

As minimal and maximal schedules are parallel, one's chance of casting a pivotal vote is the inverse of twice the horizontal distance between these schedules, as shown in Equation (8.6).

$$\pi = 1/(n_2 - n_1) = 1/[(6,000 - 4,500)] = 1/1,500 \tag{8.17}$$

Numbers of votes for the left and right parties depend on the cost of voting, $C$, and the choice of $x$ by the angel of chance. Suppose once again that $C = 20$, so that $C/\pi = 20/[1/1,500] = 30,000$ implying that one votes rather than abstains if and only if one's absolute value of $B$ is greater than 30,000. Connecting $B$ with $C/\pi$ in accordance with Equation (8.9) above, values of $n_3$, $n_4$, $n_5$ and $n_6$ can be derived from the equation

$$90,000 - 20n + x = z \tag{8.18}$$

where $x$ is either 0 or 30,000 and where $z = 30,000$ when the voters' valuations curve crosses the horizontal line is a distance $C/\pi$ above the horizontal axis and $z = -30,000$ when the voters' valuations curve crosses the horizontal line a distance $C/\pi$ below the horizontal axis.

Values of $n$ on Figure 8.6 are computed from Equation (8.18). Specifically,

$n_3$ is the value of $n$ when $x = 0$ and $z = 30,000$

$n_4$ is the value of $n$ when $x = 30,000$ and $z = 30,000$

$n_5$ is the value of $n$ when $x = 0$ and $z = -30,000$

$n_6$ is the value of $n$ when $x = 30,000$ and $z = -30,000$

The computed values of $n$ turn out to be

$$n_3 = 3,000, n_4 = 4,500, n_5 = 6,000 \text{ and } n_6 = 7,500.$$

Out of a total population of 10,000, 4,000 people choose to vote and 6,000 people choose to abstain. That these numbers are independent of $x$ is a consequence of the postulated linear form of the voters' valuations schedules.

Artificial as it is, this example suggests an important principle about who votes and who abstains. In so far as voting is from self-interest rather than from a sense of duty, it is the extremists who vote and the moderates who abstain. One votes if and only if the value of a win for one's preferred party exceeds 30,000. Everybody else abstains. Symmetries in the example prevent this consideration from influencing the outcome of the election, but, as will be discussed below, there is no guarantee of such symmetry in other, more realistic situations.

## Qualifications and exceptions

Figure 8.6 illustrates that there *may* be an equilibrium – with some people voting for the left party, others voting for the right party and still others choosing to abstain – in circumstances where each person knows his own preference but has only a rough idea about the distribution of preferences in the rest of the population, and, above all, where those who vote do so out of pure self-interest rather than from a sense of duty. The figure does not establish that there *must* always be an equilibrium or that the outcome is necessarily a reflection of the will of the electorate.

### A sure winner

The locations of maximal and minimal valuation schedules in Figure 8.6 were chosen to ensure that both parties have some chance of winning the election. The maximal schedule delivers a win the left party, the minimal valuation schedule delivers a win for the right party and some schedule in between delivers a tie. That need not always be so. Regardless of what value of *x* is chosen by the angel of chance, significantly higher schedules than those in Figure 8.5 would deliver a sure win to the left party, and significantly lower schedules would deliver a sure win to the right. This is, however, a consequence of the postulated uniform distribution of *x*. A normal distribution would have yielded some probability of winning to both parties. Though it is probably rare for a political party to have absolutely no chance of winning in a two-party race, the possibility cannot be ruled out altogether.

### Evidence about the angel of chance

Nationwide randomization requires people to know their own values of *B* without at the same time having more than a general idea of the preferences of the electorate as a whole. Nobody must know which voters' valuations schedule the angel of choice has selected. But, suppose I observe that my value of *B* has risen significantly since the last election. Might I not infer that the angel of chance has chosen a relatively high schedule for the electorate as a whole, pushing $n_L$ in Figure 8.3 beyond $N/2$ and removing the possibility of a tied vote? That is possible, but it is not the only possibility. The increase in my value of *B* may be for reasons unconnected with the concerns of the rest of the electorate. More interestingly, if the angel of chance has increased my value of *B*, there may at the same time be upward shifts in both the highest and the lowest valuation schedules in Figure 8.4, increasing the chance of a win by the left party but leaving the horizontal distance between the schedules (and the corresponding chance of casting a pivotal vote) unchanged.

Similarly, a person who observes his own valuation to be as high as the intersection of the highest schedule with the left-hand axis of Figure 8.4 or as low as the intersection of the lowest schedule with the right-hand axis must know either that his own valuation is very unusual or which schedule the angel of chance has chosen and which party is destined to win the election. Anybody who observes his own value of $B$ to lie between the intersection of the highest and lowest schedules with the left-hand vertical axis must know that the angel of chance has selected a voters' valuations schedule within a restricted portion of the full range of feasible schedules bordering on the highest possible schedule, and anybody who observes his value of $B$ to lie between the intersections of the highest and lowest schedules with the right-hand axis must know that the scheduled is confined in the opposite direction.

This difficulty is more apparent than real. A way out is to change the postulated shape of the voters' valuations schedule as shown in Figure 8.7 with all possible schedules intersecting at both vertical axes. The pattern of schedules in Figure 8.7 serves to suppress everybody's knowledge about which schedule the angel of chance has chosen by bunching all schedules together at the maximal and minimal values of $B$ (shown in the figure as $F$ and $-G$), so that neither the person with the highest $B$ nor the person with the lowest $B$ nor anybody in between can have any idea which among the set of feasible voters' valuations schedules the angel of chance has chosen. Values of the five relevant variables, $n_3$, $n_4$, $n_5$, $n_6$ and $\pi$, would be determined simultaneously from Equations (8.10) and (8.14) for the postulated shapes of the voters' valuations schedules. Alternatively, the voters' valuation schedules need not touch the axes at all. They can be asymptotic to the axes, implying that a few very high valuations can never be ruled out.

The important consideration here is that imposition of common upper and lower limits to the voters' valuations schedule is a device imposed to make uncertainty precise. In practice, voters would have no more than a vague idea of the location of the true schedule on election day, with no firm boundary between what may and what may not happen.

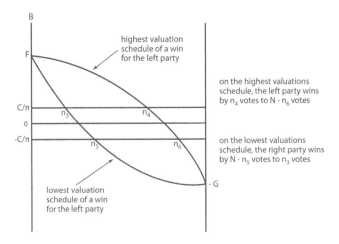

*Figure 8.7* Valuation schedules with common maximal and minimal values.

### Bias in favour of small groups with strong preferences

A situation can easily arise where a majority of the population prefers one party, but where the other party wins the election because its supporters place higher values on a win for their preferred party and are therefore less likely to abstain. The electoral triumph of a small group with strong preferences is illustrated in Figure 8.8 where the voters' valuations schedule is flatter to the left than to the right. Think of $B(n)$ in Figure 8.8 as the true schedule selected by the angel of chance, and suppose the highest and lowest schedules are sufficiently above and below the true schedule that both left and right parties are seen as having some chance of winning the election, allowing everybody some probability, $\pi$, of casting a pivotal vote.

If voting were costless, $m$ people would vote for the left party because, as the figure is drawn, $m > N/2$, signifying that the left party wins the election. But when voting is costly, $n_L$ people vote for the left party, $N - n_R$ people vote for the right party, but $(N - n_R) > n_L$, signifying that the right party wins the election. This is not an implausible outcome. Rich people may well place the greater dollar value on a win for their preferred political party and have a greater incentive than poor people to vote rather than abstain. With a kinked voters' valuations schedule as in Figure 8.8, a majority of the population prefers the left party to the right, but a decisive minority with a sufficiently strong preference for the right party enables the right party to win the election.

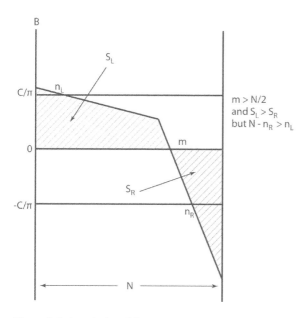

*Figure 8.8* A majority of the population prefers the left party to the right party and the left party supplies the larger aggregate surplus, but the right party wins the election.

... for large electorates, no matter how great the proportion of the electorate that prefers a particular outcome, that outcome is likely to lose the election if the opposing outcome is preferred by an expected majority of voters with a sufficiently large incentive to vote.

Campbell (1999: 1203)

### Social welfare

Parallel to the possible discrepancy between numbers of supporters of each party and numbers of votes cast is a second possible discrepancy between the outcome of the election and social welfare. Figure 8.3 showed the net gain (or loss as the case may be) to society as a whole from a win by the left party to be the difference between the gain $S_L$ to left-party supporters from a win by the left party and the gain $S_R$ to right-party supporters from a win by the right party. As the figure was drawn, the party favoured by a majority of the population supplied the larger net gain as well. That need not always be so. As illustrated in Figure 8.8, the voters' valuations schedules could be tweaked so that $S_L < S_R$ despite the fact that $m > N/2$. A relatively indifferent majority of the population may prefer that shopping on Sunday be allowed, while a passionate minority prefers that shopping on Sunday be forbidden. The dollar value of the potential loss to the minority may well exceed the dollar value of the potential gain to the majority.

Surplus has so far been graduated in dollars to ensure that $B$ and $C/\pi$ are commensurate. Nevertheless, if one party tends to favour the rich while the other tends to favour the poor and if the disputed public policy is to narrow the distribution of income, then it may be of some interest to measure surplus in utils as well. For any given voters' valuations curve, the surpluses, $S_L$ and $S_R$, measured in dollars as illustrated in Figure 8.8, are

$$S_L = \int_0^v B(n)\mathrm{d}n \tag{8.19a}$$

$$S_R \int_v^N -B(n)\mathrm{d}n \tag{8.19b}$$

where $v$ is the value of $n$ such that $B(v) = 0$. With a common utility of income function, the surpluses, $S_L$ and $S_R$, can be transformed from dollars to utils, $U_L$ and $U_R$. Expressed in utils, the surpluses become

$$U_L = \int_0^v [u(y^L(n)) - u(y^R(n))]\mathrm{d}n \tag{8.20a}$$

$$U_R = \int_v^N [u(y^R(n)) - u(y^L(n))]\mathrm{d}n \tag{8.20b}$$

where $u(y^L(n))$ and $u(y^R(n))$ are the utilities of income of person $n$ depending on which party wins the election. Equation (8.20) is constructed on the assumption that everybody's utility of income function is the same. Otherwise, each person would have his own version of Equation (8.20).

## Salvaging the incentive to vote

The chance of casting a pivotal vote has been examined thus far on the working assumption that people are exclusively self-interested, voting or abstaining as the case may be according to whether $\pi B > C$ in Equation (8.1) and ignoring $D$ altogether. Other motives for voting may be less affected by the chance of casting a pivotal vote.

Voting may be *pleasurable* rather than costly. Tullock (1967) suggested that people's willingness to vote rather than to abstain might be explained by the possibility that voting is not costly at all. Voting for a political party might be like supporting the local football team or voting for the American Idol or congregating in Times Square on New Year's Eve.

Voting may be *expressive* rather than instrumental as described in Brennan and Hamlin (1998) and in Hillman (2010). Expressive voting creates 'the utility ... of satisfying ... one's party allegiance' Fiorina (1976: 395). 'A person may support Gary Hart for the same reason he buys a Cuisinart: to show his friends that he likes fresh ideas, is part of a new generation, or that he is not yet solidly middle class' (Glaser, 1987: 259). Expressive voting is a two-edged sword. One may express good will toward one's fellow citizens by voting for a party expected to provide essential social services to the poor. One may express allegiance to the upper classes, the One True God, the master race or the glorious leader (Hamlin and Jennings, 2011). There is also something fishy about expressing oneself in a secret ballot. On the other hand, one's benefit from expressing oneself to oneself should be unaffected by the chance of casting a pivotal vote.

Voting may be *influential* regardless of whether or not one's vote is pivotal. Looked upon so far as an unambiguous choice between this and that, voting is sometimes looked upon instead as a basis for compromise between extremes. Stigler (1972) proposed a rudimentary model of this sort. Alesina and Rosenthal (1995) have worked out a much more elaborate model of compromise within legislature and between legislatures and the presidency. Competing interests may be reflected in vote shares and may influence outcomes in accordance with the probabilistic voting theorem (Austin-Smith, 1987). A person's vote may communicate to the rest of the electorate that the party one votes for is supported by a significant share of the population (Meirowitz and Shotts, 2009).

Voting may be *sociotropic*. One's value of $B$ in Equation (8.1) may be the net benefit from a win by the party one prefers not just to oneself, but to others as well as described in Edlin, Gelman and Kaplan (2007, 2007). Specifically, reproducing equation (2) in Edlin, Gelman and Kaplan (2007), it may be supposed that

$$B = B_{self} + \alpha NB_{others} \tag{8.21}$$

where $B_{self}$ is the dollar value of the benefit to oneself, $B_{others}$ is the *average* dollar of benefits to others, $N$ is population and $\alpha$ is a parameter. Accounting for the benefits to others in this way increases $\pi B$ considerably. Suppose, for example, that $N = 100,000$ and $\pi = 1/10,000$. The expected value of the gain from voting to oneself, $\pi B_{self}$, is likely to be much less than $C$, but the expected value of the gains to all others, $\pi \alpha N B_{others}$, could easily exceed $C$ as long as the parameter $\alpha$ is not too small. The expression $\pi \alpha N B_{others}$ could be interpreted as the value of $D$ in Equation (8.1).

There are several difficulties with this explanation of why people vote. People may differ in the others about whom they are concerned. 'Others' may be one's family, one's social class, people in one's neighbourhood, or the nation as a whole. Benefits to others may be compared as dollars' worth or as utils. Recognizing that it normally costs taxpayers more than one dollar to transfer an extra dollar to the poor, the benefit, $B_{others}$, from a win by a party intent on redistribution of income may be seen as positive or negative depending on the curvature of a person's utility of income function. People inclined to vote for the benefit of others may be unconfident that their assessments of aggregate gain are any more accurate than judgments of other voters supporting a different party on sociotropic grounds.

Utility aside, there is a problem in in placing a dollar value on one's valuation of the welfare of others. Like all dollar values, $B_{self}$ and $\alpha N B_{others}$ must be what a person would be willing to pay. To say that a person values a win by the left party at \$1,000 is to say that he would be would be willing to pay up to \$1,000 to obtain that benefit or that he would be willing to accept anything over \$1,000 to avoid losing it. (The latter measure would be the larger of the two.) The dollar value, $\alpha N B_{others}$, that a person attaches to the gains of others must be similarly defined. It is the amount one would pay to secure those gains or the amount one would accept to remove them, an amount much less than the dollar value of the gains themselves. Consider a country with 20 million people where, if everybody votes, one's chance of casting a pivotal is, say, 1/(2 million). Suppose also that every person's income is \$50,000, so that the national income is \$1 trillion, and that politics is a contest between left and right. Imagine a person in that society who believes a win for the left party would increase the national income by 1 per cent, equivalent to \$10 billion. How much would that person be prepared to pay to secure a win for the left party? Clearly, that person cannot pay \$10 billion, and nobody with an initial income of \$50,000 would be so altruistic as to forego \$10 billion to procure an equivalent amount for the rest of the nation. Imagine a person who would sacrifice a quarter of his income for this gain to the rest of the nation. A person prepared to give up \$12,500, to procure a 1 per cent increase in the national income for certain would be prepared to give up only 0.625¢ (\$12,500/2,000,000) to procure a 1/(2 million) chance of procuring that gain, an amount well short of any reasonable cost of voting. The value of $\alpha$ in Equation (8.21) would have to be very, very small. Sociotropic considerations may augment the benefit of voting, but not by enough to dispense with the paradox of not voting altogether.

Voting may simply be *dutiful*. People may vote rather than abstain because voting is seen as the right thing to do or in the belief that large turnouts in elections are a requirement for the preservation of democratic government, regardless of which of the competing parties is thought to yield the greatest benefit for the nation as a whole. On the duty to vote and the role of social pressure in reinforcing such duty, see Gerber, Green and Larimer (2008). Meanings of the duty to vote are discussed in Chapter 7. As with expressive voting, one's willingness to vote out of a sense of duty ought not to be much influenced by the chance that one's vote is pivotal. It should be sufficient for the voter to appreciate the prisoners' dilemma that a duty to vote is intended to circumvent.

\*\*\*

The starting point of this chapter was the vast discrepancy between estimates of the chance of casting a pivotal vote. Estimates based on the record of past elections suggest that the chance is small. Estimates based upon a commonly employed model of voter behaviour suggest that the chance is infinitesimal. Specifically, for a constituency of about 100,000 voters, Blais' evidence on Canadian elections suggests a chance in the order of 1-in-5,000, while a variant of Beck's model of person-to-person randomization suggests a chance in the order of 1-in-10 billion. The discrepancy is important for its implications about the role of self-interest and duty in the decision to vote or abstain.

The alternative model of a person's decision to vote or abstain is consistent with a chance of casting a pivotal vote not dramatically different from that suggested by the historical evidence. Person-by-person randomization assigns all voters the same probability of voting left rather than right. Nationwide randomization assigns eligible voters with distinct monetary values of a win for their preferred party, positive if the preference is for the left and negative if the preference is for the right, with strength of preference represent by the absolute value. This simplifies matters enormously. Voters can then be lined up on a schedule from left to right, and uncertainty in the outcome of an election can be looked upon as arising from random shifts, left or right, in the schedule as a whole. When voting is strictly self-interested, people with high absolute valuations of a win for their preferred party choose to vote and people with low valuations choose to abstain.

Nationwide randomization has several virtues. It is very simple. It gives rise to small but not infinitesimal estimates of the chance of casting a pivotal vote, estimates broadly consistent with the history of past elections. It links each voter's chance of casting a pivotal vote to other voters' behaviour in response to the uncertainty they face. It shows how uncertainty governs people's choices to vote or abstain. It shows how self-interested abstention by a significant portion of the electorate may alter the outcome of an election, switching victory from one party to another. It shows how outcomes of elections when everybody chooses to vote or abstain from self-interest alone may be biased in favour of small groups with intense preferences and may not be best for the community as a whole. Abstentions need not cancel out. The fewer people vote, the more does the outcome of an election come to depend organization of the electorate rather than voters' preferences. The chance of a person's vote turning out to be pivotal is significantly larger than the model of person-by-person randomization would suggest, but still much too small to induce a significant proportion of the population to vote on self-interested grounds alone. A duty to vote remains essential for the preservation of democratic government.

## Notes

1　This chapter was originally an article in *Rationality and Society* (Usher, 2013).
2　Suppose the outcome of an election is equally likely to be anywhere between a win for the left party by $x$ votes over and above 50 per cent and a win for the right party by y votes over and above 50 per cent. If so, the chance that an additional person's vote is pivotal – switching the outcome of the election from a win by the party the person votes against to a win by the party the person votes for – is $1/(x + y)$. The route to this result depends on whether the number of voters is even or odd. Suppose, for convenience, the additional person votes for the left party. That person's vote can only be pivotal when either i) but for that person's vote, the election would have been tied and the right party would have won the coin toss to break the tie, or ii) but for that person's vote, the right party would have won the election by one vote and the left party goes on to win the coin toss to break the tie created by that person's vote. As a matter of simple arithmetic, the first route is only possible when the number of votes cast is even, in which case the gap between the number of votes for the right party and the number of votes for the left party must be even too, and only $(x + y)/2$ outcomes are possible between a win by $x$ votes for the left party and a win by y votes by the right party; the probability of a tie becomes $2/(x + y)$ and the chance of a pivotal vote – a tie followed by a win of the coin toss by the left party – becomes $1/(x + y)$. An analogous argument leads to the same result when the total number of votes is odd.
3　'The probability that a single vote is pivotal is negligible in a large election. Hence small voting costs should dissuade turnout' Feddersen and Sandroni (2006: 1271).
4　Suppose a person's cost of voting is $20 and the person's value of a win for the preferred party is $12,000, so that, according to Equation (8.1), the chance of casting a pivotal vote required to justify voting rather than abstention is 1-in-600. Uncoordinated voting does not pay if the chance of casting a pivotal vote is 1-in-10,000, but voting as part of a pact of 50 voters does pay because it raises the chance of a win for the preferred party from 1-in-10,000 to 1-in-200. Every member of such a voting pact supplies an externality to every other member. On the other hand, if each person has a 1-in-100 billion chance of casting a pivotal votes, a pact of 50 voters acquires a 1-in-2 billion chance of being pivotal which is still much too small to induce anybody, or any fifty-person group of people, not to abstain.
5　The chance of a win by the left party is $(56 - 50)/(56 - 46)$ which is 60 per cent.
6　Note that

$$S_L - S_R = \sum_{n=1}^{N} y^L(n) - \sum_{n=1}^{N} y^R(n)$$

which is the difference between the national income as it would be if the left party wins and the national income if the right party wins. Diminishing marginal utility of income is ignored.

## References

Alesina, A. and Rosenthal, H. (1995) *Partisan Politics, Divided Government and the Economy*, Cambridge: Cambridge University Press.

Austin-Smith, D. (1987) Interest groups, campaign contributions, and probabilistic voting, *Public Choice*, 54(2), 123–39.

Beck, N. (1975) A note on the probability of a tied election, *Public Choice*, 23(1), 75–9.

Blais, A. (2000) *To Vote or Not to Vote: The Merits and Limits of Rational Choice Theory*, Pittsburgh: University of Pittsburgh Press.

Brennan, G. and Hamlin, A. (1998) Expressive voting and electoral equilibrium, *Public Choice*, 95, 149–75.

Campbell, C. M. (1999) Large elections and decisive minorities, *Journal of Political Economy*, 107(6), 1199–217.

Chamberlain, G. and Rothschild, M. (1981) A note on the probability of casting a decisive vote, *Journal of Economic Theory*, 25, 152–62.

Edlin, A. S., Gelman, A. and Kaplan, N. (2008) Vote for charity's sake, *Economists' Voice*, available online at http://works.bepress.com/cgi/viewcontent.cgi?article=1075&context=aaron_edlin [accessed 2 September, 2015].

Edlin, A. S., Gelman, A. and Kaplan, N. (2007) Voting as rational choice: why and how people vote to improve the well-being of others, *Rationality and Society*, 19(3), 293–314.

Fiorina, M. P. (1976) The voting decision: instrumental and expressive aspects, *The Journal of Politics*, 38(2), 390–413.

Feddersen, T. and Sandroni, A. (2006) A theory of participation in elections, *American Economic Review*, 96(4), 1271–82.

Fischer, A. J. (1999) The probability of being decisive, *Public Choice*, 101(3/4), 267–83.

Gelman, A., King, G. and Boscardin, W. J. (1998) Estimating the probability of events that have never occurred: when is your vote decisive?, *Journal of the American Statistical Association*, 93, 1–9.

Gelman, A., Silver, N. and Edlin, A. (2008) What is the probability your vote will make a difference?, NBER working paper no. 15220.

Gerber, A., Green, D. P. and Larimer, C. W. (2008) Social pressure and voter turnout: evidence from a large-scale field experiment, *American Political Science Review*, 102(1), 33–48.

Glaser, A. (1987) A new theory of voting: why vote when millions of others do?, *Theory and Decision*, 22(3), 257–70.

Good, L. J. and Mayer, S. (1975) Estimating the efficacy of a vote, *Systems Research and Behavioral Science*, 20(1), 25–33.

Hamlin, A. and Jennings, C. (2011) Expressive political behaviour: foundations, scope and implications, *British Journal of Political Science*, 41(3), 645–70.

Hillman, A. (2010) Expressive behaviour in economics and politics, *European Journal of Political Economy*, 26(4), 403–18.

Ledyard, J. (1984) A pure theory of large two candidate elections, *Public Choice*, 44(1), 7–41.

Meirowitz, A. and Shotts, K. (2009) Pivots versus signals in elections, *Journal of Economic Theory*, 144, 744–71.

Mulligan, C. and Hunter, C. G. (2003) The empirical frequency of a pivotal vote, *Public Choice*, 166, 31–54.

Myerson, R. B. (1998) Population uncertainty and poison games, *International Journal of Game Theory*, 27, 375–92.

Owen, G. and Grofman, B. (1984) To vote or not to vote: the paradox of nonvoting, *Public Choice*, 42, 311–25.

Palfrey, T. R. and Rosenthal, H. (1985) Voter participation and strategic uncertainty, *The American Political Science Review*, 79(1), 62–78.

Riker, W. and Ordeshook, P. C. (1968) A theory of the calculus of voting, *The American Political Science Review*, 62, 25–42.

Stigler, G. (1972) Economic competition and political competition, *Public Choice*, 13, 91–100.

Tullock, G. (1967) *Toward a Mathematics of Politics*, Michigan: University of Michigan Press.

Usher, Dan (2013) An alternative explanation of the chance of casting a pivotal vote *Rationality and Society*, 26(1), 105–38.

# 9 The problem of equity[1]

Allocation of the national income among citizens has always been a source of conflict, the conflict seems to have intensified in recent years, and this is reflected within the economics profession by a growing interest in the measurement and explanation of the distribution of income. We try to determine whether inequality is increasing over time and to explain observed inequality by social class, education, chance, the life cycle, and so on. However, studies of the income distribution have for the most part been directed away from what I would consider to be the central problem. The principal conflict within Western societies is not about the spread between the incomes of the rich and the poor. It is among people or groups of people to determine who shall be rich and who shall be poor. It is exemplified by the allocation among four people of four slots with fixed incomes of, say, $25,000, $20,000, $15,000 and $10,000, where nobody is initially identifiable as rich or poor and where the four people themselves must decide who is to occupy each slot. Resolution of such conflict need have no impact upon the distribution of income in the statistical sense.

The serious and divisive conflicts over the allocation of national income among citizens are not about matters such as the progression of the income tax or the level of welfare payments where the interest of the rich and the interest of the poor are directly opposed. The really difficult political decisions, the decisions that provoke debate in parliament or embitter dominion–provincial relations, are those like the allocation of oil rents between the East and the West, the granting of tariffs or other privileges to industry, and the determination of wages, where the initial incomes of the parties in the dispute are not central to the dispute itself. In particular, difficulties in the setting of wage rates are much the same for doctors, members of parliament, civil servants, teachers, construction workers, postmen or hospital orderlies.

The purpose of the chapter is to enunciate and defend the proposition that the increasing conflict over the allocation of income among people in Canada, as in other Western countries, can at least in part be attributed to an attenuation of the 'standard of equity' in dealings between the government and the economy. I begin by reviewing the usages of the term equity in economics. In doing so, I object to the recent usage of the word equity as a synonym for equality, and I try to define equity in a different but fairly precise way, making what I believe to be the crucial distinction between inequity where a specific standard is violated and *anequity* where no standard applies. Then I try to show that the maintenance of some standard of equity is a prerequisite for democratic government, and that the outcome of the competitive process in a market economy is the standard of equity we apply because we can find no other. Finally, I try to show that some attenuation of our standard of equity is the unintended consequence of the developments in Canadian institutions. The moral, if there is one, is not that we should preserve our standard of equity undiminished in all circumstances, but that attenuation of the standard of equity should be recognized as a real cost. Laws or institutions which are likely to attenuate the standard of equity should be avoided unless it can be shown that the harm in the attenuation of the standard can be justified by substantial benefits of some other kind.

## The definition of equity

In this section I review some definitions of the word 'equity' in common speech and in the literature of economics, and I propose a definition of my own. My definition is similar in many respects, but not quite identical, to the usual definition of horizontal equity. It is distinguishable from horizontal equity in its application to a broader range of circumstances, it is more clearly differentiated from efficiency, and it is better suited for the analysis of the range of problems I wish to discuss.

The Shorter Oxford English Dictionary defines equity as follows (with Latin pronunciation and dates deleted):

a   1   (general) The quality of being equal or fair; impartiality or even-handed dealing
2   That which is fair and right
3   (jurisprudence) The recourse to general principles of justice to correct or supplement the ordinary law
4   In England, Ireland and the US, a system of law existing side by side with the common and statute law (together called law in the narrower sense), and suspending these when they conflict with it
5   An equitable right i.e. one recognizable in a court of equity
b   The ordinary shares of a company as opposed to the preference shares.

The definition includes the following comment on item 4:

In England equity was formerly administered by a special class of tribunals, of which the court of Chancery was chief; but since 1873 all branches of the High Court administer both law and equity, it being provided that where the two differ, the rules of equity are to be followed.

The term equity found its way into economics through public finance. For some time, the practice in public finance has been to assess the tax structure and the composition of public expenditure under the headings of efficiency interpreted as Pareto optimality, vertical equity represented by the degree of equality in the distribution of income among people, and horizontal equity defined formally as 'treating like cases alike' but restricted in practice to the maxim that people with equal incomes, comprehensively defined, should be obliged to pay equal amounts of tax. More recently, the word equity, without the qualifiers horizontal or vertical, has come to be used in place of the term vertical equity. In articles with titles such as 'the trade-off between equity and efficiency in cost–benefit analysis' or 'equity and efficiency in the pricing of the services of public utilities', the word equity has become a synonym for equality. On this interpretation, one outcome is more equitable than another if it entails a more equal distribution of income.

Identification of equity with equality is unnecessary and unfortunate. It is unnecessary because there is already a word to denote what equity is beginning to mean. The word equality is quite satisfactory and has the advantage over equity that it denotes what it denotes without the ethical overtones that the word equity has acquired. Nothing would have been sacrificed if the word equity had been replaced by the word equality in the titles referred to above. The usage of equity to mean equality is unfortunate because, as I try to show in this chapter, equity has another meaning for which there appears to be no substitute at all. I want to condemn certain policies because they are inequitable and to convey my belief that equity is an important aspect of economic policy. The current terminology of economics does not permit me to do so.

Equity for the purposes of this chapter is a political virtue in the economic realm. A government acts equitably in the passage of laws or the formation of economic policy by respecting and preserving the allocation of the national income among citizens in accordance with generally accepted rules provided outside of and independently of the political arena. Equity is in one sense an objective of economic policy, and in another sense a constraint. It is an objective in that a society where equity is respected is likely to be a better place for most people than a society where it is not. It is a constraint in placing bounds upon public policy. One might think of efficiency and equality as the objectives of economic policy and of equity as a constraint, but the constraint is social rather than technical. Governments can choose to ignore considerations of equity, but ought not to do so.

This usage of equity corresponds quite closely to the usage of the term in common speech. We speak of the tax system as equitable or otherwise. We speak of punishments as meted out in an equitable or inequitable manner. Private acts are not as a rule described in this way. We do not speak of robbing a bank as inequitable. Nor is it inequitable if the value of my house declines because the neighbourhood where I live becomes unfashionable, though it would be inequitable if the decline were due instead to a sudden upward re-evaluation of my house for tax purposes when similar houses are not assessed accordingly. One can, of course, be equitable or otherwise in dealings with one's children, but that is a kind of politics.

Strictly speaking, if equity is allocation in accordance with rules, then the term equity cannot be applied to the rules themselves. However, the terms equity and inequity can be applied to laws or to acts of parliament because, and in so far as, an act of parliament may be assessed with reference to provisions of a written or unwritten constitution specifying who has the right to what. The critical distinction is between acts of parliament and rules about the allocation among people of the national income, where the rules are to some degree outside of parliament and not normally subject to legislation. The distinction is not and cannot be exact or immutable, for rules about the allocation of income must be modified by legislation from time to time. We shall return to this matter when we come to discuss the content of the rules.

Equity, in this sense of the term, is similar in many respects to the concept of horizontal equity, so much so that the reader will not go far wrong if he thinks of the one when I refer to the other. Both require an external standard and are meaningless if no such standard exists. The standard for horizontal equity is the ordering of pre-tax incomes. If the pre-tax income of Mr A is larger than the pre-tax income of Mr B, then the tax system is judged horizontally inequitable unless the post-tax income of Mr A is larger than the post-tax income of Mr B. I argue in this chapter that the standard for equity without the qualifier is also to be found in the private sector of the economy, but the term equity has been deliberately defined here to encompass a wide range of possible standards. One might ask why horizontal equity, or equity in a broader context, is desirable. One might ask why, for example, if bricklayers earn $10,000 and carpenters earn $15,000, should parliament not impose a special tax and subsidy so that bricklayers have post-tax incomes of $15,000 and carpenters have post-tax incomes of $10,000. One might ask why the pre-tax ordering of people on the scale of rich and poor is worth preserving at all. This chapter is an attempt to answer such questions.

Equity and horizontal equity are also alike in that neither is tied to any particular distribution of income in the statistical sense. Whether taxation is horizontally equitable, or public policy is equitable as defined in this chapter, is independent of the properties – the coefficient of variation or the Gini coefficient – of the statistical distribution of income. Equity and horizontal equity are about conformity of the allocation of income to the rules of society, whatever those rules happen to be. The statistical distribution is what it is regardless of who turns out to be rich and who turns out to be poor.

Equity and horizontal equity both are at variance with the two principal competing theories of justice as applied to the evaluation of political and economic institutions – utilitarianism and the maximin principle – because both theories look to a property of the distribution of income or utility as the objective for society as a whole. For utilitarianism, the objective is the sum of the utils of all citizens, an objective which may, with certain subsidiary assumptions, be approximated by a function of the average income and the standard deviation. For the maximin principle, the objective is the income of the worst off person. Both theories enable economies to be compared or proposals for reform to be assessed in accordance with the shape of the income distribution.[2]

To put the matter in another way, equity differs both from utilitarianism and from the maximin principle because these theories assess institutions 'from behind the veil of ignorance'. They evaluate alternatives in the eyes of someone who does not know his place on the scale of rich and poor. For such a person, all institutions giving rise to one and the same distribution of income would be equally desirable. Of course, proponents of these theories could argue that someone behind the veil of ignorance would choose institutions that are equitable, and I would have no objection to such a defence. I suspect, however, that proponents of these theories of justice would be unlikely to reason in this way because considerations of equity run counter to their ahistorical style of discourse and because the recognition of equity as an independent criterion must weaken the utilitarian objective or the maximin principle as a guide to economic policy. Nor would there be a clear trade-off between equality and efficiency in, for instance, the pricing of publicly provided goods like electricity and water because prior claims of equity would have to be taken into account.

Similar as they are, the concepts of equity and horizontal do differ in some respects, and there are things I want to say about equity that cannot be said equally well with reference to horizontal equity instead. In particular, I do not wish to be constrained by the association of horizontal equity with the comprehensive tax base, for I believe that the greater departures from equity occur on the expenditure side of the public accounts. Public expenditures can be every bit as unfair as tax laws in their impact upon the allocation of income among people, as attested to by the growing literature on 'tax expenditures' (see Surrey, 1973).[3]

Lapses from horizontal equity are not always inequitable. Suppose in the year 1800 there had been passed a law exempting all carpenters practising in the city of Kingston from the federal income tax. The law would surely have been inequitable at the time it was passed, for it would have increased the incomes of carpenters in Kingston at the expense of the rest of the population of Canada. But the law would eventually cease to be inequitable because the tax advantages to carpenters in Kingston would have induced extra carpenters to establish business there until, after the passage of many years, the net incomes of carpenters in Kingston and elsewhere in the country would be the same. Even the secondary advantages of the law would lapse in time. Benefits to Kingston residents of inexpensive carpentry would be dissipated as more commerce takes place in Kingston than would be warranted in the absence of this law. To some extent the benefit from the law would be capitalized in Kingston land prices, but that would be of no advantage to the present residents of Kingston who would have purchased the land they own at prices high enough to compensate for the low price of carpenters' services.

If carpenters in Kingston had been exempt from income tax since 1800, the repeal of that exemption today would at once be horizontally equitable as the term is commonly understood, but inequitable in the broader sense of rearranging incomes among citizens in an unanticipated way. One could certainly argue for the repeal of the exemption to increase the Canadian gross national product by improving the allocation of carpenters throughout the country. But that is an argument about efficiency, not equity in the usual sense of the term.

The reader may well raise an objection at this point: accept that the repeal of the exemption from income tax is horizontally equitable but inequitable in the sense of not preserving the distribution of income in accordance with agreed upon rules (for surely the exemption for Kingston carpenters was agreed upon, at least tacitly, in that it lasted over a hundred years). This is nothing more than an example of the proposition that an old tax is a good tax. Can it not, therefore, be said that the principle in this example would admit no change in the tax structure whatsoever? Can it not be said that equity is just the absence of change, while horizontal equity allows change in the direction of a certain ideal? And is the absence of change a principle worthy of respect? It must be admitted that there is some force to the argument. Equity is a conservative principle.

Nonetheless, equity and horizontal equity are closer than this objection would suggest. First, it is rare to find deviations from horizontal equity as venerable as that in the example. Most of the loopholes in the tax system are probably not fully capitalized, and the plugging of loopholes would get at least some of the original beneficiaries. Second, the conservative principle strictly applied gives no guidance about how to tax new forms of economic activity or how to respond to the discovery of new loopholes in the law. If carpenters had been exempted from tax since 1800, it would have been necessary at some point to decide whether electricians, people who work with plastics, or people who apply aluminum siding to houses are carpenters or not. A strictly conservative principle would be no help in that case, but a general principle such as horizontal equity could be applied. Third, and most important, a horizontally equitable tax system with a comprehensive tax base is thought of as an ideal tax structure from which further change could be arrested. No other tax system could command widespread appeal. Any other tax system would be seen to be arbitrary and subject to change at the whim of parliament or the instigation of a strong pressure group. Horizontal equity and the comprehensive tax base represent a standard and in a context where no other standard presents itself. This is the sense in which equity and horizontal equity do point in the same direction.

As to the broader question of whether equity is just the absence of change, the answer at this stage of the argument is that some degree of permanence in the rules for the allocation among people of the national income and other advantages is a requirement for the continuance of what most people would agree is a decent society. This line of argument will be developed as we proceed.

The definition of equity as allocation in accordance with agreed upon rules permits one to draw the important distinction between inequity and what I am inclined to call anequity. Inequity occurs when there is a standard and it is violated. Anequity occurs when there is no standard at all. This distinction may be clarified by examples. It would be an inequity for the city of Kingston to expropriate my house without compensation for the sole benefit of the other citizens of Kingston. That would be inequitable because there is a clear and agreed upon standard for the use and disposition of property, a standard according to which I, and I alone, have the right to use or to sell a house I have acquired through purchase in the appropriate way. The house could be expropriated with 'just compensation', but that is another matter. A situation I would be inclined to describe as anequity can arise in a public decision about the location of an airport. Suppose there is a general agreement among the residents of a city to build a new airport at one of a number of sites, but each person wants the airport located away from his house to avoid the noise and inconvenience. The situation can be described as anequity because there is no clear standard to determine where the airport ought to be located. Residents in the vicinity of each potential site band together to exert what influence they can to locate the airport elsewhere. The reason why the location of the airport generates so much public discussion and so much concern is that we really have no principle for the equitable location of airports. Our standard of equity simply does not apply in that case.

In general, it is difficult to say a priori what an appropriate standard of equity might be, for a wide and diverse range of standards is possible. Even a wholly random process might be thought of as equitable. Suppose, for instance, that ten people must divide a sum of money among themselves. They might agree to select ten unequal shares and to allocate the shares randomly. The resulting distribution of income would be unequal, but it would be equitable as the term used in this chapter because the method of allocation was accepted by all ten people in advance. Alternatively, full equality of income could serve as a standard of equity and may do so in some remote tribes but, and this is the important point, it is not, in fact, the standard of equity for the allocation of the national income among citizens in any complex industrial society.

So much for definitions. I have defined equity as distribution in accordance with agreed upon rules, but I have not advanced the subject very far, except perhaps to raise in the reader's mind two questions he might not have been inclined to put before. What is the standard of equity in our society and why is it important to have a standard of equity at all? I shall try to deal with these questions in reverse order in the next two sections.

## The political basis of equity

Though equity pertains to dealings between government and the economy, its purpose in our society is not primarily economic. The purpose of equity is as a defence and as a prerequisite of democratic government. To explain this proposition, I must digress into an elementary problem in the theory of voting. Imagine a perfect democracy in which all citizens participate as members of parliament. Suppose that decisions in parliament are made by majority rule, that every citizen is selfish as generally postulated in economic theory, and that parliament is to decide upon the allocation of the total national income, $Y$, among the $n$ citizens of the country. A fair allocation might be to divide income equally, so that each citizen gets $Y/n$. Parliament is unlikely to establish a fair allocation in this sense of the term. If all voters act in accordance with their own self-interest exclusively, as we suppose they do, a coalition of just over half the voters would form to appropriate all of the income for its members. When $n$ is odd and the coalition contains a bare majority of $(n + 1)/2$ members, the resulting allocation of the national income might be that each coalition member gets an income of $2Y/(n + 1)$ – just under twice what they would get if the national income were apportioned equally among all citizens – and those who are excluded from the coalition get nothing.

One cannot say a priori how the membership of the coalition is determined or who its members would be. Nor can one rule out the possibility that bargaining among members of the majority coalition will lead to an unequal distribution of the prize. But there is pressure for equality of reward within the coalition because, if Mr A demands a relatively large share for participating in the coalition, the other members can threaten to exclude Mr A altogether, replacing him with Mr B who would otherwise be excluded and would like to get in on any terms.[3]

The essence of the problem is that a group of people who behave selfishly as assumed by economists and who are constrained to divide income or other advantages among themselves will necessarily do so in a very unequal manner – the majority taking all it can and leaving the minority with only enough that any further reduction in the minority's portion would, one way or another, diminish the total to be allocated so as to make the majority worse off than it would otherwise be.

This line of reasoning has discouraging implications for viability of democratic government. Democratic government works when the outcome of majority rule voting is accepted as binding by majority and minority alike. The minority must acquiesce to the verdict of the majority, and members of the majority coalition must commit themselves to the continuance of an arrangement in which they could eventually be outvoted through the emergence of a new majority coalition from which they are excluded. But if majorities behave as this analysis suggests, then sooner or later a situation must arise where a minority finds its position completely unacceptable and resorts to extra parliamentary means to overturn the decision of the majority, or a majority, fearing the defection of some of its members, employs its authority over the government's monopoly of the means of violence to dispense with elections so as to preserve for itself the privileges of office. Democracy could disintegrate all at once or in bits and pieces as groups within society use progressively stronger means to gain their ends.

I am not asserting that government in Canada, United States, Great Britain and similar countries is actually unstable or is destined to disintegrate as described above. Rather, I am calling attention to a potential source of instability to focus upon how democratic government defends itself and, in particular, to explain how alternative economic arrangements may bolster or undermine the defence of democratic government against the instability of faction. A partial solution to the problem of faction is the establishment of a federal constitution within which the power of the central government is constrained by the power of the states, and the power of the states is constrained by the power of the central government. The mischief of faction in one legislature would neutralize the mischief of a faction in another. It is difficult to say how strong a defence against faction the federal system of government might be. I am not inclined to take sides on this issue because I wish to emphasize a different aspect of the problem.

Another defence against faction – not so much a defence as a way in which actual democratic government differs from the simple model of direct democracy we have been considering – is that potential conflict is defused through representative government. There can as a rule be no representative in parliament of postmen, doctors, or lawyers exclusively because each member of parliament has to obtain a plurality of votes in his constituency. No trade can command enough votes in any riding to elect a member of parliament without the support of many other trades, and any trade not included in the winning coalition in one constituency might well be included in the winning coalition in another.

I would not deny that this defence is real. Some potential conflict is defused by representation. The election of one member of parliament from each constituency is better in this regard than direct representation (if that were feasible) or proportional representation. However, representation cannot be relied upon to eliminate the problem of faction altogether. There are too many issues for which one constituency's gain is another's loss, and there are too many constituencies in which a single interest is so dominant that the member of parliament from that constituency cannot help identifying with it. Farming in the prairies, textiles in some parts of Quebec, automobiles in Oshawa, are all examples of trades dominating constituencies and of interests that successful candidates for office have to represent.

As a defence against faction, the effectiveness of representative government depends to a large extent on what the government is accustomed to do. If the government took upon itself to determine the entire allocation of income among trades or among citizens – if parliament attempted to set incomes of farmers, textile workers, owners of capital, doctors, postmen and so on – then members of parliament would be irresistibly drawn to form coalitions to advance the predominant interests in their constituencies. This happens already to some extent, but the advantages of participation in the winning coalition and the cost of being outvoted would increase significantly with the influence of parliament over the economy. The power of the majority party to aid or harm a region would increase, the outcome of elections would become progressively more important, the intensity of political conflict would grow, considerably more effort would be devoted to electing a favourable candidate and, as decisions of parliament begin to matter more and more, extra parliamentary means would be increasingly used to influence parliament's vote. Representation may reduce political conflict to some extent, but is most unlikely to stop conflict altogether. The problem of faction would arise all the same, albeit in a somewhat changed and possibly less intense form.

A third defence against faction in a pluralistic society is the absence of a permanent majority. The coalition which forms over some particular issue dissolves when the issue is resolved and a new coalition forms for the next. Thus people who fail to get their way on one issue are not inclined to rebel because they know that they may well get their way the next time. Furthermore, as Buchanan and Tullock (1962) have emphasized, logrolling allows a minority with a very strong interest in some issue to prevail over a majority that is only moderately concerned with that issue, by giving way on other issues with which the minority is less concerned. However, this defence tends to break down when a permanent majority can identify itself by a badge that persists for a long time. Race is the most durable badge but, unfortunately, language and religion will often do.

A fourth defence against faction lies in the fact that many issues are 'single-peaked'. An issue is single-peaked when all possible outcomes can be expressed as numbers on a scale and when voters' preferences systematically vary along that scale. An example would be the dollar value of the old age pension. The old would of course want the pension to be as large as possible. Preferences of other voters would depend on the voters' wealth, the intensity of their sense of altruism and, especially, their age, for the older one is the less one has yet to pay in tax into the pension fund and the sooner is one's own pension to be expected. However, if one's preferred value of the old age pension depends strictly upon age – the older the person, the higher the pension preferred – then there can be identified a median voter whose first preference prevails in a pairwise vote with any other option, and there is likely to be a considerable penumbra of voters on either side of the median who are reasonably pleased with the outcome. But not all issues are single-peaked. Issues that are not single-peaked – such as the division of oil rents between east and west or the determination of wages – are the most conducive to social conflict.

All of these defences against faction – the federal system, representative government, the absence of a permanent majority for a considerable range of issues, and the presence of many single-peaked issues – are certainly helpful and possibly necessary for the preservation of democratic government, but another defence is as important as any of these. In our society, there are matters which should not come before parliament at all. Parliament is expected to respect civil rights. The Constitution of the United States specifically limits the extent to which a person may be interfered with by the government in his enjoyment of 'life, liberty or property', and other countries have built these inhibitions into their political traditions without necessarily enshrining them into a written constitution.

There is a comparable inhibition in the economic sphere. The problem of faction, as posed above, is essentially economic. It concerns the allocation of total income among citizens. I believe that the main economic defence against faction is to arrange matters so that parliament need not allocate income at all. If parliament cannot allocate without invoking the evils of faction, then let the allocation of incomes among people be determined elsewhere. Bounds are placed upon the gain from a favourable vote and the harm from an unfavourable vote. People are willing to accept the outcome of majority rule voting because they know there are limits to what they can lose from an adverse decision of the majority. Parliament is freed to concentrate on those matters, such as the administration of justice, foreign affairs, the regulation of the economy, transport and communication, where allocation of income is not the primary concern.

The ideal is that issues of common concern to all citizens are resolved in the public sector while the allocation of the national income among citizens is determined outside of the political realm. It must be recognized that there can be no strict and thoroughgoing exclusion of allocation from the public sphere. Government must exercise some influence over the distribution of income, not merely because it cannot avoid responding to interest groups or to a general concern over poverty or hardship, but because any decision of government has allocative consequences and must influence the ranking of incomes to some extent. A decision to offer foreign aid is beneficial to Canadians in certain export industries. A decision to build a new hospital or prison is beneficial to construction workers. The ideal of placing the allocation of the national income outside of and beyond the reach of the public sector can only be attained imperfectly.

That, however, may be enough. People who would not entrust their entire incomes and livelihoods to the mercies of a potentially hostile majority in parliament might be quite willing to abide by decisions of parliament if assured that the most they stand to lose from an adverse vote is kept within reasonable bounds.

The idea of equity is related to this last defence of democratic government. If there is an allocation of income outside of parliament, then parliament can act equitably in decisions that affect the distribution of income to some extent. To take the simplest possible example, if we accept the outcome of a market economy, appropriately regulated as the standard of equity, then the equitable wage for carpenters hired in the public sector is the going wage of carpenters in the private sector, no more no less. The equitable impact upon the allocation of income among citizens of demands exercised through the public sector – demands, for instance, for more public buildings or for a network of roads – is whatever the impact of those demands would be if they could have been channelled through the private sector. Equity, in this sense is a curious virtue, for it would have no force in a society without democratic government.

## Equality as a standard of equity

An obvious and immediately appealing solution to the problem of equity is to make everyone equal. Consider once again a legislature composed of $N$ members who vote upon an allocation of total income among themselves. It might be supposed that the problem of faction could be circumvented by an agreement to divide income equally so that each person gets a $1/N$ share of the total. The difficulty with such an agreement is that it would be in the interest of any coalition of $(N + 1)/2$ people (where $N$ is odd) to break the agreement, voting instead for an allocation in which each member of the coalitions gets a $2/(N + 1)$ share of total income and people outside of the coalition get nothing. Conceivably, this difficulty might be averted and a regime of full equality maintained because everyone believes equality to be equitable or because nobody who understands the dangers of faction is prepared to take the first step along that road. I maintain, on the contrary, that full and complete equality will not serve as a standard of equity in a complex society. There is, as I shall argue in the next section, much to be said in favour of using the public sector to promote some degree of equality, but full and absolute equality would fail as a standard of equity because the standard is unstable, inefficient and incomplete.

The standard is unstable because the voter bears too great a cost if the standard is not universally respected. With full equality of income, all voters know that they have much to gain by entering a majority coalition, if such a coalition can be formed, and have literally everything to lose if a coalition is formed from which they are excluded. One may be content with an equal share as long as one is confident that no coalition will form, but if one hears of a coalition forming or suspects there is one, one is driven to establish a coalition in self-defence. An arrangement in which income is divided equally among the citizens cannot last. It will give rise to coalitions eventually.

The standard is inefficient because, if everyone were guaranteed the same income, there would be no incentive to work, to acquire skills or to save for the future. The difference in total national income between a fully equal society and a society where effort and productivity can be rewarded would probably be greater than most people would be prepared to tolerate. There is, in effect, a trade-off between efficiency and equality. Full equality is probably farther to one side than all but a very few people would be prepared to go.

The standard is incomplete because inequality of status, which is every bit as humiliating as inequality of income, cannot be dispensed with in a complex modern society. We could, in principle, arrange for everyone to have the same income but we cannot arrange for everyone to have the same job, or the same degree of authority over other workers in the hierarchy. There can only be one prime minister, 265 members of parliament, one president of each major industrial undertaking, and somebody has got to dig the ditches, drive the trucks, work in the mines and collect the garbage so that the rest of us can live comfortable lives. To some extent, inequalities of status could be compensated by income differentials, but I cannot see much scope for this procedure because it is hard to imagine how truck drivers, for example, could be paid enough to compensate them for not being prime minister at a salary high enough to enable the prime minister to do the job effectively.

The illusion that we can create a society in which everybody has an equal share of the rewards arises, I think, from an excessive concentration upon an economic model in which a homogeneous, infinitely divisible stuff called 'income' serves as the measure of the produce of the economy and as a surrogate for the bundle of goods, services and rewards which the individual obtains through the use of his resources in the market. The first step toward realism is the recognition that not all rewards can be homogenized in the same way.

Inequalities of status are inevitable in a modern technological society, and something like the problem of faction would surely arise, even with perfect equality of money income, if places in the hierarchy had to be decided in parliament without any recognized standard as a guide. In fact, it is probably more than can be expected of people to suppose that those who occupy the senior positions in society will not, one way or another, arrange for themselves to have material advantages over the rest of the population; I know of no society where this is not so. There may even be a trade-off between inequalities of income and inequalities of status. The point is not that inequalities of status necessarily hurt more when incomes are equalized, though this may be so. It is rather that a society which relies less on potential income differentials as a goad to economic performance would have to rely more on hierarchy and command. In such a society, the hierarchy would be more comprehensive and more powerful than our own. The civil service would in the end be the only channel of advancement, the drive to command rather than to be commanded would become stronger, and, all things considered, the inequalities among people and the political tensions they entail are unlikely to be less.

## The competitive economy as a standard of equity

The argument now stands as follows: our brief discussion of voting would suggest that the attempt by a democratic government to determine the complete allocation of income among citizens would increase the virulence of faction and would sooner or later lead to the breakdown of democracy itself. A defence against faction – not the only defence, but the one we are concerned with here – is to take allocation out of the public sector in so far as possible and to use the allocation of income in the private sector as a standard of equity when the public sector cannot avoid influencing the distribution of income to some extent.

Two questions arise automatically at this point. The first is whether I am not placing too much reliance on the private sector in expecting it to allocate incomes without public intervention, whether the private sector can supply a standard of equity at all. The second is why the set of outcomes in the private sector is or should be accepted as a standard for public decision-making. I shall try to deal with these issues in turn, though the discussion in each case will be less conclusive than I would like.

As for the first question – whether the competitive economy constitutes a potential standard of equity, regardless of whether that standard is actually adhered to – the answer at a fairly abstract level is unambiguously in the affirmative. That is, after all, what the theory of general equilibrium is about. From the simplest demand and supply diagram to the most elaborate mathematical theorems about the existence of equilibrium, the whole point and purpose of the study of general equilibrium is to show that there are conditions, not impossibly stringent, under which an allocation of goods and services is determinate, given the initial distribution of ownership of factors of production. The resulting allocation is Pareto optimal, but this feature is less important in the present context than the mere fact that income is allocated. The theory of general equilibrium is typically constructed in a model with no public sector at all. Unrealistic though this may be, it serves to demonstrate that a competitive economy can determine all prices and allocate the entire national income endogenously, and can, therefore, provide a standard that may be respected in decision-making by the public sector. The private sector supplies a standard of equity that the public sector may or may not choose to adopt.

The standard is unavoidably dependent upon an initial allocation of property. The theory of general equilibrium typically postulates an allocation of property among people, with no explanation of how the allocation came to be what it is and no explicit recognition that the allocation of property is the outcome of a social convention which could have been established differently. For the competitive economy to serve as a standard, the present distribution of property (including title to the earning power of one's skills) and the rules for changing ownership of property through inheritance or sale must be accepted. Rules need not be completely impervious to change and need not be thought of as inviolate forever, but there must be a stable core of rules determining who gets what if the private sector is to supply a standard of equity at all. Henry Simons (1948: 5) has put the matter as follows:

> Commutative justice [by which I think Simons means more or less what I mean by equity] simply takes for granted an existing distribution of capital, among persons, families, communities, regions, and nations. Large-scale organization, and supranational organization especially, must start from a status quo. All participants will, generally speaking, be far better off with co-operative production, division of labour, and exchange. A few, to be sure, may prosper by altering the distribution of existing possessions, that is, by theft, robbery, or war. But every violent or arbitrary redistribution impedes or disrupts the elaborate, co-operative production on which all depend; and no large group anywhere can possibly gain enough from redistributing wealth to compensate for its probable income losses from the consequent disorganization of production. Economic cooperation, like supranational organization, must largely accept possessions as facts.[4]

The degree of acceptance of the existing distribution of property and of the rules for the transmission of property varies from one situation to the next. Not many of us would be inclined to begrudge a small farmer the title to his farm or the right to pass it on to his children, though we may have serious reservations about the extent to which the very rich should be allowed to pass on their property or status in the community. A certain flexibility – which may attenuate the standard of equity to some extent – is surely possible without abolishing the standard altogether, but some respect for the status quo and some allowance for inheritance is required if there is to be a standard of equity at all. It is a moot point how far the standard of equity can be attenuated before it ceases to play its political role as a defence of democratic government.

The standard of equity may change from time to time for a variety of reasons. Conditions which were once acceptable to the majority of voters may in time be seen as intolerable; the change in attitude to slavery in England at the turn of the nineteenth century is a case in point. Technical change may affect the standard of equity as has recently occurred with regard to environmental matters. The property of a pulp and paper firm once included the right to dispose of waste products in the nearest convenient river. It does so no longer because we have come to understand the full cost of waste disposal and to place a higher value on clean water.

Admittedly, too frequent or too drastic a change in the standard of equity can degrade the standard to the point where there is no standard at all – the situation I am calling anequity – especially, if people come to believe that a majority in parliament is fully prepared to change laws in whatever way is necessary to benefit itself at the expense of the minority. But the standard of equity need not be inviolate entirely and forever to serve as a defence against faction. Some change is surely compatible with the existence of a standard at any moment of time. Change is disruptive to equity insofar as it is seen as ad hoc and as indicative of more change in the near future. Change reinforces equity insofar as it is seen as reflecting important concerns in society, such as the abolition of slavery, and as leading to a state of affairs from which little further change is contemplated. Just as the application of a law can be adjusted at the fringes by judicial interpretation without threatening the core and central meaning of the law itself, so can the rules about the production of goods and the allocation of income among people be altered from time to time by the enactment of new laws or by changes in the scope of activity in the public sector, without abandoning equity altogether. There would no doubt be some line beyond which equity becomes meaningless, but it is difficult to draw that line, just as it is difficult to say at what point a law is nullified through reinterpretation.

When the standard of equity is provided by the private sector of economy, there must necessarily arise a conflict between equity and equality. Governments may, and usually do, wish to narrow the dispersion of income between rich and poor, even at the risk of attenuating the standard of equity to some extent. However, equality and equity may be less at odds than one might suppose. Of all changes in the allocation of income among people, the most generally acceptable and the least painful are those, such as increasing the progressivity of the income tax, which are purely equalizing in the sense that the rich become poorer and the poor become richer with no corresponding change in the ordering of people on the scale of rich and poor. It would not be altogether wrong to think of equity as the preservation by the public sector of the ordering of incomes that emerges in the private sector. The two are not fully identical, but a great reluctance by members of parliament to enact laws that interchange rich and poor, would eliminate most of the advantage in the formation of factions. The gap between rich and poor may be narrowed from time to time, but the rich will remain relatively rich, the poor will remain relatively poor, and the amount one stands to lose from an adverse decision in parliament is not so large as to destroy the willingness of the typical voter to abide by the decision of the majority.

In the same vein, a method of allocation of the national income that does not entail great disparities of income is probably more stable than a method of allocation in which some people are very rich and many others are desperately poor. One becomes less apprehensive about decisions of the majority when there is a floor below which one's income cannot fall. A worker has less fear from losing his job through, for instance, a reduction of the rate of tariff on the goods he produces when medical services, the education of his children, a minimum income and some relocation payment are guaranteed, than if he alone bore the full cost of unemployment. Equalization becomes the counterpart to civil rights in the economic sphere.

Both these considerations – the constraint upon the harm to the losers when redistribution is strictly equalizing and the concern to limit the cost of an adverse vote in parliament – go a long way toward explaining the appeal of the negative income tax to conservative economists who tend on the whole to be relatively unsympathetic toward public intervention in the economy to aid the needy. Of all interventions, the negative income tax is the most purely redistributive, for its main impact is to establish a floor, or lower limit, below which no person's income may fall.

Strictly equalizing redistribution of income may be less divisive than one might at first suppose because redistribution may be a single-peaked issue that can be resolved in accordance with the tastes, desires and opinions of the median voter. In particular, it has recently been shown that under certain conditions, the progressivity of the income tax is a single-peaked issue (Atkinson, 1974). Depending on his income, each voter has his own preferred degree of progression of the income tax. When the rate of progressivity is increased, there is a fall in the national income from the resulting economy-wide marginal disincentive to work and save. Each person's preferred degree of progressivity is where his gain, if any, as a net recipient of redistribution is just balanced on the margin by his loss from the general reduction in the national income. One's optimal degree of progressivity is, of course, a decreasing function of one's pretax income; the worse off one is, the more progressive one would want the income tax to be. The optimal tax rate of the voter with the median income is the rate that parliament will choose. The median voter has his way in this case because no coalition can form with enough support to sustain any other outcome. This is radically different from the situation postulated above where people must vote on an allocation of the total income among themselves. There exists a stable outcome in one case but not in the other.

Equalization aside, the efficacy of the private sector as a standard of equity depends critically upon the role the public sector chooses to play. Economics contains a theory of the autonomous private sector, but the private sector cannot be fully autonomous when decisions affecting the rights of property and the returns to factors of production are made on a day to day basis in parliament. Influence of government over the private sector is inherent in the need for government to supply public goods, maintain law and order, and establish the limits of permissible economic behaviour. The government cannot avoid setting the rules for the private sector. It must decide which ways of making money are legitimate and which are not. Theft is prohibited by definition, markets are established and regulated, selling to the highest bidder and taking of interest are usually but not always allowed, while monopolization is usually but not always constrained. Typically, rules are intended to hold for a long time and to apply universally, influencing the allocation of the national income in ways that cannot be fully anticipated at the time when the rules are established. By contrast, government may or may not undertake projects or programmes for identifiable persons or groups of people, setting prices and wages, granting subsidies or passing legislation for particular classes or trades at the expense of the rest of the population.

The allocation of income in any given society may be thought of as lying on a continuum with full political allocation at one pole and full market allocation at the other. The closer a system is to market allocation, the more precise and unambiguous is the standard of equity that the private sector supplies. The closer an economy moves to the other pole, the more parliament must involve itself with allocation of income and the more attenuated the standard of equity becomes.

Finally, as to why the outcome of the market economy is accepted as a standard of equity (accepted, that is, by those who do accept it) despite the essentially arbitrary and unequal distribution of resources among people at birth, all that really can be said is that, imperfect as it is, the standard supplied by the market is the only standard we have. We can modify it a bit, changing the rules from time to time, but we cannot replace it with a better standard because there is none. Pure equality is technically unavailable for the reasons set out earlier. The competitive economy with at least some degree of private ownership is society's only defence against the problem of faction.

## The development of anequity with special preference to Canadian economic policy

The private sector can supply a standard of equity, but it may not be permitted to do so. Parliament may accept the allocation of income that emerges from the private sector, or it may take upon itself to establish an allocation that it considers more just, fair, or politically expedient. This is not simply a matter of the government choosing to abide or not to abide by a standard that the private sector supplies regardless. The standard of equity is imperfect at best (recall the example of the airport as discussed earlier) and it can be rendered more or less perfect by government activity. The standard of equity in an economy with extensive price and wage control and extensive public subsidization of industry, firm by firm, is not the same as the standard of equity in an economy without these features. As price control and subsidization become more and more extensive, there comes a point at which it is questionable whether there remains a standard of equity at all.

The problem of equity, as I see it, is not just that economic policies may be inequitable. It is that policies may attenuate the standard of equity itself. The principal danger is anequity rather than inequity, the dissolution rather than the violation of the standard. Equity may be attenuated as Britain is alleged to have acquired its empire 'in a fit of absence of mind'. Without quite realizing what we are doing, we may be creating conditions where the allocation of income has to be determined in parliament because it can no longer be determined elsewhere. We may be imposing obligations upon parliament that parliament cannot bear, intensifying conflict over the allocation of income, while at the same time weakening parliament's defence against faction. Policies that seem reasonable enough, looked at one by one, may be leading us in a direction we would prefer not to go. This general proposition will be discussed with reference to several aspects of economic policy that have become increasingly important in recent years: public employment, subsidization of people and firms, contraction of the market sector, price and wage control, and effacement of the line between the public and private sectors.

### *Public employment*

Wages in the private sector of the economy are a standard of equity for public sector employment, but the standard is necessarily attenuated as the public sector expands. The larger the public sector, the less guidance does the private sector supply, and the more contentious does wage setting in the public sector become. An example should make this clear. There is not much of a problem in setting doctors' wages in the public sector (in the ministry of health or in the army) when the doctors hired in the public sector constitute a small portion of the doctors in the country as a whole. Doctors in the public sector are paid the going wage of doctors in the private sector. The Civil Service Commission might not think of itself as following the market, and might be concerned to set a fair or just wage for the doctors it employs, but the wage is market-determined regardless, as long as the Civil Service Commission hires the best doctors for the money. A high wage draws forth a first class medical service. A low wage draws forth a less competent cadre of doctors. In effect, the supply curve of quality corrected medical services to the public sector is flat and wages are set accordingly.[5] This is no longer true when all medical services are provided in the public sector. (The important consideration is that fees are set in the public sector; the independence of doctors in the conduct of their practice is not relevant to the problem at hand.) The public sector is now confronted with a rising supply curve of medical services from which a price–quantity combination must somehow be chosen. The government has no option but to set fees for the medical profession, knowing that it is at the same time determining what the incomes of doctors should be.

The government is a monopsonist, and parliament must decide whether and to what extent its monopsony power is to be used. The government might try to duplicate a competitive solution, but there would seem to be no particular incentive to do so. The government might try to exploit its monopoly power to the full, providing doctors with as small an income as is in the interest of the general public, other than doctors, to provide. Alternatively, there may emerge a bilateral monopoly. Doctors may organize to bargain as a unit, and parliament may desist from exerting its ultimate authority over the terms of employment. All that economists really know about bilateral monopoly is that there is no determinate outcome within the confines of economic analysis. The outcome evolves in a complex political process quite unlike the impersonal equilibrium in a competitive economy. Employment of the whole of any trade within the public sector – policemen, firemen, teachers or doctors – leads to monopsony or bilateral monopoly, with the latter as the more likely case. The larger the public sector, the more contentious does public sector wage setting become, the greater the strains on parliament, and the less reliance can be placed on the private sector as a standard of equity.

### Subsidization

Subsidies may be granted by governments to other levels of government, to people or to firms. Equity in dealings among levels of government is outside the scope of this chapter. A brief examination of subsidies to people will concentrate on the proposition that these may constitute less of a threat to the standard of equity than is sometimes supposed. I shall have most to say about subsidization of firms.

People receive subsidies for a variety of reasons, from the recognition of outstanding services to the state, to the encouragement of home ownership, to the reward for inventive activity. The most important reason for subsidies is to prevent destitution. Subsidies are offered to the old, the unemployed, widows with children and others who, for one reason or another, are incapable of earning a living wage. Pressure from the recipients, some of whom might cause no end of havoc if their minimal needs are not met, reinforces the natural concern of each citizen to place a limit below which no income may fall. This concern is as much a matter of insurance as of altruism. Everyone grows old. Anyone might find himself unemployed. No one can be so sure of his competence or good fortune not to recognize that he may have to go on welfare some day. Subsidization of the old, the unemployed and the very poor undermines the standard of equity to some extent because the amount of the subsidy has to be decided in parliament without guidance from prices and wages in the private sector. On the other hand, the harm from political allocation in this instance may be more than compensated by the assurance that a universal minimum standard of living will be maintained. People are more willing to entrust their living to the outcome of the competitive market when the worst that can happen to them is limited to some extent.

There is no comparable justification for subsidies to firms. Gradually over the last few decades, the government of Canada has developed an elaborate network of grants for a great variety of purposes: the Regional Development Assistance Act to subsidize firms for locating in less developed regions of the country; the Automobile Adjustment Assistance Program to assist manufacturers of auto parts to adjust to the Canada–US auto pact; the Building Equipment and Accessories and Materials Program to subsidize firms for increasing productivity; the Defence Industry Productivity Program to subsidize the development and export of lethal weapons; the Employment Support Act to preserve domestic employment when import duties or similar measures are imposed abroad; the General Adjustment Assistance Program for manufacturers of textiles and clothing to improve their competitive position; the Industrial Research and Development Act; the Machinery Program to compensate Canadian users of machinery for harmful effect of the Canadian tariff on machinery; the Program for the Advancement of Industrial Technology; the Ship Construction Subsidy Regulations to compensate the Canadian shipbuilding industry for tariffs in other countries. The list is by no means complete.[6]

These programmes have in common that they subsidize firms or lend at concessional rates of interest to promote socially useful behaviour that would be unprofitable in the absence of subsidies or to compensate for the harm from other public policy at home or abroad. They are intended to be like commercial transactions between government and business in which the government pays firms for doing what the government wants done. They are not intended to be capricious. They are not intended to empower civil servants to confer benefits at will on some firms rather than others.

But that is exactly what these programmes do, for their objectives are so vague and so amenable to wider or narrower interpretation that civil servants administering programs of firm-specific subsidization have no choice but to exercise their own judgment as to when a subsidy is warranted. Who can really discriminate among investments which do or do not 'encourage new industrial employment in slow growth regions of the country' or 'enable machinery users to acquire advanced equipment at the lowest possible cost' or 'increase the efficiency of drug production' or 'improve the competitive position of the textile industry'? It is significant that, so far as I know, there is no recourse to law by a firm claiming to have been denied a subsidy improperly or to have been injured by a subsidy to a competitor. Nor could I recommend a legal remedy, except to demonstrate the arbitrariness of these programmes, because the criteria are not precise enough for the courts to decide whether they apply in a particular case.

The Regional Development Incentives Act provides a striking example of a criterion that cannot be applied in an equitable manner. The Act authorizes the Department of Regional Economic Expansion to subsidize firms for investing in less-developed regions of Canada only in those cases where 'it is probable that the facility would [not] be established ... without the provision of such an incentive'. What firm could ever prove that it would not undertake a particular investment without a subsidy? More to the point, on what grounds might one dispute a civil servant's judgment that a firm would or would not undertake a particular investment without a subsidy? In effect, the Act authorizes the Department of Regional Economic Expansion to do as it thinks best in the granting of subsidies to promote investment in less-developed regions of Canada.

These subsidy programmes undermine the standard of equity in two respects. The unavoidable lack of precision in their objectives compels administrators to exercise judgment within a wide latitude in deciding whether a subsidy is warranted. The civil service acquires considerable power and influence over the profitability of firms. Profitability comes to depend less on a firm's dealings with the public, its labour force and other firms, and more on its effectiveness in negotiating with the government. In dealing with potential grant recipients, civil servants are expected to act like the forces of nature, immune and impervious to special pleading or political pressure, but there must develop very considerable incentives to act otherwise. A member of parliament from the ruling party pleads for a subsidy to stave off bankruptcy of a firm in his constituency, which happens to be in a less developed region of the country. Bankruptcy may be inevitable without the subsidy, or it may not. Who can be sure? But when a member of parliament is involved, it might be wise to give the firm the benefit of the doubt, and to issue the grant if the case for doing so is not altogether unreasonable. Apparently, it is customary for very large grants to be vetted by Cabinet.

Subsidies breed more subsidies. Subsidies to the East provoke demands for subsidies to the West. Subsidies to one firm reduce the profitability of its competitors so that they require subsidies as well. Subsidize one trade, and all trades require compensating subsidies. Clamour for assistance creates the impression that the private sector cannot stand on its own and that the government must guide the private sector if the public interest is to be served.

There is at the same time a growing dissatisfaction with the distribution of income, especially among the poor. We may accept our status in the economy as the outcome of impersonal market forces that, if not exactly fair or just, are at least blind in their determination of who shall prosper and who shall not, that reward effort and skill to some extent, and that would seem to be irreplaceable if our political institutions are to be preserved. The poor cannot be expected to accept their status if the rich are seen to be rich as a consequence of public decisions that might equally well have favoured those who are now poor instead. One person prospers not, so it seems, because of talent, inheritance or even blind chance, but because his firm is subsidized at a critical moment in its development. Another goes bankrupt because he fails to persuade officials that his firm is progressive or that the prospects for the sale of the product are bright enough in the long run. Or subsidies may protect firms from bankruptcy to forestall unemployment among workers, insulating firms from the ups and downs of the market and socializing the risk-taking function of ownership so that, in the end, property appears purposeless and ownership falls bit by bit to the state.

### Contraction of the market sector

Growth of public employment and contraction of the market sector are two sides of the same coin, but they affect equity in different ways. Public provision of services, such as education and medical care, need not attenuate the standard of equity if services are provided equally and impartially. Problems arise when services are not provided equally and impartially. Socialized medicine is intended to take medical care out of the market so that rich and poor, the influential and the down and out, may be treated the same. The ideal is realized imperfectly. One way or another, the rich and inluential get priority of access to medical services. The prime minister and the university professor are better provided with medical care than the garbage man and the street cleaner. Superior doctors, paid the same regardless of whom they treat, choose patients from their own social class or from among those who can be expected to return favours. Knowing perfect equality of provision to be unattainable, members of parliament vie with one another to direct scarce medical resources toward their constituencies, so that politics becomes, quite literally, a matter of life and death. Medical care becomes like conscription: the rich or well connected avoid the draft, while the poor are inadequately paid for the risk and discomfort they bear. A similar difficulty arises in the allocation of higher education, but the inequities in higher education are probably greater than those in medical care because the beneficiaries constitute only 40 per cent of the population and are concentrated in upper-class families.

The most extreme and pitiful case of anequity that has come to my attention is a consequence of the incorporation into the public sector of an economic activity that might have been left to the market. There was a famine in Bengal in the fall of 1974. The distribution of grain had for some time been undertaken in the public sector. When the famine came, there was not enough grain to go around. It was widely reported in the press at that time that the government of India chose to feed people in the cities and to let landless labourers in the countryside starve because mobs in the city could riot while the landless labourers in the countryside were too dispersed to be dangerous. The government of India cannot be said to have acted inequitably. Place an activity in the public sector, and there may be no equitable allocation when equality of provision is infeasible or inappropriate.

### Price and wage control

Price and wage control must necessarily redirect the allocation of the national income among citizens from the market to parliament or to the civil service. Though there is no price control in Canada, there appears to be a gradual trend in that direction. A Prices and Incomes Commission and a Food Prices Review Board have both been charged with the task of talking prices down. Labour leaders and businessmen are expected to do their part in controlling inflation. There is a growing tendency for strikes to be settled by government intervention, especially in industries providing essential services. If trends continue, it will become difficult not to control prices as well. There is at the same time a resurgence of the theory of the just price. No one actually appeals to the medieval doctrine as such, but people moralize about prices and governments appoint commissioners to indicate when prices are unjustly high and to rebuke firms if prices are not what they ought to be. The theory of the just price can be interpreted as the proposition that there exists a God-given standard of equity in pricing, apart from the structure of prices in the market. Economists know this to be false. Governments sometimes speak and act as though it were true.

### Effacement of the line between public and private sectors

The market supplies no standard of equity unless a distinct line can be drawn between the domain of the public sector and the domain of the private sector. Public policy may tend to efface that line so one cannot say of some industries whether they are in the public sector or not. Heavily regulated industries, such as telephone, rail transport and air transport occupy a no man's land between sectors where ownership remains private but where profitability is more politically determined than elsewhere in the private sector. It is difficult to say how else these industries might be organized because they tend to be characterized by economies of scale leading to natural monopoly. On the other hand, the government is actively creating and administering monopolies in agriculture under the guidance of marketing boards, some federal and some provincial, that typically fix prices and allocate quotas among farmers to reduce total quantity supplied. As marketing boards are under the ultimate authority of parliament, a conflict is inevitable between producers who want high prices and consumers who want low prices, with no principle whatsoever by which this conflict of interest may be resolved.

There is also a growing tolerance for monopoly in labour markets, extending even to highly skilled and highly paid trades: teachers, professors and the civil service where the old rationale for unions based on sympathy for the plight of the working classes cannot hold by any stretch of the imagination. A case can even be made that we are moving in the direction of a new fascism, not the imperialism, intolerance and one party state we are now accustomed to associate with the term, but fascism in the limited and restricted economic sense of corporatism, the doctrine that 'man should not be politically articulate as a citizen but only as a worker entrepreneur, farmer, doctor or lawyer' (Gould and Kolb, 1964), and that the direction of the economy as a whole should be entrusted to an assembly of syndicates or corporations. Equity is attenuated in government sponsored monopoly because competition among corporations of trades or classes cannot be resolved by purely economic means. There is no counterpart to the general equilibrium in a genuinely competitive economy because rivalry among firms of the same trade is curtailed.

The line between public and private sectors is crossed in other ways. Governments, particularly provincial governments, are becoming more inclined to establish firms in industries which have been predominantly or entirely in the private sector, sometimes to combat monopoly power but sometimes for reasons as vague as to permit 'the people' to have a say in the management of the economy. The Canada Development Corporation would seem to provide an instance of this motive. The presence of publicly owned firms in the private sector need not corrode the standard of equity if these firms are conducted on commercial principles, without special privileges and on the understanding that they are allowed to go bankrupt if they prove to be unprofitable. It is questionable whether publicly owned firms will really be operated that way. If not, profitability in the private sector would come to depend on who the government chooses to compete with.

There seems to be developing an ideology of business, fostered especially by some of the business schools, in which firms are expected not to maximize profits by any legal means, but to act responsibly to further the aims of society as a whole. It is as though the economy were one great firm with managers – an amalgam of businessmen, labour leaders and civil servants – who move resources freely from one department to another unencumbered by the restrictions of property rights. In this atmosphere, where the line between public and private sectors is not respected, the standard of equity is eroded gradually by a subsidy here and a price control there until in time there is nothing left. Each decision by itself may seem innocuous enough, a concession to political pressure or even an act of statesmanship, but the cumulative effect of many such decisions may be to destroy the economic foundation of democratic government.

## Equity, efficiency and equality

These remarks on Canadian economic policy are not intended as a balanced or comprehensive evaluation. My objective is narrower than that. It is simply to bring equity to the fore as one of the criteria for the assessment of public policy. In some cases, especially subsidization and price control, I think considerations of equity are decisive. In others they may not be. My misgivings about recent economic policy are very ordinary misgivings, shared, I suspect, by a considerable proportion of the economics profession if not of the Canadian population as a whole. I have observed nothing that others are unaware of, and my reasons for concern are the common reasons for concern about these matters. I have tried in this chapter to deal with these concerns systematically.

We all recognize the relevance of equity informally when we gossip about politics or when we evaluate policy without reference to a rigid framework of analysis, but what we know about policy as citizens is different from what we know as economists. As economists, we are accustomed to analyse markets and to prescribe policy in accordance with two large criteria: efficiency as Pareto optimality and equality in the distribution of income. There are problems for which this stance is appropriate. In particular, I would think that macroeconomics and monetary policy can get on very well without much regard for equity because the instruments of policy are unlikely to affect the standard of equity one way or another. This chapter has focused upon issues for which equity matters a great deal.

Economists' disinclination to take equity into account is in part the consequence of a maintained hypothesis – a reasonable hypothesis for many of the problems economists are called upon to deal with – that the economy can be studied as though it were isolated from the rest of society and that, in examining the effects of economic policy, one need look no further than the economy itself. We recognize, of course, that politics can influence the economy through the tax structure or other institutional arrangements, but we typically recognize no feedback from the economy to the political realm. We take the stance of the advisor to the wise legislator or absolute monarch whose authority is pervasive and beyond question and who dictates policy for the good of the population as a whole. In these conditions, equality and efficiency would indeed be the prime considerations, and equity would be subordinate if relevant at all. Equity becomes important when economic arrangements circumscribe political arrangements, when the feasibility of this or that form of government depends on how economy is organized.

The central question in this chapter, a question as old as political theory itself, is this: what form of economic organization supports democratic government and a liberal society? The proposed answer is that no economic system can support, or even allow, democratic government unless a minimal standard of equity is maintained, that the competitive economy with some degree of private ownership and some allowance for inheritance provides the only workable standard of equity we know, and that governments in Canada and elsewhere in the western world seem to be relying more and more upon policies which can only lead to a progressive attenuation of our standard of equity and to a greater influence by parliament upon the allocation of income than parliament is equipped to bear.

## Notes

1 This chapter was originally Queen's Economics Department Working Paper No. 181, 1975. It was reproduced in Usher (1994). In the early 1970s when this chapter was written, I, like many others at the time, did not foresee the widening of the gap between rich and poor that was to take place since that time, and I anticipated a growing interference by the government in the detail of the economy. Considering how long ago this chapter was written and that the author of this chapter was a very different person from the author of this book, it seems best not to update this chapter to account for changes

in Canadian institutions or to reflect my opinions today. What has not changed is my view of equity as a requirement for democratic government. I appreciate the perceptive comments of my colleagues Professors H. Scott Gordon and Steve F. Kaliski.

2 One might well object at this point that there are other equally important theories of justice or that utilitarianism is really a broader doctrine than my description would suggest. I do not defend these usages, except to say that they are usages which have, rightly or wrongly, found their way into contemporary economic literature.

3 This example and its consequences are discussed in Tullock (1959). Recognition of the problem and its significance for the organization of a democratic society goes at least as far back as the American Revolution. As quoted at the beginning of Chapter 5, James Madison advocates representative government in preference to direct democracy to curb the abuses of 'faction' by which he refers to coalitions of the sort described in this chapter. Speaking of the majority coalition, Madison adds that 'Every shilling with which they overburden the inferior number, is a shilling saved to their own pockets' (Hacker, 1964: 19). Madison advocates representative government as a defence of property seen as a natural right of humanity. Following Tullock, I do not see property as a good or right in itself and can see no justice in one person being born rich while another is born poor. I would justify property as a lesser evil and as a standard of equity; we need the institution of private property because, without private property, parliamentary government could not be preserved.

4 Simons goes on to say that, 'A free society must be organized, not wholly but basically or primarily, around voluntary, free exchange of goods and services. The alternative is no large organization at all. A little understanding of interregional trade suggests, moreover, that supranational organization is nearly impossible save among areas, communities, or nations in which substantially free exchange prevails.'

5 A nation's supply curve of doctors may be upward sloping, but that is irrelevant when the government hires too small a proportion of the stock of doctors to affect the wage significantly.

6 For a description of Canadian subsidy programmes, see Stegemann (1973). David Lewis' (1972) little book *Louder Voices: The Corporate Welfare Bums*, is also very good, far and away the most serious and probing political campaign literature that has come to my attention. The title of the book and its general tone seem to convey a concern for equity and a sense of indignation about indiscriminate handouts to wealthy firms. It is ironic that the strongest defence of capitalism in contemporary Canadian political literature should appear under the auspices of the New Democratic Party which seems the most prone of all the major political parties to make special deals with individual firms and to efface the distinction between public and private sectors. Indeed, in the last chapter of the book, David Lewis refuses to draw the obvious moral from his analysis than these bums should not be on welfare at all, and contents himself with a vague statement to the effect that handouts should be allocated in a responsible manner.

# References

Atkinson, A. B. (1974) How progressive should the income tax be?, in E. Phelps, ed., *Economic Justice*, Harmondsworth, England: Penguin.

Buchanan, James and Tullock, Gordon (1962) *The Calculus of Consent: Logical Foundations of Constitutional Democracy*, Ann Arbor: University of Michigan Press.

Gould, J. and Kolb, W. L., (Eds) (1964) *A Dictionary of the Social Sciences*, New York: The Free Press of Glencoe, p. 141.

Hacker, A., (Ed.) (1964) *The Federalist Papers by Alexander Hamilton, John Jay and James Madison*, New York: Washington Square Press, No 10.

Lewis, David (1972) *Louder Voices: The Corporate Welfare Bums*, Toronto: James Lewis & Samuel.

Simons, Henry (1948) *Economic Policy for a Free Society*, Chicago: University of Chicago Press, p. 5.

Stegemann, Klaus (1973) *Canadian Non-Tariff Barriers to Trade*, Montreal: Private Planning Association of Canada.

Surrey, S. S. (1973) *Pathways to Tax Reform*, Cambridge, MA: Harvard University Press.

Tullock, G. (1959) The problem of majority voting, *Journal of Political Economy*, 67, 571–9.

Usher, D. (1994) *Welfare Economics and Public Finance, The Collected Papers of Dan Usher*, Vol. 2, Cheltenham: Edward Elgar.

# 10 Voting rights, property rights and civil rights

> by the same right of nature ... by which you can say, one man hath an equal right with another to the choosing of him that shall govern him, by the same right of nature, he hath the same (equal) right in any goods he sees – meat, drink, clothes – to use them for his sustenance ... if this be allowed, [because by the right of nature] we are free, one man must have as much voice as another, then show me what step or difference there is why [I may not] by the same right [take your property though not] of necessity to sustain nature.
>
> Henry Ireton, 1647, quoted in Woodhouse (1938: 58)

> If master and servant shall be equal electors, then clearly ... there may be a law enacted, that there shall be an equality of goods and estate.
>
> Nathaniel Rich, 1647, quoted in Woodhouse (1938: 63)

The circumstances of these quotations were extraordinary. In 1647, on route to the beheading of King Charles II, Oliver Cromwell's victorious army stopped at a place called Putney to fast, pray and debate the pros and cons of government by majority rule voting. Foot soldiers favoured universal suffrage. Officers favoured property qualifications. Henry Ireton and Nathaniel Rich were officers in Cromwell's army. The claim in these quotations is that property cannot be secure unless franchise is restricted to property holders. Otherwise, the power of the vote would enable a majority the poor to expropriate the minority of the rich completely.

The argument itself is more general. If, with universal franchise, a majority of the poor can expropriate the property of the rich, so too, even with restricted franchise, can a majority of the electorate – any majority identified on economic, class, religious, ethnical or geographic lines – use the power of the vote to expropriate the corresponding minority. The rewards of expropriation may not be as large as under universal franchise, but the principle is the same. The danger in majority rule voting is not just of servants displacing masters, but of any coordinated majority of voters expropriating the corresponding minority and of any elected government employing its authority over the army and the bureaucracy to block all further elections and to dominate society permanently. There would seem to be no escape within government by majority rule voting from the exploitation and impoverishment of whatever group a majority of voters chooses to exploit and impoverish. The argument is that government by majority rule voting does not and cannot work, for there is nothing to stop a majority of the electorate from using the power of the vote to expropriate the corresponding minority, and there is too much at stake for a government in office to risk loss of office in an election.

Yet 'impossible' as it may be, universal franchise is maintained in a great many countries today without at the same time removing all distinctions between rich and poor. Servants, or their contemporary equivalents, could employ the power of the vote to dispossess masters altogether, but they choose not to do so despite the inevitable inequality of income when the means of production are privately owned. The reason for such restraint can only be that expropriation is not in the interest of the would-be expropriators. Groups that could expropriate must have no incentive to do so. Groups that would expropriate must be unable to do so. Why might that be so?

A tentative answer to this question is supplied in Chapters 3 and 9. In Chapter 3 on voting about the redistribution of income, it was shown that, at least in so far as redistribution is by means of a negative income tax, redistribution is advantageous to the median voter but never to the point where inequality is wiped out altogether. Servants can take comfort from the fact that their incomes are increased. Masters can take comfort from the fact that some of the advantages of wealth and the ordering of people on the scale of rich and poor are preserved. In Chapter 9 on the problem of equity, it was shown that government by majority rule voting does not work without a prior distribution of income, or property rights from which people's incomes are derived, that citizens agree not to vote about, confronting servants with the choice of either accepting property rights, systematically redistributed in accordance with the preference of the median voter, or abandoning democracy in favour of some other form of government.

This chapter deals with three additional questions about rights. How can the inevitable inequality of property be justified? What are the boundaries between intrinsically equal civil rights and intrinsically unequal property rights? Where do rights come from? Examination of these questions is preceded by definitions of rights and a brief reconsideration of the exploitation problem. Two models of the emergence of government by majority rule voting are discussed briefly in an appendix.

## Definitions

Voting rights entitle citizens to participate in the choice of legislators and executives. Civil rights create a sphere of autonomy protected by the state from other people and from the state itself. The 'rule of law' tells citizens what they may and may not do, supplying protection from arbitrary government and helping people to predict the behaviour of others. Freedom of speech, freedom to associate with whomever one pleases and the right to work subject only to the discipline of an impersonal market all contribute mightily to what one thinks of as the good life, while, at the same time, creating an environment where creativity and innovation may flourish. Property rights assign things to people, including land, capital and the produce of one's own labour.

All rights are exercised within complex rules specifying exactly what the holder of rights is entitled, forbidden or required to do. Voting rights are exercised within rules about the conduct of elections, decision-making in the legislature, powers of legislators and executives, and voters' access to information. The right to vote for the glorious leader is, strictly speaking, a right to vote, but it is not what is usually meant by the phrase. As is often said, property rights are people's rights not over things, but over other people with regard to things. They are an elaborate set of rules that the legislature can and does alter from time to time with profound conse-quences upon people's places on the scale of rich and poor. Ownership of houses is as close as property rights come to rights over things, but, even there, owner-ship is not absolute. I may not build an unfenced swimming pool in my back yard because the rights of little children to wander takes precedence over my right to do what I please with what I own. Every town has an elaborate set of rules about such matters as fencing between properties and the location of apartment build-ings, grocery stores and factories, rules that the city council may change from time to time. Within civil law, a line must be drawn between free speech and slander.

An essential ingredient of all modern rights is the right to establish and partic-ipate in voluntary associations with legally specified privileges, obligations and restrictions, notably but not exclusively political parties and business corpora-tions. Political parties are associations of voters and politicians converting votes of citizens scattered across the country into decisions about who forms the govern-ment and telling citizens what in the end they are really voting about. The right to vote would be almost worthless without political parties bound by elaborate rules, some legally binding, others customary, about how they may be formed, partic-ipation in public debates, internal governance, campaign advertising and so on.[1] Corporations are associations of owners of shares in a centrally organized enter-prise. Charities, trade unions, political action committees and condominiums are all associations with legally prescribed privileges and obligations. Rights of asso-ciations are recognized because, and insofar as, they are useful or even necessary in a prosperous and democratic society.

In the early nineteenth century, most businesses were small enough to be man-aged by a single owner who hired workers and who bore full responsibility for failure. Today, most businesses are too large to be run except as corporations with hierarchies of managers, thousands of stockholders protected by limited liability and boards of directors with legally specified privileges and obligations.[2] In this environment, a great part of the wealth of the nation is held in pension funds, insuring the ultimate holders of wealth against the double risk of poverty in the event of an unusually long life and of the failure of any given firm.[3] The corpo-ration is a complex legally specified association, accommodating huge economies of scale in production with a unified administration of far more capital than any one person is likely to possess, while at the same time allowing people to invest their savings without knowing in detail how the business is run. It is a democracy of owners. In ordinary voting, all people are equal. In corporations, all shares are equal. Shareholders vote for boards of directors who, in turn, appoint the executives who actually run the firm within legally binding rules blocking the exploitation of minority shareholders by, for example, restricting the payment of dividends to some majority of the shareholders. The corporation is endowed by the state with limited liability, exempting shareholders from responsibility for debts in the event of bankruptcy, so that the most shareholders have to lose is the shares themselves. It is a fictional person with some but not all of the rights of actual persons; it is taxed, has some freedom of speech in elections, but not, of course, a right to vote. An economy of large corporations supplies the scale in production, research and innovation required for prosperity and progress, but is at the same time a world of oligopoly with vast inequality of income and influence on public policy. There is an inevitable conflict of interest among shareholders, executives, workers and the general public over the specification of the rights and duties of the corporation: monopolization, donations to political parties, entitlements in the event of bankruptcy, workers' rights to form unions, the powers of unions over workers, and so on.

Though societies can assign voting rights and civil rights unequally – as where franchise is limited by income or aristocrats are exempted from certain laws – these rights are potentially equal. Society can be so arranged that everybody's voting rights and civil rights are the same. Not so with property rights. Property rights are inherently unequal. Even if everybody were assigned equal amounts of property today, the working of the market is such that their holdings would turn out to be very different tomorrow. Together, voting rights, civil rights and property rights keep democracy afloat.

Democracy may be defined as 'rule by the poor' (on the assumption that the poor constitute a majority of the population) or as 'a system of government based upon majority rule voting together with whatever arrangements are necessary to keep the system afloat'. The former is more or less consistent with Aristotle's statement that 'the real difference between democracy and oligarchy is poverty and wealth. Whenever men rule by reason of their wealth, whether they be few or many, that is oligarchy, and whenever the poor rule, that is democracy' (as quoted in Finley, 1972: 13). The latter is essentially Dunn's description of modern representative democracy:

> that our own state and the government which does so much to organize our lives, draws its legitimacy from us and that we have a reasonable chance of being able to compel each of them to continue to do so, They draw it, today from holding regular elections in which every adult can vote freely and without fear, in which their votes have at least a reasonable equal weight, and in which any uncriminalized political opinion can compete freely ...
>
> Dunn (2005: 19–20)[4]

One might be inclined to suppose these definitions to be essentially the same, at least in so far as a majority of the population has less than average income.

The difference is in the qualification to the latter definition 'with whatever arrangements are necessary to keep the system afloat', for 'necessary arrangements' may entail a substantial and unavoidable degree of inequality of income, authority and status. What matters is not whether there are rich and poor, but whether such inequality as there may be is consistent with the preservation of a system of government with majority rule voting.

## The fragility of majority rule voting

Government by majority rule is a delicate institution that must be actively defended if it is to be preserved. Threats to government by majority rule voting may arise from an unwillingness of voters and governments in office to play by its rules and from difficulties with the rules themselves.

Citizens and politicians may not behave as government by majority rule voting requires. The contrast between political and commercial markets shows what may be at stake. The fundamental theorem about the competitive economy is that markets run on self-interest alone, that an outcome which is in some sense best for everybody emerges when each person acts – buying, selling or working – in his own interest exclusively. The theorem is, of course subject to a host of qualifications and exceptions, but enough of it survives the transition from textbook to actual markets that self-interest can be trusted to generate satisfactory outcomes in large segments of the economy. Something beyond mere self-interest is required in the political realm where duty and compromise have indispensable roles to play. A sense of duty must direct the citizen to vote rather than to abstain, for, as discussed in Chapter 7, the chance of one's vote influencing public policy is almost always too small to justify the cost of the time and trouble of voting on grounds of self-interest alone. Voting is like the private provision of a public good. Everybody gains when everybody votes but it is in nobody's interest to vote as long as others' behaviour is not conditional on one's own. Duty must kick in where self-interest alone will not do. Compromise is required of politicians rather than voters. It is indispensable for the formation of party platforms where different preferences have to be reconciled. It is indispensable for the formation of governments when no single party wins a clear majority in the legislature, as is almost always the case with proportional representation and is often the case with first-past-the-post as well. It is indispensable for setting the schedule of progressive taxation. It is indispensable when the two houses of the legislature are dominated by rival political parties. There is no guarantee that the required duty and compromise will always be forthcoming.

Disenchanted with the give and take of ordinary democracy, voters may elect the glorious leader who will henceforth dispense with elections or use the authority of the state to dispense with any serious opposition. The police and civil service may be directed to conceal information unfavourable to the government in office. Newspapers and television stations may be taken over or co-opted. Whistleblowers may be harassed or imprisoned. Elections may be rigged. Or, claiming to defend the country from chaos or disorder, the army may simply take over the state. Governments with dictatorial tendencies may be elected because they are seen to be strong and because voters do not care enough about the preservation of democracy to take warning signs seriously. Constitutions and courts can sometimes serve as temporary impediments to emerging dictatorship, but constitutions can be amended and sympathetic judges can be appointed. Both Hitler and Mussolini were elected by populations that knew, or should have known, what they were doing. Ideally, misconduct by the government in office will break the bonds of authority, so that a miscreant government or a cadre of generals will cease to be obeyed, but this is not always the case. There is no clear line between the elected dictator and the miscreant government that gradually assumes dictatorial power.

The exploitation problem is an ever-present danger from which there are two possible escapes. The first is intrinsic to the exploitation problem itself. The very compromise and sense of duty required for the operation of majority rule voting is also required for the exploitation of minorities. Compromise is required for the allocation among members of the predatory majority of their disproportionate share of the national income and of positions of authority in the administration of the state. A sense of duty among members of the predatory majority is required to ensure they vote in unison. Whether democracy works depends in part on whether people's loyalties are to their faction or to society as a whole.[5]

Government may be designed to impede exploitation. Divided government, checks and balances, and countervailing power can be thought of as blocking the formation of predatory coalitions by balancing majorities at one level or branch of government against different majorities at others. Hence, the division of the legislature into two houses, and the division of authority among legislature, executive and judiciary in the hope that a predatory majority in one place will be blocked by another predatory majority elsewhere.[6]

Democracy's other escape from the exploitation problem is to confine voting to domains of life where the problem either does not arise at all or where losses and gains are small enough to be tolerable. Government by majority rule voting can only be sustained by generally respected constraints protecting all citizens from impoverishment at the hands of predatory majorities. There may be no bright line between what may and what may not be voted about because almost every public decision has winners and losers, but some public decisions are clearly on one side or clearly on the other. Politicians in office must be blocked from punishing their rivals, as deposed kings might be executed by their successors. There must be no Bills of Attainder.[7] Whether or not I am punished for a crime must not depend on whether or not I support the party in office. Who is prosperous and who is destitute must not depend on the outcome of the election. On the other hand, since virtually every public decision affects different people differently, the continuance of democratic government requires that people be prepared to accept some loss without giving up on the system altogether. The great virtue of the negative income tax is the preservation of most of people's incomes and of people's ranking on the scale of rich and poor, so that, if one political party favours a relatively high tax rate and the other favours a relatively low rate, supporters of both parties can accept defeat with some degree of equanimity. A majority of servants may safely vote away most of the burden of servitude, but it must not be empowered to establish a new regime in which former servants become masters and former masters become servants. Cost–benefit analysis replaces political determination of which projects to undertake with clear rules favouring no person or group a priori and benefiting everybody in the long run.

As discussed in Chapter 9, defence of government by majority rule voting from the exploitation problem requires a *system of equity* protecting citizens from predatory majorities by confining majority rule voting to what can be safely voted about and, at the same time, attending to tasks that have been exiled from the political realm. A system of equity must preserve the right to vote, for government by majority rule voting cannot be sustained if minorities can be disenfranchised and if the corresponding majorities may, in turn, disenfranchise minorities within it until there are almost no voters left. Nor can government by majority rule voting be sustained in a society without civil rights, for no party in office would willingly risk loss of office in an election if its supporters could be arbitrarily imprisoned by its successor. A system of equity must contain a non-political allocation of the national income to avoid voting about people's incomes one by one. That non-political allocation of income is supplied by a prior allocation of property rights, broadly defined to include markets where people's incomes are determined in accordance with their ownership of human as well as physical capital. Maintenance of property rights requires the tacit consent of the majority of the voters with less than average incomes and who, like Ireton and Rich's servants, would seem to have much to gain from voting away the privileges of the rich or, at a minimum, establishing a regime of full equality of income, but who desist from doing so because democracy itself would be at stake. Voting rights, civil rights and property rights are of value in themselves and as components of a system of equity without which democratic government cannot be sustained.

## The justification of property rights

The natural starting point for evaluating arguments about the justification of property rights is a powerful argument that they are not justified at all because they are inherently unequal and because of their origin in ancient theft. Against this background, two types of justification may be considered: moral justification of property rights as good or worthy to be preserved in themselves, and technical justification that property rights are a requirement for what we see as a good society, as a foundation for prosperity and as necessary for the maintenance of democratic government.[8]

### *Property as theft*[9]

William the Conqueror stole England from the original English, installing his soldiers as the new lords of the land. Europeans stole America from the native Americans. Each tribe's land had at one time been taken by force from some other tribe. Much of people's wealth today is inherited, directly or indirectly as when rich people provide their children with opportunities and education that poor people cannot afford. Inherited wealth is not in itself theft, but it is surely a departure from equality that cannot be accounted for by the virtue or industry of people who are wealthy today.

Even when wealth is earned rather than inherited, income disparities may be far larger than can be accounted for by people's skill, diligence and marginal contribution to the national income. High incomes may be the outcome of successful speculation, buying land, stocks or goods today when the price is low and selling tomorrow when the price is high. Speculation differs from ordinary work because the speculator's gain may be at the expense of somebody else, with no net contribution to the national income. The speculator's gain from anticipating the location of an airport may be nothing more than a transfer of income to the speculator from the original owners of land nearby. Effort devoted to discovering which prices will rise and which will fall may, from a nationwide perspective, be wasted. This is not invariably so because acquired information may influence investment, but there is here no guaranteed equivalence between income and marginal product. High incomes may be gifts from the government, acquired by lobbying or bribes to public officials, as the Russian 'oligarchs' acquired property privatized at the dissolution of communism. High incomes may be acquired by monopolization that is formally illegal but not always effectively prevented. Some high incomes are 'trust wages' offered to reduce the likelihood of cheating one's employer by shirking or other means. Stock options as compensation to CEOs may, at least in part, be trust wages designed to align the interests of senior executives with the interest of stockholders. People in positions of trust may earn more than their marginal products or than what they might have earned elsewhere. Successful entrepreneurs may be the beneficiaries of publically financed research, economies of scale and network externalities; the entrepreneur's profit from being the first to recognize an opportunity for a new product may be far larger than the loss to society if that particular entrepreneur had not come along. It seems unlikely that the national income would be a billion dollars smaller if a randomly chosen billionaire had never been born.

There are many reasons why high incomes may be undeserved; high incomes may originate in ancient theft, inheritance, speculation, trust wages, the peculiarities of economies of scale or cheating. Even when incomes are true reflections of marginal products of labour and capital, there may be a case for equalization because the marginal products themselves are a consequence of the social environment, inheritance, schooling and the community in which one is brought up. The case for permitting inequality of property and income in circumstances where property can be equalized through majority rule voting is not that the rich deserve to be rich. If there is such a case, it must be that the complete levelling of incomes would be harmful even to the intended beneficiaries. It would not be a case against all redistribution of income or for the absolute sanctity of all property rights. Property rights are inevitably unequal, with some billionaires and many paupers. Whether and to what extent such inequality is to be tolerated depends upon how inequality can be mitigated, and upon the trade-off between equality and prosperity in the economy as a whole.

### Inalienable rights

Private property is sometimes looked upon as right or good in itself. Maintain private property though the heavens fall, and not, as will be argued below, because the heavens will fall if you do not. Variants of this doctrine see property rights as the will of God, as indisputably and unchallengeably worthy of preservation, as justified by first possession, as acquired by the application of labour and as the outcome of a social contract. A theological mandate for property rights can be found in the Seventh Commandment, 'Thou shall not steal.' God could hardly object to stealing if property rights themselves were not mandated by some higher power. A secular equivalent of the divine commandment is Robert Nozick's (1974: ix) assertion that

> Individuals have rights, and there are things no person or group may do to them (without violating their rights). So strong and far-reaching are these rights that they raise the question of what, if anything, the state and its officials may do.

Both the theological and the secular variant of this assertion are open to the objection that rights and commands do not come arbitrarily out of the sky, but are grounded in human needs and are what they are because human life is in some sense better when the commands are obeyed. God may be seen as a utilitarian who would not prescribe rules except for the benefit of humankind, leaving open the question of whether and how property rights are beneficial.

Property rights may justified by 'first occupation'. I pick up a pebble on the ground, and it is mine. I discover ore underground, or catch fish in the sea, or occupy formerly unoccupied land, or fence off an unused piece of land unchallenged for a prescribed number of years. By first occupation, the ore or the fish or the land become mine. The standard objection first occupation as justification for private property is not that the argument outright wrong, but that it is back-to-front. Possession becomes the root of title because the law prescribes it so, and not by celestial decree. It is often in the public interest for the law to grant title on the strength of possession, but that is not always so, and, without law, there can be no title either. As the best way of bringing fish to the dinner table, it is usually in the public interest for fishermen to be granted title to the fish they catch, but not, for instance, when a species of fish is endangered. Invention is promoted by patents granted to the inventor for a fixed number of years and subject to a variety of conditions that the law prescribes.[10]

Closely associated with and subject to much the same objection as the principle of first occupation is the doctrine associated with John Locke that property rights are acquired by the application of labour.

> That the earth and all inferior creatures be common to all men, yet every man has a property in his own person; this nobody has any right to but himself . . .

Whatsoever he then removes out of the state that nature hath provided and left it in, he hath mixed his labour with, and joining it to something that is his own, and thereby makes it his property ... For this labour being the unquestionable property of the labourer, no man can have a right to what that is joined to, at least where there is enough and as good left in common for others.

Locke (1690)[11]

Robert Nozick dismissed the argument with the observation that if I own a can of tomato juice and if I pour the tomato juice into the ocean, I cannot by that act be said to own the ocean, even if nobody has poured tomato juice into the ocean before. The early American settlers could acquire 40 acres by occupying the land because, and only because, American law entitled them to do so. Law, not mere settlement, was the source of title. It seems doubtful whether the 'mixing of labour' argument would carry much weight except to property holders seeking any excuse to justify their holdings. There is also an important ambiguity in the final clause: 'at least where there is enough and as good left in common for others'. Would a person who acquired property yesterday when property was plentiful still be entitled to his entire property tomorrow when property has become scarce?

Property rights may be justified by appeal to a social contract, a mythical unanimous agreement among all citizens, made long, long ago, to respect and live by the rules we have today. The myth can be used in two distinct ways. It can be used, as Thomas Hobbes (1651) used it in justifying absolute monarchy, to justify existing inequalities on the grounds that, since some such inequality is inevitable in what we see as a good society, we had better put up with the inequality we have, for the only alternative is reenact the bloody episodes from which existing inequalities emerged. In this usage, social contract may be looked upon as a story about obedience to the laws of the land and to the sovereign who prescribes and enforces those laws as the only alternative to the 'miseries and horrible calamities, that accompany a civil war, or that dissolute condition of masterless men, without subjugation to laws and a coercive power to tie their hands from rapine and revenge' Hobbes (1651: 120).[12]

The social contract can also be looked upon as what we would all agree upon in a great comprehensive constitutional convention today. This variant of the social contract requires an explanation of why people who are now relatively poor and disadvantaged would ever agree to a contract perpetuating their poverty and disadvantages. The standard exposition presumes people to adopt the constitutional convention 'behind the veil of ignorance' where everybody understands the consequences of alternative laws and customs but does not know what his place in society will be, and imagines himself as having equal chances of occupying each and every slot – from beggar to millionaire – once the veil is lifted. Inequality is still historically determined, but people's willingness to put up with present inequalities comes to depend on whether the hypothetical person behind the veil of ignorance is as well off as possible. On this view, the doctrine of the social contract merges with utilitarianism. The two interpretations of the social contract also differ in that the first justifies society as it is, while the second may be a prescription for reform, for it is entirely possible that people behind the veil of ignorance would opt for rules very different from the rules in force today.

The social contract is a useful way of thinking the organization of society, but it is insufficient as a justification for property rights. Something more is needed. It must be explained why respect of property rights (as they are, or perhaps as modified in some respects) would be part of the social contract, why people in the imaginary constitutional convention would unanimously agree to preserve the distribution of property today. One must examine the consequences of property rights, and decide whether property rights are conducive to as desirable a society as people are able to construct. In what follows, it will be argued that, despite the dubious origin of existing property rights, a society which respects existing property rights is the best attainable in this imperfect world, though rules surrounding property rights can be designed to take account of their vices as well as their virtues.

### A requirement for prosperity

Years ago, in his class on microeconomics, Milton Friedman, holding up ordinary lead pencil, would ask, 'Who knows how to make a pencil?' The answer was 'Nobody'. The pencil manufacturer knows how to combine lead, wood, eraser material, metal to fasten the eraser and paint into a pencil and where to buy these ingredients, but, considering just the metal, they have no idea how to forge the appropriate metal from the raw material taken out of a mine or what mining machinery to employ or how to make such machinery or how to convert petroleum into gasoline to run the machinery; and the person who does know how to convert petroleum into gasoline has no idea how to make a pencil. People know about their immediate technology and about market prices of what they buy and sell. Prices incorporate all one needs to know about all the other technologies and all the other industries on which one depends. At every stage of production, prices, and prices alone, guide the actors in the economy, enlisting their self-interest in the service of the common good.

The two central propositions in economics can be thought of as emerging from this simple observation about prices: that, subject to well-known qualifications, an economy with a given distribution of resources and where people deploy their land, labour and capital in response to market-determined prices is i) autonomous requiring no central planner to decide what to produce or how to allocate output among people, and ii) efficient in that no central planner, however knowledgeable, powerful and benevolent, can redeploy resources and reallocate outputs to make everybody better off. An 'ideal' planner might rearrange the economy to make some people better off at the expense of others – and the change may even be desirable on some moral criterion – but, starting from a competitive equilibrium, additional benefits cannot be provided to some people without at the same time harming others. Actual planning is far from ideal; an economy based on markets with a given distribution of property is almost certainly more efficient than any fully planned can ever be because a fully planned economy has lost the information that market prices would otherwise supply. An economy based upon private property and the price mechanism supplies what people want with the least expenditure of resources. That

> the division of labour has reached the extent which makes modern civilization possible we owe to the fact that it did not have to be consciously created but that man tumbled on a method by which the division of labour could be extended far beyond the limits within which it could have been planned.
>
> Hayek (1944: 50)

Suppression of prices by planning also removes much of the incentive to innovate that a well-functioning market automatically supplies, for the innovator can no longer gain from increasing the efficiency labour in the production of established goods or from introducing new products. Private property is the engine of prosperity.

Markets are not entirely efficient or autonomous. Markets are dependent on a vast infrastructure that only government can supply. Private property is meaningless without public oversight, specifying precisely who has the right to what, resolving disputes about the boundaries between people's property rights, determining when innovation is patent-worthy, specifying compensation for the taking of private property for public use and punishing attempts to grab other people's property by force. Private property requires public determination of the content of property rights which must be constantly revised by the courts or legislature in the light of changing technology and society. Private property requires a rule of law. Property cannot protect itself; the state must supply the army and the police without which property is meaningless. Only the state can establish the rights and obligations. The benefits of private property cannot be realized without a network of roads, airports and other publicly supplied means of transport and communication. Private property is the beneficiary of publicly supplied research as the source of new products that the private sector can profitably develop and supply. Public supervision of the economy is required to reduce the incidence of industrial accidents and of pollution of the atmosphere. Unregulated markets can generate harmful extermalities as when the atmosphere is polluted by usage of petroleum for heating or driving. There is, nevertheless, a sphere within which prices and incomes are determined autonomously, no central authority is required to determine who gets what, and the market is efficient in that no planner can rearrange production to make everybody better off.

### The defence of majority rule voting

Over and above its role as a source of productivity, property – the private ownership of the means of production – is a requirement for the maintenance of democratic government, supplying an allocation of incomes and tasks without which the exploitation problem would be intolerable. To say this is not to say that any and every limit or constraint on property rights is catastrophic or to deny that excessive concentration of wealth may be destructive. It is to say that a core of property rights is required, that, without private ownership of the means of production, democratic government is destined to self-destruct.

Imagine a society without property rights. Imagine a communist democracy where the means of production are publically owned, income is allocated equally 'from each according to his ability, to each according to his needs', but public decision-making is by majority rule voting. In such a society without market-determined wages and prices, the economy must be administered by a planning commission with full authority to assign people to jobs, from janitor to the socialist equivalent of the CEO, in each and every industry, and to set people's incomes accordingly, herding the entire population into one vast bureaucracy from which there is no escape. Tasks which markets perform anonymously – creating order without orders – must then be performed by the state.

Notwithstanding the ideal of equality, it is unlikely that true equality among citizens could be maintained. Public ownership of all property would automatically place control of all means of communication – radio, newspapers, television and so on – under the authority of the state, to sing the praises of the glorious leader and to denigrate any potential opposition. The authority of the planner over the economy cannot be exercised without at the same time empowering the planner to enrich or impoverish any person for any reason, and it is more than one can expect of fallible people to suppose that such authority would not be misused. Upper ranks of the bureaucracy would see to it that they live well as befitting their disproportionate contribution to the welfare of society. Nor is it likely that the criminal justice system would remain independent. Upper ranks of the bureaucracy automatically acquire the incentive and the means to block or rig majority rule voting that threatens their authority or their privileges. Inevitably, a democracy without property rights would give rise to a *new class* with more authority over economy and society than can be constrained by majority rule voting.[13]

With the entire allocation of jobs and the entire distribution of income at stake, the temptation of majorities to exploit the corresponding minorities, and of the party in office to use the full authority of the state to remain in office indefinitely, would be irresistible. With no private sector to absorb people removed from office in an election, politicians out of office would be entirely at the mercy of their successors and could be plunged from the top to the bottom of society, from masters to servants, from CEOs to janitors. With so much at stake, no government in office would be prepared to risk loss of office in an election, and there would be little hope for democratic government.

Even if leaders could somehow be induced to behave democratically, the exploitation problem would persist in another dimension. With every job in the nation at stake, there develops an irresistible temptation on the part some majority of voters to grab all the prestigious, high level and interesting jobs for themselves, leaving nothing but menial work for the excluded minority. A predatory majority may be formed on religious, ethnic or geographical lines, or may be no more than associations of otherwise unconnected people seeking to reserve the good jobs for themselves. Once again, the difficulty is not that one group is inherently exploitative, but that majority rule unconstrained by some system of equity prior to and independent of politics creates conditions where the first group to organize is in a position to grab the entire prize.

There is a moral dimension:

> Just as the democratic statesman who sets out to plan economic life will soon be confronted with the alternative of either assuming dictatorial powers or abandoning his plans, so the totalitarian dictator would soon have to choose between disregard of ordinary morals and failure ... the readiness to do bad things becomes a path to promotion and power.
>
> Hayek (1944: 135;151)[14]

Government by majority rule voting and private ownership of the means of production must stand or fall together. Property rights may be modified without endangering democracy, but they cannot be dispensed with altogether.

Government by majority rule voting simply does not work without some non-political mechanism to allocate the national income among citizens and to determine who does what job, how much each person is paid and who occupies the top posts in the industrial hierarchy. One can imagine a grand bargain, a great social contract, in which these matters are agreed upon, but agreement today can be overturned by a majority in the legislature tomorrow. To be viable, a social contract must be such that no majority in the legislature has an interest in seeing the contract overturned.

In the end, the justification of property rights is that we need them. Despite its dubious origin in ancient theft and despite the inevitable inequality of income in markets dependent on the existing distribution of property, the private ownership of at least a substantial part of the means of production is a requirement both for prosperity and for democratic government. Existing property rights are tolerated if not actively defended by the rich and poor alike.

It is important to recognize what has, and what has not, been established. Government by majority rule voting requires property rights to escape from the exploitation problem where some majority of voters, a majority based upon income, ethnicity, religion, geography or anything else, employs the power of the vote to expropriate the greater part of the national income for itself, creating a situation where no government dare risk loss of office in an election because loss of office would be a descent for the government and its supporters from the top to the bottom of society. It has been shown that private property cannot be abolished without abolishing democracy too.

What has not been shown is the degree to which property rights can be safely confined. It has not been shown that the dire consequences of the total abolition of private property extend to the slightest modification of whatever anybody chooses to call property rights. The question remains as to how narrowly property rights may be conceived without placing democracy itself in jeopardy. Property rights may be defined with or without an obligation to pay whatever taxes the legislature sees fit to impose and may be circumscribed by regulation to a greater or lesser extent. The scope of property rights is determined not by divine intervention or even by constitutional decree, but by their social consequences.

As was shown in Chapter 3, systematic redistribution of income is no threat to government by majority rule voting because the gap between rich and poor is narrowed without altering people's places on the scale of rich an poor and without removing disparities of income altogether, and because there is a limit to the amount of redistribution that the median voter, in his own interest, is willing to impose. It was also shown that, though the rich prefer less redistribution and the poor prefer more, no political party dares to deviate too far from the first preference of the median voter. Democracy can live with that because it is in the interest of no majority of the population to see democracy overthrown and because property rights, inclusive of an obligation to pay whatever redistributive taxes the legislature is inclined to impose, ward off the worst of the exploitation problem.

## The boundaries of property rights

To claim that democracy needs property rights leaves open the question of how far property's vices may be suppressed or modified without risking the loss of property's virtues. Over and above the pure redistribution of income, property rights may be expanded or contracted in the drawing of lines between voting rights, civil rights and property rights.

### The porous border between the rights of property and the powers of the state

In the chapter on voting and redistribution, it was assumed that each person's pre-tax, pre-transfer income is a given fact of life, and that there is a fixed allocation of property, including property in one's own labour, from which people's incomes are derived. Incomes can be redistributed through taxation, but gross incomes and the property rights from which they are derived are fixed. Useful as it may be in the explanation of redistribution, the assumption hides aspects of property rights that may be a source of contention between rich and poor and may give rise to a variant of the exploitation problem in majority rule voting.

Some or all of the national income is intrinsically held in common, accruing in the first instance to the state which has no alternative other than to choose who the ultimate beneficiaries are to be. The extreme example of common income is where the entire national income accrues as rent from natural resources such a petroleum and must be apportioned among citizens by the government because there is no other way to do so. Immigrants might be admitted as paid workers, but citizenship would be severely restricted because additional citizens would acquire a share of a fixed income at the expense of the original population.[15]

Water can be very much like oil. It has been argued that the foundation of many despotic societies has been hydraulic,[16] that despotic societies have arisen and been preserved where agriculture is irrigated from a single canal or network of canals that must be dug and maintained by a vast army of corvee workers directed by a single great bureaucracy with absolute authority over who gets water and how much, so that every person's livelihood and food supply is at the mercy of the ruler and his minions. Property may still be private, but income is in effect common because a scarce and indispensable factor of production is controlled by the state. Once again, majority rule voting is unsustainable because government has full authority to determine who shall prosper and who shall not. The bureaucracy, which must necessarily be hierarchic, would come to dominate society completely, would never tolerate interference by an elected parliament, and would reserve the lion's share of the national income for itself.

Something like common income, but much less ominous, arises from the need in every society to specify the content and limits of property rights. What we call property is a thousand rules, all subject to modification by the legislature, affecting people's incomes industry by industry, region by region or one by one. Externalities – effects of transactions on people not party to the transaction or on society as a whole – may be taxed, modified or stopped. The prohibition of monopoly may be more or less broadly enforced. Carbon emissions may be taxed or reduced by, for instance, cap-and-trade rules. DDT was banned completely. Recognizing that most people cannot know which drugs are safe and which are not, the government establishes a food and drug administration to restrict access to some drugs except when prescribed by a doctor and to ban other drugs altogether. Government must choose the progressivity of taxation on people and corporations, and how heavily, if at all, to tax capital gains and imputed income from residential property. Minimum wage laws and unemployment insurance support the poor at the expense of the rich, and may be adjusted in ways benefiting some groups of workers at the expense of others.

Industry may be regulated or subsidized for a variety of reasons. Regulation of financial markets – the separation of investment banking from commercial banking, the prohibition of banks from trading on their own account and the designation of some banks as too big to fail – creates a conflict of interest between the average citizen and the owners and executives of banks. Tariffs protect specific industries and may be beneficial to workers and owners of capital in one industry at the expense of the rest of the population. Owners and executives of drug companies are the immediate beneficiaries or victims of legislation about the length and width of patents and about liability for adverse effects of medicines. Gun manufacturers have a special interest in legislation about the ownership and usage of guns. Oil companies have a special interest in environmental regulation. Ultimately, property is a creature of the state which must determine – by law or by silence in response to actions of property holders – the precise content of property rights.

A willingness of the government to subsidize production and investment in a wide range of industries – to benefit workers in certain industries, to promote innovation, or to influence retail prices – can interfere substantially with the market. A subsidy here or a tax break there with no clear principle determining who gets what drives each and every interest group to seek special privileges from the state, empowering bureaucrats and politicians to grant privileges to some petitioners while denying privileges to others. A society where each firm's profit and each person's wage depend upon the good will of the state – exercised through earmarks to bills or subsidies at the discretion of the government in office – begins to show more and more of the features of public ownership of the means of production, forcing legislatures to make decisions with a family resemblance to the assignment of income to people, creating conditions where the exploitation problems becomes insurmountable. The more willing government is to reassign income, the more like a hydraulic state does society become.[17]

Society learns to cope with moderate influence by the legislature over the distribution of income, even though complete political control is inconsistent with democratic government. Clearly, democratic societies can manage a certain degree of public influence over people's incomes; were that not so, no democracy could ever survive. A modest amount of common income is advantageous in financing a portion of the cost of public goods or of provision for the poor. Too much common income threatens democracy. It is difficult to say where the line should be drawn.

A distinction can be drawn in this context between the *redistribution* and the *reallocation* of income, between the systematic narrowing of the distribution of income without at the same time altering people's ranking on that scale of rich and poor, and the provision by the government of benefits to select groups of people, choosing who shall be rich and who shall be poor with no prohibition against the reordering people on the scale of rich and poor. Redistribution is no threat to democracy. On the contrary, democracy may be safer with a degree of redistribution of income because, the narrower the distribution of post-tax, post-transfer income, the less the incentive of the poor to vote for a dictator promising to expropriate the rich and the corresponding incentive of the rich to support a dictator of their own in self-defence.[18] The line between redistribution and reallocation is respected when business is governed by rules to promote efficiency in the economy as a whole rather than to increase the incomes of particular firms, industries or groups of people.

By contrast, the unconstrained reallocation of income, the willingness of government to enrich selected people or firms for a variety of reasons, replaces the property-based determination of income in a competitive economy with an allocation where each person's income comes to depend upon the good will of the government in office. Income is reallocated when money is provided to the West at the expense of the East, when one religion is favoured over another, or when investments in selected firms are subsidized. To be sure, there is some reallocation in all democratic countries. Extensive reallocation of income creates a serious exploitation problem where the worst fears of Ireton and Rich are realized.

### Civil rights and property rights

In civil rights, all people are equal. In property rights, all dollars are equal. Both rights are essential for the preservation of government by majority rule voting, but a boundary must be drawn between them, and there is an unavoidable conflict between rich and poor over where exactly the boundary should be. The conflict plays out in many ways. One normally identifies civil rights with the rule of law where, whatever the content of law may be, it is applied blindly to everybody. Civil rights may be extended to socialized medicine designed to supply everybody with the same standard of care regardless of ability to pay. Similarly, the demogrant in the negative income tax may be seen as a civil right, the right of every person to a certain minimal standard of living.[19] Legislatures must decide how large a domain of civil rights to establish and maintain.

The constitutional principle of eminent domain forbids the government from taking people's property without due compensation. The government may expropriate and demolish your house if it happens to lie in the path of a new road, but you must be compensated. On the other hand, the government usually need not compensate you for actions (such as designating your street as one way) that reduce the value of your property without actually taking it away from you, unless the reduction in value is tantamount to expropriation. It has been argued that the principle of eminent domain should block all redistribution of income because redistribution, like the demolition of a house in the path of a new road, is necessarily a taking of income from some people for the benefit of others.[20] Most people favour a narrower specification of property rights. Another source of conflict over the scope of property rights is the duration of patents on new drugs. Shareholders of drug companies, who are for the most part rich, want long-lived patents. Users of patented drugs want generic equivalents on the market as soon as possible. Shareholders in oil companies seek to minimize environmental regulations, and are more likely than other people to believe that global warming is a hoax. Mine owners may consider safety regulations as a violation of their property rights, while miners may see these same regulations are part of their civil rights. In general, the right to use one's property, to buy or sell as one pleases, does not extend beyond the point where third parties, who may be the rest of humankind, are significantly affected. Actions on one's own land may be prohibited when such actions are harmful to other people, but there remains considerable discretion as to where the line should be drawn.

Property rights conflict with civil rights in the specifications of the rights and privileges of corporations and unions. Corporations and trade unions are artificial people with legally prescribed rights. They cannot vote, but they may be entitled to contribute to political parties and to free speech, obliging all stockholders in corporations and union members to bear their proportions of the cost of campaign contributions and political actions regardless of whether they personally favour the party or cause their organization has chosen to support. Trade unions may or may not be entitled to collect union dues from all workers and call a strike from which no worker, regardless of their preferences, is exempt. Not all shareholders approve of bargains struck between corporations and their workers.

Property rights also conflict with civil rights over the designation and punishment for crimes, as where 'the law in its majestic equality forbids the rich as well as the poor to sleep under bridges, to beg in the streets and to steal bread'. If a crime could be punished by fine or by imprisonment and if the fine were less of a deterrent to the rich than to the poor, it might be in the interest of the rich to give a convicted person the option of either fine or imprisonment, but in the interest of the poor to make imprisonment mandatory. In a society dominated by a privileged social class, the severity of punishment is likely to be greater for crimes inflicted upon, rather than for crimes likely to be perpetrated by, members of the privileged class. Hence in eighteenth century England, where franchise was restricted to property holders, the death penalty was imposed for minor crimes such petty theft, while corruption costing thousands of pounds was lightly punished, if at all.[21] Throughout the nineteenth century, roughly coinciding with the extension of franchise, the death penalty was invoked in England for fewer and fewer crimes until murder was the only capital crime left.

Property rights may be subordinated to a right to life when a lost and staving person breaks into and takes food from a well-stocked cabin in the woods, in the obligation to rescue people from a ship stranded at sea or when people in a boat seek shelter at somebody else's dock to avoid capsizing in a storm.

### Voting rights and property rights

These rights clash over the role of money in elections, where, for example, free speech may be interpreted as equal speech or as the right to communicate with as many people as one's resources allow. In no country do property rights extend to the outright buying and selling of votes in the manner that cars, houses and carrots may be bought and sold, but campaign contributions and campaign advertising, having some of the features of vote buying, are more restricted in some countries than in others. The rationale for the prohibition of vote buying lies in a peculiarity of the 'market' for votes. When one votes, there is a very high probability of one's vote having no effect on anything or anybody, together with a very low probability of a modest benefit to oneself plus two enormous externalities, positive to thousands and thousands of like-minded citizens and negative to thousands and thousands of people who would have preferred the other party to win the election. An immediate consequence of these externalities is that a person's vote is worth much more to a group of like-minded voters than to any one voter all by himself. If my expected gain from a vote for the party I favour (my valuation of a win for the party I favour weighted by the chance of my vote swinging the outcome of the election from the party I oppose to the party I favour) is $1, then it must be worth $100 to a hundred like-minded voters who, if they can coordinate their actions, can afford to pay up to $100 per vote acquired by mobilizing the electorate, campaign advertising or bribery. Without legal constraints on such actions, elections would be won primarily by direct or indirect purchase of votes rather than by parties offering platforms in accordance with voters' preferences.

Though there is no sure-fire method for like-minded voters to compel one another to vote, there are substitutes for compulsion. People who cannot explicitly coordinate their votes may be encouraged to vote by campaign advertising. People who cannot be bought may still be persuaded – by repetition as much as by reason – of falsehoods that cannot be easily checked or of half truths when the opposition does not have the resources to tell its side of the story to a sufficient number of voters. Interest groups may, in effect, buy candidates for office, supplying campaign funds in return for favourable policy if their candidate is elected. If it requires a certain additional expenditure on campaign advertising to procure one extra vote, then it is as though an extra vote could be bought at that price.[22]

## Where rights come from

Property rights present little difficulty. Society needs property rights as a source of prosperity and to forestall conflict among subjects over who is entitled to what. The monarch, autocrat or dictator protects, and may even establish, property rights to enhance 'his own strength and glory'. No matter that property originated in ancient theft. A principle of adverse possession secures property rights for the current owners. The right to vote is more problematic because restricted franchise conveys privileges that the enfranchised may not willingly give up.

Consider once again Ireton and Rich's objection to universal suffrage where everybody, master and servant alike, has the right to vote. The strength of their argument depends very much on what an electorate composed mostly of servants – for there are many more servants than masters – would be inclined to do. A majority of servants might try to eliminate property rights altogether in a variant of democratic communism, but this would in all probability evolve into rule by a new class claiming to govern in the name of equality but soon becoming as wealthy and as oppressive as the class of property owners that was displaced, the most glaring example in our own time being the re-emergence of private ownership of business under dictatorial government in communist China. Alternatively, property rights might be preserved together with whatever degree of redistribution and whatever ancillary laws are most likely to serve the interests of the median voter or supporters of the party in office. In either case, masters are made worse off with universal franchise than with franchise limited by strong property qualifications on the right to vote. Why then, since only parliament can establish universal franchise, would a parliament of masters willingly give up the masters' monopoly of the right to vote? How might universal franchise arise?

The standard answer to this question is 'fear', the masters' fear of revolution if franchise is not extended. In the words of a seventeenth century reformer,

> How is despotism to be reformed ... We are to remember that the despotism being legislative, it must be the very agent of its own restoration ... It was a great national effort, headed by the barons, that first subdued the mind of the despot, John, and extorted from his *fear*, Magna Charta ... And just so it is fear alone, that from the borough-faction can ever extort a PARLIAMENTARY REFORM.
>
> Cannon (1973: xiii–xiv)

There may come a moment when, if the masters do not cede franchise to servants, the servants – or some group claiming to speak in their name – will rise up and dispossess the masters completely. Better to extend franchise voluntarily than to have it taken away.

Several considerations are important for the explanation of the emergence of universal franchise. First, though enfranchised servants would use the power of the vote to alter the distribution of income in their favour, they may, in their own interest, stop well short of the full equalization of income. Recognizing the virtues of property rights as the engine of prosperity and as the requirement for the preservation of government by majority rule voting, the servants may not dispossess their masters completely. Masters become worse off than if their monopoly of franchise were preserved, but still better off than their servants and still better off than if they had been exposed to the full force of revolution. Second, revolution to sweep away all differentiations in income and status is likely to be chaotic, unpredictable and very costly. Average income per person might be substantially reduced, so that even servants become worse off than they were before. Finally, the extension of franchise is like a game between masters and servants where masters choose whether to extend franchise, servants choose whether to revolt, extension of franchise is costly to the masters but less so than revolution, and both parties act to maximize their incomes.

Emphasis in the story to be told here is not on revolution itself, but on why the extension of franchise to avert revolution may occur gradually over many centuries, as democracy evolved in Great Britain from the King's Council, through a gradual relaxation of property requirements in the nineteenth and early twentieth century, to parliament as it is today.[23] Fear of revolution may lead to the gradual extension of franchise as the prospects for successful revolution improve over time. Originally, a small extension of franchise may be sufficient to deter revolution. Gradually, an ever larger extension of franchise may be required, until, eventually, nothing but universal franchise will do. At each moment, the median voter's optimal redistribution reduces the chance of a successful overthrow of the government by just enough to deter revolution.

The story is to be told in two stages, the first about why masters might choose to enfranchise their servants, and the second about how universal franchise might evolve gradually over time.

Begin by imagining a society with a few rich enfranchised masters and many poor disenfranchised servants, where servants rebel if it is in their interest to do so, where masters grant universal franchise if it is in their interest to do so and where, once initiated, revolution is always successful. Suppose that revolution is completely equalizing but very costly, reducing average income in society as a whole, and that, for reasons set out in the chapter on voting and redistribution, the enfranchisement of servants would be less than completely equalizing but less costly. Costs may be such that it is in the interest of masters to grant universal franchise as the only way to deter revolution.

For a society with 20 masters and 80 servants, Table 10.1 shows four postulated distributions of income: the distribution prior to revolution or enfranchisement of servants; the distribution with enfranchisement of servants to avoid revolution; and two possible outcomes after the revolution with different incomes per head. The first column of the table shows masters' and servants' incomes per head as they would be with only masters enfranchised and with no fear of revolution;

*Table 10.1* Incomes per person of masters and servants under limited franchise, universal
franchise and revolution

|  | Restricted franchise | Universal franchise | Revolution, case 1 | Revolution, case 2 |
|---|---|---|---|---|
| Masters | $100 | $60 | $9 | $13 |
| Servants | $10 | $15 | $9 | $13 |
| Average | $28 | $24 | $9 | $13 |

Note: There are 20 masters and 80 servants.

the incomes are $100 per master and $10 per servant. The next column shows incomes as they would become with universal franchise. The median voter is now a servant who opts for whatever redistribution of income serves to maximize the post-tax, post-transfer of servants, taking account of the reduction in income per head from increased tax avoidance as the tax rate to finance redistribution is increased. Numbers in the second column of the table are chosen to be consistent with this constraint. Income per master falls from $100 to $60, and income per servant rises from $10 to $15, so that average income falls from $28 to $24. The final two columns show two possible outcomes of revolution. In both cases, incomes of former masters and former servants are the same, but, in one case, the postulated common income per person is $9 which is too small to make revolution advantageous to servants, while, in the other case, the postulated common income per person is $13 which is large enough to make revolution advantageous to servants unless that masters are prepared to grant universal franchise instead. In the second case but not the first, masters acquire the incentive to grant universal franchise as the only alternative to revolution.[24]

The framework developed so far may be helpful in explaining why franchise is granted, but it cannot explain the gradual extension of franchise over time, for, if all servants' incomes are originally the same, there would be no basis for deciding who among the originally disenfranchised servants are to be enfranchised and who are not. Gradual extension of franchise can be explained by replacing masters and servants with a complete distribution of income that may be constrained by whatever degree of redistribution the median voter prefers, where median in this context is among people currently enfranchised rather than among the population as a whole. To tell that story, suppose

- Franchise is restricted by income. At any moment of time, a proportion $v$ if the population is enfranchised. People already enfranchised may vote to increase franchise partially (so that $v$ increases but remains less than 1) or completely (so that $v$ becomes equal to 1).
- Redistribution of income would be undertaken by a negative income tax at the preferred rate of the median voter. Thus, the larger $v$, the smaller the income of the median voter and higher the rate of the negative income tax must be.

- Revolution turns the world upside down so that nobody knows in advance what his standing in the new distribution will be. Perhaps revolution will bring forth a glorious world of full equality of income. Perhaps revolution will ultimately give rise to a new and nastier ruling class. Designate everybody's expected income in the event of revolution by $I^R$. If $I^R$ increases over time, revolution becomes ever more attractive to disenfranchised people, so that concessions sufficient to deter revolution today may become insufficient tomorrow. Suppose this to be so.
- Revolution occurs and is successful if and only if supported by a majority of the population. Thus, to deter revolution, franchise must be extended to the point where the *median voter's* preferred rate for the negative income tax and the corresponding demogrant are just high enough to provide the *median person* with a post-tax, post-transfer income that is higher than his expected income in the event of revolution. Franchise would be gradually extended over time if, as a consequence of technical change or for any other reason, everybody's expected income in the event of revolution is increased.

The story is illustrated in Figure 10.1 with tax rates, $t$, on the vertical axis, everybody's expected income, $I^R$, in the event of revolution on the left-hand side of the horizontal axis, and the proportion of citizens enfranchised, $v$, on the right-hand side of the horizontal axis. With franchise restricted by income, the right-hand side of the horizontal axis can also be interpreted as a line-up of all voters from richest to poorest on a scale from 0 to 1.

The curve on the right-hand side of the figure shows the *median voter's* preferred tax rate, $t(v/2)$, as an increasing function of the proportion, $v$, of citizens who are enfranchised, where, as explained in the chapter on voting and redistribution, an increase in the proportion of citizens enfranchised, lowers the income

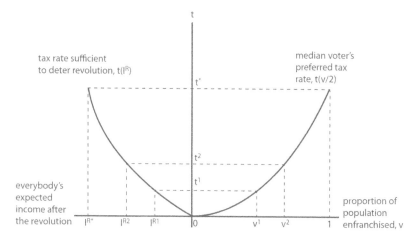

*Figure 10.1* How an increase in the benefit of revolution leads to an extension of franchise but not necessarily to universal franchise.

of the median voter, raises the median voter's preferred tax rate and increases the transfer per person. The curve shows the median voter's preferred tax rate increasing from $t^1$ to $t^2$ to $t^*$ as the proportion of the population enfranchised increases from $v^1$ to $v^2$ to 1.

The curve on the left-hand side of the figure connects everybody's expected income in the event of revolution, $I^R$, with the tax rate, $t(I^R)$, just sufficient to deter revolution by making a majority of the population worse off in the event of revolution than they would otherwise be, or, equivalently, by keeping the post-tax, post-transfer income of the *median person* (designated as ½ on the scale from 0 to 1) higher than the expected income after the revolution.[25]

Suppose the expected income in the event of revolution is $I^{R1}$. If so, the tax rate just sufficient to deter revolution is $t(I^{R1})$ shown as $t^1$ on the vertical axis. To ensure a tax rate of at least $t^1$, the proportion of the population enfranchised must be at least $v^1$ as shown on the right-hand side of the figure.

The figure illustrates the not-implausible proposition that, the smaller everybody's expected income in the event of revolution, the smaller the percentage of the population enfranchised, and the lower the rate of the negative income tax, need be. If everybody's expected income in the event of revolution is $I^{R1}$ which is relatively low, then a relatively low tax, $t^1$, is sufficient to ensure that over half the population is better off without revolution, and a relatively small proportion, $v^1$, of the population would need to be enfranchised to secure that tax rate. If everybody's expected income in the event of revolution rises to $I^{R2}$, a higher tax rate, $t^2$, would be required to keep half the population better off without rebellion and a greater franchise, $v^2$, would be required for the median voter to favour that rate. Eventually, as expected income in the event of revolution increases enough (or, more generally, society changes so as to make denial of universal franchise sufficiently painful to people already enfranchised), the transition to universal franchise becomes complete.[26] Universal franchise, at $v = 1$, is introduced once people's expected income after the revolution rises to $I^{R^*}$, an income only attainable by redistribution without revolution at a tax rate of $t^*$ which is higher than the median voter would prefer unless everybody is entitled to vote.

Figure 10.1 transforms the story of the evolution of universal franchise into a story of the gradual improvement in people's capacity to revolt if franchise is denied. The working assumption in the story – that revolution occurs and is successful when it makes a majority of the population better off – is very strong and very far from realistic, but it does point to conditions in society influencing whether or not franchise will be increased. The term $I^R$ in the story may be thought of as a surrogate for a host of related conditions: capacity of the disenfranchised to organize a revolution, capacity of the enfranchised (or the monarch as the case may be) to detect dissatisfaction among subjects and to suppress revolt, the probability of the outbreak of revolution and the probability that revolution, once begun, can be defeated.[27] Fear of revolution may be a final link in a long chain of causation. It is at least possible that the risk of rebellion would be insignificant without widespread literacy in the general population or without technology that has become available in the last hundred years. There may be changes in the technology of revolution and of suppression of revolution. Improvements in accounting may have been required for income to be partially redistributed without eliminating private property altogether or equalizing property holding completely. The median voter's preferred redistribution of income is affected by spontaneous changes over time in distribution of income and inter-generational mobility on the scale of rich and poor.

Nor is it really necessary for denial of franchise to provoke a full-fledged revolution. Especially when the enfranchised proportion of the population is already large (when $v$ is not too far from 1) franchise may be extended if the disenfranchised can make enough of a fuss to tilt the median voter's balance of costs and benefits appropriately. Enfranchisement limited to the top 10 per cent of the population may convey great privileges (though it also involves considerable cost in suppressing the remaining 90 per cent). By contrast, the median voter when 90 per cent of the population is already enfranchised may have little to lose from the enfranchisement of the remaining 10 per cent. Whatever may have induced acceptance of the enfranchisement of women, it is unlikely to have been the fear of outright revolution.

Ireton and Rich's objection to universal franchise may well have been valid in their own time but not today. Systematic redistribution of income might have been impossible in the seventeenth century before the technology of tax collection had been sufficiently developed and when income differentials were due primarily to the unequal ownership of land. A parliament with a majority of servants might have been expected to equalize land ownership completely or to institute a new upper class, placing a far greater burden on well-to-do people than redistribution does today, and constituting a significant impediment to investment and innovation. By contrast, the story in Figure 10.1 is of redistribution leaving a significant majority of the people better off than they could ever become by the abolition of prior property rights.

There is another, nastier possibility. The initial distribution of pre-tax, pre-transfer income may be wide enough and the cost of redistribution – from tax avoidance, the labour–leisure choice and so on as discussed in Chapter 4 on the revenue-maximizing tax rate – may be large enough that, even with universal franchise, the median voter for whom $s = \frac{1}{2}$ is still worse off than he would be in the event of revolution. To put the matter differently, a more drastic form of equalization of income than the negative income tax or a system of taxes and social welfare that preserves the ordering of people on the scale of rich and poor may be advantageous to some majority of the population, even at the cost of a significant fall in the national income. Perhaps land reform. Perhaps socialization of a large part of the economy. Perhaps restriction of high-paying occupations to some class of people defined on religious or ethnic lines. Perhaps subordination to the great leader. Or, fearing displacement, the masters may find a way to suppress rebellion, placing democracy itself in jeopardy. These possibilities are especially disturbing in the light of the considerable widening of the distribution of income over the last half century. Whether the United States or China will be the model for future societies may depend on how wide the distribution of income becomes and on the effectiveness of redistribution. Ireton and Rich may turn out to be correct tomorrow.[28]

The story told here is of franchise extended just enough from time to time to tip the balance against revolution. Other explanations of the path to universal franchise, emphasizing different facets of the process and complementary to the explanations offered here are discussed in the appendix on the path to democratic government.

## Appendix: The path to democratic government

Democracy may be seen as emerging in a natural sequence of stages. *Violence and Social Orders* by Douglas North, John Wallis and Barry Weingast (2006) and *The Origins of Political Order* by Francis Fukuyama (2009) are two recent histories along these lines. The books differ in their descriptions of the path to democracy, but they have much in common.

In *Violence and Social Orders*, North, Wallis and Weingast describe society as evolving from a *foraging* order, to a *limited access order* (also called a *natural state*), to an *open access order*. The foraging order corresponds to what is often described as hunter–gatherer societies, with people organized as tribes and with small enough populations to confine warfare among tribes within reasonable bounds. Limited access orders, from feudalism to absolute monarchy, are characterized by the presence of an elite with a monopoly on the legitimate use of violence and the power to appropriate for itself the lion's share of the national income, leaving little more than bare subsistence for the common people. Open access orders, representative of society as we know it in Europe and America, are characterized by the rule that 'individuals and groups may freely form organizations and enter into most economic, political, social and other activities, subject to general rules applied impersonally, such as refraining from violence' (North, Wallis and Weingast, 2006: 117). Emphasis in the discussion of open access orders is upon the universal right to form political parties and corporations.

Open access orders are only possible once three requirements, called 'doorstep conditions', are met. Somehow, within the natural state, there must be developed i) a rule of law for elites, ii) long-lived organizations in the public and private spheres and iii) consolidated control of the military (North, Wallis and Weingast, 2006: 154). Much of the book is about how the doorstep conditions evolve within the natural state. No matter how absolute the monarch may be, he cannot govern society all by himself. A monarch requires compliance of the army and the civil service. They, in turn, would be more loyal and less likely to rebel when their day-to-day affairs are governed by law rather than at the whim of their superiors. Hence the gradual emergence of the rule of law for the elites and the prospect of its extension to an ever-larger share of the population.

Minimal requirements for open access orders are government by majority rule voting and an economy with private ownership of the means of production, each composed of many interlocking customs and traditions. When one speaks, for example, of majority rule voting, one has in mind a complex mixture of mutually reinforcing arrangements: voting rules such as first-past-the-post or proportional representation, rules of order for voting within the legislature, the right to stand for office, the right to form political parties and so on, where the efficacy of each particular arrangement depends upon the presence of the rest. The right to vote is virtually worthless if the dictator chooses political parties and platforms; the right to form political parties is virtually worthless if the dictator chooses who is entitled to vote.

Though North, Wallis and Weingast define open access orders somewhat more broadly, the emphasis in their historical examples is almost exclusively on the right to form political parties and corporations. There is some question as to whether too much emphasis may have been placed on these institutions. Once property rights are secure and scientific progress is under way, the corporation with limited liability can be a great help in the creating efficient industrial organization, but the establishment of limited liability may be easy by comparison with the invention of the new technology that made the industrial revolution possible and with the establishment of property rights and the rule of law.[29]

*The Origins of Political Order* by Francis Fukuyama focuses upon the 'institutions' of modern society, defined, following Samuel Huntington, as 'stable, valued, recurrent patterns of behaviour' (2009: 242). The three institutions are i) the state, ii) the rule of law and iii) accountable government, with no distinction – like that in North, Wallis and Weingast – between states of society and doorstep conditions allowing the different stages to emerge. Intended as the first of two volumes, *The Origins of Political Order* carries the story to about 1800, with emphasis upon the emergence of the rule of law and of the unified state out of primitive or tribal governance in China, the Ottoman Empire and India as well as in medieval and early modern Europe.

Fukuyama speaks of the 'biological foundation of politics' (2009: 483), arguing that 'humans never existed in a pre-social state', that 'rational sociability is built around two principles: kin selection and reciprocal altruism', that 'human beings have a natural propensity for violence'and that 'human beings by nature require not just material resources but also recognition' (ibid.: 439–41). Together with the rule of law and accountable government, these psychological propensities are claimed to supply what is needed over and above mere self-interest for the maintenance of democratic government, in particular, to account for people's willingness to compromise in the formation of legislation and of the platforms of political parties.

*The Origins of Political Order* describes the route from the powerful state to the rule of law to accountable government, with many interesting stories along the way. Among the topics covered are how characteristics of China today emerged in empires thousands of years ago, how the rule of law as we know it today originated in the adoption of Roman law by the Catholic Church, how features of English capitalism originated from the intricacies of medieval land law, and how potential corruption in large organizations was held in check by celibacy, Janissaries or eunuchs. The analytics are not as carefully worked out as in North, Wallis and

Weingast, but Fukuyama brings together much interesting historical material and identifies patterns that might, but for this book, be overlooked.

Fukuyama adopts Dicey's definition of the rule of law that 'no man is punishable or can be lawfully made to suffer in body or goods except for a breach of law established in the ordinary legal manner before the ordinary courts of the land' (Dicey, 1885: 110). Not discussed by Fukuyama, or by North, Wallis and Weingast either, is that the law may be biased, imposing severe punishments for crimes that members of the lower class are especially likely to commit. The rule of law as established by the Glorious Revolution (given special attention on North, Wallis and Weingast) included the death penalty for hundreds of minor crimes, such as sheep stealing, that the poor might be tempted to commit but the rich would not. How class bias in the content of laws might affect the accountability of government is not discussed.

Two stories about the origin of the rule of law are both interesting but do not fit well together. The first is about the rediscovery of Roman law in the middle ages and its adoption as church law and then for identifying 'natural law' as a constraint on the actions of despotic governments. The second story is of the evolution of the English common law not from time immemorial, but as a common set of rules, developed at a time when each shire had its own unique rules, by the king's court travelling from place to place as the final judge of punishments and arbitrator of disputes.

Fukuyama's notion of accountable government is not entirely clear. To whom must the government be accountable? How exactly is it decided whether a government's actions pass whatever test accountability requires? Might a benevolent despot act accountably? What is the connection, if any, between accountability and the common good? Is accountability code for majority rule voting, and, if not, what else is required?

Fukuyama's preference for 'accountability' over 'majority rule voting' as the third defining characteristic of a desirable political order may originate from the interpretation of democracy as compromise among social classes rather than majority rule per se.

> The miracle of modern liberal democracy, in which strong states capable of enforcing law are nonetheless checked by law and by legislatures, could arise only as a result of the fact that there was a rough *balance* of power among the different political actors within society.... What we understand as modern constitutional government arose as a result of this unwanted and unplanned compromise.
>
> Fukuyama (2009: 325)

There is in both books – and, I must confess, in this chapter as well – a descent into *historicism*, defined by Karl Popper (1957: 3) as the

> approach to the social sciences which assumes that *historical prediction* is their principal aim, and which assumes that aim is attainable by the discovery

of the 'rhythms' or the 'patterns', 'laws' or 'trends' that underlie the evolution of history.

Popper's concern was to avoid imagining society 'being swept into the future by irresistible forces'(1957: 160). His main target was the Marxist progression from feudalism to capitalism to communism, allowing one to see oneself upon the very cusp of history, where the best one can hope for is to speed up the process or to make it less painful. Popper drew a distinction between history as prophesy and as an aid to piecemeal social engineering, rejecting the one and favouring the other. He saw the search for patterns of history as assisting piecemeal social engineering, for you cannot fix society, bettering institutions here and there, without some notion of where society is going and how innovation is likely to affect its course. Malthus' prophesy of permanent impoverishment was of enormous use to humankind not because it was correct, for it was not, but because and in so far as it promoted the piecemeal social engineering to ensure that it was not. Similarly, *Violence and Social Orders* and *The Origins of Political Order* chart a course, suggesting what can be done to move society faster along that course if and insofar as that course is socially desirable, and to change course if it is not.

Little is said in either of these books about the stability of democracy. Does history come to an end with the establishment of democracy, as suggested by the title of an earlier book of Fukuyama, *The End of History and the Last Man* (1992), or is there a temporary or permanent reversion to an earlier, more autocratic society? Specifically, there is little recognition of the exploitation problem in majority rule voting by which a majority of voters – any majority based upon religion, ethnicity, locality and especially income – can employ the power of the vote to exploit the corresponding minority completely or of the possibility of the evolution of technology and economic organization giving rise to a new uncontrollable ruling class. It is simply assumed in both books that all interested parties can compromise successfully as long as there is not too much at stake.[30]

Written as though democracy were secure come what may, these books are too sanguine in my opinion about the risk to democracy from a widening of the distribution of income, the intransigence of factions and the evolution of technology. It is one thing to argue that secure property rights preserve government by majority rule voting by limiting the ability of the majority – of any majority – to confiscate the property of the corresponding minority. It is quite another thing to argue that compromise within open access orders is sufficient to preserve democratic government forever.

## Notes

1  The authors of the American constitution saw political parties as corrosive to democratic government, and hoped to banish political parties altogether in the new United States of America. See Hofstadter (1969).
2  The story is told in Chandler (1977). Once upon a time, the principal transfer between generations was the inheritance by children of the family farm. Today, parents are more

concerned about giving children a decent education than about leaving anything to children when the parents are gone.

3  In Canada, out of a total wealth of about $9 trillion, a third is held in the form of housing and another third is held in the form of pension funds. In the year 2012, total assets were $9.4 trillion of which $3.3 trillion was in principal residences and $2.8 trillion was in private pension assets, *Statistics Canada*, Survey of Financial Security, #205-0001. The Canadian national income in the year 2012 was $1.5 trillion.

4  Dunn's book traces the meanings of the word 'democracy' from its origins in ancient Athens, through the French revolution, to the present day.

5  For pessimistic views about the exploitation problem in multi-ethnic societies see Rabushka and Shepsle (1972), Chua (2003) and Mann (2005).

6  On the logic and history of countervailing power, see Gordon (2002).

7  'No Bill of Attainder or ex post facto Law shall be passed', Article 1, section 9, clause 3 of the US constitution. Similar constraints are imposed in the written or unwritten constitutions of all democratic countries.

8  Philosophers refer to these species of justification as deontological and consequential. For a history of the justification of property rights, see Schlatter (1951). More recent writings are cited in Usher (2000).

9  'All ownership derives from occupation and violence. When . . . we follow the legal track back, we must necessarily arrive at a point where this title originated in the appropriation of goods available to all. Before that, we may encounter a forcible expropriation from a predecessor whose ownership we can in turn trace to an earlier appropriation or robbery. That all rights derive from violence, all ownership from appropriation or robbery, we may freely admit' Von Mises (1951: 43).

10  For opposing views about the principle of first possession, see Epstein (1979) and Lueck (1995).

11  John Locke, *Two Treatises of Government*, Thomas J. Cooke ed. Hafner Press, 1947, 134. The quotation is from the second treatise published in 1690.

12  Elsewhere, on p. 463, Hobbes remarks that if 'the right of kings did depend on the goodness of William the Conqueror, . . . there would perhaps be no tie of the subjects' obedience at this day in all the world: whereas they needlessly think to justify themselves, they justify all the successful rebellions that ambition shall at any time raise against them and their successors. Therefore I put down for one of the most effectual seeds of the of the death of any state, that the conquerors require not only a submission of mens actions to them for the future, but also an approbation of all their actions past; when there is scarce a commonwealth in he world, whose beginnings can in conscience be justified.'

13  The term 'new class' was coined by Milovan Djilas an ex-communist, to describe the de facto rulers of a communist society as the natural successors of the capitalist class that communists claim to have abolished in establishing a classless society. '. . . the ownership privilege of the new class manifests itself as an exclusive right, as a party monopoly, for the political bureaucracy to distribute the national income, to set wages, direct economic development, and dispose of nationalized and other property' (1957: 44).

14  The quotation is a juxtaposition of two quotes from pp. 135 and 151 in a chapter entitled 'Why the worst get on top'.

15  *Common income* is similar but not identical to *common property*. Common property is exemplified by the commons in medieval villages and by fish in the sea. As defined by Gordon (1954), it is property that everybody has a right to use. The state does not decide who may and who may not make use of such property, and, typically but not invariably, each user's benefit from the property diminishes with the number of people using it. By contrast, common income accrues in the first instance to the state and must be apportioned by the state, equally or not, at the discretion of the government. There are cases in between with characteristics of each.

16  This term 'hydraulic' society is from Wittfogel (1957). Wittfogel, also a disillusioned ex-communist, saw the despotic societies in ancient China, India and the Middle East as originating in the need for a vast bureaucracy to administer canals and irrigation, a bureaucracy that soon came to dominate the rest of society.

17  Avoidance of piecemeal public subsidization was a large part of Milton Friedman's rationale for the negative income tax (Friedman, 1962).

18  'We can have a democratic society or we can have great concentrated wealth in the hands of a few. We cannot have both' Louis Brandies, quoted in Bartels (2008: 284).

19  The proportional income tax to finance the demogrant in the negative income tax is a useful construct for creating an unambiguous measure of the degree of redistribution, but a given demorgant could be financed by progressive taxation and it is usually efficient to do so.

20  For a development of this argument in the context of an informative and thoughtful exposition of the principle of eminent domain, see Epstein (1985).

21  Why, asked an eighteenth century commentator, should a highway robber 'committed perhaps for a trifle, or the mere relief of his necessities' be executed, 'whilst another who has enriched himself by continual depredations, for a course of some years, shall not only escape with impunity, but, by a servile herd of flatterers and sycophants, have all his actions crowned with applause' Thompson (1975: 259).

22  Conflict between intrinsically unequal property rights and equal voting rights is exemplified in the *Citizens United* decision of the United States Supreme Court overturning the McCain–Feingold Act that had limited the amount of money any person or corporation may contribute to a political campaign. Wealthy donors or corporations may now contribute as much as they choose to political campaigns.

23  The story of the extension of franchise in the United States is told in Keyssar (2000).

24  This picture of the transition from restricted franchise to universal franchise has much in common with Acemoglu and Robinson's (2006) model of the passage from 'dictatorship' to 'democracy', but with at least one important difference. There is no place in Acemoglu and Robinson's model for the case in the second column of the table where large income differences between masters and servants persist even under a regime of universal franchise. Society's choice in their model is between substantial inequality of income in a regime run by and for the 'elite' and full equality of income in a regime of universal franchise. Acemoglu and Robinson interpret democracy as full equality of income rather than as government by majority rule voting with some disparities of income preserved.

25  In *Economic Origins of Dictatorship and Democracy*, Acemoglu and Robinson (2006) raise and deal with an interesting objection. If redistribution is required to deter revolution, a legislature with limited franchise might redistribute without at the same time increasing franchise at all. Their response to this objection is that, as franchise is harder to reverse than taxation to finance redistribution; extended franchise provides the beneficiaries of increased redistribution with insurance that redistribution will not be revoked in the event that conditions change.

26  From Equation 3.11 in the chapter on voting and redistribution, it follows that, when deadweight loss is from tax evasion, the tax rate, $t(I^R)$, just high enough to deter the *median person* from revolution is the value of $t$ in the equation $I^R = Y^{med} - t(1 - t/\beta)(Y^{av} - Y^{med}) - t^2 Y^{med}/2\beta$, where the right-hand side of the equation is the post-tax, post-transfer income of the *median person*, $Y^{av}$ and $Y^{med}$ are the pre-tax, pre-transfer incomes of the average person and the median person on the entire scale of incomes from 0 to 1, and where $\beta$ is an indicator of the efficiency of tax collection. Think of the curve connecting $I^R$ and $t$ on the left-hand side of the figure as derived from that equation. When franchise is restricted by income to a proportion, $v$, of the population and when a negative income tax at a rate $t$ is imposed, the post-tax, post-transfer income of the *median voter* becomes $I(v/2)$

where $I(v/2) = Y(v/2) - t(1 - t/\beta)(Y^{av} - Y(v/2)) - t^2 Y(v/2)/2\beta$, where $Y(v/2)$ is the pre-tax, pre-transfer income of the median voter. The median voter's preferred tax rate, $t(v/2)$, for the rate for the negative income maximizes $I(v/2)$ in this equation. Necessarily, $t(v/2)$ is a decreasing function of $v$, as shown by the curve on the right-hand side of the figure. The first of these two equations identifies the tax rate sufficient to deter revolution. The second equation identifies the extent of franchise required to procure that rate.

27 Gradual extension of franchise was discussed in Usher (1990) and in the chapter called 'Transitions' in Usher (1992).

28 The spectre of the complete expropriation of property holders played a central role in the debate about universal franchise between James Mill and T. B. Macaulay 200 years ago. Mill advocated universal franchise. In support of franchise restricted to property holders, Macaulay, writing in 1829, had this to say: '... under a system of universal suffrage, the majority of the electorate return the representative, and the majority of the representatives make the law ... If, indeed, every man in the community possessed an equal share of what Mr. Mill calls the objects of desire, the majority would probably abstain from plundering the minority. A large majority would offer a vigorous resistence; and the property of a small minority would not repay the other members other community for the trouble of dividing it. But it happens that in all civilized communities there is a small minority of rich men, and a great majority of poor men. If there were a thousand men with ten pounds apiece, it would not be worthwhile for nine hundred and ninety of them to rob ten, and it would be a bold attempt for six hundred to rob four hundred. But if ten of them had a hundred thousand pounds apiece, the case would be very different. There would then be much to be got and nothing to be feared' quoted in Lively and Rees (1978: 118).

29 In describing complex phenomena, it is often difficult to say what is central and what is peripheral. Are property and voting central to modern democratic government, or is its central feature the right to form political parties and corporations? One is reminded of the blind men and the elephant. My radio would be useless without the dial that allows me to choose among stations. The dial may be looked upon as the essence of radio, while the process of transmitting information with or without wires may be looked upon as a mere doorstep condition for the emergence of radios. That may be a reasonable point of view if one happens to be a producer of dials. Otherwise, for the rest of us, it is not a very helpful way of thinking about radios.

30 The *locus classicus* of the doctrine that compromise will prevail is Robert A. Dahl, *A Preface to Democratic Theory* (1956). Dahl contrasts 'Madisonian democracy' – not what James Madison favoured, but what he feared – where the exploitation problem is uncontainable with what he called the American Hydrid in Polyarchical Democracy where compromise is destined to prevail. 'Prior to politics, beneath it, enveloping it, restricting it, conditioning it is the underlying consensus on policy that usually exists in a society among a predominant portion of the politically active members. Without such a consensus no democratic system would long survive the endless irritations and frustrations of elections and party competition' (ibid.: 132).

# References

Acemoglu, Daron and Robinson, James, A. (2006) *Economic Origins of Dictatorship and Democracy*, Cambridge: Cambridge University Press.

Bartels, Larry M. (2008) *Unequal Democracy: The Political Economy of the New Guilded Age*, Princeton: Princeton University Press.

Cannon, John (1973) *Parliamentary Reform, 1640–1832*, Cambridge: Cambridge University Press.

Chandler, Alfred, D. (1977) *The Visible Hand; The Managerial Revolution in American Business*, Belknap Press.

Chua, Amy (2003) *World on Fire: How Exporting Free Market Democracy Breeds Ethnic Hatred and Global Instability*, New York: Doublebay.

Dahl, Robert, A. (1956) *A Preface to Democratic Theory*, Chicago: University of Chicago Press.

Dicey, A.V. (1982[1885]) *Introduction to the Study of the Law of the Constitution*, Indianapolis: Liberty Classics.

Djilas, Milovan (1957) *The New Class: An Analysis System*, New York: Praeger, p. 44.

Dunn, John (2005) *Democracy: A History*, Penguin Canada, pp. 19–20.

Epstein, Richard (1979) Possession as the root of title, *Georgia Law Review*, 1221, 121–43.

Epstein, Richard A. (1985) *Takings: Private Property and the Power of Eminent Domain*, Cambridge, MA: Harvard University Press.

Finley, Moses (1972) *Democracy Ancient and Modern*, New Brunswick: Rutgers University Press, p. 13.

Friedman, Milton (1962) *Capitalism and Freedom*, Chicago: University of Chicago Press. Chapter 12.

Fukuyama, Francis (1992) *The End of History and the Last Man*, New York: The Free Press.

Fukuyama, Francis (2009) *The Origins of Political Order*, Cambridge: Cambridge University Press.

Gordon, H. Scott (1954) The economics of a common property resource: the fishery, *The Journal of Political Economy*, 62, 124–42.

Gordon, Scott (2002) *Controlling the State: Constitutionalism from Ancient Athens to Today*, Cambridge, MA: Harvard University Press.

Hayek, Friedrich A. (1944) *The Road to Serfdom*, Chicago: University of Chicago Press.

Hobbes, Thomas, *Leviathan* (1651) Michael Oakeshott, ed., Oxford: Basil Blackwell (undated).

Hofstadter, Richard (1969) *The Idea of a Party System, The Rise of Legitimate Opposition in the United States 1780–1840*, Oakland: University of California Press.

Ireton, H. (1647–9) *Puritanism and Liberty being the Army Debates from the Clarke Manuscripts with Supplementary Documents*, edited by A. S. P. Woodhouse, 1938. London: J. M. Dent and Sons, p. 63.

Keyssar, Alexander (2000) *The Right to Vote: The Contested History of Democracy in the United States*, New York: Basic Books.

Lively, J. and Rees, J. (1978) *Utilitarian Logic and Politics*, Oxford: Clarendon Press.

Locke, John (1690) *Two Treatises of Government*, Thomas J. Cooke ed. 1947, New York: Hafner Press.

Lueck, David (1995) The rule of first possession and the design of law, *Journal of Law and Economics*, 38, 393–436.

Mann, Michael (2005) *The Dark Side of Democracy*, Cambridge: Cambridge University Press.

Nozick, Robert (1974) *Anarchy, State and Utopia*, New York: Basic Books, p. ix.

North, Douglas, Wallis, John and Weingast, Barry (2006) *Violence and Social Orders*, Cambridge: Cambridge University Press.

Popper, Karl, H. (1957) *The Poverty of Historicism*, London: Routledge & Kegan Paul.

Rabushka, Alvin and Kenneth Shepsle, Kenneth (1972) *The Politics of a Plural Society: A Theory of Democratic Instability*, Columbus, OH: Merill.

Rich, N. (1647–9) *Puritanism and Liberty being the Army Debates from the Clarke Manuscripts with Supplementary Documents*, edited by A. S. P. Woodhouse, 1938. London: J. M. Dent and Sons, p. 58.

Schlatter, R. (1951) *Private Property: the History of an Idea*, London: George Allen and Unwin. *Statistics Canada*, Survey of Financial Security, #205-0001.

Thompson, E. P. (1975) *Whigs and Hunters, The Origin of the Black Act*, New York: Pantheon Books, p. 259.

Usher, Dan (1990) The birth of the liberal society, Queens Economics Working Paper #770, January.

Usher, Dan (1992) *The Welfare Economics of Markets, Voting and Predation*, Manchester: Manchester University Press.

Usher, D. (2000) The justification of property rights, in *Ethics and Capitalism*, edited by John Douglas Bishop, Toronto: University of Toronto Press,

Von Mises, Ludwig (1951) *Socialism*, New Haven: Yale University Press.

Wittfogel, Karl (1957) *Oriental Despotism: A Comparative Study of Total Power*,   New Haven: Yale University Press.

Woodhouse, A. S. P., (Ed.) (1938) *Puritanism and Liberty being the Army Debates (1647–9) from the Clarke Manuscripts with Supplementary Documents*, London: J. M. Dent and Sons.

# 11 Assessing the citizen-candidate model[1]

Citizen-candidate models – specifically Osborne and Slivinski (1996) 'A model of political competition with citizen-candidates' and Besley and Coate (1997) 'An Economic Model of Representative Democracy' – can be looked upon as part of a larger enterprise by economists to explain politics on the same principles that are employed to explain markets. For politics as for markets, we seek to explain aggregate outcomes as equilibria emerging from uncoordinated actions by rational, self-interested people, to determine when outcomes are, in some sense, in the public interest, to identify sources of inefficiency and to provide a platform for prediction and for reform. It is argued here that the outcome of this exercise in political model building is rendered interesting and informative by revealing the very opposite of what the authors sought to discover, an irreducible core where no equilibrium prevails and public choice can only emerge as a consequence of negotiation and bargaining.

Economists' first attempts at modelling democratic politics were focused on the amalgamation by voting of individual preferences into social decisions. Central in this literature was the median voter theorem: when the choice among policies can be represented by the choice of points on a left–right continuum and when every voter's preference among points is single peaked, the first preference of the median voter prevails in a pairwise vote with any other option. In particular, the first preference of the median voter, *if there is one*, must prevail in voting about bills in parliament as long as bills can be seen as emerging from a chain of pairwise votes in which every option is included somewhere along the chain. The focus was on voters, not politicians. As candidates for office or as office holders, politicians were shunted aside by two critical assumptions: that their only aim is to get elected and that they are truth tellers who do in office what they promise as candidates.

> Thus politicians in our model never seek office as a means of carrying out particular policies: their only goal is to reap the rewards of holding office *per se*. They treat policies purely as means to the attainment of their private ends, which they can reach only by being elected.
>
> Downs (1957: 28)

The model worked well enough as long as preferences were single-peaked, but trouble emerged as soon as this assumption was relaxed.

- Collective preference as expressed through voting may be intransitive, even though no voter's preferences are intransitive. A person who chooses option $\alpha$ over option $\beta$, option $\beta$ over option $\delta$, but option $\delta$ over option $\alpha$ would be deemed irrational, even insane. Yet the electorate may vote for option $\alpha$ over option $\beta$, for option $\beta$ over option $\delta$ and for option $\delta$ over option $\alpha$ without any voter behaving irrationally. Among the implications of this 'paradox of voting' are that it may be disadvantageous to vote sincerely, for, if voters do vote sincerely, the agenda setter can choose a sequence of pairwise votes from which his own preferred option emerges as the winner.
- Voting about platforms of two or more single-peaked issues – such as military expenditure and expenditure on health care – may be cyclic, even though both issues are single peaked one at a time.
- Voting about the allocation of the entire national income is especially perverse. When people vote selfishly and uncooperatively, as *homo economicus* would surely do, there is no platform that cannot be defeated by some other platform in a pairwise vote. The most likely outcome would be limited cooperation. A deal would be struck among the members of some group, bound together by a common badge, such as race, language or locality, to share the entire national income among themselves, leaving nothing for outsiders. Voting about the allocation of the entire national income is so divisive, and its outcome so unsatisfactory, that government by majority rule voting would be impossible unless the unrestricted allocation of the national income were removed from the political realm through a system of property rights protected by a written or unwritten constitution.
- Once elected, politicians may break their promises to the electorate, enriching themselves, serving their own social class at the expense of the rest of the population, or selling public policy to the highest bidder.

If that is what is to be expected when the economists' picture of mankind is extended from the market to the political arena, then it is hardly surprising that many democracies are overthrown and it becomes somewhat mysterious that democracy ever works at all. Something more would seem to be required, either selfless cooperation among politicians or a better model of how self-interest plays out in the political arena.

Citizen-candidate models break the artificial bounds in the older literature between people voting for candidates and legislators voting for policies, incorporating both into a model of a democratic process where voters and candidates are drawn from the same population. The key assumptions are the very opposite of Downs' assumptions in the quotation above.

1  Politics is the choice of one out of a set of available options.
2  Everybody has preferences over options.

3    Everybody is fully aware of everybody else's preferences.
4    Anybody may run as a candidate for office.
5    The office holder adopts whatever option he personally prefers. No promise to do otherwise would be believed.
6    In voting and in deciding whether to run for office, people act individually, rationally and selfishly, without altruism and without deliberate cooperation.
7    The office holder in these models becomes an elected dictator, governing all alone with no legislature and no political parties.
8    In the event of a tie between candidates, the winner of the election (to become the all-powerful office holder) is determined by lot. This assumption is important because ties emerge frequently in the world of the citizen-candidate model.
9    The models are atemporal with no explicit reference to past or future.

Assumptions 5 and 6 are the core of the citizen-candidate model. The electoral equilibrium emerges from the absence of cooperation or commitment, placing the model solidly within the realm of *homo economicus*. Introduce altruism, commitment or cooperation, and anything becomes possible. In so far as the equilibrium is efficient, the bare citizen-candidate model may serve as a platform for identifying 'political failure' associated with aspects of politics assumed away in the minimal formal model.[2]

Assumption 9 requires some interpretation. To say that a model is atemporal may mean i) that there is literally no past or future (so that the world comes into being on January 1 and dissolves on December 31) or ii) that nothing changes over time (so that today is just like yesterday and tomorrow will be just like today). The distinction is important in citizen-candidate models because the latter interpretation, which is the only reasonable interpretation in this context, requires the elected candidate who is deemed all-powerful in the choice of policy to call a new election when his term of office is finished and to surrender office if not reelected; either that, or the citizen-candidate model must be seen as reflecting only part of a political process where much else is done behind the scenes by other departments of government not accounted for within the models. The requirement to hold new elections constitutes a constitutional constraint at the heart of the citizen-candidate model. It is of considerable practical significance because a perennial problem in the design of actual representative government is to stop the elected leader from using the power of office to remain in office indefinitely. 'One man, one vote, once' is eliminated from the model by assumption rather than by any check within the political process.[3] On the other hand, citizens' unwillingness to vote for a promise-breaker in future elections may induce selfish politicians to keep their word today.

The two articles – Osborne and Slivinski (1996) and Besley and Coate (1997)– were written independently but have much in common. Both incorporate voting for issues and voting for people in the same framework of analysis. Both dispense with the artificial separation in the earlier literature between motives of voters and motives of candidates. Both describe politics as the determination through voting of one out of a set of feasible policies. Both have the characteristics of the citizen-candidate model as set out above. There are also several differences.

The most important difference is in their assumptions about the scope of public policy. Osborne and Slivinski restrict the set of alternative policy choices to a left-right continuum. All policies can be identified with points on a line, and all voters' preferences are single peaked. Besley and Coate are much more ambitious. They postulate an unspecified and unlimited set of policy options among which some option must eventually be chosen. Policies may be multi-dimensional. The set of feasible policies might be anything whatsoever, no matter how complex or diverse, and not excluding the allocation among voters of the entire national income.

There are differences in the rewards of office. Osborne and Slivinski impose a fixed cost of running of office and a fixed reward to the successful candidate, over and above the reward implicit in the right to choose public policy. Besley and Coate impose a cost of running for office but no benefit to the office holder over and above the right to choose public policy. Absence of a specific reward for winning is unimportant in the Besley and Coate model because a reward can be embedded in the set of policy options.

There are differences in the behaviour of voters. Osborne and Slivinski assume people vote sincerely. Each person votes for the candidate whose policy preference is closest to his own, regardless of the candidate's chance of winning the election. Besley and Coate assume people vote strategically. In a race between three candidates, a person who prefers the policy of candidate 1 may, nevertheless, vote for candidate 2 to break a tie between candidates 2 and 3 when he knows that candidate 1 has little chance of winning the election.

The articles also differ in their stated purposes. Osborne and Slivinski employ their model for comparing electoral systems, specifically for comparing outcomes under a plurality rule and under a run-off system. The plurality rule elects the candidate with the most votes, regardless of whether or not he has an absolute majority. The run-off system allows for two successive ballots. The winner of the first ballot is elected if and only if he obtains more than 50 per cent of the votes. Otherwise, there is a second vote between the two candidates with the largest number of first ballot votes. Of special interest is the number of candidates entering the race and the validation of Duverger's law that plurality voting promotes two-candidate elections. Besley and Coate focus upon normative aspects of politics. Adapting the economists' criteria for the evaluation of markets to the study of elections, they ask whether a political equilibrium exists (It does.) and whether the equilibrium is likely to be efficient, questions of special interest in their broader framework with no constraints upon the content of the policy space. The model is well-suited for the study of political failure which can be introduced into the model by changes in assumptions about how voters or candidates behave.

The citizen-candidate models are assessed here to determine whether and to what extent they solve or circumvent problems that arose in the earlier literature on the economics of politics. The procedure is to confront citizen-candidate models with situations that proved troublesome in earlier literature and to see whether the models supply plausible outcomes.

## A simple example

Osborne and Slivinski's model is the simpler of the two, for it confines all policy options as points on a line, as in the standard median voter theorem. Imagine a society with voters' preferences representable as points, $x$, evenly spread out on a left-right scale, with 0 as the preference of the median voter. Voting is about the choice of a candidate who, if he wins, chooses his preferred value of $x$, called $x^W$. The cost of becoming a candidate is $c$, the benefit from winning the election is $b$ and utility is denominated in dollars' worth to be commensurate with cost and benefit. Specifically, $\{-|x - x^w|\}$ is the utility of a person who does not become a candidate and whose first preference is $x$ when the winning policy is $x^w$. (Since utility is ordinal, there is no harm in defining utility to be negative, as long as utility increases as one's preferred outcome gets closer to the outcome chosen by the winner of the election, and utility is largest when $x$ equals $x^W$.) The utility of the candidate who wins the election and whose first preference is adopted is $\{b - c\}$. The utility of the candidate whose first preference is $x$ but who loses the election is $\{-|x - x^w| - c\}$. The candidate who loses the election is doubly penalized, bearing both the cost of running and the loss from not obtaining his first preference.

Osborne and Slivinski show how the number of candidates depends on the gap between $b$ and $c$. The utility, $b - c$, of a sole uncontested candidate is the sum of the net gain from running for office and the value of the privilege of choosing one's preferred policy. As long as $b > c$, this candidate would prefer to remain in the race, rather than to be replaced by another candidate with a different first preference. But the candidate may not have that choice. If $b$ is more than twice $c$, a second candidate with the opposite first preference may enter the race; opposite preference means that, if the first preference of the original candidate is $x^*$, the first preference of the newcomer would be $-x^*$, and the two candidates would be tied as they must be if neither has an incentive to drop out of the race. Specifically, both candidates' expected return becomes $b/2 - c - |x^*|$, where $|x^*|$ is the expected cost of a fifty-fifty chance of an outcome of $-x^*$ when one's first preference is $x^*$, or vice versa. As long as $b > 2c$, there is some range of $x^*$ for which expected returns are positive. As $b$ increases, there is room for more candidates to enter the race.

There are problems with this formulation. First, the model requires either a plausible status quo – an assumption about what happens if nobody runs for office – or some mechanism ensuring that there is at least one candidate. For example, it might be supposed that the cost of running for office automatically falls to 0 when there is no opposition. Second, the model does not specify who becomes the candidate when $b > c > b/2$, meaning that the benefit from winning the election is sufficient to cover the cost of running, but that a fifty-fifty chance of getting that benefit is not. Third, the assumption that $b$ and $c$ are externally given constants abstracts from much of the content of electoral politics. The benefit from office may be large or small depending on the honesty of the office holders. Corrupt politicians enjoy huge $b$; honest politicians make do with smaller $b$.

Most importantly, there is no explanation of what happens if $c$ is very much larger than $b$, so that it is never in anybody's interest to run for office, even when groups of voters have much to gain from the election of one candidate rather than another. This presents no problem in practice because political parties share the cost of running for office and donors cover the cost of campaign advertising which is almost always more than the candidate himself can afford. Within the citizen-candidate model, the difficulty might be circumvented by supposing that, for example, in an electorate of $N$ people, each of the $N/2$ right-leaning people for whom $x > 0$ contributes a share $2c/N$ of the cost of the right-leaning candidate, and each of the $N/2$ left-leaning people for whom $x < 0$ contributes a share $2c/N$ of the cost of the left-leaning candidate. Satisfactory in practice, this defence is a violation of the spirit of the citizen-candidate model because it relies on precisely the cooperation and compromise that the citizen-candidate model is intended to avoid. On the other hand, cooperation is a two-edged sword. Once cooperation and compromise are introduced, it is not necessarily restricted to circumstances where everybody becomes better off.

The main proposition in the citizen-candidate models is that 'a political equilibrium exists'. The proposition is correct on its assumptions, but the assumptions are stronger and farther from electoral politics than may at first be supposed. Absence of promises and cooperation has no counterpart in actual political life.

## The paradox of voting

Imagine three people choosing among three options by majority rule voting. The people are $A$, $B$ and $C$. The options are $\alpha$, $\beta$ and $\delta$. Person $A$'s preference ordering among these options is $\alpha\beta\delta$, meaning that he prefers $\alpha$ to $\beta$ to $\delta$. Person $B$'s preference ordering is $\beta\delta\alpha$. Person $C$'s preference ordering is $\delta\alpha\beta$. Thus, in pairwise voting among options, $\alpha$ defeats $\beta$, $\beta$ defeats $\delta$, but $\delta$ defeats $\alpha$, giving rise to an intransitive social ordering. The question at hand is whether this paradox of voting becomes any less likely or less paradoxical when voting is embedded in a citizen-candidate model.

It is convenient, though not strictly necessary, to add a little structure to people's preferences. Suppose everybody's utility function is the same in the special sense that there is a common utility function defined over orders of preference rather than over outcomes per se. A person's utility can take on one of three values, $u(I)$, $u(II)$ and $u(III)$, where $u(I)$ is a person's utility if he attains his first preference, and so on. For person $A$, $u(I)$ is his utility if the outcome of voting is option $\alpha$. For person $B$, $u(I)$ is his utility if the outcome of voting is option $\beta$. For person $C$, $u(I)$ is his utility if the outcome of voting is option $\delta$. By assumption,

$$u(I) \geq u(II) \geq u(III) \tag{11.1}$$

By the rules of the citizen-candidate model, each person decides whether or not to run as a candidate, each person votes for the candidate of his choice and the winner among the candidates chooses his preferred option. As the model contains no restriction on the cost of becoming a candidate, there is no harm in supposing it to be 0 so that the cost of running for election can be ignored.

Now, depending on the strengths of people's preferences, there are two inter-esting cases. In the first, people are anxious to attain their most preferred option, but, otherwise, do not much care whether their second preferences or their third preferences prevails. In the second case, people are very anxious to avoid their least preferred option, but do not much care whether their first preference or their second preference prevails.

The limiting form of the first case is

$$u(I) > u(II) = u(III) \tag{11.2}$$

With that constellation of preferences, all three people become candidates, all candidates vote for themselves, there is a tie among the three candidates, and the tie is broken by the flip of a three-sided coin. In this case, voting within the citizen-candidate model boils down to choosing among options by lot!

The limiting form of the second case is

$$u(I) = u(II) > u(III) \tag{11.3}$$

When one's objective is to avoid one's worst option, one would always prefer a certainty of one's second preference to a lottery with equal chances of the all three options. Specifically,

$$u(II) > (1/3)u(I) + (1/3)u(II) + (1/3)u(III) \tag{11.4}$$

a condition implied by Equation (11.3) but never by Equation (11.2). Were this so, person $A$, whose first preference is $\alpha$ and whose second preference is $\beta$, would prefer a certainty of $\beta$ to a lottery with equal probabilities of options $\alpha$, $\beta$ and $\delta$. Person $A$'s best strategy is to avoid becoming a candidate. By not running for office, person $A$ assures the adoption of option $\beta$ which, while not his first choice, is at least preferable to $\delta$. Once person $A$ has dropped out, person $B$ has every incentive to remain in the race, and it no longer matters what person $C$ does. As long as person $C$ remains in the race, the election becomes a choice between options $\beta$ and $\delta$. Person $B$ wins two-to-one with his own vote and that of person $A$, and they choose their preferred option, $\beta$. If person $C$ drops out, as he would if there were a cost to running for office, person $B$ wins by acclamation.

The difficulty with this scenario is that all three people can play the same game. Consider person $C$ whose worst option, $\beta$, prevails when person $A$ is the first to drop out of the race. Person $C$ could avoid this outcome by dropping out of the race instead. Then person $A$ would acquire an incentive to remain a candidate, and person $A$'s first preference, $\alpha$, would prevail with the support of persons $A$ and $C$. Person $B$ has an analogous incentive. But three people cannot all be first to drop out of the race. Either politics reduces to choice by lot, or something outside the model must be invoked to determine who runs for office and who does not. The counterpart of the paradox of voting in the citizen-candidate model is that the model may churn out many equilibria, with no indication which will prevail.

Nothing changes when the three people become three groups of identical people as long as the number of people in each group is the same and a mechanism is devised for choosing one candidate from each group. Otherwise, if one of the three groups constitutes a clear majority of the population, its representative must necessarily win the election and its first preference prevails. A plurality (more votes than either of the other groups, but less than 50 per cent of the electorate) would do equally well when preferences are as shown in Equation (11.2), but not when preferences are as shown in Equation (11.3) because it would remain advantageous for any of the three candidates to be the first to drop out of the race. Politics would become troublesome if winning an election were advantageous to the winner and not just to the group to which they belong. A situation could easily arise where, for instance, option $\alpha$ would prevail when there is only one candidate in each group, but where option $\beta$ or $\delta$ prevails instead because two stubborn candidates split the vote of group $A$ while only one candidate emerges from group $B$ or from group $C$.

## The exploitation problem

By imposing no limits whatsoever on the scope of public policy, Besley and Coate have, in effect, designed a politics to deal with the exploitation problem. A political equilibrium in this model is an outcome where no voter wishes to change his vote, no candidate wishes to withdraw from the race, nobody else wishes to enter, and some candidate is destined to win by obtaining more votes than any other candidate or by tying with a group of other candidates and then winning the lottery among them. Besley and Coate prove, on certain assumptions, that a political equilibrium exists and is efficient. As the policy space is entirely unconstrained, the existence and efficiency of the political equilibrium must extend even to the case where voting is about the allocation among voters of the entire national income. Voting about who is to be rich and who is to be poor would seem to be no less feasible than voting about anything else.

To test this contention, consider a society of $N$ people with a fixed national income, $Y$, to be allocated politically, and suppose for the moment that there is no cost of running for office. Politics is now about the choice of a vector $\{y^1, y^2, y^3, \ldots, y^N\}$ where $y^i$ is the income assigned to person $i$ and where there are no constraints on any $y^i$ except that every $y^i$ must be greater than or equal to 0 and that the sum of all $y^i$ must be equal to $Y$. It is obvious what happens. Everybody becomes a candidate, everybody votes for himself, there is a massive tie with one vote for each candidate, the winner is determined by lot, and the winner grabs the entire national income for himself, since, by assumption, office-holders are unconstrained and completely selfish. If person $w$ is the winner of the lottery, then $y^w = Y$ and $y^i = 0$ for all $i$ not equal to $w$. The citizen-candidate model assigns the entire national income to one person chosen by lot with nothing left over for anybody else. Notwithstanding the extreme inequality, this outcome is strictly speaking efficient. It is Pareto optimal because, when one person gets everything, there is no way to rearrange the economy to make at least one person better off without at the same time making anybody else worse off. It is Pareto optimal for the 'Dear Leader' to exploit the rest of the population for his own prosperity and glory. On the other hand, this perverse efficiency is not what most people have in mind when including efficiency among the attributes of a good society.

A distinction can be drawn between efficiency ex ante and ex post. Ex post, the outcome in the citizen-candidate model is efficient in the trivial sense that there is at least one person, the elected dictator, who cannot be made better off by any reassignment among people of the national income. Ex ante, the outcome is not efficient at all. As long as people's utility of income functions are concave, each and every person is better off with an equal share of the national income than with an equal chance acquiring the entire national income in a winner-take-all lottery with the national income as the prize. Everybody prefers a sure income of $Y/N$ to a gamble with a $1/N$ chance of an income of $Y$ and a $(N-1)/N$ chance of no income at all. As long as people are risk averse, a benevolent dictator or cooperation among people could make everybody better off ex ante than they would be in the outcome of the citizen-candidate model.

Even ex post efficiency disappears with the introduction of a cost, $c$, of running for office. To keep matters simple, suppose that $c$ is less than $Y/N$, that there is some mechanism in society enabling anybody and everybody to obtain the required cost of running for election, that the net national income available for consumption is automatically reduced by the sum of all candidates' cost of running for election and that the successful candidate is empowered to choose the allocation among people of the remainder of the national income. The outcome is the same as before, except that the income of the winning candidate becomes $Y - cN$ rather than $Y$. Once again, everybody runs for office, every candidate gets one vote (his own), and the elected candidate is determined by lot. If person $w$ is the winner of the lottery, then $y^w = Y - cN$ and $y^i = 0$ for all $i$ not equal to $w$.[4]

In an earlier draft of their article, Besley and Coate proposed an ingenious solution to the exploitation problem. Suppose society consisted of $N-1$ selfish people and 1 altruist. As office holder, each selfish person would assign the entire national income to himself, leaving nothing for anybody else, but the altruist would divide the national income equally because he deems that to be the fair and honourable thing to do. Since everybody's preferences are common knowledge, the only possible outcome is for the altruist alone to run for office and to be elected unanimously. Every selfish person reasons as follows: if I run for office and vote for myself, and if everybody else does likewise, I have a $1/N$ chance of acquiring the entire national income coupled with a $(N-1)/N$ chance of acquiring nothing. On the other hand, if I vote for the altruist, he is bound to win because he would then acquire at least 2 votes (his own and mine) in circumstances where nobody else would ever acquire more than 1 (his own). On winning and becoming the office holder, the altruist supplies me with a sure income of $Y/N$ which, as a risk averse person, I prefer to the gamble where I and everybody else run for office and vote for oneself. Since all selfish people reason as I do, we all vote for the altruist, and the altruist wins unanimously.

There is a nastier possibility. Once it becomes possible for a candidate to commit to something other than what is best for himself alone, there is no limit to what may transpire. If saints may commit to full equality of income, sinners may equally well commit to sharing the entire national income among some sinful majority of voters. The exploitation problem comes roaring back, and the virtues of the citizen-candidate model are completely lost.

Several problems may be distinguished. First, the appearance of an altruist seems at variance with the spirit, if not with the letter, of the rest of the model. The overriding objective of the economics of politics is to explain politics in the way economists explain markets, as the outcome of universal greed. To postulate altruism is to depart from that enterprise. Second, it is hard to see how, in practice, the altruist would be identified in a world where everybody else is rigidly selfish and where it is in the interest of each candidate to claim the mantle of selflessness for himself. Presumably the altruist wears a halo. Third, and most important, through the universal altruist wins unanimously in a contest where everybody else is strictly selfish, he must lose out to a candidate with a more limited scope of concern. For example, in a society where just over half the population is of religion $J$ and just under half the population is of religion $M$, a candidate whose altruism extends no further than to the adherents of religion $J$ – who believes fervently that adherents of religion $M$ are unworthy of prosperity – must win in a pairwise vote with a universal altruist. This religious candidate wins against the universal altruist even in the case where everybody else is strictly selfish and not particularly religious. Suppose the population consists of $N_J$ adherents of religion $J$ and $N_M$ adherents of religion $M$, where $N_J > N_M$. The religious candidate can offer an income of $Y/N_J$ to each adherent of religion $J$ as compared with an income of $Y/(N_J + N_M)$ which is all that the universal altruist could offer. All adherents of religion $J$ vote for the religious candidate, he wins, adherents of religion $J$ acquire incomes of $Y/N_J$, and adherents of religion $M$ acquire incomes of $0$.

The exploitation problem arises with no less vehemence in the citizen-candidate world than it did in the earlier literature of the economics of politics. The moral of the story remains that the scope of electorally determined policy must somehow be restricted if democratic government is to work at all. Difficult as it is to locate the appropriate boundary between public and private spheres, it is evident from this example that there must be some minimal domain of property rights, for the allocation of the entire national income cannot be determined as the outcome of the vote.

## The Nash equilibrium as a criterion for order in the political realm

Both versions of the citizen-candidate model rely heavily upon the Nash equilibrium, where each person's action is the best response to the actions of every other person in society. Among candidates and voters, there is a Nash equilibrium when it is in the interest of no candidate to drop out of the race as long as all other candidates hold fast, it is in the interest of no person not already a candidate to become one, and nobody wishes to change his vote as long as every other person's vote remains unchanged.

The Nash equilibrium is imported into the political realm from the world of perfect competition where people respond to prices rather than to other people and where it is reasonable to assume that each person looks upon prices as invariant, or, to be more precise, as not sufficiently responsive to one's own actions to make that response worth considering when deciding what to do. Politics is different. Consider once again the two-candidate equilibrium in the Osborne and Slivinski model where policies can be represented as points on a line, where the distribution of all voters' first preferences is uniform and where the first preference of the median voter is at 0. With the appropriate balance between the cost of running for election and the benefit of being elected, there can be a Nash equilibrium with two candidates whose first preferences are at $x$ and $-x$ as long as $x$ is not so large that a third candidate with a first preference of 0 can acquire a third or more of the votes. This outcome is a thorough-going Nash equilibrium, but it may not yield the determinacy that a Nash equilibrium is normally supposed to convey.

To see why, consider a third potential candidate whose first preference among all alternatives is at $x - \varepsilon$ where $\varepsilon$ is a small positive number. As long as the two original candidates hold fast (as they are assumed to do in the Nash equilibrium), this potential third candidate would desist from entering the race. By doing so, and as long as neither of the other candidates withdraws, the new candidate would take more votes from the candidate whose first preference is at $x$ than from the candidate whose first preference is $-x$, delivering the election to the latter candidate. By entering, the would-be candidate would be twice harmed, once by having to bear the cost of running for election and again from switching the outcome of the election from equal chances of $-x$ and $x$ (which is very close to his preferred alternative) to a certainty of $-x$. It would seem that no third candidate has an incentive to enter the race.

But if the reward for office is substantial, a third candidate might try to muscle out the one of the two original candidates. The interloper may address the original candidate at $x$ as follows:

> We both know that, unless one of us drops out, that awful person whose first preference is $-x$ is sure to win. If you drop out, you will forgo the reward for winning but you will at least attain a policy outcome that is insignificantly different from your first preference because, in a contest between a candidate whose first preference is $-x$ and a candidate whose first preference is $x - \varepsilon$, the latter is bound to win. I might add that I myself am very stubborn, and, having entered the race, would consider it an unacceptable humiliation to withdraw. You being reasonable, should withdraw instead.

One cannot say a priori what the original candidate would do, but it is not inconceivable that he would withdraw.

Notwithstanding the applicability of the Nash equilibrium in large markets, it is a dubious concept for explaining interactions among actual or potential candidates in an election, for it takes no account of the influence of one's actions (and people's realization of that influence) on the actions of other people. It allows for each potential candidate to choose whether to run for election depending on who else is running already, but not on who else might choose to run, or who might withdraw from the race, in response to one's choice.

A distinction can be drawn among three, rather than just two, types of behaviour: *sincere* behaviour where one supports what one favours regardless of the consequences, *strategic* behaviour where one acts to procure what one sees as the best attainable outcome given what others are doing, and *manipulative* behaviour where one acts to procure what one sees as the best attainable outcome taking account not just of what others are doing, but of how others would respond to one's actions. One may think of the Nash equilibrium as the appropriate notion of equilibrium for the analysis of large competitive markets where each participant sees himself as too small a part of the market to have any significant effect upon the market price. Reliance on the Nash equilibrium becomes dubious when and to the extent that politics is manipulative. The citizen-candidate models invoke a Nash equilibrium for interactions among a small number of candidates for office.

Consider just two people, $A$ and $B$, whose actions, $a_A$ and $a_B$, are chosen from sets of available options and whose utilities, $u^A$ and $u^B$ are functions of both person's actions. A Nash equilibrium is a pair of actions, $a_1^*$ and $a_2^*$, such that

$$a_A^* = \text{argmax}(a_A)u^A(a_A, a_B^*) \tag{11.5}$$

and

$$a_B^* = \text{argmax}(a_B)u^B(a_A^*, a_B) \tag{11.6}$$

Each party chooses a strategy to maximize utility when the strategy of the other party is looked upon as invariant.

A manipulative equilibrium is a pair of actions, $a_A^{**}$ and $a_B^{**}$, such that

$$a_A^{**} = \text{argmax}(a_A)u^A(a_A, a_B^{**}(a_A)) \tag{11.7}$$

and

$$a_B^{**} = \text{argmax}(a_B)u^B(a_A^{**}(a_B), a_B) \tag{11.8}$$

where the functions $a_A^{**}(a_B)$ and $a_B^{**}(a_A)$ show anticipated responses to one another's actions. Person $A$ might be inclined to take one action if assured that person $B$ would not respond by changing his behaviour, but to take a different action in anticipation of person $B$'s response. With a choice restricted to actions $a_A^1$ and $a_A^2$, person $A$ may reason as follows: if I choose action $a_A^1$, person $B$ will react by choosing action $a_B^1$, but if I choose action $a_A^2$, person $B$ will react by choosing action $a_B^2$. In choosing between actions $a_A^1$ and $a_A^2$, person $A$ anticipates not a fixed response $a_B$, but a pair of responses $a_B^1$ and $a_B^2$. Thus, person $A$ chooses $a_A^1$ in preference to $a_A^2$ if and only if $u^A(a_A^1, a_B^1) > u^A(a_A^2, a_B^2)$. Person $B$ makes a similar calculation based on his expectation of person $A$'s behaviour. The sets $a_B(a_A)$ and $a_A(a_B)$ can be thought as the expectational penumbra of the actions of persons $A$ and $B$. As anticipations, these sets may but need not be consistent with one another. It is difficult to say how best to incorporate a manipulative equilibrium into a citizen-candidate model or whether such an equilibrium would exist in the political realm. There may be no political equilibrium. The economist's ideal may turn out to be elusive.

## The cost of running for election and the probability of winning

Three important aspects of politics are assumed away by the assumption that each candidate bears a fixed cost of running for election.

1   The cost of running may be too high for any one candidate to bear all alone, but not prohibitive for a group of like-minded people – in effect, a political party – to bear collectively in financing the candidacy of one member of the group.
2   A candidate's probability of winning may depend on the amount of money spent on his campaign.
3   The authority of office may be subdivided among partially competing jurisdictions: federal, provincial and local government, two houses of parliament, executive, legislature and judiciary.

The first of these considerations has been discussed earlier in the chapter. Millions of voters may have a stake in an election, with much to lose if their preferred candidate is not elected, but the cost of candidacy to the candidate may be higher than the candidate's benefit from winning the election. The obvious solution, sharing the cost among the candidate's supporters, is contrary to the spirit of the citizen-candidate model that seeks to explain voting in the absence of cooperation.

On the other hand, cooperation is always at the mercy of free-riders. Though everybody in group $A$ stands to gain from financing a candidate collectively, it is in the each member of the group to refuse to pay his share as long as he is confident that others in the group will not refuse to pay theirs. If people in group $B$ are cooperative while people in group $A$ are not, a candidate from group $B$ might run unopposed and group $B$'s preferred option would be chosen. People do cooperate voluntarily within political parties and for charitable purposes. To what extent society can depend on voluntary cooperation is an open question. In the citizen-candidate model there is none, but the model takes no account of the possibility that the cost of running for office exceeds any person's benefit from the right to choose from among the options at stake in the election.

A curious feature of the citizen-candidate models is their treatment of uncertainty. Outcomes of elections are completely certain in one sense, but completely uncertain in another. Elections are completely certain in the sense that voters know when they step into the ballot box either which candidate will win or which candidates will be tied, and they know that all tied candidates have the same chance of winning the election. Elections are completely uncertain in that voters do not know what the outcome of the coin toss will be. A candidate's probability of winning is restricted to just three values: 1, 0 and $1/W$ where $W$ is the number of candidates with any chance of winning the election. The probability is 1 when a candidate is sure to win. The probability is 0 when a candidate is sure to lose but remains in the race regardless because, as shown by Besley and Coate in an ingenious example, his presence in the election affects other candidates' chances of winning. The probability is $1/W$ when a tie among $W$ candidates will be broken by the flip of a $W$-sided coin. Every voter is assumed to know the preferences of every other voter and of every candidate in the election.

This feature of the citizen-candidate model leaves no place for campaign expenditures to influence the electorate. Voters are assumed to be knowledgeable enough and rational enough that campaign advertising could not convince anybody of anything and would be altogether ineffective. The nature of the cost of running for election, $c$, is left unexplained. It is best thought of as a registration fee rather than as expenditure to inform voters of one's candidacy or to persuade voters that one is the superior candidate. A huge aspect of democratic politics is postulated away.

Instead of restricting a candidate's chances to 0, 1 or $1/w$, it might be supposed that a candidate's chance of winning the election is influenced by campaign advertising and other expenditures to get oneself or one's candidate elected. With only two political candidates, left $(L)$ and right $(R)$, the left candidate's probability of winning, $p$, can be thought of as

$$p(x^L, x^R, c^L, c^R) + \varepsilon \tag{11.9}$$

where $x^L$ and $x^R$ are the policies adopted by the two candidates, $c^L$ and $c^R$ are their chosen campaign expenditures, and $\varepsilon$ is a random variable reflecting the inevitable uncertainty of political life, swings in the mood of the electorate, a candidate becoming suddenly ill, a scandal, and so on. Typically, a candidate's chance of winning depends upon the time and effort of his supporters and well as upon the amount of cash spent on his behalf, but $c^L$ and $x^L$ need not be independent. Interpreting $c^L$ as efforts by the party faithful, the value of $c^L$ may depend on the left candidate's choice of $x^L$; the more leftish his policy, the more time and effort his supporters can be expected to supply on his behalf. Policy influences voters directly when preferences are invariant, and indirectly through the behaviour of contributors and activists. More importantly, since campaign expenditures are likely to be much larger than any one candidate can muster all alone, effective candidacy would require cooperation among large groups of people and the need for such cooperation becomes part of the rationale for the establishment of political parties. The citizen-candidate is a more extreme abstraction than might at first be supposed.

There is a similar problem with the specification of the reward for office. Osborne and Slivinski postulate a fixed monetary reward. The difficulty with this specification is that the problem of controlling leaders is swept under the rug. The thwarting of dictatorship – not the elected dictator in these models, but the real predatory dictators of this world – is an ongoing objective of democratic government, an objective that is sometimes achieved and sometimes not. A dictatorship, elected or otherwise, would be uncontrollable. Beyond the confines of the citizen-candidate model lie other political institutions and a division of powers that somehow holds democratic government together.

## Constitutional constraints, mixed government and property rights

A theory of representative democracy might be expected to yield a political analogue of Adam Smith's invisible hand, a political equilibrium analogous to the competitive equilibrium in a market economy. There is, however, an essential difference between economic and political equilibrium. An economic equilibrium stands upon an allocation of property rights, presumed to be enforced by the government. A political equilibrium must stand on its own, for there is no government behind government to keep government in check. Adherence to political rules must be endogenous. A theory of representative government must include an explanation of why rules are obeyed. The contrast between political and economic equilibrium is especially marked with regard to the distribution of income. Efficiency – that nobody can be made better off without making others worse off at the same time – may be a sufficient criterion for evaluating the equilibrium in a competitive economy because a tolerable distribution of income may be entailed in a prior distribution of property rights or because a government that enforces property rights is empowered to narrow the distribution of income. Forces outside the formal model may ensure a distribution of income not so unequal as to undermine the required support for the system of property rights in the population as a whole. Except for people's willingness to abide by the rules, there are no such forces ensuring a satisfactory political equilibrium. Some check is provided within the citizen-candidate model by the assumption that voters are entirely aware of the all candidates' preferences, but this assumption is insufficient in two respects. It is grossly unrealistic and, more importantly, it is inadequate for the task when, as is customary in economics, everybody is assumed to be unreservedly self-interested. In politics, the rules of entitlement are constitutional constraints.

Two constitutional constraints are especially important within the citizen-candidate models: constraints on the authority of the elected leader, and constraints on the set of policy options. The former is common to both versions of the model. Citizens must obey the elected leader, but he, in turn, must be prepared to call a new election when his term of office is up and to make way for his successor if that is what the voters decide. The latter constraint is different in the two models. Osborne and Slivinski restrict the authority of the elected leader to the choice of a point on a left–right continuum, excluding all else from the political realm and relegating the rest of life to the private sector, to civil rights or to fixed custom. Besley and Coate empower the elected leader to choose an option from among a set of feasible options taking 'account of both technological and constitutional constraints on policy choices' (1997: 87), but nothing more is said about the nature of the constraints and no specific constraints are incorporated in subsequent analysis. Presumably, the exploitation problem could be circumvented by a constitutional ban upon *ad hominem* taxation and upon decisions manifestly favouring one group over another, but that would leave unanswered the question of why such a ban would be respected. There are several difficulties here:

Constitutional constraints required to render a citizen-candidate regime tolerable may be more restrictive than can be imposed in practice. Modern government has many tasks to perform and many decisions to make. Democratic government is designed to empower leaders to do the country's business without succumbing to the temptation – irresistible when an all-powerful leader is literally unconstrained in the execution of his tasks – to convert oneself into a real dictator as opposed to the innocuous elected dictator of the citizen-candidate models. The nation's work must be done without at the same time empowering leaders to lord it over the rest of society, taking the lion's share of the national income for themselves, denying rights to opponents and preserving their privileges in perpetuity. This may require constitutional constraints above and beyond the assumptions of the citizen-candidate models.

A reasonably vibrant private sector is commonly believed to be required for the preservation of democratic government. As discussed in preceding chapters, the authority to allocate the entire national income would be too great a prize for the elected leader. A leader with such authority over his fellow citizens would be unlikely to relinquish that authority at the whim of the electorate, for leaders voted out of office would be entirely at the mercy of their successors. Exiles from public service – dismissed whistleblowers, critics of public policy or opponents of the party in power – need a refuge in the private sector to escape consignment to a life of poverty. This consideration presents no problem for the Osborne and Slivinski version of the citizen-candidate model, for the postulated one-dimensional set of policy options cannot encompass the allocation of the entire national income. It places a severe restriction on the set of options in the Besley and Coate version of the model.

An organizational restriction is equally important. Government must not be organized as a single great hierarchy. There is a venerable doctrine in political theory that the formidable powers of government can only be contained and democracy can only be preserved when government is divided into legislature, executive and judiciary, each with its own domain of authority. Mixed government is more than just a division of labour. It is advocated in the hope that the excesses of each branch of government will be constrained by the rest. Necessary as it may be as a defence against dictatorship, mixed government is the antithesis of the key assumption of the citizen-candidate models, assumption 5 above that the office holder adopts whatever policy he prefers.

There is another way of thinking about constitutional constraints. In a contest of brute strength, people are not too far from equal; any person can be defeated by any two other people, or at most by three or four. Thus, if the elected candidate is to exert his will upon thousands or even millions of other people, choosing his own preferred policy from a set of feasible policies, it must be because others are prepared to obey. Obedience is procured by the threat of punishment imposed by officials, each fearing that he will be punished if he fails to do his part. The simplest such *expectational equilibrium* is based on a governmental hierarchy with an absolute leader, an emperor or a Stalin, at the top. A written or unwritten constitution may be looked upon as specifying when and how the bonds of authority are to be broken. Yes, the president (or his administration) may imprison you in a wide range of circumstances. No, the jailer will no longer hold you in captivity once the courts decree that the authority to do so is void. A constitution must be more than a 'parchment barrier'. It requires the bonds of obedience be dissolved when the constitution requires. Mixed government with overlapping spheres of jurisdiction among its branches and a reasonably large private sector may be necessary conditions for any constitution, however noble its words, to play its intended role in controlling the state.

***

Applied to elections, the Nash equilibrium has been found wanting in two connected respects. First, there may be no Nash equilibrium in dealings among candidates staking out positions and running for office. Each person's best action may depend not just upon what others are doing now, but upon how others can be expected to react to his behaviour. Uncoordinated self-interested behaviour can yield grossly inefficient equilibria, multiple equilibria, equilibria procured by coin-tossing with no counterpart in actual political life, or no equilibria at all. Even the strong assumptions in the citizen-candidate model are not always sufficient to generate satisfactory outcomes. A virtue of the citizen-candidate models is that they draw attention in the strongest possible way to the problem of how far democratic politics can rely on individual self-interest within established institutions and when conscious cooperation is indispensable. There may in the end be no thoroughgoing political analogue to the competitive equilibrium where people respond to prices rather than to one another.

Second, preservation of what most people see as a good society requires citizens to be public-spirited and may depend upon an intricate network of ill-defined constitutional constraints, incorporating reasonably strong property rights and mixed government where each branch serves as a constraint upon the ambitions, the excesses and the predatory propensities of the rest, and where spheres of authority of the different branches overlap to some extent, creating a radical and irreducible indeterminacy in democratic government. Citizens must be sufficiently public-spirited to investigate the policies of the different candidates and to vote. Citizen-candidate models postulate that nobody abstains despite the fact that one's of influencing the outcome of the election is virtually nil. The multiplicity of political institutions and the checks and balances among them require deal-making and conscious cooperation not representable as a Nash equilibrium. Legislation typically requires deals among legislators. Deals are required when the passage of laws requires the assent of two legislatures such as the senate and the house of representatives. Platforms of political parties have to be negotiated. Negotiation may lead to gridlock. Gridlock has on occasion paved the way to dictatorship. Democracy is not and cannot be just about voting. Democracy is a highly complex institution where voting must, of course, have a central role to play, but where voting has to be supported by the unpredictable and unreliable realms of negotiation and compromise. It is perhaps for this reason that democratic government has proved so difficult to transplant to countries where traditions of civil rights, property rights, negotiation and compromise have not had time to take root.

The ideal of an economics of politics is a political equilibrium comparable to the equilibrium in a competitive economy. That being ultimately unattainable, a more modest objective emerges instead: to represent as much as possible of the political realm as an equilibrium where each person does what is best for himself alone, so as to identify the minimal domain within which something more than self-interest – conscious cooperation, public spiritedness or respect for constitutional constraints – is required. Citizen-candidate models can be assessed as part of a larger enterprise by social scientists to stake out the boundary between equilibrium and negotiation, balancing the risk of a slide into dictatorship from excessive, undivided and unconstrained public authority against the risk of a slide into dictatorship from failure of the different branches of, or participants in, government to negotiate a generally acceptable public policy.

## Notes

1  This chapter is a revision of an article in *Public Choice*, Usher (2005). I am grateful for helpful comments from Tim Besley, Steve Coate, Martin Osborne, Al Slivinski, and Stan Winer. Needless to say, the usual disclaimer applies.

2  See Besley and Coate (1998: 139–56). The political failure discussed in that paper is the government's refusal, in certain circumstances, to undertake investments that would increase some people's incomes without at the same time reducing anybody else's income. Such Pareto optimal investment opportunities *might* be rejected because they would bring about a change in the political equilibrium. Consider a simple example in the spirit of Besley and Coate where the only public decision is the choice of a rate for the negative income tax and where the initial distribution of income is 51 per cent poor people and 49 per cent rich people. The elected leader would a poor person who, in his own interest, would impose a high rate a tax (perhaps as high as 100 per cent) and a correspondingly high transfer of income per person in accordance with the negative income tax. Now consider an opportunity to raise the incomes of a randomly chosen group of poor people, a group consisting of 2 per cent of the total population, up to the income per head of the rich people, without at the same time reducing the incomes of anybody else. The elected leader may well turn down this opportunity because, as a side effect, it would lower the proportion of poor people from 51 per cent to 49 per cent, transforming the rich from a minority into a majority and leading to the election of a new leader from among the rich. Being rich, the new elected leader would substantially reduce the rate of the income tax (perhaps to as low as 0), and the transfer to the poor would be reduced accordingly. Being poor,

the original elected leader may have had more to lose from the abolition of the transfer through the negative income tax than he had to gain from his 3.92 per cent chance (2/51) of being one of the lucky people whose pre-tax incomes would have been increased.

3 A curious aspect of this atemporal assumption is that, though the electoral process may remain the same year after year, the outcome of the vote need not be invariant. An important consequence of the electoral procedure in the citizen-candidate model is the multiplicity of candidates with equal chances of winning the election. For instance, in an equilibrium where two candidates have equal chances of winning the election, there is a 50 per cent chance that next year's elected leader will not be the same as this year's elected leader and that policy will differ from year to year accordingly. Full uniformity from year to year as is normally implied by the atemporal assumption would violate other assumptions of the model.

4 Besley and Coate recognize these difficulties. In their footnote 19, they call attention to inefficiencies associated with the cost of running for election and the distinction between ex ante and ex post efficiency.

# References

Besley, T. and Coate, S. (1997) An economic model of representative democracy, *Quarterly Journal of Economics*, 112, 85–114.

Besley, T. and Coate, S. (1998) Sources of inefficiency in a representative democracy: a dynamic analysis, *American Economic Review*, 88, 139–56.

Black, Duncan (1958) *The Theory of Committees and Elections*, New York: Cambridge University Press.

Downs, Anthony (1957) *An Economic Theory of Democracy*, New York: Harper, p. 28.

Osborne, Martin and Slivinski, Al (1996) A model of political competition with citizen candidates *Quarterly Journal of Economics*, 111(1) 65–96.

Usher, D. (2005) Assessing the citizen-candidate model, *Public Choice*, 125(1–2), 43–65.

# 12 The significance of the probabilistic voting theorem[1]

Citizens have two entitlements. As owners of property, inclusive of their own skill and labour power, they are entitled to the return from their property, appropriately adjusted by taxes and transfers. As voters they are entitled to influence the rules of society, including those rules that provide them with income in the form of unemployment insurance, an old age pension, welfare, and so on. Naturally, the entitlements conflict at the margin, but that is not the subject of this chapter. Of each entitlement separately, it may be asked i) whether there is a predictable outcome for society as a whole when each citizen exercises his rights in his own interest exclusively, and ii) whether that outcome is desirable in any sense of the term. For entitlement to property, the standard economists' answers to these questions are 'yes' and 'yes', subject to well-known qualifications and interpretations that need not be discussed here. That is the principal message of the fundamental theorems of welfare economics.

For voting, on the other hand, it is commonly believed that the answers to these questions are 'no' and 'no'. The first 'no' is a reflection of the paradox of voting. When self-interested people vote about the allocation of a sum of money among themselves and in the absence of cooperation within groups of voters, there is no unique allocation that defeats every other allocation in a pairwise vote; there is no voting analogue to the equilibrium allocation of goods and services in a competitive market. The second 'no' is more complex. It is based on the belief that cooperation among subgroups of self-interested voters may lead to a nasty outcome in which a majority of the population employs the power of the vote to dispossess everybody else. Contemplation of this feature of voting has given rise to a profound pessimism about the prospects for democratic government. It has been claimed that democracy must in the end provoke a radical exploitation by some majority of voters of the corresponding minority. It has been claimed that no reasonable person would trust himself and his property to the whims of the majority, as democracy requires one to do. This standard anti-democratic argument has cropped up at various times throughout history and was the basis of the classical economists' mistrust of universal franchise.[2] Few would deny that democratic government has worked better in practice than the anti-democratic argument would lead one to predict. Rather, the role of the anti-democratic argument now is to identify weaknesses in democratic society so that they may be repaired by the appropriate choice of public policy.

It is in this context that the probabilistic voting theorem is interesting.[3] Broadly speaking, the theorem signifies that there is a voting equilibrium after all, that the exploitation paradigm is an optical illusion, and that the anti-democratic argument is misplaced. In the words of one of the theorem's enthusiasts, the theorem shows 'that democratic political markets are organized to promote wealth-maximizing outcomes, that these markets are highly competitive, and that political entrepreneurs are rewarded for efficient behaviour' (Wittman, 1989: 1395). The message of this chapter is not that the theorem is wrong on its assumptions, but that the assumptions under which it is right are much stronger and less realistic than is generally realized, that the theorem does not bear the political implications claimed on its behalf, and that, for all practical purposes, the anti-democratic argument emerges unscathed from its encounter with the probabilistic voting theorem.

The chapter begins with a brief exposition of the exploitation problem in the context of the probabilistic voting theorem. Then, the theorem is proved. Finally it is explained why the theorem fails to defend majority rule voting from the exploitation problem.

## The paradox of voting and the exploitation problem

Imagine a society with three groups of voters, two political parties, and a national income conferred on society as a whole like manna from heaven. The number of people in each group is the same. Voters want income. Political parties want office. The entire national income is allocated politically. Each party proposes a platform that allocates the national income among the three groups, subject to the restriction that people within each group are treated alike. Each person casts a vote on the basis of a comparison of the offers of the rival political parties, the party with the most votes wins, and the national income is allocated accordingly. Voting is, for the moment, assumed to be *deterministic*. Each person votes for the political party that provides his group with the highest offer of income, no matter how small the gap between the parties' offers may be.

The national income is $YN$, where $Y$ is the income per head and $N$ is total population. Both $Y$ and $N$ are assumed to be invariant. There are $N/3$ people in each group. The groups are $A$, $B$ and $C$, the parties are $R$ and $D$, and the parties' platforms are

$$Y^R = \{y_A^R, y_B^R, y_C^R\} \quad \text{and} \quad Y^D = \{y_A^D, y_B^D, y_C^D\} \tag{12.1}$$

Each platform is an allocation of the national income among the three groups of voters.

The income $y_A^R$ is the offer to each person in Group $A$ in the platform of Party $R$, and the other terms are similarly defined. Necessarily,

$$y_A^R + y_B^R + y_C^R = y_A^D + y_B^D + y_C^D = 3Y \tag{12.2}$$

Political parties are somehow compelled to be honest, and to adopt their platforms as public policy if they are elected. Parties choose platforms to maximize votes, $V^R$ and $V^D$, where $V^R$ is the percentage of all votes cast for the Party $R$ and $V^D$ is the percentage of all votes cast for Party $D$.[4] Specifically,

$$V^R = (1/3)\{v_A^R + v_B^R + v_C^R\} \quad \text{and} \quad V^D = (1/3)\{v_A^D + v_B^D + v_C^D\} \tag{12.3}$$

where $v_A^R$ is the percentage of people in Group $A$ who vote for Party $R$, etc. Party $R$ wins if $V^R > 50$. Party $D$ wins if $V^D > 50$.

People are assumed to be no less self-interested as voters than as actors in the market in the usual exposition of competitive equilibrium. Each person votes for the party offering him the higher income. Thus, a person in Group $A$ votes for Party $R$ if and only if $y_A^R > y_A^D$. It is supposed, for convenience, that each group divides its votes evenly between the parties if their offers are the same. Thus, the value of $v_A^R$ is either 100 or 50 or 0 depending on whether $y_A^R$ is greater than, equal to, or less than $y_A^D$, and the values of $v_B^R$ and $v_C^R$ are determined accordingly.

In this context, the paradox of voting is that the outcome of competition between parties for votes is indeterminate. No platform wins over every other platform. If Party $D$ chooses some platform $Y^D = \{y_A^D, y_B^D, y_C^D\}$, it is always possible for Party $R$ to defeat Party $D$ by a two-to-one margin with a platform $Y^R = \{y_A^D - 2\varepsilon, y_B^D + \varepsilon, y_C^D + \varepsilon\}$ which differs from $Y^D$ by a small increase in the incomes of two-thirds of the voters and the subtraction of twice that amount from the remaining third. There is, in other words, no electoral equilibrium pair of platforms such that each party maximizes its vote by sticking to its own platform as long as the opposing party does likewise. If, prior to the election, parties could change their platforms in response to the platforms of their opponents, they would go on doing so indefinitely.

The exploitation problem arises when voters and political parties understand the paradox of voting and when binding agreements are feasible among members of a majority coalition. As long as voters in any group can act in unison, there may emerge a pact among, say, Group $B$, Group $C$ and Party $R$ in which all members of both groups promise to vote for Party $R$ on the understanding that Party $R$ establish a platform $Y^R = \{0, 3Y/2, 3Y/2\}$, sharing the national income equally between Groups $B$ and $C$, and excluding Group $A$ altogether. Party $R$ may be the first to offer a sufficiently attractive platform to two groups in what would become the majority coalition, and members of Groups $B$ and $C$ might be 'loyal' to Party $R$ because they know that any switch of allegiance to Party $D$ will set off a train of events that could lead eventually to their exclusion from a new majority coalition. Obviously, this nasty equilibrium is bad news for the prospects of a democratic society. Nobody can be expected to adhere to the conventions of majority rule voting if total impoverishment of minorities is to be expected.[5]

The exploitation problem is really two connected difficulties. The first is that voting about incomes is capricious in the sense that there is no telling who the members of the majority coalition will turn out to be. Any sufficiently large collection of people or groups will do. The second is that voting about incomes is precarious in that the losers in the process – those who find themselves among the excluded minority – appear in danger of being wiped out completely, of being left with nothing, of losing all that they might otherwise possess.

## The probabilistic voting theorem

To circumvent the exploitation problem, there is introduced a new and allegedly more realistic assumption about the behaviour of voters. Instead of supposing that each voter is exquisitely sensitive to differences in the offers of the political parties (so that, for instance, every person in Group $A$ is guaranteed to vote for Party $R$ when Party $R$ offers Group $A$ a larger income than is offered by Party $D$, no matter how small the difference in offers happens to be), it is supposed that the proportion of the people in Group $A$ who vote for Party $R$ is a concave increasing function of $y_A^R$. Specifically, for any given $y_A^D$

$$v_A^R = g(y_A^R, y_A^D) \tag{12.4}$$

with the partial derivatives $g_1 > 0$, $g_2 > 0$, $g_{11} < 0$ and $g_{22} < 0$. The percentage, $v_A^R$, of people in Group $A$ who vote for Party $R$ may now lie anywhere between 0 per cent and 100 per cent. The variable $v_A^R$ is defined in the first instance as a percentage, but can equally well be thought of as a probability, the probability that a randomly chosen person in Group $A$ votes for Party $R$. Hence the name *probabilistic voting*. Probabilistic voting allows $v_A^R$ to vary over the entire range from 0 to 100, as compared with *deterministic voting* as described earlier which restricts $v_A^R$ to the values of 0, 50 (in the event of a tie), and 100.

The main ideas in the probabilistic voting theorem are that political parties buy voters with offers of income in their party platforms and that the cost of each additional vote increases steadily with the number of votes already acquired. Suppose, for example, that income per head, $Y$, is equal to 1,000 and that all three groups' responses of votes to incomes are the same, so that the voting equilibrium, if there were one, would have to be where both parties offer equal shares of total income to all three groups, and the election is tied.

$$y_A^R = y_B^R = y_C^R = y_A^D = y_B^D = y_C^D = 1,000 \tag{12.5}$$

With deterministic voting, that outcome is unstable. If Party $D$ offered 1,000 per person to all three groups, Party $R$ could win the election with two-thirds of the vote by adding \$100 to the offers of Groups $B$ and $C$ financed by a reduction of \$200 in its offer to Group $A$, for the platform {800, 1,100, 1,100} beats the platform {1,000, 1,000, 1,000} two votes to one. Party $R$ wins the election as long as the platform of Party $D$ is unchanged, though, as pointed out above, even {800, 1,100, 1,100} can be beaten by other platforms, handing the election to the party that is last to announce its platform.

*Table 12.1* A group's percentage of votes for Party $R$ when the offer of Party $D$ is 1,000

| Offer of income by Party $R$ | Group's per cent of votes for Party $R$ |
|---|---|
| 800 | 25 |
| 900 | 45 |
| 1,000 | 50 |
| 1,100 | 60 |
| 1,200 | 65 |

Probabilistic voting avoids that outcome by causing Party $R$'s loss of votes from a decrease of \$200 in its offer to one group to exceed its gain of votes from an increase of \$100 in its offers to each of the other two groups. Continue to suppose that the platform of Party $D$ is {1,000, 1,000, 1,000} and that the response of votes to offers of income in a party's platform is the same for all three groups. With probabilistic voting, with an offer of 1,000 by Party $D$ and when the behaviour of all three groups is the same, each group might confront Party $R$ with a schedule of votes to offers of income such as that in Table 12.1.

With the votes-to-offers schedule in this table, the exploitation of Group $A$ by Groups $B$ and $C$ is no longer possible, for the platform {800, 1,100, 1,100} which won the election for Party $R$ under deterministic voting would no longer do so. Party $R$ would gain an extra 10 per cent of the votes of Groups $B$ and $C$ but would lose 25 per cent of the votes of Group $A$, reducing its overall percent of votes from 50 per cent to 48.3 per cent (equal to $(1/3)(25+60+60)$) and losing the election. By contrast, the second column of schedule would be replaced under deterministic voting by 0,0,50,100 and 100.

Generalizing this example, suppose that for any given platform, $\{y_A^D, y_B^D, y_C^D\}$, of Party $D$, the votes-to-offers functions of Groups $A$, $B$ and $C$ to Party $R$ are as follows.

$$
\begin{aligned}
v_A^R &= 0 && \text{when } 50 + S_A[U_A(y_A^R) - U_A(y_A^D)] < 0 \\
&= 50 + S_A[U_A(y_A^R) - U_A(y_A^D)] && \text{within 0 and 100} \\
&= 100 && \text{when } 50 + S_A[U_A(y_A^R) - U_A(y_A^D)] > 100
\end{aligned}
\tag{12.6}
$$

$$
\begin{aligned}
v_B^R &= 0 && \text{when } 50 + S_B[U_B(y_B^R) - U_B(y_B^D)] < 0 \\
&= 50 + S_B[U_B(y_B^R) - U_B(y_B^D)] && \text{within 0 and 100} \\
&= 100 && \text{when } 50 + S_B[U_B(y_B^R) - U_B(y_B^D)] > 100
\end{aligned}
\tag{12.7}
$$

$$
\begin{aligned}
v_C^R &= 0 && \text{when } 50 + S_C[U_C(y_C^R) - U_C(y_C^D)] < 0 \\
&= 50 + S_C[U_C(y_C^R) - U_C(y_C^D)] && \text{within 0 and 100} \\
&= 100 && \text{when } 50 + S_C[U_C(y_C^R) - U_C(y_C^D)] > 100
\end{aligned}
\tag{12.8}
$$

The functions $U_A$, $U_B$ and $U_C$ are ordinary utility of income functions with diminishing marginal utility of income, that is $U'_A > 0$ and $U''_A < 0$, etc. The role of utility in the votes-to-offers functions is to ensure that each additional dollar procures a steadily diminishing increase in the number of votes. Voters are presumed to respond to offers in accordance with their utility of income rather than income itself. The terms $S_A$, $S_B$, and $S_C$ are sensitivity parameters; for instance, $S_A$ shows how Group $A$'s vote for Party $R$ depends upon gap between the utilities of Group $A$ in the offers of the two political parties.

A specific votes-to-offers function of Group $A$ in response to Party $R$ is illustrated in Figure 12.1. The function has three branches: a lower branch where Party $R$ gets no votes because its offer is too small, a middle branch where Group $A$'s votes are divided between Party $R$ and Party $D$, and an upper branch where Party $R$ gets all of Group $A$'s vote because its offer is significantly higher than that of Party $D$. On the middle branch, Group $A$'s vote for Party $R$ is a concave function of the offer of income by Party $R$ when Party $R$'s offer is neither too much below nor too much above the offer of the Party $D$. With an offer of 1,000 by Party $D$, the figure shows how $v^R_A$ varies with $y^R_A$.

Nobody in Group $A$ votes for Party $R$ unless the income offered to members of Group $A$ by Party $R$ is at least 607, the lowest value of $y^R_A$ for which $v^R_A > 0$.[6] Beyond that point, the votes-to-offers curve is concave and rising until $y^R_A$ reaches 1,649, at which $v^R_A = 100$ and beyond which the votes-to-offers curve is again flat.[7] Group $A$'s vote is evenly divided between Party $R$ and Party $D$ when $y^R_A = 1,000$: with identical offers, the election is tied.

The shape of the votes-to-offers curve in Figure 12.1 depends critically on the offer to Group $A$ by Party $D$. If $y^D_A$ exceeded 1,000, the curve would be lower, signifying that the minimal offer by Party $R$ would need to exceed 607 and the offer required to capture all of Group $A$'s votes would have to exceed 1,649. With the same parameters, the votes-to-offers functions of the other two groups would be the same as well.

The 'proof' of the probabilistic voting theorem is now straightforward. The electoral equilibrium is a pair of platforms, $\{y^R_A, y^R_B, y^R_C\}$ and $\{y^D_A, y^D_B, y^D_C\}$, each maximizing a party's total vote, $V^R$ and $V^D$, subject to the income constraint and with due regard to the platform chosen by the other party. The equilibria are identified by the first-order conditions[8]

$$S_A U'_A(y^*_A) = S_B U'_B(y^*_B) = S_C U'_C(y^*_C) \tag{12.9}$$

where $y^*_A$, $y^*_B$ and $y^*_C$ are the incomes in the common equilibrium platform, subject to the income constraint that

$$(1/3)(y^*_A + y^*_B + y^*_C) = 1,000 \tag{12.10}$$

It follows immediately that a person's income in the electoral equilibrium is an increasing function of his sensitivity to offers; the greater $S_A$, for instance, the smaller is $U'_A$ in equilibrium, and the larger $y^*_A$ must be. Suppose $Y = 1000$ and

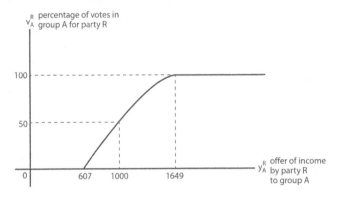

*Figure 12.1* Group $A$'s response of votes to offers of income from Party $R$.

Note: $S_A = 100$, $U_A = \ln(y)$ and $y_A^R = 1000$.

all utility functions are logarithmic. By symmetry, if $S_A$, $S_B$ and $S_C$ are the same, then $y_A^* = y_B^* = y_C^* = Y = 1,000$. But, if $S_A = S_B = 100$, while $S_C = 200$, then Equation (12.9) requires that $1/y_A^* = 1/y_B^* = 2/y_C^*$, so that $y_A^* = y_B^* = 750$ while $y_C^* = 1,500$.

## A critique of the theorem

As developed so far, the probabilistic voting theorem is open to the objection that it proves too much. It supplies a complete distribution of income among voters based entirely on political propensities and without reference to property rights at all. Strictly speaking, the Rockefellers are not rich because they own a great deal of property, but because they are especially sensitive to the offers of the rival political parties. Or, to put the same point more generally, the standard theorems of welfare economics supply one equilibrium distribution of income based on ownership of property, the probabilistic voting theorem supplies a second equilibrium distribution of income based on sensitivity of voters to offers of political parties, and there would appear to be no reconciliation between the two.

This conundrum is evaded in practice by restricting the application of the theorem to policy parameters rather than to incomes. Thus, for example, the utility functions of voters and the platforms of the political parties might be defined over a set of tariffs on all traded products or over a set of taxes and public expenditures.[9] Formally, the transformation saves the theorem, but it presents new difficulties of its own. The theorem becomes ambiguous in its implications because there is no universal connection between platforms and utilities. A high tariff on one good need not have much effect upon the welfare of the people who are affected by that tariff, while a low tariff on another good may affect people's welfare significantly. Thus, it is not always obvious whether a difference between platforms is large or small. More importantly, there is no explanation within the theory of why public policy is restricted, for example, to tariffs, why a political party that is free to choose tariffs as the theorem requires is not also free to choose incomes directly, and why, if a political party is somehow prevented from setting people's incomes at will, it should not also be constrained in its choice of tariffs. The conflict between the two equilibria is not so easily resolved.

The source of voter insensitivity to platforms of political parties is also problematic. Presumably, voters are somewhat insensitive to political platforms because they are committed to one party over another or because they are uninformed. Consider commitment first.[10] If some voters in Group $A$ persist in voting for Party $R$ even though $y_A^R < y_A^D$, it may be because these voters are drawn to Party $R$ for reasons other than pecuniary gain. When voters behave in this way and on the assumptions of the probabilistic voting theorem, the natural response of Party $R$ is to capitalize upon these voters' behaviour, offering a somewhat lower income to Group $A$ than to other less committed groups. The socialist party ignores the interests of workers and the conservative party ignores the interests of capitalists because each party already has their support. To carry the argument to its logical extreme, if there really were a constituency for which 'every child that's born alive is either a little Liberal or a little Conservative', the sensitivity parameter of that constituency would be zero, and neither party would offer that constituency any income at all. The fully committed are condemned to starve in the world of the probabilistic voting theorem where voters are loyal to political parties but political parties are not loyal to voters.

The absurdity arises from the implicit assumption that commitment is exogenous, that political parties need not concern themselves with the creation and maintenance of voter support, that support is just there for ever and ever, no matter what the party may do. Drop that assumption, make allowance for the role of political parties as representatives of groups in society that may have no other means of coordinating their activities, and the curious inverse relation between the support of people for parties and the treatment by parties of their supporters disintegrates. The electoral equilibrium disintegrates as well.

Voter insensitivity may also arise from the difficulty in recognizing small differences between offers of income in the platforms of rival political parties – a reasonable supposition when incomes are thought of as surrogates for the effects upon voters of mixes of policies covering many aspects of the economy and society. Full and complete sensitivity, as is formally postulated in the usual exposition of the paradox of voting, would require that, starting from a position of equality in the offers of the two political parties, either party could capture the entire vote of, for instance, Group $A$ by a 1,000th of a per cent increase in the offer to that group. Surely that is an unreasonable requirement. Surely it is more reasonable to assume that, if the offers are close, then the votes are almost evenly divided between the political parties. Nor is it unreasonable to suppose that some voters are more perceptive than others, and that variations in perceptivity among voters conform to the concavity of the votes-to-offers function as the assumptions of the theorem require. Dealing with this argument requires a closer look at the meaning of the concavity assumption.

## Local and global equilibrium

The paradox of voting and the exploitation problem are more formidable than they may seem, for they do not stand or fall with the extreme assumptions under which they have been explained. In particular, they do not automatically vanish once an electoral equilibrium has been identified. They remain as troubling as ever unless it can be shown that the equilibrium is global, in a sense to be discussed. A local equilibrium, as has been shown to exist, is not sufficient.

Proof of the probabilistic voting theorem, as presented above, requires only that the votes-to-offers function be concave in the neighbourhood of the equilibrium platform. Elimination of the exploitation problem and the paradox of voting requires that the function be concave everywhere: that the concavity be global. Consider once again the specific votes-to-offers functions in Equations (2.16) to (2.18), where all utility functions are logarithmic, where $Y$ is equal to 1,000, and where the three sensitivity parameters, $S_A$, $S_B$ and $S_C$ are the same, so that, by symmetry, the electoral equilibrium must be $y_A^* = y_B^* = y_C^* = 1,000$. If both parties choose that platform, then each has a 50 per cent chance of winning the election, and a small deviation by either party from the electoral equilibrium platform is guaranteed to lose that party the election. But the possibility of winning the election by exploiting one of the three groups of voters has not been eliminated! If the common value of the sensitivity parameters is 100, and if Party $D$ adheres rigidly to the platform $\{1000, 1000, 1000\}$, then Party $R$ can win the election with a platform of $\{0, 1500, 1500\}$.

That the equilibrium is local rather than global is illustrated in Figure 12.2 with total votes, $V^R$, for Party $R$ – where $V^R = (1/3)(v_A^R + v_B^R + v_C^R)$ – on the vertical axis and Party $R$'s offer to each person in Groups $B$ and $C$ on the horizontal

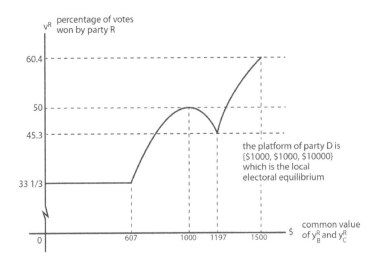

*Figure 12.2* Percentage of votes won by Party $R$ as dependent on the degree of exploitation of Group $A$.

axis. The figure is drawn on the assumption that income per head, $Y$, is 1,000, that sensitivity parameters in Equations (12.6)–(12.8) are all equal to 100, that all utility of income functions are logarithmic and that income not offered to Groups $B$ and $C$ is automatically offered to Group $A$. On these assumptions, the votes-to-offers curve of Groups $A$ in Figure 12.1 is applicable to Groups $B$ and $C$ as well.

An offer by Party $R$ of less than 607 to people in Groups $B$ and $C$ would procure a vote of 33⅓ per cent for Party $R$. As illustrated in Figure 12.1, nobody in Groups $B$ or $C$ would vote for Party $R$, but everybody in Group $A$ would do so because the residual income of 1,786 per person in Group $A$ – equal to $[3,000 - 2(607)]$ – is more than enough to capture 100 per cent of the voters in that group.

As the common value of $y_B^R$ and $y_C^R$ rises above 607, the total vote for Party $R$ increases because Party $R$ gains more votes per dollar from Group $B$ and $C$ than it loses from Group $A$. The increase continues until the common value of $y_B^R$ and $y_C^R$ rises to 1,000, which is the local equilibrium where both parties win 50 per cent of the votes by offering the same income to all three groups of voters. But as common value of $y_B^R$ and $y_C^R$ increases beyond 1,000, the total vote for Party $R$ declines, at least as long as there are votes to be lost from Group $A$. The low point in the fortunes of Party $R$ is reached when $y_A^R$ has fallen to 607, the common value of $y_B^R$ and $y_C^R$ has risen to 1,197 (equal to ½[3,000 – 607]) and the total vote for Party $R$ has been reduced to 45.3 per cent – equal to $(2/3)\{50 + 100[\ln(1,197) - \ln(1,000)]\}$.

Thereafter, an increase in common value of $y_B^R$ and $y_C^R$ leads to an increase in the vote for Party $R$ because there is still room for the votes by Groups $B$ and Group $C$ to increase, but people in Group $A$ have no more votes to withdraw. The maximum possible offer to people in Groups $B$ and $C$ is 1,500, at which Groups $B$ and $C$ cast 91 per cent of their votes for Party $R$ – their votes are $v_B^R = v_C^R = 50 + 100[\ln(1,500) - \ln(1,000)]$ – and Party $R$ wins the election with a vote of 60.4 per cent (equal to $(2/3)91$).

Small deviations from the local equilibrium cost a party votes, but exploitation still thrives because a party can still win the election by means of large deviations benefitting some majority of the electorate at the expense of the rest.

Much depends on the size of the parameters, $S_A$, $S_B$ and $S_C$, indicating the groups' sensitivities of votes to offers of income. Consider $S_A$ in Equation (12.6) which is reflected in the shape of the votes-to-offers curve in Figure 12.1. In principle, $S_A$ could be anywhere between 0 and infinity. At one extreme where $S_A = $ infinity, the votes-to-offers curve in Figure 12.1 becomes a vertical line located at 1,000 on the horizontal axis or whatever the offer of Party $D$ happens to be. People in Group $A$ would vote for Party $R$ if $y_A^R > y_A^D$ or for Party $D$ if $y_A^D > y_A^R$ no matter how small the difference in offers may be. Deterministic voting is restored and the exploitation problem is inescapable. At the other extreme, where $S_A = 0$, the votes-to-offers curve in Figure 12.1 becomes a horizontal line at $v_A^R = 50$ or whatever the constant term in Equation (12.6) happens to be. In effect, this assumption divides Group $A$ into two sub-groups of extremists, one that always votes for Party $R$ no matter how small its offer of income happens to be, and the other that never does so no matter how large its offer of income to Group $A$ happens to be. Curiously, neither party would offer any income to Group $A$ in this case because Group $A$'s votes are insensitive to offers of income; $y_A^R = y_A^D = 0$. Income in party platforms would be redirected to other groups for which offers of income can be expected to procure votes.

In between, the votes-to-offers curve would be like that in Figure 12.1, but with the possibility when $S_A$ is small enough that the curve cuts the vertical axis at some value of $v_A^R$ between 0 and 50. Then, exploitation of Group $A$ may or may not be possible depending on the sensitivity parameters of the other two groups. Universal concavity of the votes-to-offers curve requires that somebody in Group $A$ continues to vote for Party $R$ even when Party $R$ is prepared to deprive Group $A$ of income altogether. It requires voters to be so insensitive to platforms of political parties that they never run out of votes to withhold, even though progressively more votes are withdrawn with every decrease in income.

The probabilistic voting theorem yields an electoral equilibrium, even for the allocation among voters of the entire national income. This implication of the theorem is at variance with a longstanding tradition in political theory, going back at least as far as Aristotle, that democracy is unstable unless circumscribed; that the range of issues about which people vote must be constrained because the alternative is discord, faction, instability, and, ultimately, the collapse of democracy itself.[11] Civil rights and property rights, with a prior distribution of property among citizens, must to some degree be placed beyond the grasp of the vote if democracy is to work at all. The critique of the probabilistic voting theorem in this chapter can be looked upon as a defence of that older tradition against the view that voting can be safely unconstrained.

## Notes

1   This chapter is a slight revision of an article in the *Canadian Journal of Economics*, Usher (1994). Thanks for comments and suggestions from Dan Bernhardt, Robin Boadway and Raghbendra Jha.

2   This was a common view among the classical economists. Their reasons for distrusting universal franchise and their general preference for property qualifications are examined in Grampp (1948). Articles in the famous debate on universal franchise between James Mill, who favoured it, and T. B. Macaulay, who was opposed, are reprinted in Lively and Rees (1978). As discussed in Chapter 10, the anti-democratic argument was used by Oliver Cromwell against the Levellers in the Putney debates in 1647.

3   For a simple exposition of the probabilistic voting theorem together with a good review of the literature, see Mueller (1989). For a more thorough treatment, see Calvert (1986). Mueller includes a discussion of the circumstances in which an electoral equilibrium might be optimal.

4   It is arguable that political parties seek not maximize votes, but to win elections, which may or may not be the same thing. To say that political parties maximize votes is in some respects like saying that hockey teams maximize scores. In a sense they do, but a team is, as a rule, not less satisfied with a win of 4 goals to 3 than with a loss of 8 goals to 9. Similarly, a party that seeks to maximize votes would presumably maximize expected votes as well, in which case, in a two-party race, it would prefer a 30 per cent chance of winning 80 per cent of the votes together with a 70 per cent chance of winning 49 per cent of the votes to a certainty of winning 51 per cent of the votes. This implication of the hypothesis is clearly false. Furthermore, as William Riker pointed out many years ago,

vote-maximization is at variance with the 'size principle'. A rationally administered political party may prefer to win by a margin that is safely above the 50 per cent mark but is not overwhelming. The reason is that a party with the support of an overwhelming majority of the electorate is prone to fission as a bare majority of its supporters comes to realize that they could do better for themselves in a new party with a smaller base of support and no need to placate superfluous adherents. A party with too large a base in the electorate is intrinsically undisciplined and unstable. On the size principle, see Riker (1962). The vote-maximization hypothesis is usually attributed to Downs (1957).

5  There are six possible nasty equilibria: Groups $A$ and $B$ voting for Party $R$, Groups $A$ and $B$ voting for Party $D$, Groups $A$ and $C$ voting for Party $R$, and so on. They are known in game theory as bargaining sets.

6  $y_A^R = 607$ is the solution to top line of Equation (12.6):

$$0 = 50 + 100[\ln(y_A^R) - \ln(1,000)]$$

or equivalently $y_A^R = 1,000\, e^{-1/2} = 607$.

7  $y_A^R = 1,649$ is the solution to bottom line of Equation (12.6):

$$100 = 50 + 100[\ln(y_A^R) - \ln(1,000)]$$

or equivalently $y_A^R = 1,000\, e^{1/2} = 1,649$.

8  As seen by Party $R$, the Lagrangian of the problem is

$$\mathcal{L} = V^R - \lambda[y_A^R + y_B^R + y_C^R - 3Y]$$

where $V^R = (1/3)[v_A^R + v_B^R + v_C^R]$

$$= 50 + (1/3)\{S_A[U_A(y_A^R) - U_A(y_A^D)] + S_B[U_B(y_B^R) - U_B(y_D^D)]$$
$$+ S_C[U_C(y_C^R) - U_C(y_C^D)]\}$$

Differentiating with respect to $y_A^R$, $y_B^R$ and $y_C^R$, the first order conditions become

$$\delta\mathcal{L}/\delta y_A^R = S_A U_A'(y_A^R) - 3\lambda = 0$$
$$\delta\mathcal{L}/\delta y_B^R = S_B U_B'(y_B^R) - 3\lambda = 0$$
and  $$\delta\mathcal{L}/\delta y_C^R = S_C U_C'(y_C^R) - 3\lambda = 0$$

implying (12.9) in the text. If all three utility functions, $U_A$, $U_B$ and $U_C$, are the same, and all sensitivity parameters, $S_A$, $S_B$, and $S_C$, are the same as well, then, by symmetry, the equilibrium platform has to be $\{Y, Y, Y\}$. If Party $D$ deviated from that platform, Party $D$ would lose the election.

9  For an example of this procedure, see Magee, Brock and Young (1989).
10  This interpretation of the theorem is favoured by Howitt (1990).
11  The best exposition of this point of view is still Hayek (1946). See also Berg (1956), Brennan and Buchanan (1985) and Usher (1981).

## References

Berg, E. (1956) *Democracy and the Majority Principle*, Gothenburg: Scandinavian University Books.

Brennan, G. H. and Buchanan, J. M. (1985) *The Reason of Rules: Constitutional Political Economy*, Cambridge: Cambridge University Press.

Calvert, R. L. (1986) *Models of Information in Politics*, Chur: Harwood Academic Publishers.

Downs, A. (1957) *An Economic Theory of Democracy*, New York: Harper and Row.

Grampp, W. D. (1948) The politics of the classical economists, *Quarterly Journal of Economics*, 62(5),714–47.

Hayek, F. (1946) *The Road to Serfdom*, Chicago: University of Chicago Press.

Howitt, P. (1990) *Candidate preference versus uncertainty in models of probabilistic voting*, Mimeo, University of Western Ontario.

Lively, J., and Rees, J. (1978) *Utilitarian Logic and Politics*, Oxford: Oxford University Press.

Magee, S. P., Brock, W. A. and Young, L. (1989) *Black Hole Tariffs and Endogenous Tariff Theory*, Cambridge: Cambridge University Press.

Mueller, D. C. (1989) *Public Choice II*, Cambridge: Cambridge University Press.

Riker, W. (1962) *A Theory of Political Coalitions*, New Haven: Yale University Press.

Usher, D. (1981) *The Economic Prerequisite to Democracy*, Oxford: Basil Blackwell.

Usher, D. (1994) The significance of the probabilistic voting theorem, *Canadian Journal of Economics*, 27(2), 433–45.

Wittman, D. (1989) Why democracies produce efficient results, *Journal of Political Economy*, 97(6), 1395–424.

# Index

For Product Safety Concerns and Information please contact our EU
representative GPSR@taylorandfrancis.com
Taylor & Francis Verlag GmbH, Kaufingerstraße 24, 80331 München, Germany